OLIVIA DE HAVILLAND

OLIVIA DE HAVILLAND

Lady Triumphant

Victoria Amador

UNIVERSITY PRESS OF KENTUCKY

Scholarly publisher for the Commonwealth,
serving Bellarmine University, Berea College, Centre
College of Kentucky, Eastern Kentucky University,
The Filson Historical Society, Georgetown College,
Kentucky Historical Society, Kentucky State University,
Morehead State University, Murray State University,
Northern Kentucky University, Transylvania University,
University of Kentucky, University of Louisville,
and Western Kentucky University.

Editorial and Sales Offices: The University Press of Kentucky
663 South Limestone Street, Lexington, Kentucky 40508-4008
www.kentuckypress.com

Unless otherwise noted, photographs are from Photofest.

Library of Congress Cataloging-in-Publication Data

Names: Amador, Victoria, 1955– author.
Title: Olivia de Havilland : lady triumphant / Victoria Amador.
Description: Lexington : The University Press of Kentucky, 2019. | Includes bibliographical references and index.
Identifiers: LCCN 2018056745| ISBN 9780813177274 (hardcover : alk. paper) | ISBN 9780813177281 (pdf) | ISBN 9780813177298 (epub)
Subjects: LCSH: De Havilland, Olivia. | Actors—United States—Biography.
Classification: LCC PN2287.D4 A625 2019 | DDC 791.4302/8092 [B]—dc23

This book is printed on acid-free paper meeting
the requirements of the American National Standard
for Permanence in Paper for Printed Library Materials.

Manufactured in the United States of America.

Member of the Association
of University Presses

For G., S., K., J., and R., with endless gratitude and love.

CONTENTS

INTRODUCTION

Olivia and Me

In 1967 and again in 1969, *Gone with the Wind* was reissued to American theaters in a 70mm wide-screen print, introducing the classic to a new generation of filmgoers thirty years after its first release. Even then, the film was discussed with a mixture of admiration and concern for its representation of the Confederate, slave-owning South, yet it was still seen as a masterpiece. Along with many other viewers, I was first exposed to the film in 1969, and its grandeur possessed me.

As a young teenager in a tiny Wisconsin farming and manufacturing community, I did two things to facilitate my dreams of a wider world—I read compulsively, and I saw virtually every film that played at the local movie theater, escaping through the written word and the art of cinema. I had read *Gone with the Wind* in 1968, a rite of passage for many American girls of the time, often encouraged by their older relatives and teachers who had loved the Pulitzer Prize–winning novel by Atlanta's Margaret Mitchell. Over a long, frigid Christmas holiday, I was captivated by the panoramic American history and histrionics, by the plot and the characters, by the archetypal American reinvention story of a woman and a nation divided, but particularly by Scarlett O'Hara.

I don't think it was a coincidence that this Civil War–era heroine in a Depression-era film seemed prescient when I became obsessed a few years later with David Bowie's anthemic 1974 "Rebel, Rebel." Like me (and virtually every other young person in the Western world), Scarlett was on a mission to live life as she chose. Even more relevant to me and to many other young women, she was, in many ways, a protofeminist. Scarlett didn't like limits or being treated like a child when she knew exactly what she wanted—power, self-determination, and a self-forged identity. She wanted romance with Ashley Wilkes and was ruthless about it. She loved her family and Tara despite herself, and she used every skill, talent, attraction, and strategy she had to fight for their survival. Scarlett didn't have the awareness to see the personal as political, but she did refute the limitations on her gender and her defeated land. Above all, she wanted to do every and any damned thing she desired.

But what about Melanie Hamilton Wilkes? Too nice to emulate. A true personification of Patmore Coventry's treacly tribute to Victorian-era domestic enslavement, "An Angel in the House." Melanie was a loyal friend to Scarlett, but who could possibly want to be that good? Melanie wasn't flashy or outwardly fierce; she wasn't funny, wasn't particularly captivating. Margaret Mitchell's description of Melanie offers a character who seems pallid compared with Scarlett:

> She was a tiny, frailly built girl, who gave the appearance of a child masquerading in her mother's enormous hoop skirts—an illusion that was heightened by the shy, almost frightened look in her too large brown eyes. She had a cloud of curly dark hair which was so sternly repressed beneath its net that no vagrant tendrils escaped, and this dark mass, with its long widow's peak, accentuated the heart shape of her face . . . a sweet, timid face but a plain face, and she had no feminine tricks of allure to make observers forget its plainness. She looked—and was—as simple as earth, as good as bread, as transparent as spring water.[1]

Melanie was a lovely role model for someone bucking for sainthood. She was not, however, an immediately obvious heroine for a troubled teen.

Or so I believed until I saw the film when it finally came to my little Wisconsin town in 1969. I went back several times, alone and with friends. It is the only epic I've ever tolerated, and it became my favorite all-time film: the Technicolor, Clark Gable, Vivien Leigh's magnificence in one of the greatest female screen performances in cinema history, the supporting cast, the Civil War, the sweeping music, the story of survival. Certainly, I was enraptured with Leigh's Scarlett, as I expected to be. What was unexpected, however, was my newfound appreciation of Melanie. As portrayed by Olivia de Havilland, Melanie was as indomitable as Scarlett.

I knew de Havilland's spirited work from her many films with Errol Flynn shown on television. Her maleficence in *Hush . . . Hush, Sweet Charlotte* and *Lady in a Cage,* both viewed at the cinema when I was a burgeoning obsessive filmgoer, was delicious to me. But in the actress's Melanie, I saw a character with strength and gentleness, true manners, and an authentic spirit.

Her Melanie captured more of Margaret Mitchell's evaluation of that Hamilton girl: "Ashley had sat on a stool at Melanie's feet, apart from the other guests, and talked quietly with her, smiling the slow drowsy smile that Scarlett loved. What made matters worse was that under his smile a little sparkle had come into Melanie's eyes, so that even Scarlett had to admit that she looked almost pretty. As Melanie looked at Ashley, her plain face lit up as with an inner fire, for if ever a loving heart showed itself upon a face, it was showing now on Melanie Hamilton's."[2]

Olivia's Melanie was no second chorus to Scarlett's beauty or fire; Olivia's Melanie was suddenly interesting. After all, Melanie married Ashley (played by Leslie Howard) and gave birth during the siege of Atlanta; she cradled the weeping Rhett Butler (played by Clark Gable) when he feared Scarlett would die; she was aware of the gossip about Ashley and Scarlett and loved them both regardless; she was the best friend any woman could have. Scarlett was my idealized self; Melanie was the self I might become. I decided to write a fan letter.

Vivien Leigh had died two years earlier, in 1967, of tuberculosis. Leslie Howard had been shot down in 1943 while flying a mission during World War II. Clark Gable had suffered a heart attack in 1960 shortly after completing work on *The Misfits.* Olivia de Havilland, thankfully, was alive and well and living in Paris with her second husband, Pierre Galante, *secrétaire général* of *Paris Match,* and her two children. So I typed a fan letter on my new manual typewriter with a script font—ladylike, I remember thinking, feminine and strong, as I banged on the keys. I told her how much I loved her performances in *Gone with the Wind, Captain Blood,* and *Hush . . . Hush.* I asked her about Gable, Leigh, and Howard; told her I wanted to be an actress; thanked her for her attention; and sent the letter off to Paris (I had found her address in *Who's Who* and *Current Biography*). I was thirteen years old.

Remarkably, several weeks later, a neat airmail envelope arrived with a French postage stamp. It was from Olivia de Havilland. It is a miracle I didn't tear it to bits in my haste to open the letter. And there, on tissue-fine stationery, was a typewritten response to my letter, answering my questions about Leigh ("a consummate actress"), Gable ("a true gentleman"), and Howard ("wonderful to work with"). She also affirmed, as she has in countless interviews, that Melanie "is the role I most loved playing and she is very real, indeed, to me."[3] The actress even included an autographed photograph of herself as Melanie—of course, I desperately wanted one, but I hadn't requested it for fear she would think I was writing solely for that purpose—signed in dark blue ink in her distinctive, curving hand (a good example appears in a note she writes in *My Cousin Rachel*). The screams of joy are still echoing off the barns in central Wisconsin, and the framed photograph sits before me as I write this.

I showed every human being I had ever met the response from Olivia, as she became known to me and my mother (who also knew and loved her films). I decided to write back so she wouldn't think I was just another fan braying for a photo. I remember suggesting that we become pen pals, and I shared my interests with her, which included the Green Bay Packers, horror films, cats, and becoming a stage actress. I also learned from further research that she had a son named Benjamin from her first marriage and a daughter named Gisèle who was only a year younger than me, so I thought Olivia might be particularly kind to a young person near her daughter's age. Thus our correspondence began, and it has continued for forty-nine years (she was always "Miss de Havilland" in our correspondence until the spring of 2016, when she asked me to call her "Miss D"; since her 2017 damehood, she is "Dame Olivia").

I sent Olivia everything about myself—newspaper clippings reviewing plays I was in or announcing scholarships I'd won; invitations to all my graduations (alas, she never attended any). I even sent her articles about herself that I thought she might have missed. I asked questions about her films: Did she keep her costumes? A few. Was Errol Flynn a good kisser? I knew the answer to that just by watching them onscreen together, and she was far too elegant to answer. Was she really friends with Bette Davis? Very good friends indeed.

In later years, when I studied and worked in Europe, I sent her endless requests to meet me in Paris; it became my favorite city, in part because my favorite correspondent lived there. She always declined. But she continued to answer my letters, typewritten replies on her trademark Della Robbia blue paper. Sometimes years passed between notes (there was a long silence when her son had died, and another long break when she was nursing her ex-husband, who was suffering from lung cancer); sometimes two or three would arrive in a flurry. I kept every one. Now that we email, I receive fewer typed notes, but I hear from her even more regularly and still scream happily, if more restrainedly.

Our exchanges weren't always terribly profound—how could they be? But we found enough common ground to sustain our correspondence. Olivia's kindness to me as I matured was generous beyond belief. In 1973 she offered a handwritten P.S. to one note: "Special good luck to you for this last year of school—may your grades be excellent, and your plans for the future clarify."[4] I wrote to her in 1981 about my decision to move into academe and teaching rather than pursue an acting career, and she wisely advised me, "If you think of your teaching as a form of communication (this is mainly what acting is, too) and of the immense need people have to articulate and organize their own thoughts, and to convey them intelligibly, you may find creative ways to teach those courses of yours which will satisfy you very deeply."[5]

When I completed my PhD, she kindly wrote, "Dear Dr. Victoria, isn't it wonderful to be able to address you this way!"[6] Olivia had intended to major in communications at Mills College before those plans were derailed by Max Reinhardt and a Warner Brothers contract, and I always felt this shared interest forged a special bond between us. In an email interview with *People* in honor of her 100th birthday, she mentioned regretting that she hadn't attended college and observed, "'The scholarship I won in 1934 is still waiting for me!'"[7] I smiled at the thought that she might have been my teacher or my colleague. In some ways, with our correspondence and with the writing of this book, she has been both.

I've annoyed her, certainly, at times. She didn't mince words when I first mentioned reading *Sisters,* the late Charles Higham's biography of Olivia and her sister, Joan Fontaine. She dismissed the book, saying, "I have nothing whatsoever to do with this book and have not even read it. Friends have told me, however, that it is full of inaccuracies of every sort and that its author, Charles Higham, is most irresponsible."[8] A few years later, in an academic paper I'd written about John Huston's *In This Our Life* (1942), I returned to the infamous Higham bio, which contained several pages on the making of the film and Olivia's affair with the director. I sent the published article to the actress, who very kindly said, "I found it extremely interesting and wonderfully perceptive. Accurate, too."[9] She then requested photocopies of the pages from Higham's book that I'd quoted.

Despite her generous appreciation of the essay I'd written, Olivia was outraged by the information in Higham's book: "His description of the atmosphere on the set . . . is unrecognizable, and his incredible fiction about Bette [Davis, her costar in the film] coming to 2337 Nella Vista to read some selections from Job while the two of us shared a hot tub, is so outrageous and has rendered me so indignant that it will be difficult for me to function normally for the rest of this day!" Yet, with her teasing cleverness, she went on to write, "On the other hand, John Huston did, indeed, cross the threshold of that small vine-covered house, but he certainly did not read the Bible while there."[10]

Olivia's wit has always been present in her performances, in interviews, and in our correspondence, too. She gave me a nickname—"Victoria A. and B.," the second letter for my then married name. When I divorced, I became "Victoria A." again.

Her generosity to me over the years has been remarkable. When I was in Paris for my fiftieth birthday, my customary requested meeting was denied due to her ill health, but she sent a bountiful basket of fifty roses to my hotel, along with a long, handwritten note (on the Colette-blue paper) asserting that the "50s are *marvellous* years—enjoy them to the fullest!"[11] I still have the letter, the dried petals, and the basket.

Regrettably for me, yet understandably, Olivia continued to ignore or avoid my repeated requests for a meeting in Paris. Why should she consent, after all? I was not a renowned journalist or a working actress, and she had a busy life, as well as numerous other correspondents and a wide fan base. Olivia was also a very discreet, very private person. Even though I had gone to university with the partner of her longtime agent Jim Wilhelm, and even though another friend's acquaintance worked with the American Cathedral in Paris, which she attended regularly, those connections weren't door-openers either.

So the years and the decades passed. Olivia was now in her mid-nineties. I was an academic, presenting papers about her career for conferences and writing about her for various publications. We continued to correspond, and the fan in me refused to give up. Every time I visited Paris over the years, I always sent a letter with my travel details and a request for a visit; she always politely and regretfully declined. It must have been terribly annoying, but Olivia was always gracious in her refusals.

Then, in August 2010, I was in Paris for three days with a friend, and I took a bolder step. As usual, I'd written to Olivia to tell her I was coming and hoped for a meeting—after all, I was now middle aged and she was a walking miracle—and heard nothing. I'd decided to have roses delivered to her home when my steadfast travel companion, Jane, made a bold suggestion—why not go to her home with the flowers and my business card and ring the bell? If she wasn't in, I could leave the flowers for her. If she was in, who knew?

So, fortified by a couple of glasses of wine and a now-or-never false courage, that's exactly what I did. Olivia's house was on a short, elegant street dominated by consulates and stately buildings, the street sign ringed by ivy. The house itself was tall and narrow, with four stories and a basement level; it was painted a soft, burnished yellow-gold, fronted by a black iron fence and a dark iron door. The light from one of the upstairs rooms facing the street cast a warm, peachy glow. *La maison* was as elegant and discreetly situated as its owner.

After taking a moment to compose myself and possibly change my mind, I boldly rang the doorbell. Surprise! The iron door in the gate immediately swung open, and standing there was a young American woman, very pretty, dressed casually, and curious about this person standing before her bearing blooms. I introduced myself and showed her my card and learned that she was Olivia's assistant. Then I babbled a bit—Olivia and I had been correspondents for over forty years, I just happened to be in Paris, and I wondered if I might briefly pay my compliments. The very poised assistant kindly invited me to wait in the entryway—*mon Dieu!*—while she delivered my bouquet to Miss de Havilland. She walked up the several concrete steps to the door of the house, and I followed.

I had crossed the sacred threshold. On that hot August day, I was frozen with anticipation. I sat demurely on a wooden bench in the cool, nineteenth-century, flagstoned entryway, across from a large drawing room with another large room beyond it. To my left was the open front door; to my right was a steep staircase carpeted in red, at the top of which was a landing and, certainly, the actress. The drawing room was very formal, and it looked unused, like something frozen in time. It was very proper, heavily French, and elegant but cold—literally—despite the sweltering August heat. Clearly the life of the house existed beyond this proper, somewhat old-fashioned reception room.

Then I heard muffled voices—the young woman and the actress. I recognized the mellifluous tones, low and honeyed, even if I couldn't hear the precise words. My heart was pounding. I might finally meet the woman who had become almost like a family member, whose career and personal life I had followed faithfully, whose presence in my life, however limited, had given me tremendous pride and conferred on me a dusting of starlight by only a few degrees of separation.

Suddenly the young woman came downstairs, smiling sadly. Miss de Havilland appreciated the roses but wasn't prepared to receive visitors. I understood. I also smiled sadly, thanked her assistant, and hurried away, embarrassed and disappointed and, I have to confess, in tears once I had put some distance between me and the house—crying partly to release my previous emotions and partly because the tale of our faraway acquaintance wasn't getting the ending I needed.

I met Jane at a sidewalk café near Shakespeare and Company, and she congratulated me for my resolve while handing me a stiff drink. I exulted a bit as my first response faded. Upon reflection, and aided by another cocktail, I realized that calling on a legendary movie star unannounced and being turned away with civility seemed apropos of Olivia de Havilland and indicative of the character traits that inform much of this study of her life and work.

Olivia is elegant, she is friendly, she is humorously self-aware in interviews, but she is reserved and protective. This careful approach may be attributable to her sudden fame and youth (she was nineteen) in 1935 Hollywood, or to the difficult relationships she had with her family, or to her frustrations at Warner Brothers, or to her decision to abandon the Hollywood lifestyle for Paris in 1953. Her reticence may be natural; it may be intentionally cultivated. In 1950 the Hollywood Women's Press Club chose her as "the winner of Least Cooperative Actress," and she "did not acknowledge the honor."[12]

In any case, Olivia's discretion has served her well. Since her final screen performance in 1988 in the television movie *The Woman He Loved,* she has maintained a dignified but only occasionally visible and well-managed profile. She has increasingly kept the wider world at a distance, maintaining the image of a velvet glove hiding an iron hand, offering up a lady of elegance with a life far more interesting than the public could imagine. That persona informed her career choices, which sometimes, ironically, limited her potential as effectively as Jack Warner's studio leash, yet it also preserved her reputation as the last grande dame of America's golden age of cinema.

The failure of my first attempt at direct contact with Olivia did not dissuade me. In August 2012 I was back in Paris for my friend Steven's sixtieth birthday. I had emailed Olivia that we would be in the city for a week and would love to call on her. This time, when she wrote back, the heavens opened and the angels sang: we were invited to tea! At last, my private audience with Olivia de Havilland was going to happen.

Thrilled, Steven and I bought an enormous bouquet of roses the size of a small child and took the Metro and a taxi to the sixteenth arrondissement. We walked down her street, which was familiar to both of us after years of pilgrimages to the tall, narrow town house where the star lived. We rang the bell to the heavy iron gate. We rang again. Then we rang a third time.

A young woman appeared, not the same one from two years earlier, but just as sweet and welcoming. I recognized the thoughtful, compassionate look. "Didn't you receive our message?" she asked. "Miss de Havilland is ill." Our hearts sank. "But do you want to come in while I take this bouquet to her?" Hope! We stood in the same entryway where I had waited two years before. There was the same coolness to the air, the same beautiful floor tiles, the same formal living room, and the same red-carpeted stairway to heaven. After a few minutes' wait that felt eternal, the assistant descended. Olivia was too ill to receive us, but she loved the bouquet. "I'm so glad," I replied, as both Steven and I smiled. "I thought it might be too large."

"Miss de Havilland appreciates extravagance," her assistant replied charmingly. We left, but we were far less disappointed than might be expected. After all, Olivia had our flowers, we had brightened her day, we had both passed through the iron gates, and we had the great satisfaction of being close to our favorite star.

Immediately, I sent her an email, wishing her good health and noting that if she was feeling better in the next few weeks and felt like a visit, I would fly in at her convenience. I didn't expect anything, but I couldn't help thinking, "I've gotten into the house twice now. Perhaps the third time will be the charm." It was. Two weeks later, she invited me for coffee and *macarons.* With no hesitation whatsoever, I flew to Paris from Edinburgh, where I lived, to see her.

This time when I arrived, again bearing sumptuous blooms, the iron gate was ajar. Her assistant, Meghan, greeted me, smiling. The reception room was warm this time, not chilly; it was scented by ivory candles, and rose-shaded lamps cast a comforting light. A tray of macaroons rested on an elegant serving table to the left of a burgundy velvet settee. The silk Chinese screens radiated a golden glow. I chatted nervously with Meghan, almost trembling with anticipation. And then in she walked, vigorously, wearing a white silk blouse, a black skirt, and a pearl necklace. Her white hair was styled in a chic chignon. Her hand reached out to me. Olivia de Havilland—at last! After forty-three years of correspondence, we were finally sitting down together, and the long-awaited meeting began.

Our three hours together flew by. We drank coffee, nibbled macaroons, discussed the present and the past; much of our conversation informs this book. We also discussed our personal lives; much of that will remain private. Her assistant took our photograph together. When I offered *bises* on both cheeks in farewell, I was above the clouds. Life couldn't have been better.

Then, in August 2013, I was going to be in Paris again, staying for a month this time. Again, Olivia de Havilland invited me to visit, this time for champagne and canapés. Her assistant greeted me (as usual, I was bearing an extravagant bouquet) and led me to a sequestered walled garden. It was sundown, and I sat beneath a huge chestnut tree, illuminated by candlelight, a bottle of Mumm's chilling on a white hostess cart. Flowers were in bloom; a spherical, Japanese-influenced fountain bubbled quietly. The white wrought-iron settee was covered invitingly in plush white draping.

I breathed in the moment, memorizing every detail. Then the actress made her entrance, this time wearing a beautiful velvet maroon caftan and the same white pearls, her hair in a silver chignon. She offered the same welcoming hand and smile. This time we spoke for four hours, through the gathering dusk and into the evening. We drank champagne and talked about John Huston (I had met his daughter Allegra and interviewed Anjelica), her favorite roles, her daughter's recent marriage, and her garden. She asked me about my life. We laughed and spoke thoughtfully, always with *joie de vivre.* Her assistant took a photograph of us toasting, me looking wide-eyed and contented, Olivia looking regal. When I left, I kissed her hand good-bye, and the trip back to my Paris flat was fueled with a fizzy happiness and a tremendous sense of good fortune at being able to spend time with a real legend.

The goddess had smiled upon me twice. What more could I want? Another visit, of course. In April 2014 I was back in Paris for a conference, but Olivia was suffering from respiratory and back issues and wasn't receiving guests (I wondered if her poor health had somehow been precipitated by the death of her sister, Joan Fontaine, in December 2013); even her old friend Turner Classic Movies host Robert Osborne had been unable to see her, according to her new assistant, Mimi. Nevertheless, at Olivia's urging, Mimi agreed to meet with me at a café near Olivia's home. Over wine and cigarettes, Mimi and I spoke about her work with the actress—like most of Olivia's assistants, Mimi was a lively and charming postgraduate student. It was the next best thing to being in Olivia's drawing room and garden.

This seemed likely to be the end of our encounters, and I was grateful to have met Olivia at all. Time had passed, I had secured the contract for this book and had started my research, and Olivia had recovered from her illnesses of 2014. By the time February 2015 rolled around, I had taken a semester's leave from my university and planned to spend several months working on the first draft of this manuscript. Carpe diem, I thought, so I wrote to Olivia and asked if she would be open to another visit, expecting a charming declination. And *quelle surprise*—she said yes!

A week later I was in Paris, again accompanied by my friend Jane. This time, as befits a grand lady, Olivia was ensconced at the Saint James Hotel while her home was being renovated. She still lives there today, in an airy blue suite designed with a distinctive Chinese aesthetic.

Hidden behind a tall wall in the sixteenth arrondissement, the Saint James is one of the most elegant hotels (and private clubs) I've ever seen. The grand Napoleon III building, with whimsically elegant updates by interior designer Bambi Sloan,[13] is entered through a circular courtyard and up a flight of impressive stone steps. Jane and I sipped cocktails in the leopard-carpeted library bar as we waited for Olivia's newest assistant, the adorable Stefanie (another postgrad student), to escort me to Olivia's suite. This time, in addition to a fragrant and flamboyant bouquet of roses, I arrived bearing a bottle of pink Taittinger champagne (Olivia had emailed me that Stefanie was searching for the rose bubbly because "it's so much more festive"[14]), *macarons* in honor of our first tête-à-tête, and a silk scarf.

When Stefanie arrived, I left a contented Jane in the bar, and we went to the second floor to the star's suite, which was decorated *de la façon chinoise* in beautiful royal blue and turquoise, similar to her signature writing paper. We walked through the entryway, and there, resplendent in a black velvet and gold embroidered caftan, stood my hostess, the divine Olivia de Havilland. Her white bouffant hair was swept up elegantly, as always, and her favorite pearls circled her neck. Her skin was glowing, her smile welcoming, her voice strong, and her memory sharp. We shook hands, shared *bises,* sat together, and, for the next four-plus hours, did justice to more than one bottle of pink champagne. We were like old friends catching up, discussing what we'd been doing and how we'd been. She had just been the subject of a lovely profile in *Entertainment Weekly* entitled "The Last Star," in which she had exclaimed, "'I'm certainly relishing the idea of living a century. Can you imagine that? What an *achievement.*'"[15] We discussed that goal, and with her characteristic energy and enthusiasm, she told me about her home improvements, her pleasures of daily life, and her improved health. Even more flattering to me, she asked about *my* life, remembering details from our first meeting three years before. I had sworn that this time, I was going to leave early. After all, Olivia was ninety-eight years old. Instead, I stayed even later, and rather than take the Metro to my hotel, I asked Stefanie to call a taxi due to the bubbly we had imbibed, whereas Olivia was all poise and warmth. When I saw my friend Jane at our hotel, we toasted to Olivia.

We met for the fourth time only eight months later, in November, again at the Saint James Hotel. This time I flew to Paris not so much to obtain material for this book—she had been most generous in emailing answers to my questions (it had become her favorite way of dealing with interviewers)—but just to see this amazing woman with whom I had finally established a friendship. In addition to roses and champagne, I brought a bottle of her favorite scent, which, I discovered after an inquiry to her assistant, was Chanel No. 5 (I had expected it to be a Dior fragrance, given her love of that fashion house's designs). We spent several hours discussing her relationship with her mother, for whom she had enormous respect and gratitude, as well as contemporary politics, film, and education. I left my first edition of her 1962 memoir of Parisian life, *Every Frenchman Has One,* and she kindly autographed it and sent it to me shortly thereafter.

On July 1, 2016, Olivia turned 100 years old. Tributes from around the world appeared in the media, and the star celebrated at the Saint James with close friends and, of course, with champagne. *Vanity Fair* ran a tribute article in May that asked, "Is 100 the new 70?"[16] And despite the remarkable number of gifts she received to commemorate this wonderful milestone birthday, she emailed me a week later to thank me for my flowers. In December 2017 we enjoyed our fifth meeting, and again I needed a taxi to take me to my hotel after too much intoxicating wine and conversation.

This book examines Olivia de Havilland's long and rich life, hoping to inspire in readers a renewed appreciation for her career. She is still known to the public primarily because of her appearance in *Gone with the Wind;* its seventy-fifth anniversary was celebrated in 2014 with another theatrical release. However, her reputation as an actress and her stature as a Hollywood star, as well as her recognition as the woman who changed the studio contract system, have also ensured the public's enduring interest. In February 2011 at the Cesar Awards, when Jodie Foster introduced de Havilland, who was sitting in the audience, Olivia received a spontaneous standing ovation; the clearly moved actress was acknowledged by industry members seventy-five years younger than she. And at the age of ninety-four, she was awarded both the Legion of Honour in France and a Presidential Arts Medal in the United States—stunning achievements. These aren't just awards for longevity; they signal that the media and popular culture fans are broadening their vision and appreciation of female artistry. (However, the American Film Institute [AFI] can't be accused of such progressiveness. Although the AFI has been giving its Lifetime Achievement Award since 1973, only ten women have received it—none of them Olivia. She hasn't received a Kennedy Center honor either.)

De Havilland was born during World War I on the first day of the Battle of the Somme. Her first film role was only eight years after the first talkies. Yet her regular appearances in the press and in person have asserted her lasting fame, even if that fame is connected in most contemporary minds with *Gone with the Wind* and, to a lesser extent, *The Adventures of Robin Hood* (and now with her depiction in the FX series about Bette Davis and Joan Crawford, *Feud*).

What else does her lengthy legacy entail? De Havilland is one of a select group that has won the best actor or actress Academy Award at least twice, and she has five nominations, along with numerous other film awards. She costarred in one of the most famous films in history. She broke Hollywood's contract system by winning her landmark lawsuit against tenacious Jack Warner when Bette Davis couldn't. Her second husband, Pierre Galante, engineered the photo opportunity that brought Grace Kelly and Prince Rainier of Monaco together. Her move to Paris in the mid-1950s marked a return to her European heritage as well as a prescience concerning the career of *une femme d'un certain âge* in Hollywood. It also inspired the risqué-titled *Every Frenchman Has One* (referring to his liver), reissued by Crown Archetype in June 2016 in time for her centenary. Inevitably, every article that addresses sibling rivalry gives the actress and her late sister, Joan Fontaine, a name check; even the *Vanity Fair* profile of Olivia in May 2016 was part of its special "Sisters" issue.

Thus, Olivia de Havilland has achieved lasting respect and visibility among her peers and the media. Yet we don't really know much about her. Her love affairs with powerful men like Howard Hughes, James Stewart, and John Huston have not been scrutinized as closely as those of other actresses. She's been a staunch Democrat for years yet never publicly espouses her political beliefs, unlike so many of her colleagues. Her film and television work has always been well received, and as late as 1986 she earned a Golden Globe (and an Emmy nomination) for her role as Dowager Empress Maria in the television remake of *Anastasia* with Amy Irving. Yet she doesn't have the same cachet as a Katharine Hepburn or a Bette Davis, despite outliving them both and winning two Oscars. On AFI's top-fifty Hollywood legends list, her name is shockingly missing.

Why isn't de Havilland recognized as one of those legends? There may be several reasons. She lacks a late career-defining role like Davis's and Crawford's in *What Ever Happened to Baby Jane?* or Hepburn's in *On Golden Pond.* Arguably, her last great starring film role was as Catherine Sloper in 1949's *The Heiress,* although she worked when she wanted to for the next forty years. She was never driven by financial or artistic need to stay in the public eye. She wasn't camp; no drag queens dress up as Olivia or one of her characters. Her daughter, Gisèle Galante, has lived a circumspect life as a journalist as well as the administrator of her late husband Edward Broida's estate and art collection. Her quiet remarriage to Andy Chulack in September 2011 did not receive much press. The closest Gisèle has come to gossip was in the 1980s, when she briefly dated French pop heartthrob Johnny Hallyday. Joan Fontaine's 1978 autobiography *No Bed of Roses* pulled no punches about her version of her relationship with her sister, but Olivia has not yet published her long-awaited memoir. She is discreet, protected by French privacy laws and her own generational inclination toward unobtrusive public behavior.

It is that poise, however, that limited Olivia's later career in some ways. So often, she made choices that positioned her as a respectable matron rather than as visceral actress. Perhaps her prettiness and her later motherhood led her to select roles of propriety after the hard-won battle for career freedom. Although she plays a mature seductress opposite the young Richard Burton in 1952's *My Cousin Rachel,* and she enjoys clinches with Robert Mitchum and Rossano Brazzi in later films, she developed a mature, humorous, self-aware protagonist persona who was unwilling to risk emotional or psychological experiments in her roles or performances.

There are two major exceptions to this persona: her hag horror–Grand Guignol roles in 1964 in *Lady in a Cage* and *Hush . . . Hush, Sweet Charlotte.* Perhaps being back in Los Angeles for these films led her to scream along with Bette and Joan and other aging actresses, but it also inspired her to let loose and display a rawer, less controlled complexity in the characters she played. Although these two films have been dismissed as part of the 1960s move to black-and-white B-list horror-thriller films with former A-list stars, they show Olivia's potential to be more than a gentlewoman in a Christian Dior suit.

In exploring Olivia's private and public lives, it has been challenging to find sources that illuminate beyond the fan magazine articles and the polite interviews. A few years ago, I sent a letter to the actress and told her I was thinking of writing a book about her. Often, years would pass before she replied, but this time, a letter appeared in two weeks. In it, Olivia was gracious enough to say, "It is very gratifying to learn that you are considering . . . writing a critical biography of some of my work; I wish you great good fortune therewith." With that letter came a copy of *Paris* magazine that contained a recent interview "almost free of error."[17] A letter that arrived several weeks later offered the caution that "almost nothing accurate is known about my life."[18] True enough. Olivia has shared facts, details, and reminiscences, but she has very wisely shared the private woman with only her inner circle.

Her resolve to maintain the persona she had crafted for more than eighty years was certainly realized in the month before her 101st birthday on July 1, 2017. Queen Elizabeth II had bestowed a damehood on Olivia in early June, making her the oldest person to ever receive the honor. This was a delayed but moving recognition for the actress, who, although a naturalized American citizen, was born to English parents. Olivia issued a statement to *People,* saying she was "'extremely proud that the Queen has appointed me a Dame Commander of the Order of the British Empire. . . . To receive this honor as my 101st birthday approaches is the most gratifying of birthday presents.'"[19]

She was also getting a great deal of press as a result of Ryan Murphy's FX miniseries *Feud,* the delicious tale of the legendary Bette Davis–Joan Crawford relationship. Catherine Zeta-Jones portrays Olivia—who is both narrator (in an imagined 1978 documentary) and participant—as elegant and as loyal to Davis, and her career savvy and her measured, articulate public incarnation are represented.

I emailed her in February 2017 and asked whether she'd watched *Feud* and, if so, what she thought of Catherine Zeta-Jones's portrayal of her. She offered an interesting reply: "Many thanks for the forewarning! My assistant, Stefanie, assures me she will be able to arrange a viewing here of each of the episodes."[20] Apparently, that didn't happen, as Olivia issued a "gorgeously dismissive" response to the *Hollywood Reporter*'s inquiry about her opinion of *Feud*'s depiction of the relationship between Davis and Crawford and of the 1963 Oscar ceremony that features prominently in the series:

> I have received your e-mail with its two questions. . . . I would like to reply first to the second of these, which inquires of me the accuracy of a current television series entitled *Feud,* which concerns Bette Davis and Joan Crawford and their supposed animosity toward each other. Having not seen the show, I cannot make a valid comment about it. However, in principle, I am opposed to any representation of personages who are no longer alive to judge the accuracy of any incident depicted as involving themselves. . . . As to the 1963 Oscar ceremony, which took place over half a century ago, I regret to say that I have no memory of it whatsoever and therefore cannot vouch for its accuracy.[21]

Alas for Ryan Murphy Productions, much of *Feud*'s portrayal of Olivia is not historically accurate. The producers never ran a script by Olivia and never even engaged in a conversation with her. Fatally, I believe, they included a scene in the episode entitled "And the Winner Is . . . (the Oscars of 1963)" in which Olivia (Zeta-Jones) complains about "my bitch sister" Joan Fontaine to Davis (Susan Sarandon).[22] When I saw that, I thought, "Uh-oh. Big mistake there. There is no way that Olivia would okay that."

She didn't. Murphy, who claimed he hadn't wanted to disturb her, must have been unaware of Olivia's successful lawsuit against Jack Warner in the 1940s. So, on the day before she turned 101, Olivia's lawyers filed a suit in Los Angeles against Ryan Murphy Productions. As reported by *Deadline:*

> Her portrayal by Catherine Zeta-Jones in the anthology series damaged her "professional reputation for integrity, honesty, generosity, self-sacrifice and dignity. . . . Olivia de Havilland did not give her permission for FX Defendants to use her name, identity, or likeness in *Feud* or any of the promotional materials used by the FX Defendants to advertise themselves, their products and services," states the complaint charging infringement of right of publicity, invasion of privacy and unjust enrichment that was filed Friday in Los Angeles Superior Court. "FX Defendants knew that they did not obtain Olivia de Havilland's permission to use her name, identity, or likeness in their documentary or the advertisements of their products and services," the 33-page filing adds.[23]

Melanie Hamilton Wilkes stood at the top of the stairs again, sword in hand, ready to vanquish any Yankee—or any Hollywood producer—daring to attack. Scarlett who?

Olivia's protection of her legacy is understandable, and she will not be misrepresented, misquoted, or mishandled by anyone. Her fierceness is quite formidable. Hence, this biography presents both her life and her work as accurately as possible, offering the reader a perspective on the actress and her career that is both respectful and candid—no easy task. Balancing my lifetime of fandom with the biographer's task of providing an accurate interpretation of her life and times was daunting. It is my hope that Olivia de Havilland and her many admirers will find this work an extravagant bouquet of roses, replete with beautiful scents and textures and colors—and the occasional thorn.

1

AN ENGLISHWOMAN ABROAD

Olivia Mary de Havilland's entrance into the world was in some ways typical of a child of English expatriates during World War I. Such children were born into privilege, thanks to ambitious parents who were seeking their fortunes in faraway countries. Yet within three years of her birth, Olivia's life (and the British Empire) took a new direction in a new world. For Olivia, this resulted in a career of changing personas, evolving artistic interests, shifting nationalities and countries, and routed gender expectations. It also suggested the resilience, determination, and bravery that have taken her, as of this writing, to her 102nd year.

Olivia was born in Tokyo, Japan, on July 1, 1916, to two British citizens—Lilian Augusta Ruse, a talented music and voice student and later teacher, and Walter Augustus de Havilland, a Cambridge graduate and lawyer. Outwardly, they seemed typical of their class at the end of the Edwardian era; however, some quirks would soon become apparent: Lilian had performing aspirations that she passed on to her first daughter, Olivia, and to her second child, born seventeen months later, Joan de Beauvoir. Walter, a patent attorney working for a British firm in Tokyo, had aspirations to live the life of a mikado once he arrived in Japan and was somewhat successful in that pursuit.[1]

Lilian Augusta Ruse was born in Reading, Berkshire, England, on June 11, 1886. She studied voice and music and was accomplished enough to win two three-year scholarships to Reading Musical College.[2] In fact, according to Olivia, "Starting at the age of fifteen . . . she was trained as a teacher of Choral Singing. . . . And it was Choral Singing which she taught in Tokyo's Anglican community—starting . . . in 1907."[3] That year, Lilian traveled to Tokyo to accept the position and was reunited with her brother, Ernest, who taught music at Waseda University.[4] Many British men and women made their fortunes in the East in the nineteenth and early twentieth centuries, but for Lilian to venture to Japan without a husband showed a bravery and a confidence that would be passed on to both Olivia and her sister.

It was there that Lilian first met Walter de Havilland, who became smitten with the younger woman. He proposed, but she rejected him and returned to England in 1911. Beginning in January 1912, she studied acting with Sir Beerbohm Tree while working as his assistant at his academy, now known as the Royal Academy of Dramatic Arts (RADA).[5] Olivia noted that Lilian "was prompted to embark on this adventure by a remark made by another Tokyo resident, a lady playwright who, after hearing my mother sing a solo one Sunday morning at St. Andrew's Church in Tokyo, said to her, 'You have a beautiful voice and I would like to write a musical play for you.' To which my mother replied, 'I know a lot about music and singing, but nothing whatever about acting.'"[6]

It is interesting to watch Lilian, billed as "Lilian Fontaine," in the 1945 film *The Lost Weekend.* She has one brief scene as the mother of Jane Wyman's character, who is dating the alcoholic played by Ray Milland. While waiting with her husband in the lobby of a hotel, Lilian's character analyzes her daughter's suitor, unaware that he is sitting behind her and listening to everything she says. Lilian speaks in a cultured voice, using that mid-Atlantic–British cross-dialect that matrons in Hollywood films adopted in the 1930s and 1940s. She is substantial, almost coquettish, in her brief scene. In one moment, when she appears in profile, she reveals the heart-shaped face of Olivia. In the next moment, the angle reveals the high cheekbones of Joan. It's not much screen time, but it was an important accomplishment for Lilian, who, according to Joan's autobiography, *No Bed of Roses,* possessed a post-Victorian self-control as well as "taste, discrimination, good manners, love of the arts, intellectual clarity, the highest morality in all things."[7]

Not unlike Bette and Bobby Davis and their mother, Ruthie, the de Havilland–Fontaine girls breathed the air of the redoubtable Lilian, whose inspiration and grit were paired with the brusqueness of her class and age. Joan's relationship with Lilian was troubled, and the actress felt she didn't know her mother very well; Olivia's view of her mother was more appreciative. She said, "A total misconception exists regarding my mother's gifts, her background, and her intentions for her children. She wanted to bring us up in a normal way, consistent with her own upbringing and with our infancy in Japan."[8]

Olivia's father, Walter, was born on August 31, 1872, a thoroughly British colonial descended from Guernsey ancestors. The de Havilland family tree is a remarkable one. Olivia researched Lilian's family and traced them only as far as "1839 and a lady school teacher in Cambridgeshire," but the de Havilland line goes back for hundreds of years. There is a family coat of arms and an important relationship to Sir Geoffrey de Havilland, the great aviation pioneer. Olivia "did not know until I was 15 years of age that there was a connection between me and Sir Geoffrey." They met later, however, and "Sir Geoffrey, himself, sent me a chart which makes my paternal lineage (and his) quite clear," indicating that they were cousins.[9] Olivia even attended the University of Hertfordshire's dedication of its de Havilland campus in 1997, in recognition of Sir Geoffrey's technological contributions to aviation history. He built the Tiger Moth, Mosquito, and Comet at the Hatfield site where the campus is located.[10]

After attending Cambridge, Walter went east, as many young men of his class did at the start of the twentieth century (including Lilian's brother). Perhaps in rebellion against the strictures of his Episcopalian minister father, the Reverend Charles Richard de Havilland, and the limitations of the island of Guernsey, Walter was drawn to a different sort of island—exotic and far from the Church of England morality with which he grew up. The burgeoning international business scene in Tokyo was a perfect place for Walter to establish his career as a patent attorney in a comfortably upper-class milieu while creating a new persona for himself. This required a suitable wife.

Walter returned to England at the start of World War I and tried to enlist in the British army. At age forty-two, he was deemed too old to serve, but this disappointment resulted in a positive outcome when he and Lilian were reintroduced. This time, she accepted his proposal, albeit in a reckless way—she "tossed a crown to help her make a decision"—and they were married in 1914.[11] That rather cavalier action foreshadowed the couple's marital dynamic. Nevertheless, it was a good marriage for twenty-eight-year-old Lilian; she was actively involved in the socially acceptable pastimes of choir and amateur performance, but it was time for the young woman to establish the status and lifestyle that marriage would afford. Walter was tall, distinguished, solvent, well connected, and, if not handsome, then certainly commanding. Lilian was a little *jolie laide,* not a beauty and somewhat inclined to stoutness, yet she had a trained voice and a commanding manner of her own. It should have been a perfectly convenient partnership. After they married, Walter and Lilian returned to Japan.

Although there was a significant age difference (fourteen years), this probably would not have been an issue if the couple had been better suited to each other. Lilian was bright and accomplished and played the role of the expatriate wife well enough, yet she was ambitious for herself and later for her daughters, not in terms of a career but certainly in terms of social and creative opportunities. Her dramatic temperament was not a comfortable fit with Walter's more patrician, taciturn nature. Walter wanted an adoring wife and children, but he also wanted the freedom that an aristocratic male deserved—he wanted to have his wife and his geisha servant, too.

When Olivia Mary arrived two years later, she was not the desired first-born son, but she possessed the intelligence, drive, and ambition expected of a boy. Her early years in Japan "had an enduring effect upon [her] life." She compared her childhood in Tokyo with her later life in Paris, where "I hear a foreign language all day long." Her house in Paris is "surrounded by embassies," which is "the very milieu in which my parents lived in Tokyo."[12] As she shared with a group of art and film conference attendees in Osaka, Japan, in November 2014, she still remembers "how to count to eight in Japanese."[13]

With a loving mother, a successful father, and a baby sister (Joan arrived on October 22, 1917), Olivia's world was one of cherry blossom privilege. World War I was raging in Europe, but the de Havillands were safely ensconced in Japan, away from it all. For a few years, life in Tokyo was very good for the family. Olivia's mother was enjoying success as a singer and a hostess. Olivia remembered:

> As part of the official program prepared for the four-day State Visit of HRH Prince Arthur of Connaught to the Court of the Emperor of Japan, a celebrated British Amateur Theatre group presented, to great acclaim, an operetta entitled *Kismet,* starring my mother and a leading man. The fame of this production apparently spread far and wide.
>
> At that time, my mother had enjoyed a significant position in Tokyo's foreign diplomatic and business community as the wife of Walter Augustus de Havilland. . . . The couple entertained sumptuously in their great big white house with its spacious grounds and staff of nine, including a Chinese chef and a coachman.[14]

And yet, the good life did not last. The birth of a younger and frequently sickly sibling, and then Olivia's own bout with bronchitis at age three (she has struggled off and on with respiratory ailments all her life), led to upheaval.[15] Lilian decided to move her daughters from Japan for their health. The entire family arrived in San Francisco on March 1, 1919, and almost immediately Olivia came down with a fever and tonsillitis and Joan contracted pneumonia.

Following medical advice, Lilian decided to stay with her girls in California. Postwar California was a better option for Lilian than England, as the weather was warm and the West Coast was readily accessible from Japan, where Walter returned a week later owing to "unexpected circumstances."[16] His quick departure put space between Lilian and Walter, which was not a hardship for either of them; their incompatibility included his infidelities outside the home and then his installation of a mistress-cum-housekeeper named Yoki-san.[17]

Olivia expressed admiration for Lilian's "capacity to cope" during this trial, which left her mother "alone in a foreign country with two small children . . . and the urgent search for convenient and reasonable quarters. . . . She rose to this daunting situation astonishingly well and did the same with all of the other challenges which followed." As to Walter's disappearance from her life, Olivia said, "I have no recollection of any social problems related to the absence of a paternal presence."[18] This cold, clipped affirmation of life after father reflects the distant relationship the adult Olivia had with Walter. After a few months in the Vendome Hotel in the Santa Clara valley, Lilian settled her two girls in the charming city of Saratoga, first living in Lundblad's boardinghouse and later in their own home.[19]

Support from Walter was insufficient, so Lilian worked in a milliner's shop, gave dramatic readings at women's clubs, and occasionally performed in plays; she would later teach voice and music. She wasn't a career woman, but it quickly became clear that she would have to raise her children without Walter, which she managed to do. She eventually built them a charming cottage in Saratoga and even employed a housekeeper. Olivia adored her mother and asserted, "I think my independent spirit was greatly nourished by her example. . . . Because my sibling and I were . . . entirely in the care of our mother, we were at the very center of her life and had her full attention. Long before either of us enrolled in first grade, she taught my sibling and me how to read and write. . . . Though she loved and needed marital life, [she] could live quite satisfactorily without it, if need be."[20]

Lilian accepted that her marriage was over. She returned to Japan in 1924, staying for almost four months to negotiate a divorce from Walter (leaving the children with the housekeeper, Mrs. Hatfield).[21] He married his Japanese lover three years later.

Lilian wasn't alone for long. She met George Milan Fontaine at a New Year's Eve ball at the Vendome Hotel.[22] Divorced with one son, he was co-owner and general manager of Hale Brothers, a San Jose department store. George was very attracted to Lilian, and she certainly welcomed his attentions.

They courted, and two months after her divorce was final, in April 1925, Lilian married George. His position and income made life financially easier for Lilian and her daughters, but his temperament and inflexibility would lead to problems later.

Both Olivia and Joan were extremely bright, and Lilian taught them articulation, voice, deportment, literature, and discipline—attributes that would stand them both in good stead later. Olivia, whose nickname was "Livvie," initially attended Saratoga Grammar School. She was happy there, and she "sensed a kind of equality between the two sexes . . . all the teachers were women and the girl students, generally speaking, were better at their studies than the boys." This strengthened her self-confidence, as did being chosen to recite at the school assembly every Columbus Day and competing in the Santa Clara County spelling bee (despite being "defeated . . . by a boy!").[23] When Lilian "urgently needed a major operation" in the late 1920s, it was decided that the girls should temporarily attend a local convent school, but because of her divorced status, Lilian's initial request was turned down.[24] Fortunately, Notre Dame Convent allowed both children to attend while Lilian convalesced. The discipline and rigor, as well as the familiar smells and bells of Anglicanism, provided a positive interlude for Olivia, who was an excellent student—quick, energetic, and popular. She was athletic as well—enjoying good health after her early years of illness—and she loved dogs (one of her party tricks was a great dog bark, which she would use in *Princess O'Rourke*).

During this time, Olivia developed a love of reading: "John Steinbeck and F. Scott Fitzgerald have a singular and permanent place among my favorite American authors. So do Henry James, Herman Melville, and Edith Wharton. And top of the list, is the great . . . Leo Tolstoy."[25] Olivia attended Los Gatos Union High School from 1930 to 1934. She was active and happy, bright and accomplished, and pretty, with long, naturally wavy hair and a trim figure. She was never intimidated by the boys and sensed no inequality between the genders—"in every field girls and boys enjoyed the same privileges."[26] That kind of empowerment served her well when she took on one of the big boys in Hollywood: Jack Warner.

She found her teachers to be supportive and inspirational. In fact, she contemplated becoming a teacher herself "because my own teachers contributed so much to my life and because I realized how invaluable teachers are in influencing and shaping the culture and character of a country: whole civilizations depend upon them. I still think of teaching as one of the 'sacred' professions."[27] Her teachers "inspired their students to pursue many interests. As a result, my school activities were so broad . . . that my ambition at the time was to be the first woman president of the United States. It was a vast disappointment to me when I learned that, should I become an American citizen [which she did on November 28, 1941], I could never aspire to that high position as I was born outside of the USA."[28]

Olivia recalls her high school experience with great fondness, and her involvement in extracurricular activities gave her enormous pleasure, as did her intellectual pursuits:

> Early on, I was elected Secretary of my class and a member of the Student Council. When I ran for Secretary of the Student Body, I won. I went out for debate and with my partner, Jimmy Gibb, won a majority of our debates. I also won the Miller Public Speaking Cup (my subject was Woodrow Wilson); and in my senior year I was selected as Editor of the *Wildcat,* the school annual. Kay Ellis was the Valedictorian of my graduating class in June of 1934 and I was co-Salutatorian with Keats Pullen, who later turned out to be an atomic scientist (our grades were very close but mine were better than his).[29]

Olivia demonstrated an interest in theater by becoming secretary of the drama club.[30] She also joined the glee club and played various sports, even lettering in field hockey.[31]

Olivia was shy, but like the *Twelfth Night* character for whom her Shakespeare-loving mother named her,[32] she learned to function well under another persona—a stereotypically "masculine" persona in terms of her energy, courage, and agency. She was offered the lead in *Alice in Wonderland* by the Saratoga community theater, and she recalled, "'I really felt I was Alice and that when I moved across the stage I was actually moving in Alice's enchanted wonderland.'"[33]

While Olivia was laying the groundwork for her future, she was also developing autonomy. Her relationship with her sister was never close—Joan was younger, more fragile, and needier—and this lack of an intimate sibling bond contributed to Olivia's independence. Her father was also absent and played little to no part in Olivia's young life; Walter didn't return to the United States until 1940. She loved her mother, but Lilian was busy being a wife, which brings us to her stepfather, George Fontaine. Although Olivia liked Fontaine enormously when she first met him, he was extremely controlling, which led to difficulties. Joan (who took his last name as her stage name) escaped George by returning to her father in Japan, a reunion she described in *No Bed of Roses* as peculiarly incestuous. Olivia's escape was different.

Fontaine was dictatorial and disapproved of a theatrical career—rather ironic, given the woman he married. He forbade Olivia's participation in extracurricular activities, particularly theater (which she circumvented, exhibiting a rebellious streak that persisted throughout her life), and imposed an 8:15 p.m. curfew, so early that the two girls had to study by flashlight.[34] When Fontaine wouldn't allow her to play Violet in the junior class production of *Mrs. Bumpstead-Leigh* (a popular comedy from 1929), sixteen-year-old Olivia moved out of the house in 1932.[35] Lilian, being a Victorian conservative in many ways, would not contradict her husband and allowed Olivia to leave. However, Lilian's bridge club raised $200 toward her expenses (which Olivia repaid), and the teenager moved into the home of a family friend. Olivia performed in the play, while tutoring in math, working in the public library, and babysitting to cover her expenses.[36]

She also experienced her first love. Olivia fell for seventeen-year-old Peter Dwight Whitney in the summer of 1932. Peter was the cousin of her best friends in Saratoga, the Goodrich girls (no relation to Olivia's first husband), and "it was a case of instant attraction. Peter was a brilliant student and had won a scholarship to Yale. Before he left for the fall term, immediately after kissing me for the first time he asked me to marry him. I instantly said yes, and not many days afterward he slipped an engagement ring on the proper finger."[37] This was another bold move for sixteen-year-old Olivia, and for two years the young lovers wrote to each other and pined. However, when Olivia's interest in acting became clear and Peter realized she wanted a career, he said "that if I became an actress I could be his mistress but he would not marry me. This ended our relationship."[38] Silly Peter.

Olivia had learned a very valuable lesson one would not expect a young woman from a refined European background to know so early in life: she was self-sufficient. She could make her own living and live her own way. Father figures would come and go in her life—curiously, and at the risk of sounding too post-Freudian, when it came to men, she had a type. Olivia's father was tall and imposing. Although her stepfather was not as physically impressive, he occupied a position of power. Her first husband, Marcus Goodrich, was another tall man with a powerful physique and a healthy ego. Other beaus included Jimmy Stewart, Howard Hughes, and John Huston—all long, tall drinks of water with a love of adventure. She would love and be loved by these men, but she would live on her own talent and wit. No one would caretake or dominate Olivia. In that respect, she was far more Scarlett than Melanie, and her ability to live her own way, with or without a tall, handsome Prince Charming, was inspirational and typical of Olivia—the steel and the softness combined.

The teenaged Olivia's courage to strike out in her own direction rather than be a dutiful stepdaughter reflected her mother's gumption, to use a good American southern term. She might be the prodigal daughter, but she remained close to her mother while living the life she wanted to live. She knew what she wanted.

It is that intelligent direction that marks so much of Olivia's screen work. One trait that sets her apart from other actresses of her generation is the thoughtfulness of her performances. Even at her most youthfully luscious, in her early screen appearances in 1935 and 1936, she was more than the starlet's cliché of "spirited" or "spritely" or "winsome." She wasn't hyperenergetic like Hepburn or hypermannered like Davis. She was both accessible and inaccessible, pretty and patrician, melting and iron-spined.

In the summer of 1934, right after Olivia graduated from high school, she was cast as Puck in the Saratoga community theater production of *A Midsummer Night's Dream.* Like so many young thespians, she found a supportive community in the theater, and she was exploring the possibilities of her talents.

Saratoga was good to Olivia and her family, and the actress remained fond of the town. In a letter from October 1977, Olivia noted that while filming *The Swarm* in Los Angeles, producer Irwin Allen had given her a few days off before her final scene was filmed. The actress headed north to Los Gatos Lodge, the "part of California which I know best. The pretty village of Saratoga, where I grew up, is only four miles away, the familiar green mountains are near at hand, frost coats the grass in the morning, the maples are turning red, and the days are golden in the October sun."[39]

Saratoga was the perfect location for *A Midsummer Night's Dream,* a luminous Shakespearean celebration of youthful passion. Although Puck was not an ingenue role (Olivia would soon have many opportunities to play such parts), the character's puckishness suited the lithe, athletic young woman. There was an enormous amount of publicity at the time because the Hollywood Bowl was also staging the play, directed by renowned European director Max Reinhardt. He was one of a panoply of talented theatrical and film personages to escape Europe for Hollywood in the 1930s and find a burgeoning industry willing to pay generously—despite the worldwide Depression—for their talents.

With tremendous good luck, and "through the intervention of friends," Olivia "met Felix Weisberger, the casting director for Reinhardt. . . . Olivia only requested permission to watch Reinhardt's rehearsals, but Weisberger asked her to audition."[40] That was a fortuitous break, and Olivia was offered the opportunity to be understudy to Jean Rouverol, the understudy of actress Gloria Stuart (rumored to be a close friend of Olivia's, but untrue according to the actress herself), who was cast as Hermia. She would have to go to Los Angeles, but she would still be able to attend Mills College, a women's liberal arts college in Oakland, in the fall (Olivia wanted to teach and had won a full scholarship in drama and speech arts). There was only one course—the lovely Livvie left Peter Whitney and Saratoga behind and embarked upon a really big adventure. Like something out of Warner Brothers' great theatrical myth-making musical *42nd Street,* Olivia went to Los Angeles a kid, a nobody, and within a year became a star.

2

FROM STARLET TO LITTLE STAR

In *Melanie Remembers,* a 2004 documentary, Olivia de Havilland recalls how she managed her loan-out to David Selznick for *Gone with the Wind* by appealing to Jack Warner's wife, Ann, for help. She had to use this subterfuge because, though popular with audiences, she had very little clout with the studio. As she described her career at that time, "I was a star, that's true. But I was a little star, a sort of mini-star."[1]

This was an accurate assessment of her position in Hollywood from 1935 to late 1938. Olivia was a contract player at Warner Brothers, appearing in several prestige productions, wearing chic contemporary designs or luxurious period costumes, tossing her ringlets to indicate her sassy smarts. But beyond playing a spirited young woman across several centuries, what she desired were roles that tested her as an actress. That is why she ultimately left Warner Brothers and risked her career for the chance to shine brighter. Nevertheless, from the age of eighteen to twenty-three—from her screen debut in 1935, through her first films with Errol Flynn, to her first Oscar nomination and first significant test of her talent in *Gone with the Wind*—Olivia led a relatively charmed life, both financially and professionally. In just five years, despite her frustrations, the starlet became a star—a little star, perhaps, but luminous.

Her opportunity to participate in Max Reinhardt's *A Midsummer Night's Dream* must have seemed like a dream—or a Hollywood movie. Olivia told a British Film Institute audience in August 1971, "It was sort of a cinema script in itself, which of course all of our lives are."[2] To go from playing Puck in the Saratoga community theater production to being an understudy at the Hollywood Bowl was a move of Shakespearean proportions. So fortuitous were the many elements that aligned for Olivia that her breakthrough really was the stuff acting dreams are made on. However, had she not had talent and intelligence, she would merely be a footnote rather than one of the last survivors of the golden studio era.

Olivia went to Los Angeles as a minor participant in this theatrical happening, and then "a further miracle occurred." Leading lady Gloria Stuart was filming at Warner Brothers, so Olivia took the role of Hermia during rehearsals with Reinhardt. Then, five days before the opening, Stuart had to bow out because of her work schedule. Olivia recalled, "I was receiving this banquet rather than a sandwich. . . . September 17, 1934, 26,000 people . . . in the audience was William Powell, Bette Davis, Joan Crawford, Jean Harlow . . . and that was the way the story began."[3]

A press release by Robert Taplinger, director of publicity for Warner Brothers, noted that Olivia "then went on the road with [*Midsummer*], playing in the open-air Greek Theatre at Berkeley, in San Francisco and in Milwaukee."[4] During the tour, Olivia received some good news: "I was summoned back to Hollywood from Milwaukee, by the astonishing announcement that Professor Reinhardt was going to make the 'Dream' into a motion picture . . . and that they wanted to test me for the part."[5]

That the play was filmed at all was extremely fortunate for Olivia and out of character for Warner Brothers. A production of such scintillating glamour, and potentially small box office returns, seemed more suited to Metro Goldwyn Mayer (MGM), a studio known for its elaborate spending and literary adaptations. Warner Brothers decided to film Reinhardt's *Midsummer Night's Dream* to assert its artistic ambition, a rather surprising and costly decision. But Warners was an interesting place—a mixture of urban social dramas and Busby Berkeley musicals, tight budgets and an international pool of technical talent, Al Jolson blackface yet more roles for African American players than any other major studio.

It also had great up-and-coming stars recognized more for their acting skills than their glamour—James Cagney, Humphrey Bogart, Bette Davis (known as the fifth Warner Brother). The studios were run by ambitious moguls, and as Olivia conceded years later, "They were extraordinary people. And they had suitable respect for the talent at their service. They knew how to make use of it and develop it."[6] In many ways, Warner Brothers seemed to be the perfect studio for Olivia, a serious young actress who wanted a real career. But like Bette Davis (who was eight years her senior), Olivia would find that the mix of artistry and economics, central to the film business, was often incompatible, and the bottom line took precedence over the ambitions of contract players. In a rather prescient comment, Taplinger said of Olivia, this "radiantly healthy youngster," that her "ambition—perhaps like that of every other young actress, runs toward the strongly dramatic things of the screen. She knows she is not yet old enough for them. . . . But some day."[7]

The DVD of *A Midsummer Night's Dream* includes Olivia's screen test as Marianne, suggestive of the heroine of the French Revolution, and her youth and inexperience are very obvious. She wears a frilly housemaid's cap and a peasant's dress and has two scenes—one in which she pleads before a magistrate, and the other in which she learns that her mother is dead. In the first, she's awkward, unsure of what to do with her arms and hands, overdirected to the point of melodrama; she declaims theatrically, her technique for a Hollywood Bowl audience rather than the camera. But she's endearing. Her initial entrance shows her petitioning the magistrate like a meek little girl, saying coyly, "I want to see the king." She simultaneously maintains eye contact and simpers like a child—"I want to tell him how things really are."[8] This scene is awkward, with abrupt shifts in beats, but Olivia's face is mobile, expressive. Some of the phrasing is odd, and she has a slight French accent that comes and goes. At one point, she even appears to break character, laughing inappropriately, but the little trooper keeps going.

The second test scene cuts to Marianne's house, where she slices bread and giggles youthfully with her brother, mugging for the camera. But when she discovers their mother is dead, Olivia owns the moment. Slowly she moves over to the body, grabs the blanket, and covers her mother's face, never taking her eyes from the corpse as she drops her head theatrically. We see potential in the untrained girl who pulls the dust cap off her head as she weeps; her diction is lovely (Lilian would have been proud), and her outrage is palpable as a bill collector comes to take their furniture.

When Warner acquired *Midsummer* and Reinhardt, it also acquired Olivia de Havilland. Earning a contract with a major studio at the age of eighteen was an enormous accomplishment, for there were thousands of young actresses with more experience, all vying for their big break. Warner's many backstage musicals showcased lines and lines of lovely faces, dancing and smiling their way into anonymity, but Olivia stood out.

Because of her youth, "the contract had to be approved by the Court and a guardian appointed. Quite naturally, this role fell to my mother and it was one she fulfilled wonderfully. . . . However, [she] was not at all involved with my work, which was a very private matter between me and the roles in which I was cast."[9] Even then, her innate independence was evident.

The studio contract system was one of the best training grounds for serious young actors. Unlike in Britain, which had the Royal Academy of

Dramatic Arts, there were few training programs in the United States for professional theater aspirants. The best route for serious American actors was to take acting classes or work with acting coaches, gain experience in regional and summer theater, and then, with luck, move on to Broadway or a lucrative contract with a studio. During the Depression and World War II, the best talents from both coasts and from Europe found a future in Hollywood.

Olivia's contract with Warner Brothers ran for seven years—if her option was picked up, plus any suspension time—and it guaranteed that she would be performing and networking with the best talent on the West Coast. Olivia's success was gratifying to her mother Lilian, who had maintained her own theatrical interests. Lilian, who would go on to become a teacher of performance at a variety of California institutions, including Stanford, was very pleased that Olivia was appearing in such a prestigious production. Olivia also paved the way for her sister Joan's acting ambitions. Whatever the tension and competition between them, Olivia's success led to interest in Joan. Sibling rivalry existed between the young women, but Olivia provided the template for Joan's career.

Above all, Olivia's contract with Warner was the pathway to everything she desired—an intelligent career, an opportunity to learn, exposure to the wider artistic community, financial security, and self-determination. Healthy, trim, and pretty rather than beautiful or seductive (other than having a canine tooth capped, her good looks were all natural), Olivia possessed the ability to play the all-American girl as well as the romantic European heroine in a range of genre films. She was disciplined and bright, and although she never went to Mills College, she was an autodidact whose intelligence and curiosity led her to become a fine writer and an independent artist. And she was a single woman, which made her the subject of countless movie magazine profiles but also allowed her to date some of the most eligible and interesting men in Hollywood.

The importance of studio photographs in promoting a career should not be underestimated. At this time, Olivia began collaborating with photographer Scotty Welbourne, and many of his snapshots appeared in fan magazines. As she remembered in 1995, "Scotty was one of the studio's excellent team of portrait photographers and the first photographer with whom I worked soon after arriving at Warner's in mid-December of 1934. I always enjoyed our sessions which were harmonious and creative."[10] The Warner Brothers machine was behind Olivia; her light was brightening.

In her screen debut as Hermia, Olivia costarred with future MGM superstar Mickey Rooney in the role of Puck. Olivia's eulogy for Rooney in 2014 recalled "a little boy passing easily as a nine-year-old when you are really thirteen. You hand me your work copy of *A Midsummer Night's Dream,* climb onto the banquette beside me, place your head upon my lap, and ask me to awaken you nine lines before your cue."[11] Hermia's romantic interest, Lysander, was played by Dick Powell, Warner's leading juvenile male star. In addition, the supporting cast was impressive—comedians Joe E. Brown and Frank McHugh, beauties Jean Muir and Anita Louise, and the tragic Ross Alexander (who would work with Olivia again in *Captain Blood* but commit suicide in 1937). Erich Wolfgang Korngold, who arranged the glorious Mendelssohn score, had worked with Reinhardt in Vienna on a variety of projects.[12] This was the beginning of Korngold's long career with Warner, including creating the magnificent score for *The Adventures of Robin Hood* (1938), starring Olivia and Errol Flynn.

According to the trailer for *A Midsummer Night's Dream,* the studio planned to charge $2.20 for first-run seats.[13] Considering that a movie ticket normally cost 25 cents, this was a significant decision by Warner Brothers. The film still wouldn't make any money, given the cost of the production, but in those days, the movie factories were willing to produce worthy pictures just to demonstrate the legitimacy of the film industry.

There was an enormous amount of publicity for *Midsummer,* and the DVD's special features include many of these short film promotions. "A Dream Comes True" details the production and uses backstage film of the actors; it also shows footage of the premiere, including a young Olivia hidden by the microphone and swathed in a white mink that's too large for her. "Warner Bros. Studio Café" features Joe E. Brown and Pat O'Brien bantering about how great the movie is, and a long short called "Shake Mr. Shakespeare" shows various characters coming to life and singing. In "Presenting," the film's leading actors—Dick Powell, Ian Hunter, Jean Muir, Frank McHugh, Anita Louise, and Olivia—emerge from behind a curtain, flanked on either side by palms, to a trumpet announcement. The men sport white tie and tails, the women wear evening gowns, and each addresses the audience directly while discussing Professor Reinhardt and his shimmering spectacle.

Olivia, announced as "Olivia de Haviland" (the second *l* is missing both here and in the film's opening credits), looks very young but very poised. Her Hollywood hairstyle seems youthfully silly, and her studio-chosen dress—a simple long, dark gown with a white-sequined V-neck collar and cuffed sleeves just above the elbow—is conservative and not particularly flattering. She wears a hat perched above her left eye. Even so, she is tremendously appealing. She begins to speak in a waist-up one-shot:

> Ladies and gentlemen: I know it isn't polite to intrude one's private life upon other people. But I would like to tell you why I think I'm the luckiest girl in the world. When an actress gets what is called in Hollywood "a break," which means that she's assigned to her first part, it isn't very often that she's allowed to play in a large production. Therefore, you can imagine how amazed I was [in this first direct address to her audience, we can hear Olivia's trademark lengthening of vowels for theatrical emphasis] when they told me that Max Reinhardt was going to let me play the part of Hermia in *A Midsummer Night's Dream,* and Max Reinhardt as you know is the greatest genius of all directors.[14]

Olivia delivers her first comments with sincerity, perfect diction, and lovely simplicity. Then the camera cuts to a full close-up. Her eyebrows aren't overplucked in the style of the day, and her eye makeup is subtle. Her bow mouth and open face are soft, her dimpled chin charming. She continues:

> This great Shakespeare classic represents a glorious effort to produce a picture which will influence the entire future technique of the talking screen. Its beauty, its lavish mounting, and its unbelievable photographic effects can't [she uses the British pronunciation *cahnt*—another Olivia-ism] possibly be described adequately. I do hope you'll see it, and then perhaps you'll forgive me for having intruded now to tell you about it.[15]

The film itself is exquisite to look at, but it feels longer than two hours and thirty-five minutes, given the overture, the exit music, and the intermission, not to mention Mickey Rooney's obnoxious performance as Puck. Still, James Cagney and Joe E. Brown are great fun as Nick Bottom and Francis Flute. The dances choreographed by Bronislava Nijinska (sister of renowned ballet dancer Vaslav Nijinsky) capture a spritely mixture of elegance and ephemerality. Mendelssohn's music conducted by Korngold embellishes the action beautifully.

Visually, the film is almost surreal in its splendor. The epic crowd scenes of scantily clad fairies dressed in silky silver fringe dancing and frolicking through the lush woodland set—all twinkling water, glistening leaves and clouds, and various fauna and flora—are completely enchanting. There is even a unicorn walking through a dry-ice fog in the moonlight. As for the chastely erotic fairies awakening during the midsummer night to misbehave, the film gives us loads of lissome girls in Isadora Duncan garb. So sharply yet mistily photographed, the film can only be fully appreciated on the big screen.

Olivia has little to do as Hermia, who is in love with Dick Powell's Lysander, but as the juvenile leads, they are fresh and fun together. She is styled beautifully; her unpretentious youth and natural loveliness are highlighted by her loose, curling hair worn in a center part, an embellished Elizabethan collar, and iridescent gowns. Olivia runs, she smiles, she kisses, she recites the verse fairly well, but otherwise, there's not much to do except look pretty. Still, she gets more screen time than Jean Muir.

Olivia is learning on the job here. As in her screen test, she has a tendency to cut some of her lines a bit short, or flutter her hands in front of her mouth too much in a gesture of concern, or bite her lower lip, which became a characteristic action of hers. At this point, she is what Ted Sennett accurately describes in *Warner Brothers Presents* as "well-meaning but arch or saccharine . . . enchantingly beautiful and vapid . . . lovely and demure as usual."[16] She is sweet and breathless and petite, yet she utilizes the alto range of her trained voice (thanks to Lilian). She moves in the elaborate garments so well and she connects so beautifully with Dick Powell that when they kiss, it's a luscious adolescent moment. When the young lovers walk through the enchanted woods and Powell tenderly kisses her eyes and then sings to Olivia, it's her Ruby Keeler moment. Later, when she leans back in the forest with her arms above her head to rest, it is a sensual move that anticipates her potential sexuality. By the time the film closes with Mendelssohn's "Wedding March" and the lines, "Lovers to bed. 'Tis almost fairy time,"[17] Olivia has been established as a romantic starlet with the grace and poise of someone ten years older. She receives sixth billing, but given the seasoned performers, the enormous sets, the huge cast, and the epic production values, that's not bad for a film debut.

While not successful at the box office, *Midsummer* helped establish Warner as a major studio in Hollywood; Louis B. Mayer and the Selznick-Thalberg units weren't the only purveyors of class and classics. It was important for the studios to create thoughtful, prestigious films, particularly given the production code and Breen office strictures from 1933 onward. Warner spent $1.5 million on a film that didn't recoup its costs,[18] although it earned respectable reviews. Importantly, the film won two Academy Awards—one for Hal Mohr's cinematography by write-in vote, and a well-deserved editing Oscar for Ralph Dawson.

MGM released its own Shakespeare film the next year. *Romeo and Juliet,* starring Warner Brothers fixture Leslie Howard and the reigning queen of MGM, Norma Shearer, was produced by her husband, the powerful Irving Thalberg. This reflected a competitive recognition of Warner's growing influence as a Hollywood power broker.

Although *A Midsummer Night's Dream* was Olivia's first film, it required several months to edit and complete the special effects, as well as construct the publicity campaign to launch the film and its young stars. Thus, movie audiences were introduced to Olivia not as the delicious Hermia in this magnificent fantasy but in the "genial if ramshackle little comedy" *Alibi Ike* (1935).[19] *Alibi Ike* was based on a Ring Lardner story about baseball, so at least its inspiration was respectable. It starred comedian Joe E. Brown, he of the wide mouth, tiny eyes, and voice like a fire alarm. Brown was popular with the public, and this film was designed to showcase him in the role of Ike, a good-natured baseball player who always has an excuse for what goes wrong. Olivia was cast as the girlfriend, Dolly, and she was not happy: "They did rather see me as an ingenue. And I was quite upset when they cast me immediately after in *Alibi Ike*. . . . I began this career which I saw in the most illustrious terms—with Shakespeare—and I had quite other ideas about my career."[20]

The role of Dolly could have been played by any starlet in a hundred-mile radius, and for Olivia, this was an abrupt shift, a "rude shock to be transported from the euphoria of the Reinhardt milieu to the workaday business of a routine movie product such as *Alibi Ike*."[21] When the young actress protested her casting to production executive Henry Blanke, she fired the first shot in what would be her tempestuous career at Warner Brothers; Jack Warner responded that she was under contract and had a job to do.[22] Despite her promising talent, Olivia was only one of a stable of actresses at the studio, and she would have to prove herself unique.

Olivia, a trooper, offers a spirited performance opposite Brown as his much-too-young love interest. The pairing is actually disconcerting and discomfiting, given their age difference; the forty-four-year-old Brown was more than twice her age and was not a dashing leading man, which might have made her attraction to him more believable. Olivia was too cultured and serious for this cheery schlock; someone like fellow contract player Joan Blondell would have been much more appropriate and believable. Olivia has been styled like every other 1930s Warner Brothers ingenue, and even her hairstyle is too tight and fussy. Despite Brown's rather naïvely sweet persona, there is no chemistry whatsoever between them.

Olivia's strength was never girlish comedy. Thus, when she's leaving town on a train and tells Brown, "I've had a grand visit," her wide-eyed breathlessness and very tight-lipped kiss of her leading man seem extremely forced. A particularly awkward moment occurs when Olivia and Brown go on a boat ride. He paddles as she reclines prettily, and he asks sheepishly, "Do you like me enough to be alone with me for a long time?" Of course she does, and of course, he tips the canoe as he's proposing and she reaches over to hug him. "Didja get wet?" he asks stupidly.[23] According to Tony Thomas, the film crew, knowing that Olivia had come to this slapstick comedy from Shakespeare, "dunked her in a pond to teach her a lesson in humility." Demonstrating the stern stuff of which she was made, when Olivia filmed the canoe scene, she held her breath and didn't come up for a while, terrifying everyone.[24]

The closing scene is Ike and Dolly's marriage. Wearing an unattractive veil, Olivia looks pained as the groom promises he'll never use another alibi. When the crowd urges him to kiss the bride, Ike kisses the minister instead. One has to wonder whether, at the end of this shoot, Olivia was regretting her decision to pass up classes at Mills College. Certainly, none of Olivia's early films would pass the Bechdel test.[25] At least the *New York Times* review of *Alibi Ike* gave her special mention: "Bringing up the rear guard of the cast, and doing it quite well, too, [is] Olivia de Havilland, a charming newcomer who will be seen next Fall in the role of Hermia in 'A Midsummer Night's Dream.'"[26]

After such a debut, it would be understandable if the starlet began to have doubts about her seven-year, $200-a-week contract with Warner Brothers.[27] She was an essentially untested and untried actress who had earned job and financial security during the Depression. And yet, was it all worth it?

Bette Davis made *Dangerous* in 1935 and won that year's best actress Oscar—not so much for that role as for her stunning breakthrough portrayal of the doomed Mildred in *Of Human Bondage* (1934). Olivia was not unaware of Davis's talent and accomplishments at the time, although it would be two years before they worked together, and it would take a few more years for them to become friends. Bette provided the role model for Olivia's desired career. As she said at the ceremony commemorating Davis's American Film Institute lifetime achievement award in 1977:

> Bette had the career I most admired. It was the career I wanted to have, because she was a pioneer, a revolutionary, in that she wanted to play real human beings, good and bad, lovely or ugly, whereas, I

> fear, most actresses wanted only to be beautiful and romantic. But not Bette. She was the only young actress to combine character work with stardom. All actors and actresses want the Academy Award. Bette won two, and later on, so did I. I must say this—if I owe mine to anyone, I owe them to Bette. She was the inspiration of my career. And I'm thrilled that she is the first woman to be honored in this way. It's *so* appropriate.[28]

In 1936 Davis would try to break her contract with Warner Brothers and even traveled to London in the hope of obtaining a more sympathetic judgment, but she lost. It must have dawned on Olivia that she would face the same battles for good roles.

The young actress had little time for regrets, however, because fast on the trail of the disappointing *Alibi Ike* was another forgettable comedy, *The Irish in Us*. At least this film featured James Cagney (Bottom in *Midsummer*) as her love interest and good support from Pat O'Brien and contract comic Frank McHugh, all battling for her affection. However, the advertising emphasized the Irishmen in the leads—a three-leaf clover image in the trailer features the three of them—while Olivia, who looks lovely in the trailer, is mentioned only as "the cause of it all!"[29]

One of the interesting social aspects of Warner Brothers was how the Jewish immigrant Warners supported other minorities. Warner was exceptional among the big-seven studios for its regular casting of African Americans—in stereotypical roles, of course, but employing them nonetheless. Similarly, some of the studio's greatest stars of the 1930s were Irish, another group of émigrés who experienced prejudice in America.

This tale of three Irish brothers—Cagney, O'Brien, and McHugh—offers standard Irish characterizations and plotlines. McHugh is a fireman, O'Brien is a policeman, and Cagney is a fight promoter who has to step in when his boxer is too drunk to fight. The plot revolves around their tensions as brothers, and that tension is increased when Olivia, playing O'Brien's love interest (and the daughter of the police captain), is wooed away from him by Cagney. That the actors are almost twice her age is typical of Hollywood casting, then and now, and although Cagney's youthful charm works well here, O'Brien seems more fatherly than suitorly. That the "girl" has little to do beyond looking pretty is also typical, then and now.

Still, Olivia is charmingly flirtatious with O'Brien, and she wears her jaunty hats and trim, feminine suits beautifully. She's very cute when Cagney first spots her under her car, trying to change her own tire. Feisty, bouncy, smiling, and funny, she's a thoroughly modern girl who provides "a comely balance of realism between the self-confident antics of Cagney and the often-grim-faced displeasures of O'Brien."[30] She offers cold lemonade from a thermos and turns their "disagreeable" first meeting into something rather sweet.[31]

Like her role in *Alibi Ike,* Olivia's part could have been competently acted by any Warner starlet. However, the film gives her the opportunity to play a character who displays a mature sexuality. There is a balcony scene during the firemen's ball, after Olivia and Cagney have danced cheek to cheek and they find themselves alone in the moonlight (Olivia's date, O'Brien, is otherwise occupied). Here, Olivia's youthful smile is reminiscent of her sister Joan's dreamy look five years later in *Rebecca,* as she dances with Laurence Olivier. Her hair in a curly bob, Olivia wears a beautifully fitted satin evening dress with revealing décolleté, and when she turns around to see the view from the balcony, her smooth back is revealed by the cut-to-the-waist gown. Her voice is warm, with an alto timbre. She's much more confident than Cagney, and her kiss with him is solid. They have an easy chemistry, a mature romantic connection that will be on display again in *The Strawberry Blonde.* And of course, despite the tension between the brothers, all is resolved in a happy ending.

At this point in her career, Olivia was described as "a very pleasant young lady with no airs about her, even though she is a full-fledged screen star" and she "still suffers terribly from stage fright."[32] A *Film Weekly* feature called her "Hollywood's Normal Girl [with] the wide-eyed beauty of a fawn, and much of its characteristic alertness, with the quiet confidence and docility of a fluffy kitten." Nothing could have been further from the truth, but as the writer pointed out, at this stage in her career, "she could not hope for the more excitingly dramatic role of the girl who snatches the man away from the girl he married."[33] That kind of evaluation contributed to Olivia's transformation from kitten to jungle cat.

Her leading man in her fourth film would be a handsome, charming, youthful lothario who would charm her onscreen and off. His adoration would not only contribute to her status as a Hollywood legend but also lead to the first great adult romance of her life.

3

LIVVIE AND ERROL

The cinematic partnership of Errol Flynn and Olivia de Havilland remains a memorable one for film fans, given that they costarred in eight films over six years, found stardom in their first movie together, and were two beautiful young actors with authentic chemistry during the golden age of Hollywood. Errol Flynn, the impossibly handsome, daring, self-mocking, and intensely romantic action star, and Olivia de Havilland, the impossibly pretty, feisty, self-aware, and intensely romantic supporting star, provided strong box office returns for Warner Brothers through their popular historical action films and their best-known collaboration, *The Adventures of Robin Hood* (1938). As important as their screen partnership is in Hollywood history, their offscreen relationship has contributed to their enduring popularity. Flynn was married throughout the years they worked together, from 1935 to 1941, and they are remembered not only for what they created but also for what was never meant to be.

Olivia has always been extremely protective of their relationship, not only because she managed her career carefully but also because their partnership is part of cinematic history and should be honored. And of course, she loved Flynn. As she admitted in 2009, to no one's surprise, "'We were very attracted to each other. In his autobiography, *My Wicked, Wicked Ways,* he wrote about falling in love with me. Yes, we did fall in love and I believe that this is evident in the screen chemistry between us. But his circumstances at the time prevented the relationship going further. I have not talked about it a great deal but the relationship was not consummated. Chemistry was there though. It was there.'"[1]

Olivia demonstrated her iron-butterfly will where Flynn was concerned when she took Michael Caine to task for claiming in his 1992 autobiography *What's It All About?* that she'd confessed to having sex with Errol Flynn on the Warner back lot. According to Caine, Olivia had told him that she got the nickname the "Iron Virgin" because she refused to sleep with the rakish

Flynn, and Flynn had bet the stage crew $100 that he could change that nickname. Caine went on to write, "She pointed to a certain spot in the hills behind the studio. 'That's where Errol won his $100,' she said naughtily."[2]

When Caine's book appeared, Olivia, who was seventy-six years old at the time, contacted her beloved friend Robert Osborne at the *Hollywood Reporter* and issued a rejoinder: "'I think Michael Caine is a very fine actor, a stunning actor at times, but he's turned out to be a terrible disappointment as a human being. And a very faulty writer.'" She capped that dressing-down with a wicked last comment: "'Interestingly, there was a place in the hills behind the studio where a rather memorable picnic once occurred. But it wasn't with Mr. Flynn. It was with someone else entirely.'"[3] Leave it to Olivia to charmingly put Caine in his place and then, with humor and a saucy wit, put paid to the virgin claim.

She was angry, though. She told one reporter, "I was very, very angry about Michael saying that. It was not true. [Errol] Flynn wasn't like that when I worked with him. He didn't even drink a lot in those days. He later became very unruly, but not when he was young, and he never took advantage of me."[4] She also wrote to me about the "anecdote about Errol Flynn in which Caine, with appalling and tasteless inaccuracy, cast me in a principal role. Bob Osborne . . . was almost as incensed as I over this sloppy journalism and wrote an indignant column about it, a copy of which I enclose."[5] That she sent me a photocopy of the article three years after the kerfuffle demonstrates Olivia's fierceness when it comes to managing her legacy and her relationship with Flynn.

Errol Flynn was born in 1909 in Tasmania, off the Australian coast. After a series of adventures working on ships, he found his way into the movies in a rather dreadful early version of *Mutiny on the Bounty.* An admitted lothario, drinker, and general hell-raiser, by 1935, he was married to French actress Lili Damita and under contract to Warner Brothers. Charmingly insouciant, handsome, and witty, Flynn was a force of nature and his own worst enemy. As his great friend and occasional housemate David Niven said of Flynn, "The great thing about Errol was you always knew exactly where you stood with him because he *always* let you down. He let himself down, too, from time to time, but that was his prerogative and he thoroughly enjoyed causing turmoil for himself and his friends."[6]

Warner seemed to be at a loss as to what to do with the young, athletic Flynn, just as the studio seemed unable to find the right project for Olivia after *A Midsummer Night's Dream.* But fortuitously, the two actors were brought together for *Captain Blood.* (Historian Rudy Behlmer and Robert Osborne, in the DVD extras for the film, discuss the popularity of big swashbucklers like Douglas Fairbanks in the silent era.) Warner, in an ongoing effort to extend its profile beyond Busby Berkeley musicals and gangster films, had decided to make the film version of Rafael Sabatini's best-selling book, with Robert Donat in the lead. However, Donat passed on the project, and the studio had no one under contract who wasn't busy on other movies. By this time, Flynn had made two films with little impact, but Ann Warner, Jack's wife, had seen Flynn and recommended him. The studio tested and retested Flynn, but it was also considering Ronald Colman, George Brent, and even MGM star Clark Gable. However, Flynn shone in the tests, so the studio gave him the film and top billing.[7] This was a gamble for Warner Brothers. *Captain Blood* was an A-list picture, and studios sold films on the backs of their stars. But the moguls were gamblers, and it soon became clear that in this project, they had a winner.

As for Olivia, although she might have preferred a more challenging role, at least she wasn't playing the "girl" again. *Captain Blood* showed her off as a beautiful, intelligent young starlet in an expensive, lively production, and it promised to be an exciting shoot. Olivia noted, "I was terribly excited. They had tested Bette Davis. And then, they were going to test *me!* Well, I reported to the set, and saw this tall young man in costume, ready to make his test. We were very formal with each other, but I thought, 'Oh, oh. He is the handsomest, most charming, most magnetic, most virile young man in the entire world.'"[8]

As Arabella Bishop, a young British girl, Olivia's diction is precise and clipped—mother Lilian had taught her well. The nineteen-year-old Olivia is fresh, blooming with youth and fun, dressed becomingly and ethereally in white gowns designed by Milo Anderson. She appears onscreen for the first time on horseback and rides sidesaddle like an expert. Olivia remembered, "To prepare for *Captain Blood* and Arabella Bishop's horseback riding episodes, I took lessons from a Hungarian riding master at a well-known stable located somewhere between Warner Brothers studio in Burbank and Griffith Park. I still have the riding ensemble made for me by a famous English, Beverly Hills tailor, Pesterre, especially for these lessons. I loved horseback riding."[9]

She also has great chemistry with Flynn, who was delighted to test with "a young woman of extraordinary charm . . . with warm brown eyes, a soft manner."[10] Along with Basil Rathbone as the archetypal villain (he duels with

Flynn in *Captain Blood* and then again in *Robin Hood*), the film costarred Ross Alexander (who was also in *Midsummer*), an actor on the verge of stardom that never happened. The great supporting cast also included Donald Crisp and Lionel Atwill, ensuring solid performances.

Michael Curtiz was the perfect helmsman for an action picture. A remarkably versatile studio director, Curtiz also steered such diverse films as *Casablanca* and *White Christmas*. The Hungarian was known for his interesting use of the English language (giving David Niven the title of one of his memoirs, *Bring on the Empty Horses*). Harry Warner had seen one of Curtiz's films in Europe and brought him to Hollywood in the mid-1920s. During his long career, Curtiz proved that he could do everything and was particularly good with action, utilizing a European style in terms of shadows, angles, and setups.

Despite concerns about the budget and the two young stars' ability to carry the film, *Captain Blood* was a big box office success. As journalist Bob Thomas noted, Jack Warner recognized that Olivia and Flynn were a "winning couple."[11] Flynn became an instant star in one of the most amazing career launches in Hollywood history. "He just lights up the screen," Robert Osborne noted. He went on to say, "Lo and behold, they got two for the price of one, because Olivia became a star. . . . She has a brightness and a sensibility and sort of a whole elegance about her that was several steps above most of those decorative leading ladies that were in films."[12] The trailer for the film also trumpeted her star power in conjunction with Flynn, who was "teamed with the Girl who has won the hearts of MILLIONS . . . CHARMING . . . TALENTED . . . Olivia de Havilland."[13]

Flynn plays Irishman Peter Blood, a seventeenth-century physician. After soldiering for six years, he's had enough and declares himself "a healer, not a slayer." Half the town says he's a papist, and the other half says he's a coward. While Blood is treating his friend, Lord Gilroy, who was injured during the Monmouth Rebellion, soldiers arrive to take Gilroy away. Blood insults them and is arrested and charged with high treason against King James II. "It's entirely innocent, I am," he declares, but he's found guilty for helping a rebel. Nobly he protests, "I only knew my sacred duty as a physician."[14] Instead of being hanged, Blood is shipped to Port Royal, an English colony in the West Indies, to be sold as a slave.

Arabella Bishop—Olivia in satin, jaunty hat with plumes, silken brunette curls, and carrying a lace parasol—is the niece of the island's governor (played with appropriate malice by Lionel Atwill). During a slave auction, she buys

Peter for ten pounds, declaring, "It was fortunate for you that I was here to save you!" The innocent heroine is shocked when Blood retorts, "I hardly consider it fortunate to be bought by anyone by the name of Bishop."[15] From this point, they are entwined in a push me–pull you relationship. One scene in particular captures their repartee. Blood has become Arabella's uncle's doctor, so he now dresses the part and looks like, well, Errol Flynn. Under the palm trees, they ride horses (something Olivia did with aplomb in several films) and spark back and forth as they ride:

> "You bought me. I've had no lack of experiences in my time, but to be bought and sold was a new one. I was in no mood to thank my purchaser."
>
> "That I can understand."
>
> "How was I to know be'dad that a devil . . . that a devil could have an angel for a niece?"
>
> "From a resentful man, that is a pretty fair compliment."
>
> "I've resented you because you're beautiful and I'm a slave."[16]

As understanding of his situation dawns on Arabella, and as Blood releases his resentment, their sweetness, innocence, and essential chemistry shine through. Blood goes on to join forces with the evil Basil Rathbone and becomes a kind of (prescient) Robin Hood–esque pirate and finally a restored-to-glory British citizen who wins the pretty girl. In the closing two-shot, she perches on his knee, a satin bow and white lace mantilla perched on her curling tresses. She nestles into his shoulder and kisses him on the cheek, and we see the pure perfection of an idealized golden age Hollywood romance.

In this first film, the template for most of their future projects was set. Flynn plays a noble man with some kind of shadow or blot on his character. But he's spirited and handsome, courtly and intelligent. He encounters Olivia, a thoughtful young woman who is outspoken, feminine but forceful, hard to win over, and deeply romantic. After several clashes and misunderstandings, they find each other. It's a standard romantic comedy formula, but with two extraordinarily charismatic young actors who were mad for each other. It was that real-life unfulfilled romance that contributes, undoubtedly, to their best films together. It was one of those open Hollywood secrets, rather like the Spencer Tracy–Katharine Hepburn romance (the truth of which was undeniable for decades). The Livvie-Errol love affair was terribly poignant and ultimately found a sorrowful ending for two people who simply couldn't overcome their culture, their careers, and their characters to attain a happy ending in real life.

More than sixty years after their last film together, Olivia recalled a conversation they had during the making of *Captain Blood:* "He sat down and he said to me, 'What do you want out of life.' And so I said, 'Well, I want respect for difficult work well done.' And then I said to him, 'What do you want out of life?' And he said, 'I want success.' And by that he meant fame and riches, and I thought, 'That's not enough.'"[17]

When they met, Olivia was nineteen and Flynn was twenty-six. He was more seasoned in virtually every way except as a Hollywood star. Olivia was still something of an innocent, closely tied to her mother and responsible for her sister. She found Flynn irresistible—who wouldn't? But he was married, and an affair between the two of them, if discovered by the press, would have ruined her career and damaged (but not destroyed) his. The double standard of virgins and playboys has changed, but at the time, it held fast. As for Flynn, he repeatedly separated from and reunited with Lili Damita; he caroused, drank, sailed, and slept with many, many people. Although he adored Olivia, he was not the right man for such a serious young woman.

On an episode of *The Dinah Shore Show* in the mid-1970s, Olivia appeared with fellow Oscar winners Shirley Jones, Eva Marie Saint, and Shelley Winters. When the discussion turned to falling for one's costars, naturally, the attention focused on Olivia and Errol. She was charmingly, theatrically coy, staring at her fingernails, playing with her pearls, and blushing as she related this story: One night, David Niven, who was Flynn's roommate at the time, invited her to a ball. They planned to dine at his house first, so off she went to enjoy a British meal of roast beef with her charming date, who was wearing a white dinner jacket. But when they got to the ball, she was shocked when "[Flynn] takes my arm and David Niven takes somebody else's arm!" She was concerned about photographers, even though Flynn was separated from his wife at the time. They went to the Coconut Grove and "danced to 'Sweet Leilani.'"[18] She remembered the song, but whatever else she remembered was her business.

The Olivia-Errol chemistry was palpable. When they were not paired as lovers in their movies, the films lacked an interesting core and played like programmers rather than A-list pictures. Their follow-up to *Captain Blood,* for example, was the earnest action film *The Charge of the Light Brigade* (1936), also directed by Michael Curtiz. Many of the scenes are quite thrilling, and the film is designed to showcase Flynn's athletic abilities. The screenplay, by Michael Jacoby and Rowland Leigh, is *very* loosely inspired by

Tennyson's poem "The Charge of the Light Brigade," honoring the 17th British Lancers (in the film, the 27th), who lost their lives during the Crimean War (1853–1856). Combining that event with an earlier massacre in Afghanistan in 1842, the film addresses an imaginary Indian outpost called Chukoti and an evil rajah who breaks his promise to the upright British and massacres soldiers and their families, inspiring the doomed charge in retaliation and as a distraction for a larger attack. It takes so many liberties with British history that Warner Brothers issued a disclaimer at the beginning of the film. It is a man's film, with a love interest thrown in to appease the female viewers who accompanied their male partners to the movies. Despite the trailer's proclamation that the action addresses "the kisses that turned the tide of empire,"[19] the movie is an homage to British heroism, not a romance.

Olivia's role as the romantic interest offered few acting challenges. Her Elsa Campbell is engaged to Major Geoffrey Vickers, the handsome Flynn. However, she's really in love with Geoffrey's younger brother, Captain Perry Vickers, played by the also-handsome supporting actor Patric Knowles. It's just not a believable triangle. Flynn and Olivia share such a wonderful attraction that it's hard to believe she would choose Knowles when the dashing Flynn adores her. Her worried look as she makes love to Flynn while actually loving Knowles seems utterly absurd. Elsa's father, played by Donald Crisp, finds out her true feelings and orders her to honor her promise to Geoffrey, thus introducing a romantic tension parallel to the larger political crisis. She cries to her father, "I love him" (referring to Perry), and indulges in one of her few trademark movements—sulkily biting her lip.[20] Olivia is very pretty in this film—with tightly ringleted hair and mid-Victorian hoop skirts and ruffles in white satin and tulle—but other than looking attractive, there's not much for her to do.

The one exception is a vigorous sequence in which the British settlers are retreating from the besieged Chukoti outpost, and Olivia and Flynn must wade through a river crammed with panicking men, women, and children, allowing Olivia to demonstrate a physicality and a willingness to chuck into the fray. If she had to do these action films with Flynn, why didn't Jack Warner give her more opportunities to be athletic as well as feminine? In this scene, wearing a Victorian dress, she plunges into the water carrying one little girl while another clings to her. The scene is very wet and very scary, and the use of child actors in such a dangerous scene would be closely monitored if not prohibited today. Willing to become dirty and bedraggled, Olivia is a tough recruit participating in the terror and violence of those moments.

They escape, of course, and in their last scene together, before Flynn sacrifices himself for God, country, and revenge, the star-crossed hero and his distressed heroine have a final romantic moment. Flynn confronts her about her feelings for his brother, saying, "You love him, don't you." Olivia, bedecked in black frills and tulle, wrings her hands and speaks breathlessly of her love. She apologizes. He smiles, then looks away. He knows he won't be back. Despite the treacly moment, their sincerity is palpable, and when she tells Flynn that he's "the finest man I've ever known," it's genuine.[21]

The supporting cast was superb. In addition to kissing two handsome men, Olivia got to work with Spring Byington, of the barbed tongue and delivery, and the marvelously buffoonish Nigel Bruce. Also in the cast was Flynn's future partner in debauchery and decadence, David Niven. He would costar with Olivia as the eponymous hero of *Raffles* in 1939, but in 1936 he was still a novice, while Olivia got second billing. Niven was extremely fond of Flynn, but one of his descriptions may explain why Olivia kept her distance: "Errol was a strange mixture. A great athlete of immense charm and evident physical beauty, he stood, legs apart, arms folded defiantly and crowing lustily atop the Hollywood dung heap, but he suffered, I think, from a deep inferiority complex. . . . Women loved him passionately, but he treated them like toys to be discarded without warning. . . . He was not a kind man, but in those careless days he was fun to be with."[22]

Niven wrote of making *The Charge of the Light Brigade* in his charming 1972 autobiography *The Moon's a Balloon*. The actor was auditioning for the part of the brave but doomed Captain James Randall, who is shot as he tries to get past the evil attackers at Chukoti and alert another British garrison of the onslaught—a small but career-building role. Niven was happy to learn that he would be testing for the part opposite Olivia, until he discovered, "with dismay, [so] were a dozen other hopeful young actors dressed in exactly the same uniform as myself." That Olivia was forced to read with so many young actors auditioning for a supporting role indicated her lack of status at the studio; it's no wonder she "smiled a tired smile" when she met Niven for the test. He had memorized his lines, so he left the four pages of script in his dressing room. It was 100 degrees on the sound stage, and he was wearing a wool uniform, so when director Michael Curtiz ordered Niven to retrieve the script, he replied, "'You fucking well run and get it.'"[23] What Olivia thought about Niven's test is not recorded.

Olivia didn't enjoy the shoot at all. For one thing, she was bored and "at one point . . . became so envious of her fellow castmates cavorting about on horseback that she mounted one of the horses and began galloping about."[24] She was also dealing with her feelings for Errol Flynn and his for her. Flynn confessed that by the time they made *Light Brigade,* "I was sure I was in love with her. So that acting in that hard-to-make picture became bearable."[25] Olivia remembered in September 2012, "He had fallen in love with me and told me so, adding that he did not love his wife, who was abroad making a film in Morocco."[26] Flynn did not deal with this painful situation maturely, however: "Around de Havilland he is reverting to pure Flashman; in other words, a mean bully."[27] Flynn admitted, "I sprang some very obstreperous gags. There was the time she found a dead snake in her panties as she went to put them on. She was terrified and she wept . . . and it couldn't have endeared me to her. . . . I had a lot to learn about the sensibilities of young ladies."[28] An understatement.

Although *The Charge of the Light Brigade* was a great success, it didn't boost Olivia's value at Warner Brothers. The studio executives still saw her as a sweet ingenue who wore period clothing well. It is obvious that the studio considered Olivia less valuable than Flynn, particularly in the two films they made in which she plays a supporting role rather than his leading lady. Olivia's roles are scripted as distractions for the leading man, rather than his focus; as a result, the radiance they generate when involved in a real film partnership doesn't shine in those films.

Olivia's role as second fiddle to Flynn is painfully evident in both *Four's a Crowd* (1938) and *The Private Lives of Elizabeth and Essex* (1939). Interestingly, and foolishly, each of these films followed a successful romantic pairing of the two—*The Adventures of Robin Hood* immediately preceded *Four's a Crowd,* and *Dodge City* preceded *Elizabeth and Essex.* All four films showcased Flynn's appeal as a leading man, and although the breadth of genres and eras certainly demonstrated Olivia's ability to portray a variety of historical heroines, her role was essentially the same in all the films—feminine foil to Flynn. And relegating her to a supporting role in two of the four films had to show Olivia that her career growth was not a priority for Warner Brothers. She adopted the habit of becoming ill during filming and of going on suspension, and who could blame her? Her potential was already being taken for granted—and she was barely into her twenties.

Consider her role in *Four's a Crowd,* Warner's unsuccessful if harmless attempt at screwball comedy. The film, originally titled *All Rights Reserved,* was rushed into production to capitalize on the projected "hubbub of *Robin Hood.*"[29] Olivia gets second billing above costar Rosalind Russell, on loan from MGM, and she gets the opportunity to play comedy and wear attractive contemporary clothes. Still, Olivia isn't comfortable in the silly, ditzy role. She tries, but others could have done it better. Errol Flynn shows his wit and finesse in a comic part, but of course, the film is for him, not Olivia. And in the end, Roz gets Errol and Olivia gets Patric Knowles again (as she does in *Light Brigade*).

The opening credit sequence shows the four leads walking together in evening dress and black tie (a popular conceit in films of the 1930s to show what a jolly time the cast was having in Hollywood), and then the foursome is switched around so they're paired with the "right" partners. In a rather tired plot, newspaperwoman Russell (a rehearsal for her better role as Hildy in 1940's *His Girl Friday*) and publisher Knowles try to save their newspaper by luring former managing editor Flynn, now a public-relations genius, back on board. Meanwhile, Flynn tries to get Olivia's wealthy grandfather to rethink his underhanded business ethics and let Flynn handle his public relations.

No wacky but brilliant debutante like Carole Lombard in *My Man Godfrey* or Katharine Hepburn in *Bringing Up Baby,* Olivia is simply silly as spoiled Lori Dillingham. She looks delicious, she wears cute workout togs and feminine evening gowns designed by Orry-Kelly, she flirts and flounces in rather unbecoming tight curls, and she has a naughty dog that provides more comic relief than she does. Olivia gives the role of an airheaded heiress her best shot, but she's too smart, and again, she lacks chemistry with Knowles; only when her character flirts with Flynn's do we see her authentic spirit. Michael Curtiz was wonderful at directing action, he guided women like Ingrid Bergman in *Casablanca* and Joan Crawford in *Mildred Pierce* in memorable dramatic roles, and he certainly knew the strengths and weaknesses of Warner's contract actors. But screwball comedy was not his strong suit, especially not the highly sophisticated farce this film tries to be.

While Flynn is great fun—his comic potential was always underused and underrated—Olivia is simply a mad starlet. In her initial scene, she's on the telephone with her beau (Knowles), and he actually says "Kitchy kitchy kitchy" to her as she works out on a rowing machine while wearing tight whites. She is bored by her fortune and desperate for a romantic challenge. Later, in a nightclub scene, the twenty-two-year-old actress is dressed in sequined square shoulders, and she uses a perky higher range of her rich voice as she flirts coyly and sweetly while dancing with Flynn, who tells her, "I think you're adorable."[30] She's lively and energetic, and she listens to him raptly, but throughout the film, Olivia seems like a child at a table with three grown-ups. Her interactions with Flynn are fresh and familiar, but in the rest of the film, she's too frenetic. Even an opportunity to punch Knowles lacks the pepper it needs.

At least *The Private Lives of Elizabeth and Essex,* based on Maxwell Anderson's Broadway success *Elizabeth the Queen,* offers up Technicolor, Bette Davis, and a small but scintillating role for Olivia as a scheming wench of a lady-in-waiting. Davis is Queen Elizabeth, played on Broadway by the great Lynn Fontanne, whose stage roles usually provided acting challenges for MGM queen Norma Shearer (*Strange Interlude* and *Idiot's Delight*). Hollywood purchased the rights to successful Broadway shows and recast them with contract players, sometimes successfully, sometimes not. Davis gives the role fire, brimstone, and her trademark delivery and stride, but despite the elaborate makeup, she's too young for the part. More successfully, Flynn replaces Fontanne's husband and acting partner Alfred Lunt in a part more appropriate to the actor's age and persona. He acquits himself well as yet another passionate action hero (despite Davis's contempt for his abilities), and the couple's battles in love and in politics keep the film interesting and its rhythm crisp.

The documentary *Elizabeth and Essex: Battle Royal,* a DVD extra, notes that Errol Flynn and Bette Davis made *The Sisters* the year before, an entertaining turn-of-the-century melodrama about three sisters and the men they married. By 1939, that golden year in Hollywood history, both were big stars, two of the biggest at Warner Brothers. At first, there was discussion about reworking and retitling Anderson's play as *The Knight and the Lady,* but Bette insisted on top billing. She detested Flynn and didn't want to work with him, and she let Jack Warner know it; Warner would hear her coming and hide in the men's room until she left. She wanted Laurence Olivier as her costar. Nanette Fabray, who is interviewed in the documentary, remembers that Bette and Flynn would end a scene and walk off in separate directions.

Whatever they thought of each other, there is real chemistry between Flynn and Davis onscreen. That had to add to Olivia's frustration. She had worked with Bette in 1937's *It's Love I'm After,* also as a supporting actress to the big star. They had not yet formed the friendship they would enjoy in later years, and the shoot was unpleasant for Olivia.

This was another expensive production for Warner Brothers, and Olivia received third billing as the manipulative Lady Penelope. She had just finished her career-defining role as Melanie Wilkes in *Gone with the Wind,* so this was a definite comedown. She had no time off between projects and had to rush right into the role. It made her miserable and "was not a joyous return. Any thoughts that her work on *GWTW* might lead Jack Warner to promote her with first-rate starring vehicles were crushed. . . . The assignment was a painful one."[31] She wanted to complain, but strategically, according to entertainment journalist Bob Thomas, "she kept her mouth shut."[32] However, years later she said:

> Now the day I finished shooting in [*GWTW*], Jack called me back. . . . Jack said he had cast me in . . . *Elizabeth and Essex* and this time Bette Davis was Errol's leading lady and I was Bette's Lady-in-Waiting and he had put my name below the title. Now if that isn't asking for trouble. He was provoking me. He was provoking me to break my word to him and be just what he'd said I would be, which was difficult. I didn't say a word. It was very hard for me . . . I was really miserable, but I did it because I'd given him my word that I wouldn't be difficult.[33]

Michael Curtiz directed the film, and he was much more comfortable being in charge of a historical drama than he was directing the farcical *Four's a Crowd. Elizabeth and Essex* features a stirring score by Erich Wolfgang Korngold and a tremendous supporting cast, including the ubiquitous Alan Hale, Donald Crisp, Vincent Price as Sir Walter Raleigh, and ingenue Nanette Fabray. Fabray had been given a six-month contract for beginners and didn't know about marks, but Bette was patient and helped her. "I was very good in it. Kiss, kiss, kiss, kiss, kiss," Fabray said comically. Then she added, rather poignantly, "Except for me and Olivia, I think all of them are gone."[34] Fabray died in February 2018.

Of course, the film is about the tempestuous relationship between Queen Elizabeth and the Earl of Essex, Robert Deveraux. She eventually has him executed to prevent him from rising against her when she refuses to marry him and make him king. But Olivia, as Lady Penelope Gray, has seldom been so elegantly beautiful, dressed in ice-blue satins and silks by Orry-Kelly to reflect the cool calculation of her character. The upswept hair, delicate jewels, and sweeping lines of her Elizabethan gowns give Olivia a new lushness and maturity. Lady Penelope is her first post-Melanie role, and she's very dangerous in it, not only because of the character she plays but also because of her fury at being relegated to third billing below the great Bette and the dashing Errol. That heat makes this a scintillating supporting turn for Olivia.

By this time, Olivia knows how to make her few scenes count. For example, as the film opens, Essex has defeated the Spanish at Cadiz, and he is on his way to Whitehall to be greeted by Elizabeth. The big crowds are thrilled to see him, and Sol Polito's camera zooms in on a window full of ladies-in-waiting, including Nanette and Olivia. Olivia gets the close-up and sighs, "How nobly he bears himself." She's overdressed, as a young seductress should be, wearing blue feathers, a stiff lace Elizabethan collar, and blue ribbons and diamonds in her hair. Her cheeks are glowing, and she looks at Flynn with lust. But one of the other girls notices that his eyes constantly look up, "searching for the queen," and Olivia's eyes flash as she says, "An easy victory if one is a queen and may command it."[35] She gets a hard look that we seldom see before the 1940s but became more common thereafter: the look of a strong woman willing to take Jack Warner to court.

In her next major scene, Penelope is playing chess with the queen (Bette's white facial makeup is a preview of Baby Jane twenty-five years later). Davis pronounces to Olivia, "So you would take the queen's knight, Mistress Penelope? I fear you are over-presumptuous and over-inexperienced."[36] This is a two-shot, and the chess game is an interesting metaphor for the actresses' relationship with each other as well as with Jack Warner—they were threatened by and jealous of each other and constantly pissed off with Jack.

Olivia referenced those tensions when she appeared on a 1971 episode of *This Is Your Life* honoring Bette Davis. Ralph Edwards, the stalwart host, has already introduced a number of Bette's costars (including Paul Henreid) and members of her family (her mother and sister Bobby), and he is chatting with Bette about her early career. Bette wears her trademark pageboy and heavy black glasses as Edwards mentions that Bette wanted the role of Angela in *Anthony Adverse* but Olivia got it instead, and Bette nods in agreement. Then we hear, "The first time I saw Bette Davis, she scared the daylights out of me!" Bette is clearly surprised. Olivia rushes out to greet her "old pal," as Edwards calls her, looking slim in a terracotta blouson top, pencil skirt, narrow belt, bouffant hairdo, and fabulous ethnic necklace. At fifty-five, Olivia looks chic and completely Parisian next to Bette's sixty-three-year-old, aging movie queen persona. Bette rises slowly and stands confrontationally with black-gloved hands on hips as Olivia throws her arms around her. Bette is genuinely stunned, and Olivia is genuinely happy to see her dear friend and rival. We hear Davis declare under the applause, "Oh, you rat! You look marvelous." And when Edwards asks if Bette really scared her, Olivia replies with mock seriousness, "Nearly to death. We had to make three pictures for her to warm up to me," and she shrugs like a resigned but mocking teenager. Bette protests that she doesn't remember it that way, saying, "I feel I've always known and loved Olivia." "It wasn't true," Olivia corrects her, and after some eye rolling and protestation on both sides, Davis concedes, honestly, "I was probably jealous of you, you were so damned good looking." Tellingly, Olivia recalls the making of *The Private Lives of Elizabeth and Essex* and, with mock outrage, reminds Bette and the audience, "And by the way, up until that time, I had always been Errol Flynn's leading lady . . . and I was demoted to *her* leading lady! I was humiliated!"[37] Despite her jovial delivery, this was obviously a strong enough memory for Olivia to share it with a television audience.

Of course, they are discussing a film made more than thirty years before, but there are flashes of Penelope versus Elizabeth in that moment. The reunion is a reminder of the wonderfully bitchy scene in the film when the young and beautiful Penelope, playing chess with the older, more successful and less beautiful Elizabeth, takes the queen's knight, proclaiming, "I fear the queen is powerless now." The queen retorts by knocking the chess pieces off the board. But the worst is yet to come. By way of apology, Elizabeth tells Penelope to sing a duet with another lady-in-waiting (Nanette Fabray). The little vixen chooses Christopher Marlowe's ballad "The Passionate Shepherd to His Love." Olivia strums a lute while Nanette plays the harpsichord. Unable to leave well enough alone, the shrewish Penelope decides to sing Sir Walter Raleigh's answer to Marlowe, which she describes as a "tournament of song" about a "woman in love with a man much younger than herself." The queen is enjoying the concert until she hears the lyrics: "If I could be as young and fair as you. . . . In lovers' vows there is but little truth / And love cannot endure without its youth."[38] Elizabeth is furious; she breaks the mirror she gazes into and snatches a rose from the younger woman's cleavage. And after she clears her ladies out, the queen smashes three more mirrors and collapses. Olivia may not have enjoyed playing bad girls, but she played them well. The scene was probably cathartic for both actresses, who did not get close until 1942's *In This Our Life.*

Olivia's only romantic scene comes later in the film when she finally has a moment alone with Flynn. She rushes up to him, and the screen suddenly seems balanced; they're gorgeous together in Technicolor. She grabs his hands and pulls him toward the fire, saying, "I wish you loved someone who loved you better. . . . She loves you, she loves you not." She's very sincere, and she uses one of her trademarks—holding the vowels for a rounder, more suspended moment. Flynn's Essex replies, "But if we were lovers, you might [curse me]. So thank your lucky stars we're not."[39] One cannot watch this exchange and not find it poignantly ironic, articulating the situation in which the star-crossed would-be lovers found themselves. She makes him promise to be careful and seizes him by both arms as she quickly kisses him farewell.

Olivia remembered in the documentary *The Adventures of Errol Flynn:* "Many years later, I was in Hollywood, and Bette and I had meanwhile become very, very good friends. And she said to a mutual friend of ours, 'I'd love to see *Elizabeth and Essex* again. Can you arrange it—just a private showing?' And when it was over, she said, 'Damn, he's good.' She said, 'I was wrong about him all the time.' Isn't' that wonderful? She said, 'He's marvelous.' That's lovely. I wish he knew about that."[40] It's a poignant reminder of Flynn's talent and Olivia's abiding respect for his work, but of course, her own small role in the film goes unmentioned.

Despite Warner Brothers' seemingly perverse desire to chasten Olivia's ambition, the studio was smart enough to cast her as Flynn's romantic interest in four other outings. The chemistry between Errol and Livvie could not be denied, and their partnership continued to provide good box office for Warner Brothers. Although their offscreen entanglement remained unfulfilled, onscreen they continued to glow with youth and vitality and mutual adoration.

Of all their collaborations, the best known and most timeless is *The Adventures of Robin Hood.* Although almost a shot-for-shot remake of the original 1922 silent version starring Douglas Fairbanks, this film retains the insouciance of the mythic Sir Robin of Locksley, along with the vigor of Flynn and the radiance of Olivia.

The excellent DVD documentary *Welcome to Sherwood!* shares a great deal of fascinating information about the making of the film, including the early consideration of James Cagney as Robin. Warner Brothers was moving from the gritty realism that had once defined its aesthetic to more prestigious and crowd-pleasing productions, and *Robin Hood* could further that goal. Warner Brothers discovered that it had the rights to an 1890 operetta version of the Robin Hood story. Simultaneously, MGM was thinking about making the operetta starring Nelson Eddy and Jeanette MacDonald. In an unusual show of cooperation, the studios worked out a deal—Warner would produce the dramatic version, and MGM would make the DeKoven Smith operetta.

The first mention of the character of Robin Hood occurred in 1377 in *Piers Plowman.* Thereafter, the character evolved from jester to folk hero to nobleman who stole from the rich and gave to the poor. His role as a lover came with the addition of Marian in the nineteenth century. Screenwriter Rowland Leigh, the first of three to work on the script, suggested omitting Marian because she wasn't in the original ballads.[41] However, the addition of a romantic interest was recognized as a significant improvement in a variety of adaptations featuring the hero (even the title characters in Robert Louis Stevenson's *Strange Case of Dr. Jekyll and Mr. Hyde* gained two girlfriends in the first stage adaptation in 1887, a year after the novel's publication).

The casting of Cagney as Robin Hood didn't work out. The actor blew up at Warner Brothers and walked off the lot; in fact, he didn't work for the studio for more than two years. And, as Robert Osborne noted, it would be difficult to imagine Cagney donning a "little green outfit" as Robin Hood.[42] Flynn was the star of the moment and the only true choice for the role. At twenty-nine, he was handsome and healthy, with great humor and tremendous agility. He thus became the definitive Robin Hood.

The studio first hired William Keighley, a contract studio director with stage experience who was trusted and liked by Flynn. Keighley was good with many of the more intimate scenes, but he was ultimately replaced by Michael Curtiz, whose expertise with action scenes gave the film greater energy. Flynn disliked the new director's method, and the fact that Curtiz had once been married to Flynn's wife, Lili Damita, couldn't have enhanced their relationship. Despite the directorial shift, the film's flow and balance were maintained.

The wonderful cast of Merry Men includes stalwart Alan Hale as Little John, who played the same role in the 1922 Fairbanks version and in *Rogues of Sherwood Forest* (1950).[43] Foghorn-voiced Eugene Pallette is Friar Tuck, and Patric Knowles (always the sidekick to Flynn) is Will Scarlett. The sententious, Machiavellian bad men include a deliciously fey Claude Rains as Prince John, the serpentine Basil Rathbone as Sir Guy of Gisborne, and buffoonish Melville Cooper as the Sheriff of Nottingham. Complete with an archery contest, the kidnapping of Gisborne and company in Sherwood Forest, a delicious feast, and a rousing closing battle, the film's good spirits and lively Erich Wolfgang Korngold score continue to entertain generations of filmgoers.

Warner Brothers decided to shoot the film in Technicolor, a costly process that was used mostly for musicals and spectacles. However, the Warners wisely believed that yields at the box office would be worth it, and they were absolutely correct. The gloriously rich, fairy-tale quality of the photography and those jewel-toned colors vividly enhance the story's action. Technicolor also captures Olivia's glowing beauty for the generations (one can only wonder what it is like for her daughter Gisèle to watch her adored mother in her blooming youth). Olivia is the only actress to appear in five of these early Technicolor films (the others are *Gold Is Where You Find It, Gone with the Wind, Elizabeth and Essex,* and *Dodge City*), setting the bar quite high for later beauties whose reputation rested on how attractive they appeared using this technology.

Initially, Warner Brothers didn't consider the film a prestige production, despite the expense of Technicolor, the on-location shooting in Chico and at Busch Gardens in Pasadena, and the enormous cast; according to Robert Osborne, "Errol Flynn films never were."[44] Nevertheless, given Flynn's good looks, physical abilities, and popularity, the studio was willing to produce the film to support its action star. Since the studio had spent almost $2 million by the time the production ended, it was important that the film be a success. Producer Hal Wallis realized that one way to ensure success was to maintain the Maid Marian love interest, despite her absence in the original folk tales. And it seemed that the only choice for the role was Olivia. However, according to the Internet Movie Data Base, "Interoffice memos clearly indicate that Olivia was not the first choice for the role of Marian. The original actress, whose name is blacked out in each of [the] documents [archived at the USC Cinema Television Library], became pregnant out of wedlock, and could no longer accept the role."[45] Given Olivia's popularity and the chemistry she shared with Flynn, she was the next logical choice.

If the studio didn't appreciate Olivia's perfect casting, the fan magazines did. *Film Weekly* declared, "No other actress in Hollywood could have been so suitably cast as she was. . . . Maid Marian has always seemed to me to be the embodiment of all the ideal story-book heroines. And, in one form or another, Olivia de Havilland seems to be a story-book heroine in nearly all her pictures."[46] *Photoplay* declared, "Maid Olivia is perhaps as complex a piece of acting mechanism as the Brothers Warner have under contract. . . . Now twenty-two, well curved, more than pleasing to the eye . . . Maid Olivia is a tragedienne whose Medea-like . . . expressions can be almost frightening."[47] This kind of recognition boosted Olivia's confidence in her abilities.

Olivia needed confidence not only in terms of her performance but also in terms of her feelings for Errol Flynn. Even though he was married, she had strong feelings for the handsome young star. She admitted years afterward, "I'll be honest: yes, it is true [that she loved him]. But I was very shy and so this passion stayed secret. Falling in love with him was bound to happen."[48]

She also remembered, "He was magnetic, handsome, ambitious, I think tormented, and I don't know why and I don't know about what."[49]

"There was a magic there," said Bob Thomas. "Olivia was one of the great beauties of Hollywood. And she was having a bit of a romance going with Flynn at this time. The romance between them and the intelligence that Olivia brought to her role was just magical."[50] There are many off-camera casual shots of the two of them together, and their camaraderie and mutual delight are obvious.

Robert Osborne observed, "Yes, I think Olivia de Havilland is wonderfully cast, but she had a substance to her and an intelligence to her, and you can understand why he would be so smitten with her, and it's a relationship that could last."[51] When Flynn kisses her hand or gazes at her, it's tender and humble and intimate, and their adoration for each other radiates from the screen.

Olivia is lovely in the film, and she photographs beautifully in Technicolor—her cheeks blooming roses, her eyes richly brown, her sumptuous costumes iridescent. She's elegant but accessible, and her "face and voice play a major role in her appeal. She has a high forehead that accommodates gigantic period hats and her huge brown eyes above a wide mouth always outlined with dark lipstick. Together these features are hugely expressive. Every slight shift in emotions plays immediately across [Olivia's] face." Her voice "combines a lilting, musical quality with a tempering huskiness and slightly low pitch . . . [but] her laugh is what one remembers. It trills quite charmingly, even though it's never totally natural—and indeed there is always something a bit studied and affected."[52] That assessment is a bit harsh, but it captures the tone and delivery, musical and poetic, that Olivia uses for the ward of King Richard.

It is the relationship between Robin Hood and Maid Marian, a "lyrical love story infused with gallantry and goodness," that provides the romantic core of the film, wherein battling for one's king and country has more ferocity when coupled with true passion.[53] Flynn, "who at twenty-nine was at his peak and perfect for the role, with just enough seasoning," has an absolutely marvelous time leaping and dueling, riding horses, and engaging in swordplay.[54] Flynn's grin, his muscular thighs in green tights, his pageboy haircut and mustache, the green velvet and burnished suede costumes, and the actor's sheer magnetism make Robin Hood his greatest role. One cannot and should not ignore the delightfully lascivious reading Flynn gives after overhearing Olivia question her lady-in-waiting Bess, the hilarious Una O'Connor, as to how to tell she's in love. Bess asks the innocent Marian, "When he looks at you, do you feel a kind of prickly feeling?" Just then, Robin Hood enters Marian's bedroom, of all places, and gleefully comments, "And after what I couldn't help overhearing about that prickly feeling, I'm very glad I did come!"[55] It's a deliciously coded moment.

As Lady Marian Fitzwalter, Olivia "personified Maid Marian as no other actress since. . . . She is a chaste and virginal fantasy and blessed with special grace and dignity."[56] She is "every schoolboy's fantasy. Lavishly costumed and angelically framed . . . she never looked more fetching. Her Marian is a thoroughbred, fiercely independent and spirited . . . warm and desirable. . . . It was by far her finest role in her films with Flynn."[57] Olivia was always physically active in her films with Flynn. In fact, some of their most poignant scenes together feature them walking in a forest or in the countryside, two wanderers in the green world. Here, she rides sidesaddle comfortably and competently on none other than Golden Cloud, the future Trigger, adopted as Roy Rogers's equine pal. Her responses first to Robin Hood's insouciance and then to Prince John's machinations are those of an autonomous young woman. She moves swiftly and silkily as she spies on the conspirators against King Richard, and her physical comedy, such as when she reluctantly tears at her meat, depicts her as an active, not passive, heroine.

Olivia demonstrated that same strong-mindedness behind the scenes as well. Costume designer Milo Anderson, who created the heavy, flowing, jewel-toned silk-satin medieval gowns for Olivia's Lady Marian, spoke to Rudy Behlmer about the actress: "He . . . said that working with Olivia de Havilland was interesting, because [she] had her own ideas on certain things, not overbearing, but she would do research and come in with some thoughts."[58] She maintained an interest in costuming and later found sympathetic collaborators in both Edith Head and Christian Dior.

She also exhibited a strong-mindedness about her behind-the-scenes relationship with Flynn. Essentially, "the characters Flynn and de Havilland played in their films together in some respects rhymed with actual personality traits and personal histories. . . . The star discourses of the two, as fabricated by the Hollywood publicity machine and its journalistic accomplices, served to triangulate their actual life stories and the pure fiction on the screen."[59] A film production can become its own world, with its own rules and characters, and things can get complicated. Although they met when they were both quite young, their life experiences were astronomically different. While onscreen with Olivia, Flynn was loyal and flirtatious and deeply romantic; offscreen he was a "chronic philanderer with a high fancy for serial infidelities."[60] Flynn was a swordsman both on and off the screen. Though less experienced—she had dated future brother-in-law Brian Aherne during *The Great Garrick*—Olivia was certainly no innocent in terms of how Hollywood affairs worked. She affirmed, "None of my few relationships were ever 'just a lark.'"[61] Olivia was a serious young woman when it came to her career and to love. At the same time, "she was infatuated with [Flynn] from the first day they met, but she was also a shrewd judge of character and knew that he was not the kind of man she wanted in her life."[62] How could she *not* have a crush on Errol Flynn? And how could she resist the temptation? As Olivia remembered:

> I walked onto a set [in 1935] to film a silent test with a fellow Brit whom I had not yet met, took one look at the tall young man already stationed in front of the camera, and fell madly in love with him—a secret that I imparted to no-one and totally concealed from the object of my affection. In 1937, after we had made *The Charge of the Light Brigade* together, he, in his turn, decided that he had fallen in love with me and told me so, adding that he did not love his wife, who was abroad making a film in Morocco. I felt that we should not see each other until he had straightened out his situation with Lili, a condition to which he agreed. I waited for three years for news that the divorce had taken place, but the news never came. And so I finally began to look elsewhere.[63]

By the time the filming of *Robin Hood* began, Flynn and his wife Lili Damita had a reputation for battling and infidelity, and Flynn was vowing that the marriage was almost over. Lili, however, showed up on the set—including on location in Chico, California, where they filmed many of the Sherwood Forest scenes—and it was clear that although Flynn might be finished with Lili, the feeling wasn't mutual. Olivia hatched a plan to retaliate and decided: "I'm going to torture Errol Flynn. That's what I'm going to do. We had one kissing scene, which I looked forward to with great delight [when Robin Hood climbs the vines up to Maid Marian's balcony]. I remember I blew every take. At least six in a row, maybe seven, maybe eight, and we had to kiss all over again. And Errol Flynn got really rather uncomfortable, and he had, if I may say so, a little trouble with his tights."[64] Apparently, Olivia wasn't so innocent after all.

Whatever the drama happening behind the scenes, thanks to the superb craftsmanship and perfect performances, the film was hugely successful. It was nominated for several Oscars, including one for best picture, and won three—for Carl Jules Weyl's art direction in color, Ralph Dawson's editing, and Korngold's stirring score. Producer Hal Wallis won the Irving Thalberg Award for his work on the film.

Interestingly, two endings were shot. It is hard to imagine anything more charming than Marian and Robin, arms around each other, sneaking away from the band of Merry Men, happily accepting King Richard's command that they marry. The second ending shows the two lovers riding on a horse, smiling, in a beautiful outdoor scene. That discarded conclusion is memorable because it gives the viewer a sense of the days the two lovers will share, happily ever after, in Sherwood Forest.

Robert Osborne noted in the documentary *Welcome to Sherwood!*:

> I've talked to Olivia de Havilland . . . a lot about this film, and it's one she's very proud of, but she said that interestingly enough it was not considered by Warner Brothers to be a very prestigious picture. . . . And she said that broke [Flynn's] heart. And she said that years later she went to see it and she said she was kind of overwhelmed at how wonderful it was and how attractive it was and how entertaining it was. And to hear the squeals of delight of the audience that was there watching it. And so she decided she was going to go home and write Errol Flynn a letter.[65]

Olivia recounted the same story in the Flynn documentary: "I happened to see *Robin Hood* again. And I thought, 'What a wonderful movie. I've got to write to Errol.' Which I did. I said, 'If you haven't seen the film recently, run it. You will be so proud of it, so glad that you were Robin Hood.' Then I thought, 'Well, perhaps I shouldn't send it. It's sentimental. Perhaps I shouldn't.' And I didn't. And it was about two weeks later that he died."[66]

The film earned double its budget of $2 million, reminding Warner Brothers that the romantic pairing of Olivia and Flynn was the key to success at the box office. The couple had three more opportunities to work together as spirited lovers. The first, the 1939 western *Dodge City*, was also shot in Technicolor. The development of *Dodge City* was a "long and tortuous" process, however.[67] It started out as a tale about Wyatt Earp, but Earp's widow wanted payment, so the script had to be rewritten. James Cagney was discussed as the lead, but Flynn was eventually cast, his character being described as something of an adventurer-fighter to explain how a Tasmanian devil ended up in the American West. Olivia was cast as the female lead, opposite Flynn, as box office insurance.[68]

Sadly, by this point, Olivia had concluded that her career was going nowhere fast. She said, "'I was in such a depressed state that I could hardly remember the lines.'"[69] Olivia was also battling nervous and physical exhaustion, according to author Robert Matzen, and she fell apart crying in front of a journalist during costume fittings for the film. She was halfway through her contract but was "appearing in pictures she doesn't want to make. Her weight is down to 100 pounds soaking wet."[70] A neurologist friend gave her a schedule of rest and diet to help her recover her strength, but she remained exhausted and frustrated with Flynn's behavior.

Olivia's role in *Dodge City,* the lively retelling of the settling of that famous Kansas outpost, is a vigorous one. She travels in a covered-wagon caravan, wear split culottes as she demonstrates her horseback-riding skills, spars charmingly with Flynn (playing the noble sheriff), and looks like the ultimate American western heroine. Interestingly, Olivia was shot in three-strip Technicolor three times in 1939 (*Dodge City, Elizabeth and Essex,* and *Gone with the Wind*), a triptych preserving her youthful beauty in that landmark year of Hollywood cinema. *Dodge City* demonstrated her ability to perform in a variety of genres and preserved her box office appeal.

The 2005 DVD feature *Dodge City: Go West, Errol Flynn* notes that westerns were in vogue after *Stagecoach,* so it was inevitable that Flynn would be involved in them. Alan Hale's character creates a backstory to explain how Flynn, playing an Irishman in this film, ends up in Kansas: he's been everywhere, a "sort of a rover," and "he's the most moving-on man you ever saw. . . . So you see, he's either the greatest traveler that ever lived, or else he is the biggest liar!"[71] That explanation worked for audiences. Flynn attended the premiere of the film in Dodge City; he arrived on a locomotive, rode a horse in the celebratory parade, and attended a rodeo. All this publicity, along with the highly entertaining film itself, established Flynn as a western star.[72]

Just as Flynn is the last person you'd expect to see in a western, the same could be said of Olivia. She plays Abby Irving, a brave young woman who is moving west with her difficult brother (William Lundigan), part of a cattle drive led by Flynn and Hale. The brother is a dreadful boy who causes a stampede and pulls a gun on Flynn, who shoots and kills him. Abby holds Flynn responsible for her brother's death. Thus, as in almost all their movies, and in enduring rom-com fashion, they don't like each other at first. However, once they get to Dodge City, Olivia becomes the society columnist for the local newspaper and investigates corruption in the town. Flynn becomes the sheriff, and predictably, her opinion of him changes as they rid the town of the crooked men in control. After a variety of exciting events—a stagecoach race, shoot-outs, fistfights, and a barroom brawl—they marry and light out for new territories.

Olivia's character is, as always, proactive; she doesn't simply stand by, waiting to be swept off her feet. She and her wild brother are making the journey west on their own, which requires enormous courage. After his death, she takes a job, signifying her independence. Olivia's loose, flowing hair and ruddy cheeks complement her feisty heroine—an archetypal persona in Hollywood romances that hasn't changed in the eighty years since *Dodge City* was filmed.

The film, directed by the reliable Michael Curtiz and supported by Max Steiner's stirring score, was a hit. In addition to Alan Hale, it features a great supporting cast of Warner regulars, including the "Oomph Girl," Ann Sheridan, who had moved to the studio from Paramount and was rumored to be one of Flynn's many flings. Another supporting actor, Bruce Cabot, plays bad guy Jeff Surrett; in real life, Cabot and Flynn were great buddies until Cabot sued Flynn over his unfinished *William Tell* production, claiming his full salary and contributing to the project's abandonment. Victor Jory (Oberon in *A Midsummer Night's Dream* and no-good overseer Jonas Wilkerson in *Gone with the Wind*) plays an evil gunman. A wonderful treat for Gothic fans is the elegant Gloria Holden (*Dracula's Daughter*) as the tragic woman who loses her husband and son to the bad guys.

In a studio decision that once again demonstrated to Olivia that her career trajectory at Warner was not aimed toward stardom, Flynn got top billing above the title, while Olivia got second billing below the title. And, in what Olivia could have perceived as another slight from Jack Warner, although Sheridan got third billing, her name was the same size as Olivia's. Olivia may have been back in Flynn's arms, but despite—or perhaps because of—her appearance in *Gone with the Wind,* her stock was stuck. Nevertheless, they have some charming scenes together. For example, she asserts herself in a scene at the newspaper office when he tells her that her working there is "undignified. It's unladylike. More than that, you ought to be home doing needlework. Things like that." She retorts, "Sewing buttons on for some man. . . . That's a fine career for an intelligent woman."[73]

Olivia was not happy during the making of the film, and she was not dismayed when David Selznick called her back for reshoots for *Gone with the Wind,* meaning that she was unable to attend the huge premiere with Flynn and Sheridan in Dodge City, Kansas. She felt that her career was going nowhere, and Warner Brothers was reducing her to a supporting player. A month earlier, as a result of an intensive shooting schedule and her career-related frustration, Olivia had a "meltdown that had reduced her to a fetal position in bed."[74] Back to work too soon on a project she didn't want to be in, she lost weight during the shoot, something that happened frequently while Olivia was under contract to Warner, although the makeup required for Technicolor certainly conceals any ill health.

She was also angry with Flynn. For one thing, he was still married to Lili Damita. In addition, he was not supportive of Olivia's performance. He kept stealing scenes from her, and in an early moment in the film, as she tells him that she and her brother are heading west because of the death of their father, "he twirls the reins of his horse as they walk along."[75] Apparently, the cast and crew weren't fond of Olivia (no doubt her unhappiness didn't endear her to them), and they urged Flynn to take ownership of their scenes together.

While Olivia plays most of the film with a frown, she has some funny and romantic moments with Flynn. Perhaps their sweetest scene is when they are riding horses in the Kansas countryside. She wears a sporty red tartan, cap-sleeved shirt and a red, calf-length split skirt, with caramel riding boots. Her auburn hair is loose and curling. As they sit close together on the prairie grass, Flynn woos her with the story of how his father's pigs ate his mother's prize roses, resulting in six sons and a luscious rose garden. "You wouldn't dare," she says when he threatens to kiss her.[76] Naturally, he does exactly that in the beautiful late-afternoon light, and they ride into the sunset together. Offscreen, however, Olivia was about to begin dating Howard Hughes, a wonderful riposte to her faithless suitor.

Their last two films together—*Santa Fe Trail* and *They Died with Their Boots On*—rehashed the personae established in their previous films: Olivia as the feisty gal who comes to love the wildly impetuous but sincere Flynn. Both films, however, were built around Flynn, who was getting star treatment. As fond as Olivia was of Flynn, and as much as she appreciated the expertise of crew and costars, she was miserable professionally. Her films without Flynn were not tailored for her; the roles could have been played by any intelligent starlet. And particularly after portraying Melanie and getting a glimpse of the world of David O. Selznick's productions, she knew there were greener pastures out there. That her sister Joan Fontaine was under contract to Selznick and was filming *Rebecca* for Alfred Hitchcock, with Laurence Olivier, had to be bitterly painful for Olivia. She would have had to be a saint not to feel more than a little jealous of her younger sister.

After being loaned out to Samuel Goldwyn for *Raffles* with David Niven, which is an oddly incomplete and unimpressive film, Olivia was cast in a Warner remake of a film entitled *Married, Pretty and Poor.* She hated the script and refused to make the film, instead going to the premieres of *Gone with the Wind* in Atlanta and New York. The film eventually became *Saturday's Children* with a young John Garfield, and Jack Warner put Olivia on suspension for almost three months. It ended only when she agreed to make *My Love Came Back,* a weak if charming comedy.

By 1940, Olivia's contract would expire sooner rather than later, and her strategy began to change. At the ripe old age of twenty-four, Olivia had no illusions about her future at Warner Brothers, but she couldn't be constantly at war with Jack Warner. At that point, she was offered *Santa Fe Trail,* another film about the Wild West. Olivia knew this film was intended to exploit the success of *Dodge City* and take advantage of Flynn's growing star power as an action hero. Although his films were always more interesting when Olivia was the love interest, the studio considered her interchangeable with other young beauties. Olivia, however, saw in the role "some interesting qualities, including a spiritual side, an assertiveness with the male leads, and a surprising amount of screen time for an action picture."[77]

Flynn plays J. E. B. "Jeb" Stuart, a real-life US Army officer who served in Kansas in the 1850s during the expansion west, fought several battles with Native Americans, assisted in the capture of abolitionist John Brown, and later fought and died as a Confederate officer. In a rather curious casting choice, contract supporting player Ronald Reagan is George Custer; the stentorian Raymond Massey gives a weighty performance as John Brown; and the omnipresent Alan Hale appears once again as Flynn's sidekick. Olivia is the only woman of note in the film, but as usual, there's no acting challenge beyond playing a spirited heroine willing to tackle the prairie and Flynn. With the usual suspects on board, Hal Wallis produced, Sol Polito photographed, Max Steiner composed, and Michael Curtiz directed.

Set in 1854 and opening at West Point, where Robert E. Lee is the commandant, the screenplay manages to sidestep the slavery issue by making Flynn's Jeb Stuart a good guy who believes the South will settle the problem in its own way. Van Heflin's character, a northerner, supports emancipation, but he's rowdy and rude about it and is dishonorably discharged, setting up the film's real tension. The other cadets are assigned to the 2nd US Cavalry in Fort Leavenworth, Kansas, and as they graduate, we get a close-up of Livvie in white, carrying a parasol. She yells "Yippee!" when her brother graduates, as befits the spunky Kit, who smiles and exclaims, "It just popped out!"[78]

The film addresses several issues—the building of the railroad through Kansas and the prairie; the status of Kansas as a free state or a slave state; the national and personal tensions that underpinned the Civil War; the Union cavalry's mission at Fort Leavenworth, the last outpost before Santa Fe; and the doomed efforts of John Brown. These are all worthy subjects, and the romance between Olivia and Errol seems incidental rather than integral. Olivia's character, Kit Carson Holliday (so named because she was supposed to be a boy), looks more mature now, with her dark hair and a widow's peak; she climbs fences in short skirts and wears a plaid blouse with rolled-up sleeves. But the friendly competition between Flynn and Reagan over Livvie lacks drama—they actually draw straws for her, and when Reagan gets the long one, he bemoans, "Where I come from, long man loses." Her role in the larger issues of the film is minor. Olivia has some typically charming romantic scenes with Flynn, and one serious moment when she recognizes the need to free the slaves and asks, "What has pride got to do with human lives?"[79] But her role is primarily decorative.

Santa Fe Trail offers the Warners' Democratic Party philosophy in its depiction of the raid on Harpers Ferry, and Raymond Massey is wonderful as John Brown. In the scene in which Brown is hung, Olivia is the only woman there, standing next to the slaves, and Kit cries, "I'm not crying for him, Jeb. I see something else up there. Something much more terrible than just one man."[80] This is a strong dramatic moment for Olivia and for the film, predicting the Civil War. Even though she wasn't playing substantial roles, she was recognized in one of the English film magazines as having taken "her rightful place as one of the screen's natural heiresses, inheriting the Pickford-Gaynor tradition with a great deal of originality thrown in."[81] As in most of her romantic pairings with Errol, the film ends happily—with a cut to the iron horse and the wedding of Kit and Jeb. They kiss, and the train moves off into the sunset. The film was a success, but once again, it was Flynn's film.

Olivia had lost hope for an offscreen romance with Flynn, and she was becoming irritated with him. By this time, Flynn was drinking a lot and feeling far more confident in his star power, although he was still beset with insecurities about his true talent. She "admitted she was tired of him, bored to tears by his egotism and rudeness. Working with him had stopped being fun, and de Havilland craved better roles."[82] In one instance, after waiting several hours for a long setup of a night scene to be completed, Flynn decided to leave the set, and Olivia was furious.[83]

Years later, she recounted another example of Flynn's scene stealing: "There was a scene that we had rehearsed, a two-hander. I am sitting there in my silly little bonnet and he comes in and sits down beside me. Except that when we came to shoot the scene, he kicked his chair around so that his face was in the shot, but you could only see my back. That was very unfair." When asked why he would pull such an ungenerous, juvenile, unprofessional stunt, she replied, "Oh well, I think that he was annoyed because Jimmy Stewart was making another film on the same lot and kept coming over to see me. I was seeing a lot of Jimmy in 1940 . . . I suppose Errol was jealous."[84]

After this, she decided she didn't want to make another film with Flynn, who had become a liability to her career and to her emotional well-being. Flynn agreed with her, and "both informed producer Hal Wallis of their decision."[85] According to David Niven, during a press junket to Santa Fe, New Mexico, to promote *Santa Fe Trail,* the studio "assigned three men working twenty-four hours a day in shifts to keep [Flynn] sober and in his own bed, but Errol out drank and outmaneuvered the three men, and the junket lasted twice as long as planned."[86] However, as far as Olivia was concerned, she "was forced to re-evaluate Flynn yet again, for he was gentlemanly, polite, and courteous . . . and [she] began to understand the complex nature of the man with whom she had been so recently infatuated."[87]

Fast-forward one year, and life had changed for both young stars. Errol Flynn was Warner Brothers' biggest male star and at the top of his game. He was also a new father, having had a son with Lili Damita (his only son, Sean, disappeared in Cambodia in 1970 during the Vietnam War while working as a photojournalist—one trauma that Errol's early death spared him). He might be making programmer box office hits, but he was also becoming more confident in his power both off and on the screen.

Different voices were calling to Olivia. She had dated Howard Hughes and Jimmy Stewart and was no longer a naïf in the big dark woods of Hollywood chauvinism. In 1940 she met her future first husband, novelist Marcus Goodrich, eighteen years her senior and far more articulate and brilliant than her "In Like Flynn" costar (a name coined in the press during his 1942 trial for statutory rape—he was acquitted). She was outgrowing her girlhood crush.

Professionally, Olivia's loan-out to Paramount in 1940 resulted in her second Oscar nomination—and her first for best actress—this time for 1941's *Hold Back the Dawn.* That success also led her back to Warner Brothers, which demonstrated its respect for her accomplishment by, predictably, casting her in her eighth and final film with Flynn: *They Died with Their Boots On.*

Olivia and Errol had meant it when they said they didn't want to work together again. However, upon reviewing the script, "she admitted [it] was good . . . [and] was surprised to learn that Flynn had asked for her because he felt she was the only one who could handle the role. Flynn also pointed out to the Warners executives that the fan mail continued asking for a Flynn–de Havilland vehicle."[88] Flynn's move was certainly not that of a rebel but of a man strategizing to achieve greater stardom. His affection for Olivia was still palpable, but this final pairing should not be overromanticized. Flynn was calling the shots here, something he had been doing for a while.

For her part, Olivia was through having her career controlled by men. In fact, "on discovering that studio policy required that a script designated for production be first sent to makeup where the department head estimated the number of makeup people required for the project . . . [Olivia] would casually enter the department and sneak out a script or two at a time. She would read them overnight and surreptitiously return them the next morning."[89] If she couldn't demonstrate agency publicly, she would do so privately. *That* was real rebellion. *That* was swashbuckling.

She was no fool, however, and was enough of a strategist to recognize that if this film were successful, it could make the final two years of her contract more palatable. She was also clear-eyed enough to know that "the role of Libby Bacon Custer was a strong one . . . that follows the love affair beyond the altar and through the difficulties of marriage to someone not unlike Flynn himself."[90]

The film proved to be a poignant finale to a cinematic partnership that had begun six years earlier when both Olivia and Flynn were green and untested. By this time, although both were still young and attractive, each had gained significant life experience due to the nature of stardom, their frustrations with Warner Brothers, and various love affairs, including their own passion for each other that had calmed into a friendship and would fade as their careers took them in different directions.

In this last project, as always, Olivia plays the supportive woman behind the man. And as always, she is relegated to second billing. Hattie McDaniel, despite her Oscar win for *Gone with the Wind,* receives lowest billing in the opening credits. However, this film has a new energy behind it, thanks to Flynn's desire to replace director Michael Curtiz. Directed by Raoul Walsh and scored with war drums by Max Steiner, this action-filled star vehicle is a romanticized version of George Custer's defeat at the Little Bighorn. Flynn plays Custer with flamboyance, bravado, wit, and hints of tenderness, providing an entertaining if highly imaginative view of this tragic moment in American history. His Custer is far more memorable than Ronald Reagan's boyish interpretation in *Santa Fe Trail.*

In an interesting aside, Louis Zamperini, the World War II prisoner of war and Olympic distance runner whose story was made into the feature film *Unbroken* by Angelina Jolie, worked as an extra on the film. He was on the set when he received his draft notice, and his induction date came before filming would finish. Zamperini stood to earn a bonus if he stayed for the entire shoot, so just before his army physical, he "ate a fistful of candy bars; thanks to the consequent soaring blood sugar, he failed the physical. Ordered to return a few days later to retake the test, he went back to the set and earned his bonus. Then . . . he joined the army."[91] It was a brilliant ploy and rather Flynnesque in its cleverness.

They Died with Their Boots On opens at West Point, as did *Santa Fe Trail,* but three years later, in 1857. Flynn's Custer is a dandy new cadet who arrives with four dogs, a valet, a taste for raw onions, and a feathered cap. His antagonist is a rich and snobbish cadet played by Arthur Kennedy. Their tension fuels most of the film's action, but both men are too old for these roles. Flynn, at thirty-two, looks handsome but tired. Once again, he plays an American with a British accent and gets away with it, portraying a hell-raiser with a heart of gold.

A few years later, at graduation, it is announced that the Civil War has begun and that all officers and cadets must take an oath of loyalty to the United States. Anyone who can't comply must fall out. The southerners walk away as the cadet band plays "Dixie." The cadets are allowed to graduate early to fight in the war, and the officers, while discussing each man and what he might accomplish, bring up Custer: he has no regard for discipline or tactics; he has the lowest marks and highest demerits of any cadet who ever attended West Point (not unlike Ulysses S. Grant); he's aggressive, yet he has the qualities of a commander—a squadron would follow him to hell, says one sergeant.

About twenty minutes into the film, after Flynn's star power and the formulaic plot have been established, Olivia appears in a very pretty, frilly, four-tiered dress. She portrays Custer's wife, Elizabeth "Libby" Bacon, and bears some resemblance to the real-life woman, not only because of her hairstyle and the elaborate and almost—but not quite—overwhelming costumes by Milo Anderson but also because of the determination in her eyes. Libby spars with Custer on their first acquaintance—the old formula of girl loathes boy. In no time, however, their repartee leads Custer to tell Libby that he likes the idea of "walking through life with you beside me."[92] That line in fact becomes a trope in the film. There is a very rushed marriage scene in which the two look like exquisite porcelain wedding-cake figurines as they walk under a canopy of soldierly swords far too quickly for the audience to appreciate the gown or the moment—emotion sacrificed to action. Their marriage provides a frame around which the action occurs. Although Libby doesn't have much to do while waiting for Custer between battles, she supports her husband's career through to its disastrous end.

Whatever had or hadn't transpired between the two actors, the chemistry between Olivia and Errol is evident throughout the film. The ease, the fun, the flirtation, and the almost meta-performances of the leads—playing themselves and playing their roles and playing at happy endings—have a quiet authenticity. Oddly enough, just as the real Libby wrote three books about her husband and worked tirelessly to rehabilitate his image, Olivia would find herself in a similar position concerning Flynn years later.

The film follows Custer's career in the war, in Washington, DC, and then out west, including his confrontations with the dishonorable Arthur Kennedy character and his own outrageous decisions on and off the field of battle, leading to the final clash with Crazy Horse (played by a very young Anthony Quinn) and the Sioux nation. Sydney Greenstreet makes a large appearance as General Winfield Scott. The film is well paced, and the battle sequences at Manassas and the closing massacre at the Little Bighorn feature Raoul Walsh's signature realism.

Olivia carries herself with more confidence than in her earlier films—she is twenty-five now. The full, dark Victorian chignon she wears as Libby gives her both maturity and elegance. Her banter with Flynn is lively and comfortable and funny, and we can see that the two performers feel real warmth for each other. When Custer ingratiates himself by saying, in another variation of the film's slogan, "I can't imagine anything worse, ma'am, than walking through life without you," both the line and Flynn's delivery carry an authenticity that is poignant and beautiful.[93] The marriage proposal scene features Flynn climbing up to Olivia's balcony, enfolding her, and kissing her (reminiscent of

Robin Hood and Maid Marian). Shot through a softening filter, there's no talk; Olivia beams seductively with her hair down and wearing an off-the-shoulder dress. They also share a nice running gag about Custer's love of eating raw green onions and even manage to make that sexy and funny.

In their final scene together, before Custer goes off to what they both know is certain death, we see the sweetness of a friendship and a love that simply couldn't exist in real life for Olivia and Errol. A bugler is calling the troops. It's dark outside. All the soldiers are mounting up for their last campaign at the Little Bighorn. Libby is packing for George, who deliberately breaks his watch chain so that he can leave his watch for her; he pretends it's broken, and she pretends she didn't see him do it, both of them agreeing to the lie. He lifts his arms up, and she buckles his gun belt around his waist. Olivia is wearing a dark gown and heavy braids, which makes her look like a woman weighted down by too much feeling, and she gives true gravitas to the scene.

When Custer goes to fetch his orders, he finds her diary, which she dismisses as "just silly things that seem important to a woman," and he reads of her "premonition of disaster." She tells him, "Every parting has its own fears and anxieties," and "the more sadness in parting, the more joy in the reunion." Libby says, "Boots and saddles," which was the title of the real Mrs. Custer's first book about her dead hero. They kiss, deeply, and he cups her head tenderly. Then Flynn delivers perhaps the sincerest line of his career: "Walking through life with you, ma'am, has been a very gracious thing."[94] They kiss a final time, he strides out, and she collapses gracefully to the floor.

Olivia said of Flynn in *The Adventures of Errol Flynn,* "He was accustomed to getting his way, which was often very harmful to him. No sense of consequences. And I think the rest of his life really did illustrate that particular failing of his over and over again."[95] Critic Richard Schickel noted, "There is in his relationship with Olivia de Havilland something that is enormously touching because she's kind of a civilizing influence on this perpetually boyish, perpetually hot-blood-pounding type of guy." Of their final scene together, he said, "And there's a kind of a sense of doom about that scene. . . . And he's in this room, saying goodbye to this lady, and he knows and she knows that this is the end of this beautiful romance and he's going to die."[96] Olivia said:

> As we were playing that scene, I felt this extraordinary feeling of grief and loss. It was still with me when I went home. And it was

> with me the next day. I couldn't understand it until a long time later. I realized I had a presentiment that Errol and I would never work again together. And that's how it turned out to be. Of course, we did have a life together, as Peter Blood and Arabella Bishop, as Maid Marian and Robin Hood, as General Custer and his Libby, and those were happy lives, and perhaps that was enough.[97]

It would have to be enough for both of them.

Life took Olivia and Flynn in different directions after their last film. Flynn was rejected for military duty during World War II due to recurrent malaria and heart problems; he could only portray on celluloid the lives of men participating in the action abroad. He faced statutory rape charges in 1942 and was ultimately exonerated, but this contributed, along with his alcoholism, to a slowly declining career. Olivia noted in the documentary about Flynn, "His self-esteem was somehow profoundly affected and wounded, wounded by that trial, because he became a figure of fun as a result of it which he had never been before."[98] Flynn's marriage to Lili Damita ended, and subsequent marriages and children could not provide the actor with the stability he needed. The films he made at Warner Brothers became rote, and his contract ended. Despite excellent performances in *That Forsyte Woman, The Sun Also Rises,* and *Too Much, Too Soon,* too many problems with money, producers, women, and addiction led to the handsome actor's death from a heart attack at age fifty; doctors said his body resembled that of a man twenty years older. The letter Olivia had written to him about *Robin Hood* would forever go unsent. There would never be another onscreen reunion.

The benighted nature of their relationship is illustrated in a series of letters from 1969 concerning the publication by Citadel Press of *The Films of Errol Flynn.* One of the authors, Clifford McCarty (representing coauthors Anthony Thomas and Rudy Behlmer), wrote to Olivia in care of her public-relations firm in January 1969 to request that she contribute an introduction for the book, for "there was no doubt in our minds who should write it." Olivia responded almost three months later, requesting to see a copy from the Citadel series as well as "your galleys." In May, a deeply embarrassed McCarty responded that because they hadn't heard from her, "we approached Miss Greer Garson," who accepted. Olivia responded graciously that Garson was "a most attractive and appropriate choice."[99]

We can't know for certain whether the romance between Livvie and Errol was ever consummated, despite Olivia's denials. The prurient pleasures of Hollywood gossip aside, she is certainly not the kind of woman to kiss and tell. Although she took extreme umbrage at Michael Caine's false and salacious (in her opinion) story about her history with Flynn, she has danced around the issue in various interviews. She mentioned in 2009, "What I felt for Errol Flynn was not a trivial matter at all. I felt terribly attracted to him. And do you know, I still feel it. I still feel very close to him to this day."[100]

Olivia's comment was not revealing or surprising. She has always carefully, tactfully, and ferociously protected her reputation and her legacy, and over the years, she has also, rather poignantly, protected the man she costarred with in eight films. Whatever heartache the young Olivia suffered in loving and longing for the unavailable, charming, and self-destructive Flynn, one hopes it has mellowed into a beautiful memory of a golden time of youth, of Hollywood, of immortality. She can relive those moments in their eight films, as can we. *Robin Hood* and *Elizabeth and Essex* preserve their passion, but it is in *Dodge City,* on horseback, with Olivia's hair down and the golden sunset lighting them, that we see a glimpse of what they may have been to each other in real life: two friends, not quite lovers; two strong-willed, strong-minded people whose time together would be brief but memorable. Livvie and Errol—their spirited chemistry vibrant and vivid—riding off into legend together.

4

LEARNING THE JOB

Olivia's partnership with Errol Flynn gave her tremendous visibility among moviegoers, a solid if boring career, and financial security for the immediate future, but not many challenges as an artist. While she was learning her craft through a variety of films, the deeply ambitious actress wanted to tackle more substantial projects. She worked constantly from 1935 to 1943 during her time at Warner Brothers, and she often appeared in popular and successful films, yet she was generally dissatisfied. The promised land of prestigious films and directors and Shakespearean heroines had been reduced to a back lot and a starlet with a bad attitude. The films were not particularly rewarding for Olivia in terms of generating more interesting offers, even on loan-out; nor did they increase Warner Brothers' appreciation for her potential. Rather disappointingly, the roles available to a charming, bright ingenue under studio contract in the early years of talking pictures were similar to those of today—in a typical plot, a pretty, smart, sometimes smart-talking girl with a comely figure and a wide smile meets a fellow who underestimates her spunk and eventually marries her after a series of misunderstandings and misadventures. Such films still make money, but to build a truly sustainable career, an actress must aim higher.

Olivia was eight years younger than the queen of the Warner Brothers lot, Bette Davis, so Bette inspired and, to a great extent, instructed Olivia. Despite the actress's frustration with the studio, Warners crafted projects for Davis that displayed her artistry to critical and popular acclaim. No other studio actress ever had such a long run of great roles. Even Greta Garbo, Joan Crawford, and Norma Shearer at MGM were not as diversely brilliant as Bette. Olivia, however, would never earn an Oscar nomination while at Warners.

Olivia worked with a number of talented actors and actresses, as well as crew members and studio technicians, and she acquired the kind of training a contract actress was blessed to receive. By performing in various genres set in various periods, working with highly capable studio directors and costars, and studying her profession by doing, Olivia gained practical experience and developed her own technique and approach to her roles:

> At Warner Brothers, we usually had a dialogue director on a film, the best known of whom was an Englishman, Stanley Logan, who specialized in films with English casts. . . . The ostensible function of a dialogue director was to assure that the actors knew their lines before the first rehearsal. However, some of these technicians had a gift for interpretation and made constructive suggestions in the process of assuring the actors were line-perfect. . . . In time, I found that I needed to receive a script as much as six weeks in advance, and that I further needed to read my role over and over again, until the character took possession of me.[1]

Interestingly, Olivia never took formal acting classes. She developed her technique through on-the-job training and self-study. In fact, she noted, "I had no connection with Method Acting or any other style of performing. However, Joan Crawford, whom I met briefly through a young friend, sent me a copy of 'Stanislavski.' Subsequently, I read more than one of his works."[2] The idea of Olivia and Crawford bonding over the Method is one of the many strange, wonderful twists of Hollywood history.

Although some of Olivia's early films were predictable, others were quite memorable. Immediately after *Captain Blood,* for example, she won the role of Angela in *Anthony Adverse* (beating out Bette Davis), adapted from the best-selling novel by Hervey Allen. In February 2015, at a charming poster shop in Paris, I came across a large painting from a local cinema that had advertised the film in 1936. Both Olivia and costar Fredric March, in the title role, look gorgeous, dewy, and dashing in their period garb—another reminder that Olivia's star still shines brightly in her adopted hometown of Paris.

Olivia was given the saucy task of creating Angela Giuseppe, the cook's daughter whom Anthony marries, loses, rediscovers, and loses again. The impressive production won four Oscars, the most significant going to best supporting actress Gale Sondergaard (who would later be blacklisted). Despite Olivia's second billing, Sondergaard had the better role and deserved both the nomination and the award. The studio didn't give Olivia the material she needed for an award-worthy performance. Once again, the young actress was frustrated, but Olivia's nature and drive, shared with her mother and sister, would not allow her to be complacent about the direction of her career.

Twenty-year-old Olivia, with four films already in the can, is charmingly competent in the film as she matures from an innocent girl to an opera star and mistress of Napoleon Bonaparte. Directed by the always reliable Mervyn LeRoy, *Anthony Adverse* unfolds as both a stirring adventure and an ill-fated love story about "Victims of cruel fate—The spiritual orphans of the world."[3] Anthony Adverse is the product of the illicit affair of a young woman married to the cruel (and wonderfully evil) Claude Rains. The lad is abandoned at the Convent of the Holy Child after his mother dies and Rains kills his father. The nuns baptize him "Anthony" in honor of the saint. Fortuitously, Anthony is apprenticed in Leghorn (now Livorno) to a merchant who owns Casa da Bonnyfeather—and the merchant just happens to be his grandfather (Edmund Gwenn), who didn't even know he was alive! The kind grandfather realizes that Anthony is his—a child of adversity—and says, "We'll call him 'Adverse.' Now and forever, Anthony Adverse." In no time, Anthony has grown into the handsome Fredric March, and Angela, his childhood friend, is the beautiful Olivia. She is active and vigorous and rather peasant-like as they throw kisses to each other, but social class will stand in their way. He would love to marry her and buy a villa, but she doesn't believe it: "It's different now. We're not children any longer." She wishes she was a beautiful lady, and he assures her, "I'll never be ashamed of you, Angela." Presciently, she says, "You will, someday."[4] They sing together (Olivia lip-synching effectively), foreshadowing her character's future as an operatic diva.

The film unfolds as Anthony and Angela grow up, grow together, grow apart, marry, separate, conceive a son, and finally bid adieu when he takes their son to America for a better future. March is handsome and sincere, and Olivia is luscious in opulent costumes and curling locks, but their romance never strikes the poignant note it should. It may be the age difference between the actors—March was nineteen years older than Olivia. Also, the film tells his story, not hers. Again, Olivia's character supports the hero, complements him, but doesn't command the focus of the film.

Nevertheless, Olivia is exploring her lower vocal register, and there is vibrancy in her movements. She manages to age relatively realistically from a teenaged peasant girl to the lover of the great Napoleon. Olivia also holds her own with March, who would become a two-time Oscar winner but was inclined toward theatricality and a soupçon of ham. While Anthony becomes an embittered slave owner, Angela becomes the toast of Parisian society.

When she and Anthony are reunited at a masked ball after several years apart, Olivia is stunning in a blonde powdered wig and a beautiful satin Regency dress, seductively voicing her lines. When they embrace and kiss, she says, "Don't talk. Just let me hold you close to me." It is a truly romantic moment. Alas, their love is not meant to be. She has become Mlle. Georges, and he is bound for America to give their son "a new name."[5] And so it ends—a lush if predictable epic. The film's four Oscars—for Sondergaard as well as for cinematography, editing, and music—added to its status but not to Olivia's value as a gifted young performer.

Olivia followed this film with her second pairing with Errol Flynn, *The Charge of the Light Brigade* (see chapter 3). Her loveliness in the Victorian costumes certainly bolstered her reputation as a starlet who was comfortable in period dress, and the action sequences demonstrated her athleticism. Olivia also proved that she could work with director Michael Curtiz, whose raison d'etre was action rather than the development of female characters. In fact, the brigade's remarkable climactic charge was so realistic that "a number of horses were killed and many of the stuntmen injured. Due to pressure brought to bear by the Society for the Prevention of Cruelty to Animals, Hollywood was thereafter closely supervised in its treatment of horses on the screen."[6] It is a tribute to Olivia's calm professionalism that she was able to get along with the eccentric Curtiz more smoothly than Flynn did over the years.

Olivia was doing quite well by Hollywood standards at the start of 1937. She had made six films in two years and entered into a new romantic screen partnership with Flynn, she had a guaranteed salary and five more years to go on her film contract, and she had a presence in the fan magazines. One would think that Jack Warner and the studio's producers would see that the young Olivia was intelligent, ambitious, and capable of more. Perhaps they did, which may be why she was given top billing for the first time in her next film.

Call It a Day was something of a B-picture, with solid support from Ian Hunter, Anita Louise, Alice Brady, Roland Young, and Una O'Connor. Contract scriptwriter Casey Robinson adapted the screenplay from a play by British writer Dodie Smith (who would later gain fame for *101 Dalmatians*). The play had a healthy run of 194 performances on Broadway at the Morosco Theatre from January to July 1936; it was directed by the renowned Tyrone Guthrie and produced by the Theatre Guild, best known for its remarkable plays with Alfred Lunt and Lynn Fontanne.[7] In keeping with standard Hollywood practice, Warner Brothers bought the rights to the play, hoping not only to take advantage of a proven success but also to inject a tone of respectability and refinement into its movies, as well as lure theater-trained professionals to California (talking pictures required performers with good voices). Ironically, when the play transferred to Los Angeles, Joan Fontaine played the leading role of Catherine Hilton.[8] When Olivia got the part in the film, this could not have helped the sisters' relationship.

Olivia looks fresh and pretty in costumes by the great Australian designer Orry-Kelly; a thoughtful 2016 documentary about this Hollywood fixture, *Women He's Undressed,* reaffirms his importance at Warner Brothers. Photographing Olivia was renowned cinematographer Ernest Haller. As the story addresses the madcap antics of a British family, she adopts a British accent, which came naturally to her, particularly given her mother's abilities as a speech coach. Joan Fontaine maintained a British accent throughout her film career, which may have been a deliberate effort to distinguish herself from her sister, but it was no stretch for Olivia to reproduce the same. Olivia had demonstrated a burgeoning sophistication and sense of play in her characterizations, particularly in her easy interactions with Flynn, and this opportunity to play a rather lively and innocent young heroine, albeit in a smaller production, gave her some comedic training.

The film opens with the comment, "The first Spring day is in the Devil's pay."[9] From there, we see a spectrum of silly behaviors committed by the cast. The divinely funny Una O'Connor portrays a charwoman with a bad attitude. Playing Olivia's siblings are Peter Willes and Bonita Granville (who, with husband Jack Wrather, later produced television's *Lassie*). Their bemused parents, the terribly British Frieda Inescourt and Ian Hunter, watch them frolic through the film as they themselves are enticed by people not their spouses. Hilarity ensues, with director Archie Mayo "handl[ing] the proceedings proficiently but without verve or enthusiasm."[10]

Olivia's Catherine is very dreamy, spending her early mornings reading and praying to Shelley and declaring, "I wanna be alone." She argues with her mother and hates the whole horrid household. She sulks, she cries, she storms away as she asks the existential question, "What does anything matter?"[11]

The film's romantic spring day unfolds with almost all the characters pursuing love. Olivia's focus is the famous artist (Walter Woolf King) who is painting her portrait as his wife (the great stage actress Peggy Wood) watches indulgently while she tats. Olivia has a tremendous crush on him, and she stares at him longingly and then looks away tearfully. Posing in a black lace shawl over a wide tulle gown as she reads, she looks lovely and sweet (where is that painting today?). She pitches a fit when his wife leaves the room, calling him, clinging to him, weeping breathlessly. He's married, and she knows his reputation, "but . . . it doesn't seem to make any difference."[12]

A variety of madcap actions ensue, but in the end, everything is resolved. Those who are married stay married. Olivia cries because her romance has gone nowhere, but her sister comforts her by telling her that lots of people fall in love with married men. Their parents get the film's closing shot: they hold hands across their twin beds as birds tweet, violin music plays, the wind blows in, and a caged bird is happy. Despite her top billing, Olivia really has nothing to do; it's not her film in any way. No wonder the actress was beginning to see her seven-year contract as more of an obstacle than security.

Olivia made two more films in 1937 that exposed her to audiences but provided no real box office power or acting challenges. Both films dealt with life in the theater, and one wonders whether Olivia's theatrical beginnings only three years before seemed more appealing than her new stardom. She mentioned in a 1946 interview with gossip columnist Louella Parsons, "I got a chance at a stage play . . . but everybody argued me into going into movies instead. I sometimes wish I hadn't. . . . I might have got a better grounding in acting if I'd had some stage training. You have to be so facile in pictures. You haven't time to explore a character."[13]

Her second film of the year, *The Great Garrick,* is another costume drama that allows her to wear beautiful, elaborate gowns but, again, doesn't give her much to do. It was directed by Hollywood maverick James Whale, and one wonders whether the great director and the novice actress ever got together to bemoan their lot. Whale was the visionary who brought *Frankenstein, The Old Dark House, Bride of Frankenstein,* and *Show Boat* to the screen. His decision to end his directing career and the story of his subsequent years in Hollywood were beautifully, poignantly portrayed in Christopher Bram's novel *Father of Frankenstein* and in the film *Gods and Monsters,* starring Ian McKellen.

Costarring with Olivia was her future brother-in-law Brian Aherne. Aherne had the same youthful appeal and bravado as Errol Flynn, and although he was not used as intelligently as the latter, his star was on the rise. He was also rumored to be a beau of Olivia's during filming.[14] Olivia denied there was anything to it, and certainly her major crush at the time was Flynn. Nevertheless, the fact that Olivia got to Aherne first and then lost him to sister Joan was another source of irritation between them.

The film is a spritely view of eighteenth-century British theater great David Garrick, one of the first actors to make that profession respectable. There is a theater in London named after him, and he was buried in Westminster Abbey. The script, written by Ernst Vajda, is an adaptation of his play *Ladies and Gentlemen.* Again, Olivia was photographed by Ernie Haller, who would win an Oscar for *Gone with the Wind.* Art director Anton Grot created lively and elaborate sets to reflect both Drury Lane and the Comédie-Française of the mid-eighteenth century. In Milo Anderson's delicious eighteenth-century costumes, Olivia looks like a glamorous French doll. She is supported by a very young Lana Turner as well as Harry Davenport (the future Dr. Meade in *Gone with the Wind*). "Personally supervised" and produced by *Anthony Adverse* director Mervyn LeRoy, this prestigious film begins on Drury Lane in 1750—a romantic adventure "that might have happened."[15]

Beloved actor David Garrick, played with enormous energy and great scenery-chewing fun by the very handsome, very blonde Aherne, takes a curtain call after his performance of *Hamlet* and announces that he's been invited to Paris by the Comédie-Française, so this is his farewell performance of the season. The cockney rabble in the cheap seats subject him to catcalls and throw vegetables at him as they ask angrily, "Do you prefer the French?" Garrick milks it for all he's worth and declares with enormous theatricality, "You command me not to go? And I am overjoyed to stay." He kneels before his adoring fans as he reads from a blank piece of paper, claiming it's a letter from the French. Then one of the wealthy audience members in the expensive boxes calls out that he must go and teach the French! "Teach the French!" the audience chants.[16] The manipulative Garrick has gotten his way, so he bows, exits, and heads to France.

The action then cuts to Paris and the Comédie-Française stage, where the overdressed and obviously decadent company meets onstage. Melville Cooper plays M. Picard, the president of the French troupe, who calls Garrick a "conceited popinjay." They're insulted by his faux letter—we implored him to teach us to act?—and want to rescind the invitation to join their group. But Beaumarchais (played by the divinely sardonic Lionel Atwill) warns them that Garrick will try to turn the tables by claiming that they fear him because he's a better actor: "Ridicule kills—and it's true."[17] So the French actors plot to take over the inn where he will be staying en route to Paris and treat him so badly that he will leave France. Unfortunately for them, Garrick knows actors when he sees them, and a comedy of errors ensues when the French players take over the roles of the inn's servants. The first act of the film is very talky and extremely theatrical, shot almost like a stage play, but it's also quite energetic, and the actors have great fun overacting all over the place (Lana Turner as a giggling young actress pretending to be a giggling young maid is delectable).

Half an hour into the action, Olivia makes her entrance in an elaborate fur and brocade concoction that threatens to engulf her petite form. This late entrance—demonstrating that she is viewed as pretty but unessential by both the studio and the scriptwriters—gives the film's real stars, the action men, time to establish themselves. The Countess Germaine De Le Corbe's coach has overturned, and she desperately needs a room. With her prettily overdone costume, elaborately curled coiffure, and proper British accent, Olivia is utterly adorable. Garrick is convinced that she is another actress, so he offers his own room. Of course, the French actors don't know who she is, and she thinks she's just spending the night at an inn, so the charade continues: "The play must go on."[18]

More French farce and miscommunication occur as Garrick decides to seduce the countess and expose her as a fraud. Who can blame him, though, given how luscious Germaine looks in her gauzy, dreamy, décolleté-revealing peignoir? A frog in her bedroom prompts screams, and Garrick (the prince she must kiss instead of the frog) comes to her rescue, declaring that she is Juliet and he is Romeo. Garrick and Germaine share a wistfully romantic moment as they leave the inn and wander by a gleaming pond right out of *A Midsummer Night's Dream*. As they gaze in the water and talk, Germaine's musical voice becomes deep and lovely; her pretty, heart-shaped face reflects how enamored she is as her companion garishly recites Shakespeare. And when Garrick reveals his true identity, she is thrilled! "I'm talking to the great David Garrick!"[19]

But the course of true love . . . the actors in the inn continue their charade, engaging in a variety of madcap antics. Garrick and his valet, Tubby (played with trademark drollness by Edward Everett Horton), decide they will let Germaine "pretend" to be a frightened ingenue, and when she runs into Garrick's lascivious arms, he bawdily declares, "She'll no longer be an amateur."[20] She is outraged, they part, and more antics ensue.

However, all's well that ends well for the Great Garrick. Several weeks later in Paris, he is playing—who else?—Don Juan. In this last act of the film, the theatrical scenes, sets, and costumes and the authentic sense of anticipation of a live performance are captivating. Picard reveals to Garrick that Germaine was not a member of the theater troupe, and Garrick, to his credit, is aghast that he has hurt such a "sweet, loving little heart!"[21]

So Garrick decides to tell the audience that he cannot perform—"I've found happiness and I threw it away!" he declares. Fortunately, however, the prompter has run into Germaine and explained the situation; he holds up a chalkboard telling Garrick that he is forgiven. Germaine is sitting prettily in a box, wearing an utterly glorious, lace-bedewed gown, glowing at Garrick as he tells the audience, "For the first time in my life, I can hardly find words. Because for the first time in my life, I am in love." She smiles, bites her lower lip, and throws him a flower. The audience follows suit, and the actor throws his understudy off the stage as he shouts, "Let's ring up the curtain!"[22] Significantly, Olivia gets the last shot—a close-up in which she is smiling prettily.

The Great Garrick is a theatrical film about the theater, and while it is sometimes static and talky, its production values are impressive, its cast is adept, and its humor is very British, very arch, and occasionally very funny. Olivia is the innocent ingenue, but she is also elegant and committed to the material, proving that she can play a comedic heroine. She was given the opportunity to build on those skills in her next project.

Olivia's third film of 1937 finally brought her face-to-face with Bette Davis. According to Olivia in 1977, when she appeared on an episode of *This Is Your Life* honoring Davis, this first professional meeting was not the beginning of a beautiful friendship. That was understandable. Davis was already a great star, and she was eight years older than Olivia; she did not go out of her way to be friendly to the younger actress. There might have been shades of *All About Eve* in their relationship at the time: Bette was fighting for every good film role she could get, and Olivia was doing the same. Bette needn't have worried. *It's Love I'm After* is a fun but forgettable romantic comedy, "further proof of [Olivia's] then-subordinate stature at the studio."[23] Leslie Howard was given top billing, followed by Davis and then Olivia in third place. It's a screwball farce about life in the theater, and it's not the best work of any of that trio. Olivia's love interest is Patric Knowles, who once again plays her callow beau, and Archie Mayo directs without particular flair. At least Orry-Kelly designed the contemporary costumes, which Olivia wears fetchingly.

Howard and Davis play engaged couple Basil Underwood and Joyce Arden (a witty double mockery of Shakespeare's green world). Not unlike the Lunts in their stage and film success *The Guardsman,* they are two egotistical actors who love and loathe each other both onstage and off. Olivia plays Marcia West, a gaga fan, a shallow future Melanie as she watches her future Ashley play Romeo from a balcony. Ironically, Howard had just played that role opposite Norma Shearer for MGM. Whether the scriptwriters or Warner or Howard himself wanted to somehow disparage that production, Howard seems to be over the role. Olivia, wearing a sexy halter dress, sighs dreamily and rests her chin on her hand in her first appearance in the film, watching Basil from her box in the theater. Knowles grabs her hand, but she shakes him off and leans onto the balcony railing to watch. Leslie looks up at the box, and Bette chastises him. Eric Blore, the witty man Friday in many films of the 1930s and 1940s, plays Howard's unimpressed dresser, Diggs. When the couple begins to spar, he murmurs, "Here they go again."[24] That sparring is the essence of the film.

Like Germaine with Garrick, Olivia's Marcia is madly in love with an actor, mistaking the onstage romantic ideal for the real man offstage. In this film, however, she rather formulaically ignores her nice boyfriend and her idol's wife. As the droll Spring Byington (one of the most versatile supporting actresses of the era) tells the hapless Knowles, "You're everything a girl should want and doesn't,"[25] which also rather aptly summarizes Knowles's acting career. At Knowles's request, Howard agrees to behave extremely caddishly toward his young admirer in an effort to put Olivia off and allow her boyfriend to win her back; naturally, this simply makes her more determined to win Howard's love.

This positioning of Olivia between two men was nothing new in her films. In fact, "being one corner of a love triangle or quadrangle became a hallmark of de Havilland's characters."[26] She's actually rather perfect as an obsessed young fan; her endless energy is as shimmering as her satin gowns, and her manic eyes are like two feverish dark spots as she declares to her idol in his dressing room, "I'm—I'm nobody. . . . You're my ideal. . . . I love you." And then Olivia delivers with breathless sincerity this speech: "Someday when you're old and forgotten and when you feel that awful loneliness that comes to those that have been adored and are now forgotten, then perhaps you'll remember tonight and be grateful to me." Howard makes her straight lines funny as he comments, "I don't know what I've been worshipping," and he tells Blore, "There was no young lady, Diggs. . . . Merely a lovely wraith who appeared from nowhere, and disappeared into nowhere. And completely daffy."[27]

Daffy and labored describes the ensuing action. Howard and Davis spar, Blore and Byington deliver dry comments, and Knowles plays the hapless young male lead rather haplessly. Olivia, however, is straining a bit. Her character should be dizzy and slightly mad, and despite her best efforts, Olivia's native intelligence overwhelms her dreamy debutante. It may be the result of rather desultory direction by Archie Mayo or a tired script by Casey Robinson, but Olivia's best comedic moments are always when she is an ironic commentator on the action.

Of course, all ends well. After much romping and miscommunication, Olivia realizes that Knowles is the boy for her, and in an amusing moment with Bette, she says, "You may have your husband back now. . . . You're a very sweet person, Mrs. Underwood, and believe me, you have all my sympathy." Bette realizes that Howard was telling the truth about his intentions toward Olivia, and she tells him, "You seem like a new man. . . . There seems to be a halo around your head." They decide to fly to Las Vegas to get married, but then they start arguing; Howard pushes Bette off the couch, and she pushes him over. As the film ends, Blore's Diggs is crying, the couple is kissing, and Howard declares, "This is the life, eh, Diggs?"[28]

It wasn't necessarily the life for Olivia, though. Her frustration with her career was growing, and as 1938 dawned, she seemed to be on a treadmill, making film after film that gave her an income and visibility but certainly didn't provide much creative gratification. Her personal life wasn't terribly fulfilling either. Olivia casually dated Howard Hughes (they shared a love of flying), but so did everyone else in Hollywood, including her sister. Joan Fontaine was now working in films, and although her career wasn't much more interesting than Olivia's, the competition couldn't have been comfortable. A fan magazine article from 1941 looked back on her career and noted, "Olivia's sweet demureness was sometimes broken by a fit of tantrums and a flash of anger from her large eyes, but it didn't seem to get her anywhere much. You felt that, even if she did summon up enough positive personality to say boo to a goose, she would be overcome with tears of contrition immediately afterwards."[29]

And so the films continued. But there were some compensations for both Olivia and her audience. Her next project—*Gold Is Where You Find It*—would be filmed in Technicolor, and Olivia would be seen onscreen in all her luminous beauty. That she appeared in five Technicolor films in 1938 and 1939 isn't given enough attention in terms of that process's history and importance. In *Gold,* the colors are so burnished that she seems hand-tinted. This paean to California's agricultural history offers a "farmer and the cowman" scenario, albeit between the solid, all-American wheat growers and the greedy gold miners whose hydraulic methods pollute the waters that nourish the soil.

The film is very much a typical Warner Brothers socialist tract, pitting the "natural" individual against the ruthless gold-monger. Given the nightmare of the Dust Bowl, the film presents California as a land of milk and honey, of green fields and luscious land opportunities, which, in the late 1930s, it still was. Tony Thomas notes that the film "has somehow slipped into movie obscurity, and undeservedly so," for it is a "prime example of cinematic Americana . . . it shines with optimism about the American experience."[30] The trailer trumpeted the glowing "New Technicolor."[31] It certainly "pretties up a feud," as Frank S. Nugent commented drily, but the intensity of the Technicolor made it "difficult for anyone to sympathize with the ranchers when mud overflows their fields. It was such beautiful mud."[32] That's not a bad thing for a rousing adventure about the American dreams of gold and land in late 1800s California.

Perhaps even the film's title—*Gold Is Where You Find It*—was a kind of instructive comment for a restless and dissatisfied Olivia, along with "bloom where you're planted" and "make lemonade out of lemons." She may have found herself in period garb again—this time, the clothing of 1870s California—but she looked wonderful in color. This epic tale of the beginnings of the state's growth from a landscape to be mined and pillaged to an agricultural wonderland has become, over time, a romantic tribute to the Anglo settlers of the region.

The film is clearly on the side of the farmers, with the majority of the plot revolving around engineer George Brent, who sees the error of his ways thanks to his feelings for Olivia and her farmer father, Claude Rains. Despite playing a seventeen-year-old ingenue (which the twenty-two-year-old Olivia does convincingly), the actress has a more substantial role than usual. Olivia's vigor delights as a young woman who maintains her own fifty acres of orchards. She is shown tilling the earth by controlling a horse-drawn contraption confidently, full auburn hair glowing in the California sun. Clearly director Michael Curtiz thought enough of Olivia's appeal to direct her to flip her long curling locks behind her as she ploughed furrows. While initially appearing as a spritely tomboy of sorts, Olivia's character matures as the trouble between her father and the miners unfolds.

The Ferris family—the aptly named, calmly confident Serena (Olivia); her brother, Lance (a young and reckless Tim Holt); and her beloved father, Colonel Ferris (played with authority and compassion by Rains)—have a strong stake in the future of California. The film's rose-tinted poster portrays Rains, Olivia, and Brent in an aura of such glowing health that the actors seem positively radioactive, but Olivia's lusciousness blooms from the screen. Her costumes are extremely girlish and frilly, emphasizing a doll-like youthfulness, yet Serena's warm contralto voice and gradual, believable maturation overcome conventional expectations.

As the daughter of the charmingly paternal Rains (who wears a hairpiece that makes him resemble a Viennese composer more than a wheat farmer),

Olivia displays a familial chemistry with the older actor, who also developed a fond working relationship with Bette Davis. Her scenes with Holt capture all that is idealized in sibling relationships in 1930s Hollywood cinema. Somehow, it all works. Olivia is always sincere and intelligent in her delivery; the maturity she showed at eighteen in *A Midsummer Night's Dream* and at nineteen in *Captain Blood* rests below the surface in her initial scenes as an enthusiastic teenaged orchardist. And as tensions grow, her innate calm provides the organic, Mother Nature core of the film's mission.

As far as attraction between Olivia and the debonair Brent, there isn't much, but that's not entirely her fault. When I asked her what it was like to work with certain actors, she shared quite a lot about other costars, but about him, she wrote, "George Brent was a nice fellow, easy to work with, compatible, but difficult to know."[33] The Irish Brent always retained a diffident onscreen persona, and despite his three pairings with Olivia, their onscreen interactions are professional but passionless. Brent and Bette Davis were known to have an off-and-on affair for several years, so his reserve may have been due to his various wives and Davis's watchful eye. His affect was generally one of understated, wary objectivity. In *Gold,* the action surrounding the struggles in the Sacramento Valley in the 1870s takes primacy over any romantic or familial subplots, so the lack of a connection is incidental.

It's a scenically stunning film, shot on location "around Perris, California, the site of its historically accurate story."[34] Contemporary viewers can only marvel at how spectacular the state was eighty years ago. Directed by Michael Curtiz (who, as one of Warner's most prolific directors, was adept at virtually *every* genre), the battles between the farmers and the miners are rigorously apropos to this tale of a struggle over land. Olivia worked with Curtiz many times, of course, and here she fulfills the physical and character demands the director imposed. Olivia knew what her role was, and she delivered, but always with a personalized twist.

As an action ingenue, Olivia's performances consistently showed "a certain vigor."[35] Today's action stars get enormous amounts of press about their training and diets in preparation for physically demanding roles. Olivia and other contract players just got on with it. She plows her orchard, she digs an irrigation ditch by hand, she climbs her apple trees to pick and prune, and she battles beside her father—all of it done easily and occasionally messily, with her face begrimed by the effort.

This film was followed by the iconic *The Adventures of Robin Hood,* Olivia's second film in Technicolor and her third pairing with Flynn in as many years. That she received the plum role of Maid Marian indicated the studio's awareness of the power of that partnership, and this was Warner Brothers' biggest-budgeted film thus far.[36] Following up *Robin Hood* with *Four's a Crowd* made good box office sense for Warner Brothers, as audiences clearly enjoyed films that starred Flynn and Olivia. Here, Olivia is cast in a role she doesn't do terribly believably—"a girl who giggles a good deal too much . . . [and] it is difficult to imagine her character having a sensible thought inside her pretty head."[37] Everyone tries their best, but "screwball comedy was not the forte of either Flynn or Olivia."[38] (Both films are discussed in detail in chapter 3.)

Her final film in 1938 was another programmer released that November. Originally titled *For Lovers Only, Hard to Get* is a good-spirited but unremarkable romantic comedy with music.[39] Olivia plays yet another spoiled rich girl—certainly a stock character in the 1930s, but not well suited to Olivia's type; she can play comedy, but she can't play dumb. She is reteamed with her first screen beau from *A Midsummer Night's Dream*, Dick Powell (he's now Busby Berkeley's great star), and they're fun together. Certainly Olivia is game, and Powell is cute, but there's not much for them to do. As always, Olivia is spirited and charming, but there is nothing unique in either the role or her performance.

In addition to Powell, Olivia is reteamed with two great supporting actors—Bonita Granville and Melville Cooper. Olivia plays the bored and spoiled Margaret Richards, who keeps two nasty little Chihuahuas and tussles with her younger sister, Connie (Granville). Her biggest challenge is that she seems to be suffering from ennui. To escape, she rushes out of the house, jumps into the butler's (Cooper) car, and speeds off, but it runs out of gas. She bites her lower lip as she blares her horn at a gas station/motel, and who should work there but all-American boy Bill Davis (Powell). She has no money, and they snipe back and forth. She tells him to bill the $3.48 to her father, who owns the oil company that provides the station's gas, but he refuses, so she revs her engine and backs into a truck. Their compromise? He'll let her work it off. She has to make every bed in the motel and sweep and dust. He even swats her with a broom!

When she gets home and complains to her father (the funny and charming Charles Winninger), he sides with the pump jockey. The spoiled brat Olivia then announces, "I'll get even with him—you just watch my smoke!"[40]

The plot unwinds when Margaret meets Bill again and pretends to be her own lady's maid. They take a subway ride, crash a banquet, and go to the top of the Empire State Building (rather Busby Berkeley–ish activities), and she discovers that Bill is actually an architect who has a swell idea for auto courts. All he needs is a rich investor to fund his ideas. She suggests that he go see Mr. "Spouter" Richards—her father—and she tells him how to get past the secretary. Of course, the first effort doesn't work, and after much madcap action, Richards asks, "Who told you to come in and ask for Spouter?"[41] When Bill tells him it was his daughter's personal maid, Maggie Case, Richards catches on and invites him to dinner. When he arrives, Olivia answers the door in a maid's uniform. It's a fun scene for Olivia to play—she didn't do much physical comedy—and there's a real charm to it.

What follows is the sweetest scene in the film: Powell and Olivia, lovely and lip-biting in a picture hat, are in a rowboat in the park. He sings the new song "You Must Have Been a Beautiful Baby" by Harry Warren and Johnny Mercer, "which, within months of the film's release, was being sung by hipsters all over America."[42] It's difficult to keep a straight face while being sung to, but Olivia seems charmed by Powell's voice, and the entire sequence is utterly lovely. Naturally, they fall in love, but the course of true love is never smooth. Olivia confesses to her father that she's changed her mind about Powell. Powell's plans come to fruition, thanks to her dad. Olivia pulls up to the gas pump again, but this time her beau is overseeing the building of his architectural dream. Her father arrives with flowers and a judge, there are some grumbles and arguments, and they finally wed as they call out, "Hey, Pops! Thanks!" Melville Cooper's butler gets the last line: "Amazing!"[43]

By 1938 Olivia is familiar to film audiences, despite being in the business for only three years. She is the subject of both cover and feature articles in many movie magazines, thanks to Warner Brothers' publicists and fan demand. She is known as a serious, thoughtful, unspoiled girl who loves music and lives simply; she is athletic and without affectations. She makes her doubts about her career known. Just as Olivia thought she would have benefited from more stage training, she also regretted her lack of education, as "it isn't so much what you learn from textbooks but the chance of slowly maturing that it gives you. . . . I came into films without any preparation for life."[44]

The one note that suggests a flaw in her careful façade is her relationship with her sister, the "Dragon Lady." Both Olivia and Joan participated in their push me–pull you relationship, and family ties are no guarantee of compatibility. Admittedly, Olivia sowed the seeds of her feud with Joan in an interview, noting, "'My sister decided to become an actress, too. That ruined the close-knittedness of our family life.'"[45]

Despite her willingness to open up to the press, to pose in swimsuits and other novelty promotional photos, and to make a series of largely unremarkable films, Olivia's reward was not better roles. Instead, after *Hard to Get* she was cast in yet another love-triangle role—this time between two military brothers, not unlike the part she played in *Charge of the Light Brigade*. There is no clear reason for this casting choice, other than an effort to chasten Olivia for her recalcitrance, absences, illnesses, and complaints while making use of her decorative attributes.

Wings of the Navy, made almost three years before the attack on Pearl Harbor, was "a reminder that Hollywood was quite active, obviously with military encouragement, in gearing up the American public to the realization that its armed forces needed expansion in the light of what was going on in Europe."[46] This rather stirring tale of navy pilots in training offers effective airplane footage and manly roles for the male leads: George Brent, in his second project with Olivia, and the young John Payne, who would find success at 20th Century Fox and is best remembered for the charming Christmas classic *Miracle on 34th Street*. The tension between Brent as the older, more experienced brother and Payne as his ambitious, cocky sibling is the film's main strength, along with a patriotic, appealingly propagandistic vision of American military power. What the film doesn't offer is an interesting or memorable part for Olivia, who is relegated once again to the stock role of the adoring ingenue. In this case, she's engaged to Brent but falls for Payne. She's attractive, energetic, and intelligent, as always, but she has very little to do other than look concerned and then get out of the way so the men can fly and clash. Rather misleadingly, she's described in the trailer as "the cause of a private war that keeps the Navy cheering for both rivals."[47]

This film helps clarify why Olivia was a continual thorn in Jack Warner's side. He seemed incapable of seeing her as a younger Bette Davis (at least he placed her in the great star's proximity in *It's Love I'm After*) and repeatedly cast her in insubstantial supporting roles, despite her usual second billing. The young actress gave every performance, including this one, all she had, but she had little to work with. So she complained. Repeatedly.

The *New York Times* described *Wings of the Navy* as "a documentary study of the Pensacola Naval Air Training station, and its methods of turning raw recruits into seasoned pilots of combat and bombing planes." That description is quite apt, as Warner received the full cooperation of the US government. The footage of the flights, the training, and the planes is inspirational even now, and it was clearly designed to strike fear in the hearts of the

Nazis, even though the film was released six months before England declared war on Germany. The reviewer went on to note that "the educational part is so interesting that we return to the romantic part—in which Olivia de Havilland switches her affections from George Brent, the older brother, to John Payne, the younger brother (both stanch flying men) with a feeling almost akin to pain."[48]

That harsh evaluation of the subplot is rather unfair. Brent and Payne have good chemistry as brothers trying to support and challenge each other. Unfortunately, Olivia's connection with the two men isn't nearly as thrilling. There was never much of a spark between Olivia and Brent, despite the rumors that they dated briefly. It might have been due to the age difference—Brent was twelve years older than Olivia—or it might have been due to Olivia's disinterest in the film. That same year, Brent would star opposite Bette Davis in both *Dark Victory* and *The Old Maid,* two showcase films of the sort Olivia was desperate for. She's a game girl in Orry-Kelly's trim suits, but sadly, any young actress on the lot could have played her thankless role in *Wings.* Although she gives the part her usual intelligence and energy, she primarily stares adoringly, alternately, at Brent and Payne.

While 1939 was a landmark year for Hollywood cinema, for Olivia de Havilland, the films she made at her home studio were more of the same. *Wings of the Navy* was followed by another pairing with Errol Flynn, *Dodge City* (see chapter 3). This time, Olivia was allowed to be the handsome actor's love interest rather than a supporting starlet, but she was fed up and frustrated. In *Dodge City,* which is a lively and eminently watchable film, the characters head out in a covered wagon for new challenges. In real life, Olivia's resolve to do the same was growing stronger, and soon her personal and professional lives would be completely redirected. Although Olivia was only twenty-three in 1939, she was transforming into a new woman, a new actress—a real star.

5

MISS MELLY

Gone with the Wind remains one of the most beloved of all American films and the greatest success of glorious 1939, a year when so many remarkable movies were released. In 2009, Armond White, chief film critic for the *New York Press* and chairman of the New York Film Critics Circle, described *GWTW* as "the quintessential Hollywood movie" that has "long deserved to be rescued from critical disdain and given its correct place among American pop masterpieces."[1] In honor of the film's seventy-fifth anniversary in 2014, a trade magazine published to capitalize on its enduring popularity shared some remarkable statistics that "Windies"—the name for committed fans—would enjoy: the novel has been translated into thirty-two languages; 30 million copies of the book (which has never been out of print) have been sold; the original 1936 novel weighed 2.5 pounds, which is why it sold for $3 a copy; the film has been re-released to theaters eight times; and, given adjustments for inflation, the film has earned between $3 billion and $5 billion.[2]

Also in 2014, the Harry Ransom Center at the University of Texas–Austin, which houses the David O. Selznick archive, held an exhibition in honor of *GWTW*'s anniversary. It was the largest retrospective dedicated solely to the film up to that time and included "screen tests, Selznick's memos, [and] watercolor storyboards." It also covered "the concerns of civil rights leaders and African American journalists about how black people would be depicted in the film, Selznick's long search for the right actress to play Scarlett, and the film's influence today."[3] A well-researched coffee-table catalog by the show's curator, Steve Wilson, was published in conjunction with the exhibition. It featured a foreword by Robert Osborne and offered such fascinating materials as a photograph of Olivia and Vivien Leigh, both actresses with writing pads in their hands, taking notes as they listened closely to Margaret Mitchell's friend Susan Myrick offer "advice on southern etiquette and culture."[4] Myrick also served as the vocal coach for the actors' southern accents.

Equally exciting, for the first time in twenty-five years, the Ransom Center exhibition displayed three original dresses, including the famous green velvet portiere dress, which cost more than $10,000 to restore. That dress was also featured in a 2012 Hollywood costume exhibition at the Victoria and Albert Museum in London, curated by Deborah Nadoolman Landis. Having attended that show myself, I can attest to the great number of attendees crowding around that famous gown. As Osborne noted, "*Gone with the Wind* has endured and triumphed even in a very changed world 75 years later. . . . It still affects people in the same way as it did then."[5]

In September 2017, Sotheby's auctioned 321 items that had belonged to Vivien Leigh. The family had sold some of her personal belongings to the Victoria and Albert Museum, and fifty years after her death, they were ready to part with many of her other possessions. One of the most expensive items was her leather-bound script for *GWTW,* which sold for £47,000 ($60,000). I was watching the auction streamed live online, and the auctioneer announced after the sale, "This is something I've been wanting to say all of my life. Going . . . going . . . gone with the wind!" Clearly, there is still an enormous interest in the film and in the actress who portrayed Scarlett, as the sale earned over £2.2 million ($2.8 million).

The film has even become part of the ongoing discussion of racism in the United States. At the time, the filmmakers made many efforts to present the African American characters in a nonstereotypical way. However, owing to the film's depiction of those characters and its sympathy for the fallen Confederacy, the Orpheum Theatre in Memphis decided in August 2017 "that it will discontinue its annual screening of 'Gone with the Wind' over concerns that the film is insensitive."[6] Whatever one's view of the film, that it is still being shown and discussed says something about its cultural power.

Every five to ten years, the film's anniversary receives attention from the press; *GWTW* is re-released to theaters, and new deluxe DVD boxed sets become available. Turner Classic Movies' 1992 documentary *The Making of Gone with the Wind* is a delightful recounting (suavely narrated by Christopher Plummer) of the film's creation, featuring many of the actors and technical crew. Restoration of the film followed several years later, capturing forever its glory. A four-DVD set, featuring Olivia's participation in a documentary, appeared in 2004. For the eightieth anniversary in 2019, there will surely be another series of public tributes. One hopes that a bright, vital Olivia will partake in the festivities in some way. She has actively promoted the film in recent years. For example, in 2010, she wrote that in honor of the film's seventieth anniversary, "for four special showings of *GWTW,* one at the Academy in May of last year, two others held later in Georgia, and another in New York City, I composed and recorded messages which were heard just before the screenings of the film, each message fashioned to suit the particular occasion."[7]

Olivia was also a central participant in two major *GWTW* tribute events. In 1961, she returned to Atlanta (wearing her favorite designer, Christian Dior) with David O. Selznick and Vivien Leigh for the centenary of the Civil War. The event featured a grand ball as well as a screening of *GWTW.* In a March 1961 interview with Hedda Hopper, just after that reunion, Olivia showed Hopper "a memento of her recent trip . . . a beautiful gold cigarette lighter inscribed on one side with GWTW/Atlanta/1939–1961 and on the other To Olivia / from / D.O.S." Olivia noted that Selznick seemed melancholy, given that this great achievement had happened so early in his career, and this made him feel "pretty beaten down"; however, the "tremendous, warm welcome" from the attendees provided "a tremendous moment" for the producer.[8] The film was still an important part of American popular culture.

In December 1979, at the Los Angeles County Museum of Art, a gathering of "more than two dozen of the people who helped make" *GWTW* celebrated the film's fortieth anniversary. Olivia addressed the 525 guests at the buffet dinner and told them that "the missing members of the cast had sent their regrets from that 'great plantation in the sky. Rhett and Scarlett are together, you can make what you like of that,' she said, as if confiding a new item of gossip from Tara. . . . 'They'll be there and we'll all have a joyful reunion.'"[9]

In 2004, Olivia finally appeared onscreen, at the age of eighty-eight, to discuss the film and the role for which she will always be remembered—Melanie Hamilton Wilkes. In the documentary *Melanie Remembers,* shot at the Pierre Hotel in New York City, the actress participates in a forty-minute discussion of her involvement with the film. It was thrilling for fans of *GWTW* to see and hear the actress, ensconced in a comfortable chair, her silver-white hair in an elegant chignon, wearing a tailored suit and her signature pearls, recount her cherished memories of the film. Olivia explained why she wanted to play Melanie when everyone else in Hollywood wanted to play Scarlett: "It was the character of Melanie that attracted me most, because of her admirable qualities and the values that meant so much to her and meant so much to me. I wanted to perpetuate these values. And the perfect way to do that of course would be to play the part of Melanie."[10]

When Margaret Mitchell's novel was published in 1936 and then won the Pulitzer Prize, its popularity swept not just the South but the entire United States. Producer David O. Selznick received a Teletype from his New York representative, Kay Brown, that had "an urgency not typical of her other communications about story properties."[11] Selznick wisely followed her advice and purchased the screen rights for $50,000. The master of publicity then proceeded to audition virtually every actress in Hollywood and hundreds of others around the country to find his Scarlett O'Hara, not to mention his Melanie. Virtually everyone had an opinion about should play Scarlett. Bette Davis, Joan Crawford, Norma Shearer, Joan Bennett, and Katharine Hepburn were among the many actresses considered by Selznick. As for Rhett Butler, the producer considered several leading men, including Gary Cooper and Errol Flynn, but the public wanted Clark Gable.

Olivia, like millions of others, had been swept away by the novel. She noted, "I read it during the summer of 1936 while on vacation in Carmel, California, and I found it very interesting. I also immediately responded to Melanie. Scarlett may have been a great slapper, but I admired Melanie because she has qualities that are worth being valued. I wanted to play a role that embodies . . . sincerity, unselfishness, compassion, high ideals of personal conduct. . . . Yes, I wanted that role very much."[12] And, with an unwavering determination, Olivia refused to be constrained by her Warner Brothers contract and the uninspired roles she was being given.

As she wrote in a charming article for *Look* magazine in 1967, Melanie represented everything that Olivia's life *wasn't* in 1938, when casting for *GWTW* occurred: "When the role of Melanie came to me, I was 22, and angry and full of despair. Not only professional despair, because the creative roles I wanted were seldom mine, but personal despair. Despair at what seemed to be the reality of the life around me, the reality of the powerful, brutal kingdom that was Hollywood, in which there was no place for the values I had been brought up to believe in, values I believed in, not only as a human being, but also as a woman."[13] Olivia doesn't sound like a prude or a goody-goody in this article; rather, she is quite candid in expressing her frustration as she describes a Hollywood run by men:

> They had created in their own image and made the sexual symbol of the day their female counterpart. She was bitchy, she was destructive, and she saw men only in terms of use. She was capable

> of beating them at their own game, and like them, she was incapable of love. She was their ideal woman. She was their Eve.
>
> I was not that woman. Nothing I wanted to be or believed I should be was that woman. How, then, in a world where the bad and beautiful were the pearls of great price, and the good and beautiful were somehow absurd, was I to survive?[14]

Olivia wanted to play a genteel character who was loving, loyal, and thoughtful. She described Melanie as "a happy woman, she is a loving woman, and you cannot say Scarlett was loving." Being cast in *GWTW* was a huge career opportunity for Olivia, but she also wanted the challenge of portraying good-girl Melanie because "the general concept is that if you're good, you aren't interesting. And that concept annoys me, frankly. They have the same point of view about girls who are plain. They think that somebody who's intellectual is sexless. Ha ha."[15] Indeed.

She was also coming off her long-term, frustrating crush on the married Errol Flynn. All her roles opposite Flynn had been variations on one theme—pretty, spunky young gal takes on the macho Flynn and wins. But that partnership, both personal and professional, was slowing to an end. For Olivia, portraying a romantic literary heroine in the biggest, most hyped Hollywood production ever made would have eased a variety of heartaches.

Alas, she was not alone in her desire to play Miss Melly. Many actresses were considered for the part, and their screen tests, shown in *The Making of Gone with the Wind,* vary little—a collection of lachrymose readings and simpering facial expressions. Versatile director George Cukor, whose working relationship with Selznick brought many memorable films to the screen, was part of the *GWTW* team from the beginning, shooting the screen tests for Melanie and Scarlett, but without satisfaction. Even Joan Fontaine was considered, but she suggested her sister. Fortunately for Olivia, she was already on both Cukor's and Selznick's radar.

Selznick had "carefully followed the progress of Olivia . . . whom he considered a prime possibility for Melanie Hamilton." He was also aware that "the Warner family thought well enough of the actress to feature her in two of their only four Technicolor features that year—a rarity for any performer at the time. Miss de Havilland photographed beautifully in that process, which was not necessarily kind to those it came in contact with."[16] In fact, in November 1938, Selznick wrote to the vice president of Selznick International, Daniel T. O'Shea, and asserted, "'I would give anything if we had Olivia de Havilland under contract to us so that we could cast her as Melanie. . . . Warners have so far definitely refused to consider letting us have de Havilland, but I think they might be persuaded, especially if we offer them (Paulette) Goddard in trade.'"[17] In an interesting twist of fate, Goddard nearly secured the role of Scarlett before Vivien Leigh appeared on the scene, and two years later, both she and Olivia would be loaned out to Paramount for *Hold Back the Dawn,* portraying modern variations on Scarlett and Melanie.

Just reading for the role was proving almost impossible for Olivia; legally, she needed Jack Warner's approval to do so, and that was not going to happen. Olivia had been stressed and exhausted and had taken days off to protest the roles she was being offered, so Warner was not terribly inclined to do her any favors. Warner Brothers had already produced its own moonlight and magnolia epic—Bette Davis had won an Oscar for her portrayal of a southern belle with a temper in *Jezebel* (1938). So despite talk of Errol Flynn playing Rhett Butler and Bette Davis's oft-told tale that she turned down Jack Warner when he approached her about the property, the studio had no real interest in *GWTW.* Fortunately for Olivia, Cukor's and Selznick's interest in her meant that they were not going to give up easily:

> One day, the telephone rang, and the voice on the other end of the line said, "Is this Miss de Havilland?" And I said, "Yes." And the voice said, "You don't know me, we've never met, but I am George Cukor, the director of *GWTW*." He then said, "Would you be interested in playing the part of Melanie?" I said, "I certainly would." Then he said, "Would you consider doing something entirely illegal?" I said, "I might." [She says it with great mischief.] And then he said, "It would be illegal for you to come over to Selznick Studios and read for the part. Would you be willing to do that?" And I said, "Indeed I would."[18]

So much for the good girl. Olivia's decision to risk the audition demonstrated the characteristically ferocious tenacity that has characterized her personal and screen incarnations. There was no way she was going to pass up this opportunity. At the urging of Cukor and Selznick, she secretly read for the part she wanted so much.

Olivia described the audition in *Melanie Remembers.* She surreptitiously went to the Selznick studio, having been told that someone would be waiting for her. And who was waiting? "This rotund gentleman, with close-cropped, very frizzy dark hair. He was very welcoming, very kind, and said, 'I'm George Cukor.'"[19] He asked her to look over some pages and then read the dialogue to him. At the end of that first audition, Cukor said he wanted Selznick to hear her. So the next Sunday, Olivia went to Selznick's to read a scene between Melanie and Scarlett. However, Scarlett had not been cast yet, so Cukor read Scarlett's lines. Olivia noted with bemusement, "George gave the most passionate performance of Scarlett ever seen clutching the portieres as DOS [Selznick] stood two feet away. Some part of my brain could not help but think, 'This is certainly the most comic scene ever seen in the entire world.'" But Selznick was "enraptured by the scene" and said, "'I think we've found our Melanie.'"[20] Of course, being David O. Selznick, he had to throw in one small monkey wrench before confirming that Olivia had the part: "'He had me look at the screen tests of six other actresses who wanted the part and asked what I thought of them.' She said she was complimentary about them and meant it, but added with a smile: 'I didn't want to be too convincing.'"[21]

Now they had to approach Jack Warner, who was "notoriously reluctant to lend out [his] contract players."[22] Selznick began negotiations with Warner, who flatly refused, so Olivia went to see him. "I pleaded with him, I implored him." He told her that she should play Scarlett. "He was adamant. I was desperate. I had to think of something to do that would bring negotiations to a favorable conclusion. And then I did something I shouldn't have done." She had already read for the part of Melanie twice, illegally, so what did she have to lose? "I called the boss's wife, Mrs. Warner, Ann Warner, a beautiful, elegant, kind, and warm-hearted woman. And I asked her if she would consider having tea with me one afternoon, at the Beverly Hills Brown Derby." So they met for tea, and Olivia told her the story and asked for her help. "She said, 'I understand you, and I will help you.'"[23] Ann Warner did help, "although there would still be weeks of tension ahead before final permission might be granted."[24] Ann Warner had also championed an unknown Errol Flynn for the lead in *Captain Blood;* it's a pity Jack didn't listen to his wife more often.

To give Warner his due, he acknowledged in his autobiography, *My First Hundred Years in Hollywood,* "Olivia, who had a brain like a computer concealed behind those fawnlike brown eyes . . . simply went to my wife, Ann, and they joined forces in a plot to change my mind."[25] In return for Olivia, Warner Brothers received her salary of $1,000 a week; a deadline of May 4, 1939, for completion of the filming of her scenes; and Jimmy Stewart for a future role.[26]

There are several photographs of Olivia posing with Selznick, Vivien Leigh, and Leslie Howard taken on January 13, 1939, signing their contracts.[27]

In one photo, Selznick and Vivien are sitting behind a desk, Howard leans behind them, and Olivia stands in the forefront in a charming two-piece wool suit with dark, intricate floral appliqués on the jacket. She looks confident, thoughtful, contented, and rather sensually louche. In another, Olivia smiles as she peruses the script with Vivien (her hair parted in the middle in Scarlett fashion) and Howard. When those photos hit the wire services, Jack Warner could not have been completely disappointed about the loan-out: Olivia was good advertising for his studio.

Gone with the Wind finally provided Olivia with the acting opportunity she had so desperately wanted. Selznick regarded the original novel as a bible, which was important, given the number of drafts and the number of writers involved in preparing the script. Olivia's characterization stayed true to the descriptions of Melanie in Margaret Mitchell's novel, sometimes filtered through Scarlett's jealous eyes: "Oh it couldn't be true! The Twins were mistaken. They were playing one of their jokes on her. Ashley couldn't, couldn't be in love with her. Nobody could, not with a mousy little person like Melanie. Scarlett recalled with contempt Melanie's thin childish figure, her serious heart-shaped face that was plain almost to homeliness."[28] Mitchell's narrative description of Melanie is more objective, and Melanie's inner qualities are far more important than her physical failings:

> She was a tiny, frailly built girl, who gave the appearance of a child masquerading in her mother's enormous hoop skirts—an illusion that was heightened by the shy, almost frightened look in her too large brown eyes. She had a cloud of curly dark hair which was so sternly repressed beneath its net that no vagrant tendrils escaped, and this dark mass, with its long widow's peak, accentuated the heart shape of her face. Too wide across the cheek bones, too pointed at the chin, it was a sweet, timid face but a plain face, and she had no feminine tricks of allure to make observers forget its plainness. She looked—and was—as simple as earth, as good as bread, as transparent as spring water. But for all her plainness of feature and smallness of stature, there was a sedate dignity about her movements that was oddly touching and far older than her seventeen years.[29]

For Olivia, staying true to that picture of Melanie reflected her commitment to the truth of the character. Having been beautifully photographed in

Technicolor in two earlier films, it would have been understandable if the young, ambitious actress wanted to use her third color film to promote herself. But Olivia was not about to compromise this opportunity for vanity.

When she went to the Selznick studio to discuss makeup and hair, "George Cukor, who's so wonderfully perceptive, said to me, he said, 'You know, we can give you hairdresses, coiffures, and costumes and makeup that will make you look pretty or they will make you look plain.'" The actress had to decide, "and I said, 'plain.'" They followed Mitchell's description of Melanie's hair, including the wings on either side of her head and a widow's peak. Olivia explained, "Now, I didn't have a widow's peak. So very delicately, the makeup man penciled in a widow's peak, and that's the hairdress that we chose."[30] The resulting image was "not quite the pale, sickly creature of the book or of Scarlett's malignant imaginings, nevertheless she's a subdued presence, stopping distinctly short of glamour."[31]

In addition to Melanie's physical appearance, her wardrobe was an issue for the actress. Compared with the excessively theatrical antebellum confections Scarlett wears as often as possible, Melanie's wardrobe is much tamer, both before and after the war. In her first appearance in the film at the Twelve Oaks barbecue, Olivia is wearing a very beautiful dove-gray dress created by costumer Walter Plunkett, which resembles the one Mitchell describes in the novel:

> Her gray organdie dress, with its cherry-colored satin sash, disguised with its billows and ruffles how childishly underdeveloped her body was, and the yellow hat with long cherry streamers made her creamy skin glow. Her heavy earbobs with their long gold fringe hung down from loops of tidily netted hair, swinging close to her brown eyes, eyes that had the still gleam of a forest pool in winter when brown leaves shine up through quiet water.
>
> She had smiled with timid liking when she greeted Scarlett and told her how pretty her green dress was, and Scarlett had been hard put to be even civil in reply, so violently did she want to speak alone with Ashley. Since then, Ashley had sat on a stool at Melanie's feet, apart from the other guests, and talked quietly with her, smiling the slow drowsy smile that Scarlett loved. What made matters worse was that under his smile a little sparkle had come into Melanie's eyes, so that even Scarlett had to admit that she looked almost

> pretty. As Melanie looked at Ashley, her plain face lit up as with an inner fire, for if ever a loving heart showed itself upon a face, it was showing now on Melanie Hamilton's.[32]

Olivia loved the dress, of course, but was concerned that Plunkett had given it four ruffles instead of three. For many actors, attention to detail in costumes is central when creating a character, and that was certainly the case for Olivia. She went to Selznick's office for a costume parade, as did every actor appearing in the film (no wonder the producer was gulping down Benzedrine). She turned and posed, the director okayed the costume, and then as she was leaving, he said, "'Just a minute. Come back. Turn around.' I did. And he said, 'Not four ruffles, three.' Wasn't that wonderful?"[33] Interestingly, the demure hand-knitted sweater Olivia wore in two scenes in the film—at the hospital when Belle Watling approaches, and at the station during Ashley's Christmas leave—sold for $16,730 at Christie's in 2002.[34]

Olivia's commitment to the role extended to a delightful photograph taken by Fred Parrish while she and Vivien were shooting Melanie's childbirth scene. Vivien is perspiring and sitting by Olivia's bed holding a cold compress to her head, and Olivia looks exhausted as she grasps Vivien's hand and presumably reads the scene from a huge hardcover copy of the novel.[35] Susan Myrick sent a copy of the photograph to her friend Margaret Mitchell, who commented, "'The picture of Melanie in labor . . . was wonderful. John [Marsh, Mitchell's husband] says that the expression on Miss de Havilland's face is precisely the expression I wore during the time I was writing the book."[36]

Olivia's performance throughout the film is utterly believable, and she makes Melanie—a woman who seems almost too good to be true—memorable, vivid, and indelible while managing to avoid "the saccharine qualities of Melanie and create a character that was real and dimensional."[37] She carries a maturity and grace throughout the film, and "if she has little of the spark of her movies with Errol Flynn, her serenity has its own mysteries."[38]

Olivia's chemistry with Vivien Leigh is completely believable, and they mesh beautifully as Melanie and Scarlett. Melanie clearly adores Scarlett and chooses to think the best of her, whether she's dancing in mourning or marrying her sister Suellen's dusty old beau Frank Kennedy to save Tara. It's a shame that Olivia and Vivien never acted together in another project. They worked closely during the five months of the shoot, first with their beloved George Cukor, who left the production for any number of purported reasons—his dissatisfaction with the script and Selznick's constant interference, Gable's concern that the picture was being thrown to the women, Cukor's own concern that he was shooting too slowly and without enough vibrancy for a war story as well as a romantic picture—and then with his replacement, Victor Fleming. Olivia had tremendous respect for Vivien and said, "'Vivien was very professional. Impeccably prepared. . . . Vivien was born to play Scarlett, whom she perfectly understood entirely.'"[39] It is not surprising that one determined actress born to play a role would recognize and support another determined actress doing the same thing.

When Cukor left the picture, Olivia and Vivien pleaded with Selznick to reinstate the director. Olivia recalled arriving on the set one day to film the bazaar sequence, dressed in mourning. She greeted Vivien, who was "in a state of terrible distress" because Cukor was leaving and would be replaced by Fleming. Their characters had been developed, they had confidence in Cukor, and the actresses didn't see how they could play their roles without his guidance. So they went in their "widow's weeds" to see Selznick, "and for three hours we beseeched, we implored, we pleaded with David Selznick to please keep George on the film." They even drew out their hankies, but he refused, and they left weeping, "disconsolate and despairing."[40]

That night, Olivia recalled, "I had an engagement to dine with Howard Hughes. I was still wearing my makeup when I joined him at a little restaurant near the studio. And I told him this tragic tale. And he, with remarkable insight, said to me, 'Don't worry. With George and Victor, it's the same talent, only Victor's is strained through a coarser sieve.'"[41]

When Olivia rehearsed her first scene with Fleming at the helm—Melanie's first appearance in the film at the Twelve Oaks barbecue, when she and Scarlett meet—she played it "in a polite and very friendly way." After that, Fleming pulled her aside and said, "'Whatever Melanie says, she means. Now go back and play the scene again and mean it.'" So she did. "And I never forgot that piece of direction. I kept it, of course, as an integral part of Melanie's character in the interpretation. And it's really something one should remember in playing any part. And so Victor Fleming won my total confidence and maintained it straight through the film."[42]

That may be true, but Olivia also admitted to telephoning Cukor and asking for his help. "Generously, at lunch in a restaurant or over a cup of tea in his house, George would give me black-market direction. I felt ever so slightly guilty toward Vivien about making these secret visits to George until, when the picture was finished, I learned that all during the filming, Vivien had been doing exactly the same thing."[43]

Although Olivia's interaction with Vivien is wonderful throughout the film—particularly when Melanie greets Scarlett after she and Ashley have been caught in a clinch by the bitter India Wilkes (Alicia Rhett) and the gossipy Mrs. Meade (Leona Roberts), and in Melanie's deathbed scene—her scenes with Clark Gable's Rhett Butler are the most poignant, starting with their first face-to-face encounter at the bazaar, when Melanie removes her wedding ring to donate it to the cause and Rhett gazes at her with respect. Later, he carries her to the wagon during the evacuation of Atlanta, she thanks him for protecting the wounded Ashley during the Shantytown raid, and she names Bonnie Blue Butler. Then, of course, there is their great scene when Scarlett has miscarried after falling downstairs during an argument with Rhett. Their interactions are unlike any others in the film. Their connection is palpable, quiet, and steady.

Much is made of the fiery, star-crossed passion between Rhett and Scarlett and Scarlett's unrequited love for Ashley. However, the greatest romance in the film is arguably between Melanie and Rhett as portrayed by Olivia and Gable. Melanie loves Ashley completely, and Olivia's early scenes with Leslie Howard establish her rightness for him. Their sweet scene at Twelve Oaks, as they metaphorically emerge from the shadows into the light on the balcony through the double doors, is gentle and beautiful. She reassures him, "No war can come into our world, Ashley. Whatever comes, I'll love you, just as I do now, until I die."[44] Yet it is the relationship between Melanie and Rhett that really surprises and rivets our attention on successive viewings. Among the four principals, only Melanie and Rhett truly know themselves and those they love. Scarlett is obsessed, and understandably so, with the survival of her family, as well as with the hapless Ashley. Ashley cannot adjust to the postwar world, and without Scarlett's help, his family would be living in genteel poverty. But Melanie has a core of love, morality, and practicality. She sees everything and chooses the high road. Rhett's core is based on a masculine cynicism born of family rejection, ambition, and necessity. With Melanie and Rhett, what you see is what you get. Melanie sees Rhett's ability to love and his internal dignity and pain; Rhett sees Melanie's pure soul. Had the two of them come together, *that* would have been a true love for the ages.

Their deep feeling for each other is seen, fleetingly, at Ashley's bedside after he has been shot and Scarlett's Frank Kennedy has been killed. Rhett apologizes to Melanie for taking Ashley to Belle Watling's. Throughout that scene, Melanie holds the ladies together as they worry about their men. She has a pistol in her sewing basket, she reads *David Copperfield* (a sly nod to

Selznick's 1935 film), and she acts believably and prissily outraged when Rhett, Ashley, and Dr. Meade show up feigning drunkenness and lechery. After the Yankees leave and Ashley's injury is revealed, Melanie takes control yet again. When Rhett humbly offers his excuses for mentioning Belle Watling, Melanie responds, "This isn't the first time you've stood between me and disaster, Captain Butler. It isn't likely that I'd question any device of yours."[45] For a moment, she and Rhett hold each other's eyes, and in that instant, we see the true love affair of the film. Ashley is busy being noble and sublimating his Scarlett lust; Scarlett is pining, even after her daughter's birth. The only male-female relationship entirely without guile and manipulation is that of Melanie and Rhett. After the birthday party where Melanie chooses to believe Scarlett rather than the gossip about her clinch with Ashley, a drunken Rhett confronts Scarlett. He may carry Scarlett up the stairs, but it is Melanie who is on his mind when he chastises his wife about her behavior:

> So she stood by you, did she? How does it feel to have the woman you've wronged cloak your sins for you? You're wondering if she knows all about you and Ashley. You're wondering if she did it just to save her face. You're thinking that she's a fool for doing it, even if it did save your hide. . . . Miss Melly's a fool, but not the kind you think. It's just that there's too much honor in her to ever conceive of dishonor in anyone she loves. And she loves you. Though just why she does I'm sure I don't know.[46]

Clark Gable was the king of Hollywood at the time, having been crowned by Ed Sullivan on his radio program in 1938. He was a box office star, MGM's greatest male heartthrob. He had serious misgivings about being cast as Rhett Butler, not only because of the wide acclaim the novel had received but also because he didn't quite trust Cukor's direction. As Olivia noted, "'Playing Rhett Butler was an enormous responsibility for Clark and I can quite understand his qualms.'"[47] She remembered, "I had not previously met Clark Gable. He seemed to be so awesome in his superstardom that it was all I could do to say 'Good morning' and 'Goodnight.'"[48] Her shyness toward the great man dissipated a bit as the shoot continued. She learned to play Battleship with him and Vivien and proudly said in 2004, "I won a few Battleship tours."[49]

Olivia even played a practical joke on Gable during the Atlanta evacuation scene, admitting that "the spirit of the devil entered me."[50] Melanie has just had her baby, and they have to leave Atlanta. During rehearsal, Gable had no problem picking up the petite Olivia. However, on the set she had spotted a block of cement with a steel ring and a rope attached. She had a crew member move the block under the bed, and she tied the rope around her waist. Cukor called "Action!" And then, as Olivia recalled, "He comes over to the bed, and he puts his hands . . . under the comforter, and he lifts Melanie and the baby, and he lifts them, and he lifts them, and he says, 'What the devil?'" She laughs and slaps her knees and ends the tale by saying, "That big-hearted man forgave me."[51]

Their most memorable interaction is the scene in which Gable weeps with fear and guilt over Scarlett's miscarriage and injuries after their fight at the top of the stairs. Even though Gable's friend Victor Fleming was directing the scene, the actor was nervous. He had played the Irish patriot Parnell two years earlier, and although today the performance can be seen as a genuine stretch for the actor, at the time it wasn't well received because it wasn't the typical battling, ballsy, womanizing Gable. Filming a scene of genuine grief and tenderness was terrifying for the actor. Olivia remembered, "If ever there was an actor who wished he had never taken up his profession, it was Gable the day we shot that scene. He was bothered, and he balked. He fumed, and he fussed. He threatened to leave for his farm and his tractor. For he was embarrassed. Embarrassed at the naked suffering of Rhett Butler." What a tribute to Olivia's poise, calmness, and acting skill that this scene is one of the greatest in Gable's career. She said, "I shyly tried to do the same [reassure him], for I knew so well how much encouragement could mean."[52] Certainly the pouring rain outside the open window, the subtle lighting, their close two-shot as she reassures Rhett of Scarlett's love, and Gable's commitment to his profession all contributed to the beautiful moment the two actors share. But even more, Olivia's total immersion in her role as Melanie facilitates Gable's graceful vulnerability. When he covers her delicate hands with his, kisses them, and says, "From my heart, I thank you," and she places her hand comfortingly on his bowed head, it is the most purely loving moment in the movie.[53]

Olivia also spoke of how Melanie's character informed that scene: "With all her qualities, one of which I discovered was a kind of inner security that she had, I found that and, very luckily, was able to experience it. I think, too, another of her great qualities was that she was a perfectly loving woman. And it may be that it was that perfect lovingness on her part that gave her that sense of security, inner security."[54] When Scarlett tells Rhett that Melanie has passed away, he speaks quietly and sincerely of the woman he had so admired:

"Well, God rest her. She was the only completely kind person I ever knew, and a great lady. A very great lady."[55]

After three years, millions of dollars, and millions of frames of film, *Gone with the Wind* (also known as "Selznick's Folly") was ready to be shown to the public.[56] The film had three premieres—in Atlanta on December 15, 1939, followed by New York and Hollywood—just in time for Oscar consideration. Olivia knew how important this film was for all the participants: "This was an immensely daring thing, daring choice for David Selznick, because he would be presenting this film about the South, about the War between the States, about Atlantans, to them. Their war, their struggles, their story. Would they accept us? Would they accept the film? It was a tremendously suspenseful occasion." It was a thrilling time for Olivia, both personally and professionally, but her home studio tried to dampen the excitement: "Jack Warner said I couldn't go to the premiere. And I thought, 'Well, I *am* going to the premiere.' And I *did* go to the premiere."[57]

On the first of the three-day festivities surrounding the film's premiere, "crowds larger than the combined armies that fought the Battle of Atlanta line[d] up for seven miles to watch the procession of limousines from the airport to the Georgian Terrace Hotel, where most of the visiting celebrities were staying."[58] The next day, there was a huge ball at the Atlanta Municipal Auditorium, where almost 6,000 attendees, dressed in antebellum attire, danced with the film's stars. In a 2002 letter, Olivia vividly remembered what she wore to these events:

> To the ball in Atlanta I wore a pale pink net gown from I. Magnin, its ruffles edged in black lace and pale pink camellias adorning the center of the décolletage. Of course the three-strand necklace of pearls given me by my sister served perfectly (with pearl earrings from I. Magnin). To the premiere itself I wore a Saks Fifth Avenue (Sophie) black velvet gown with inserts of black lace adorning its wide skirt, and Sophie recommended with this dress a cyclamen pink (cut-glass) necklace and matching earrings—from the costume jewelry counter at Saks.[59]

One might have expected her to be glittering in diamonds at the premieres, but no: "I was brought up in the countryside of Northern California by a conservative English mother and at a time when it was considered bad taste for young women to wear any sort of jewelry until they were into their 20s—and then only something very discreet. . . . Eventually, when (at 23) I was well-established in my profession, and a costume for a great occasion . . . required some sort of jewelry to set it off, I chose only what would look well with the gown in question. . . . So jewelry was interesting only as an accessory to an ensemble."[60]

In *Melanie Remembers,* Olivia describes the thrill of the premiere in Atlanta, the massive parade, and the presence of author Margaret Mitchell. In the theater, Olivia sat with producer Jock Whitney; to his left were Margaret Mitchell and her husband, John Marsh. From the time the title flashed on the screen, "the audience was spellbound. Spellbound. Absolute silence reigned until the scene, the great panoramic scene at the Atlanta depot where we see, laid on stretchers, row upon row upon row of wounded Confederate soldiers. And I heard John Marsh say to Margaret Mitchell, 'Why, if we'd-a had that many soldiers, we'd-a won the war.'"[61] She recounts the tale in a southern accent and then coyly looks down and smiles, rather pleased with herself and the telling. She would have been happy to know that in a lengthy and often negative critique of the various actors, the script, and the film's design elements, the Marshes found her characterization as Melanie "'good.'"[62]

Although Olivia's escort to the Atlanta premiere had been Jock Whitney, Selznick's business partner and a member of the distinguished Whitney family, matchmaking was afoot. According to Hedda Hopper, Irene Selznick and super-agent Leland Hayward were in cahoots to find a proper gentleman for the actress in New York. The man they found turned out to be one of Olivia's great romances—James Stewart. Olivia told Hopper that Stewart met her at La Guardia Airport with a limousine: "'There he was, droll, charming, adorable, and shyly waiting.'"[63]

Stewart was a rising star at MGM at the time, one year away from his best actor Oscar for *The Philadelphia Story,* and a very popular bachelor in Hollywood. He had starred with Marlene Dietrich in *Destry Rides Again* (1939) and survived both the battling in the film and the offscreen love affair with the insatiable femme fatale. Stewart was a player *and* a catch. He also loved flying, which connected Stewart (a future major general in the US Army Air Force) to Olivia (related to the de Havilland aeronautics family). In fact, Olivia learned to fly, and "the name of my flying instructor . . . was Cecil Smallwood, Jimmy Stewart's instructor. I soloed once . . . and though that included a perfect 3-point landing proudly acknowledged by Cecil, I never did get over my fear and was relieved from further instructions by the catastrophic developments of December 7, 1941, soon after which all civilian pilots in the Los Angeles area were grounded."[64]

There were sparks between the two, and they laughed at their *GWTW* connection: she had secured the role of Melanie because Selznick had agreed to loan Stewart as part of the deal. So, on New Year's Eve 1939:

> Jimmy wanted to take me to Jack and Ann Warner's party. I wanted to go too but I was running a temperature . . . and I couldn't—which was just as well as I'd had a longstanding date with my old beau [according to Hopper, this was probably Howard Hughes]. At eleven o'clock that night, this old beau phoned to say he was taking me—to Jack and Ann Warner's party. When I pleaded a fever he just said, "Get dressed, Livvy, you're going, I'll be right over." He was too, and I went, and danced with *both* gentlemen until 6 a.m.! I came home completely cured.[65]

Olivia told Hopper, "Jimmy Stewart was one of the delightful things that happened to me. . . . He taught me to eat my first oysters, ordered my first old fashioned, took me to '21' the first time . . . and everything he said I thought witty and everything I said, he thought droll." According to Hopper, they dated for more than a year, and while Olivia wanted to marry Stewart, he never asked her. Olivia commented about it: "The relationship had the charm, innocence, and character of a high school romance. The kind which quite naturally leads to marriage. This was the expectation of the press, the public, my friends, and myself. Jimmy never proposed. As most women will do under such protracted and public circumstances, I decided to break off the relationship. And did so."[66]

Gone with the Wind was an enormous success, and it was clear that the film was going to sweep the Academy Award nominations. But Selznick was concerned and "noted that Hedda Hopper had voiced her preference of Bette Davis [in *Dark Victory*] over Vivien Leigh and pointed to an article about Olivia de Havilland's chances for the award that stated she had a starring role. He felt she had a better chance for an award in the supporting category and worried that she would not even be nominated if the votes were split."[67] This was a painful choice for Selznick, who put Olivia forward as supporting actress, even though her role "was, without doubt, larger than Greer Garson's in *Goodbye, Mr. Chips,* and Miss Garson was named a 'Best Actress' nominee!"[68]

Olivia was disappointed about her omission from best actress consideration. Even more painful was that she had to compete against her Warner Brothers and *GWTW* colleague Hattie McDaniel for best supporting actress. To make the situation even more awkward, the winners were leaked to the press ahead of Oscar night on February 29, 1940, with the understanding that this information wouldn't be published. However, the *Los Angeles Times* printed an early edition containing the results, so Olivia had to attend the ceremony knowing that McDaniel had won the award. For the young actress, this was a bitter loss. She later related that "she could barely get through the balance of the evening and finally stole away to indulge in tears of disappointment. But . . . it was only a short time later when she realized how important—and justified—Hattie's win really was."[69]

Nevertheless, Olivia's performance as Melanie anchors the film and gives it its moral heart. As Molly Haskell notes in her wonderful appreciation of the film:

> She loved the character of Melanie . . . this utter sincerity was part of her fineness. She captures the inner security of a perfectly loving woman in a character that, though not multidimensional, is more interesting and enigmatic than her goody-two-shoes image might suggest. Her emotions are more steadfast than those of any other character. . . . In any case, her refusal to listen to gossip, to turn on or confront Scarlett, to allow herself to be attuned to the cross-currents of adulterous feelings, gives her a moral majesty that looks more interesting today than it did at the time. . . . Maybe it's time to take another look at Lady Melanie![70]

Olivia herself has remained thoroughly committed to Melanie Hamilton Wilkes and her most memorable role. When asked in 2004 if she was tired of speaking about *GWTW,* she replied, "Not at all. Whenever I do see it, something absolutely magical happens. . . . Quite seriously. The film has that extraordinary power."[71] Olivia also affirmed, "We never imagined in 1939 that our film *Gone with the Wind* would endure decade after decade after decade. But it has. And it will no doubt endure for many, many decades to come."[72]

Olivia is one of only two actors from *GWTW* who are still alive. Alicia Rhett, who played Ashley's sister India Wilkes in her only onscreen credit, died in January 2014.[73] Mary Anderson, who played Maybelle Merriwether and had auditioned for the role of Scarlett, died in April 2014.[74] Only Mickey

Kuhn (Beau Wilkes) and Olivia remain. Olivia still receives fan mail as well as interview requests as a result of this role. Her great friend Robert Osborne reiterated at the time of the film's seventy-fifth anniversary, "'She is very proud of it; this is her legacy.'"[75]

Ironically, *GWTW* would not make life easier for Olivia at Warner Brothers. However, calling on Melanie's grit and courage, Olivia would leave the studio and change the contract system forever.

6

LEAVING THE JOB

With the remarkable triumph of *Gone with the Wind* fueling her ambition, along with her best supporting actress nomination, Olivia was no longer a babe in the woods. Securing the role of Melanie and portraying her so memorably had been an enormous coup, and it showed Olivia that with the right producer and the right studio, she could realize her potential as an actress. Affirmation of her talent might not come from Jack Warner, but at least it was coming. When Olivia turned twenty-four in July 1940, she had a much clearer view of her future at Warner Brothers, her career, and her romantic life.

Olivia didn't provide much fodder for the gossip magazines at this point, despite her occasional suspensions and clashes at the studio and her burgeoning rivalry with her sister, Joan, who had not yet made her breakthrough appearance in *Rebecca.* Olivia was seen as serious and respectably English, even though she had never visited England until 1938, when she and her mother took a short holiday break to allow Olivia to recuperate from overwork at Warner Brothers. Most articles portrayed her as a proper young woman who lived with her mother and sister, enjoyed reading the classics such as Dickens and Shakespeare, relished doing crosswords (a pleasure she continued to indulge in until she turned 100, when her eyesight became too bad to read the *New York Times* puzzles), and dressed fashionably without being a slave to glamour. She was viewed approvingly as "a very sensible young lady [who] saves her money. She has a definite financial programme that she follows, and she has a business manager."[1]

Olivia was always extremely discreet about her romances—not because she was a prude but because she recognized the power of the gossip columns and movie magazines to both build and destroy careers. She would see this most vividly in 1942, when Errol Flynn's trial for statutory rape obsessed America. This quest for privacy in the inbred world of Hollywood is one of the reasons it is so difficult to research the juicy tidbits, the dirt, and the salacious gossip connected with Olivia de Havilland—there isn't much, if any. And whatever there is often came from Joan Fontaine (who else?).

Olivia learned about discretion when her father abandoned his family for his mistress. Living in a small California town, it wasn't easy being a child of divorce, although Lilian's relatively quick remarriage to George Fontaine likely spared Olivia from whispers about having a single mother. Given her father's behavior and her dislike of the unpleasant Fontaine, Olivia was in no hurry to be controlled by a man. Having become in many ways the head of the household, she took naturally to managing her own finances and career, as well as her personal life. Raised by a Victorian mother with her own agenda, Olivia didn't need to break free of Lilian's control; in fact, she respected her mother's standards. Olivia felt comfortable making her own choices. She didn't marry until she was thirty, which was extremely unusual for the time, although she certainly had beaus before and after that marriage. Unlike for her sister, Joan, who married actor Brian Aherne when she was twenty-two, Olivia's career took precedence over everything.

Olivia's personality, position, and prettiness resulted in many gentlemen callers, so while her public persona remained eminently respectable, she was not romantically inexperienced. Her first serious boyfriend, Peter Dwight Whitney, was a teenaged "case of instant attraction" that didn't result in marriage, despite a two-year engagement.[2] Lilian's situation had shown Olivia the importance of having an independent income, so the rather antiquated idea of relinquishing a career on the wicked stage to marry a Yale man was anathema to her.

The next important man in her life was, of course, Errol Flynn. Olivia was immediately smitten while *Captain Blood* was in preproduction. She "fell madly in love with him" in 1935 but was careful not to be too foolish. The married Flynn declared his love for her in 1937, but despite his promises, he didn't divorce Lili Damita. Olivia "waited for three years for news that the divorce had taken place, but the news never came. And so finally I began to look elsewhere."[3] That pining for Flynn helps explain why she didn't marry: like her career, her heart was in limbo.

Olivia's first well-known suitor and "her first beau in Hollywood" was her future brother-in-law Brian Aherne, with whom she costarred in *The Great Garrick* (1937).[4] He was certainly attractive and seemed destined for a promising film career, having made the strange but unsuccessful *Sylvia Scarlett* in 1935 (now a cult classic). That film was an anomaly for its time, dealing with gender identity and class difference, but it was directed by George Cukor and featured Cary Grant. Aherne played Katharine Hepburn's love interest just two years after her first Oscar win for best actress.

Aherne was the type of man Olivia was drawn to time and again. One hates to offer a penny psychoanalysis of the actress, but she seemed to favor men who were lanky, adventurous, and unattainable. When I asked her about this, she replied, "It is true that I was attracted by tall men, perhaps because their height gave me a sense of security." When I asked whether there was a certain physical, spiritual, or intellectual type she was drawn to, she said, "I would say all three of the qualities you mention (rarely found together) were important to me. What was also essential was that a man excel in his profession or occupation and that we shared views about a majority of matters."[5] Aherne was very tall and athletic. Witty and somewhat cynical, he moved confidently and gave the impression of being a man of the world. While both Aherne and Flynn were very attractive, most of Olivia's beaus weren't classically handsome but rather interesting looking. They were also clever and cosmopolitan and had an air of insouciance. And without belaboring the father issue too much, most of her dates were older than she—Aherne by fourteen years. As he eventually married younger sister Joan, the actor was clearly attracted to younger women. There was no torrid affair between Olivia and Aherne, and they remained friendly enough to be on good terms as in-laws just two years later.

Another notable suitor was aviation pioneer and future eccentric Howard Hughes. Much has been written about Hughes's peculiarities as well as his series of relationships with beautiful Hollywood actresses (including Olivia's sister, Joan). Though stringier and gawkier than Aherne, Hughes certainly fit the pattern of men to whom Olivia was attracted, and his brilliance and rebellious nature appealed to the young star. Curiously, in Martin Scorsese's film *The Aviator* (2004), which delves into Hughes's growing eccentricities and his romance with Katharine Hepburn, Olivia is name-checked by actor Jude Law as Errol Flynn. Law plays Flynn like a lascivious ass in a nightclub scene, smoking constantly, flirting with Hepburn (Cate Blanchett), and grabbing a pea from the plate of the germophobic Hughes (Leonardo DiCaprio), thereby ruining his dinner. He says he wants in on the "casting session" if Howard is "seriously talking about putting carnality back on the screen. . . . I have somewhat of an eye." Flynn then invites the group onto his yacht and says, "I've even managed to coax the luscious Miss de Havilland and her equally luscious sister to accompany me. Though I fear their mother will insist on coming along, to preserve their questionable virtue. We shall assault these twin monuments of pristine Britannic beauty nonetheless. What do you say, Howard?"[6] Although the real-life Flynn frequently blustered about women, it's a vulgar moment in the film and undermines the connection between Olivia and Errol and Olivia and Howard. There is a grain of truth to the characterization of the actresses as proper girls, however. Olivia had moved into a modest home (by Hollywood standards), where she lived with her mother (though still married to Fontaine, Lilian's pursuit of a career as a performance coach meant that she spent extended periods with her girls) and her sister. Olivia and Joan were certainly neither prudes nor naïfs. However, conscious of the possible adverse effects on their careers, neither risked undue gossip.

Olivia's relationship with Hughes was brief, and it came about thanks to Errol Flynn. The two men had become friends, and during the shooting of *Dodge City,* Hughes sent a plane to the film's location to pick up Flynn so he could attend a party. However, a gossip columnist suggested that Hughes had sent the plane for Olivia, instead. As Olivia recalled their relationship in 2015:

> I met Howard Hughes on New Year's Eve of 1938–39, as a result of a bewildering item in Louella Parsons' column . . . which stated that Howard Hughes and I were engaged, whereas we had never met! Consequently, Howard Hughes called me on the telephone and said, "I understand we're engaged. Don't you think we should meet?" And so we did meet.
>
> He was soon to leave for Key West to work with Howard Hawks on a screenplay of a Hemingway novel, but we did see each other, as I recall it, through January and part of February, before his departure for Key West. Though we did not see each other often after that long absence, we remained friends. He was honest and fair, and I think of him today with affection, admiration, and loyalty.[7]

Howard Hughes was wealthy and internationally famous, and he had connections to the film industry. He was known as a ladies' man whose women included Kate Hepburn, Jean Harlow, and Ginger Rogers. He was good looking and daring, and he certainly made an interesting companion. By dating him, Olivia ensured that her name stayed in the press. But the spark just wasn't there. Olivia wanted more.

Olivia segued from Hughes to Jimmy Stewart, another lean, intellectual, successful man who made her feel comfortable. This relationship was also something more meaningful—for both of them. They met at the end of 1939, and Stewart even escorted Olivia to the New York premiere of *Gone with the Wind.* Both were thoughtful and serious about their careers, and both their stars were ascendant, although Stewart's would shine brighter and longer than Olivia's. Their relationship lasted over a year, and Olivia was certainly smitten, but Stewart remained one of Hollywood's most eligible bachelors until 1949. Before settling down, Stewart sampled the diverse delights of Hollywood actresses, including a rather torrid affair with Marlene Dietrich (before meeting Olivia). So, while Olivia was mad about the boy, and Stewart adored her, the timing was off.

The jacket of Alexander Nemerov's thoughtful monograph on the 1940s, *Wartime Kiss,* features a gorgeous photograph of Olivia and Jimmy taken by John Swope in 1940. They're having a picnic and "relax[ing] in a graceful, unselfconscious way, reclining on a blanket with a portable phonograph behind them on the grass." Jimmy is wearing a sport coat and has one hand against his eye, the other resting on his stomach. Olivia's midsection is showing just a bit between her angora sweater and her skirt, and her arms are stretched above her head. Both have their eyes closed, making the moment particularly intimate. Nemerov analyzes the photo poetically, noting that it shows a "time without time" and captures the beauty of their youth and talent: "We see two young movie stars . . . on top of their profession, on top of the world, in love with one another. . . . There they need not, should not, cannot think their own deaths." Nemerov also observes that Swope's photograph "owes its timeless feel to another factor central to the lives of Stewart, de Havilland, and Swope himself. This is their common love of airplanes, a fact not immediately apparent . . . except in a detail . . . the way Stewart and de Havilland face the sky. For each of them, flying was a way to be exhilaratingly out of reach of the world."[8] Stewart was a pilot, Swope was a pilot, and Olivia had dated aviation pioneer Howard Hughes and was the cousin of aircraft manufacturer Geoffrey de Havilland. She often flew with Stewart in his own plane, and Olivia eventually took flying lessons and made one solo flight before grounding herself. By the time she dated Stewart, Olivia had already appeared in *Wings of the Navy,* and her subsequent films *Princess O'Rourke, Government Girl,* and *To Each His Own* would feature aviation as plot devices. Flying to the moon and reaching for the stars were part of Olivia's trajectory.

It is rather sad that the relationship with Stewart ended by 1941. Their droll intelligence, mutual independence, growing talent, and versatility onscreen and off would have made theirs a wonderful Hollywood romance for the ages. Perhaps Stewart felt unready to marry at age thirty-two, as he was still building his career with MGM. It's possible that politics played a role—Stewart was a Republican and Olivia a Democrat—but given that one of his closest friends was liberal Henry Fonda, it seems that could have been negotiated. Stewart was also one of the first Hollywood stars to enlist when the United States entered World War II, which might have caused him to hesitate. As for Olivia, she was living a "'spur-of-the-moment life'" and was still quite young—in her midtwenties—when they were dating.[9]

Olivia told *People* magazine in July 2016 that she had been offered the Donna Reed role in *It's a Wonderful Life* (1947), but she turned it down: "It would have meant playing opposite Jimmy Stewart, home from the wars. I knew it would be awkward to work with him because of our many months together in a sort of high school pre-war romance, which came to an end."[10] Stewart presented her with her second Oscar in 1949, however, and although they were extremely formal at the ceremony, backstage photos show them beaming at each other. They finally appeared together many years later in the disaster film *Airport '77.* It was lovely to see the two great actors onscreen, once enough years had passed to make the experience pleasant. Stewart had a long, happy marriage, but one wishes that his and Olivia's love affair had at least been played out in film.

Olivia also briefly dated Franchot Tone, the former lover of Bette Davis and the ex-husband of Joan Crawford, another of those curious intersections among the three women. In fact, during her early to midtwenties, the only man Olivia dated who didn't fit the long, lean lothario template was the brilliant, pugnacious, and very short Burgess Meredith. Olivia dated him in 1940, attracted by his talent and charm, and he was sufficiently debonair to win Paulette Goddard away from Charles Chaplin. Olivia was serious about Meredith, but the relationship wasn't strong enough for a lasting commitment.

Despite an active love life, Olivia was more focused on her career than on marriage. After her Oscar nomination for *Gone with the Wind* and all the attendant publicity and good reviews, she found herself back at Warner Brothers, playing third string to Bette Davis and Errol Flynn as Lady Penelope in *The Private Lives of Elizabeth and Essex.* This was her fourth Technicolor film in two years, and it gave her a chance to demonstrate her versatility, playing a beautiful—truly luscious—bad girl after her role as the saintly Melanie Wilkes in *GWTW.* Olivia's Penelope strums a lute and sings a bitchy song to the aging Elizabeth; she wears sumptuous ice-blue gowns, and she has one good scene with Flynn as the ambitious Essex, questioning his loyalty to Queen Bette. But she is not the love interest in the film. She is not the focus. Even her excellent scene toward the end of the film with Davis, in which she tearfully and shamefully confesses her culpability in Essex's fall from favor, is one moment out of Davis's tour de force, nothing more.

Olivia had promised Jack Warner that if she were allowed to play Melanie, she would be cooperative. So she returned to the grind of being a studio contract player—after *GWTW,* Olivia would make thirteen films between 1939 and 1943. She "consented without visible argument" to accept two inferior if pleasant roles that any starlet would have been hard-pressed to make remarkable.[11] The first film was a loan-out to Sam Goldwyn, which Olivia didn't mind at all, despite the weak script. The more experience she got at other studios, the better. The project—*Raffles*—should have been fun, pairing her with the debonair David Niven, whose star was definitely on the rise. A remake of the 1930 Ronald Colman hit about the adventures of an elegant English gentleman and cricketer who is also a jewel thief, *Raffles* should have been a chic, surefire success, prefiguring Niven's later merriment in *The Pink Panther.* Alas, it wasn't.

Niven was frustrated because, despite his leading-man status, he wasn't getting the showcase roles he wanted. Although Niven was grateful to Goldwyn, who, the actor admitted, "had given me a chance when nobody else would touch me," he believed he was getting his best parts in loan-out vehicles.[12] Niven convinced himself that Goldwyn was taking advantage of him, and his agent, Leland Hayward, agreed. When Goldwyn offered the lead in *Raffles* to Niven, Hayward initially rejected it, despite Goldwyn's promise of "a more remunerative seven-year contract," in the hope they could get a better deal.[13] This was a risky strategy, as Niven knew, because "the black list really did exist. Too many actors who had quarrelled with their studios had sunk without trace. I might never work again anywhere." One day, while doing a costume test for another film, Niven "began to notice a man hovering about in white tie and tails. . . . Obviously he was meant to look like Raffles, the gentleman crook. . . . The name of the man was Dana Andrews."[14] Andrews, who had signed a seven-year contract, had been instructed to shadow Niven as a not-so-subtle reminder that he was replaceable. Niven signed his new contract and accepted the role.

One wishes that, given the kind of Machiavellian treatment Niven endured, the film had been a huge triumph. However, during filming, on September 1, 1939, Hitler invaded Poland. The largely British cast, including Dame Mae Whitty, was terribly concerned about family and friends back home. So the sparkle this experienced cast might have generated to lift the film was absent.

As Raffles, Niven enjoys sending London into a frenzy with his various thefts. For example, he takes the Medici Venus from a museum and leaves behind a card that reads, "The Amateur Cracksman." He then sends the piece in the post to aging actress Maude Holden so that she can claim the reward—he is somewhat of a rapscallion benefactor. It's a role that Niven plays with aplomb. Olivia, who gets second billing, wears chic clothes—as the film opens, she strides elegantly in a white gown and turban on Niven's arm—but as Gwen, the jewel thief's love interest, she is just the standard girlfriend.

The script lacks crackle, tension, and wit. Goldwyn recognized the problem and "felt everybody's nerves were making the film play flat. He wanted a script doctor to pep up the love scenes." So he hired F. Scott Fitzgerald, who "sat in a corner of the soundstage with his secretary, dashing off pages and handing them to the director. . . . After a week on the job, the author was thanked for his work with $1,200 and no screen credit."[15] Niven had discussions with Fitzgerald about the war in Europe—Niven intended to enlist as soon as possible—and although Fitzgerald was maudlin at times, Niven recalled that he was "beginning to like a lot, and perhaps understand a little, this strange, haunted, withdrawn, and massively insecure man [when] Goldwyn fired him."[16] In particular, Goldwyn disliked a quirky love scene in which Raffles tells Gwen to smile and then asks her a very important question: "'Who's your dentist?'"[17] The film could have used this kind of silly flirtation.

Olivia has several pretty scenes with Niven. When they dance together at the Ambassador's Club, she is lithe in a pale evening gown. He takes her home in a hansom cab through Piccadilly, they share a sweet kiss, and she invites him to the country for the weekend, sensing that he has a deep secret. There are many extremely British scenes, such as Raffles playing cricket and looking dashing in an open white shirt, while Gwen applauds and the other upper crusters drink beer and tea. Olivia said of the role, "'I had nothing to do with that English scene, I had nothing to do with that style of film and I was nothing to that part the way it was written.'"[18]

All in all, *Raffles* was a wasted opportunity. Niven was charming, and so was Olivia, but the declaration of war as well as the flat script resulted in an uninvolving caper movie. As a British citizen, Olivia was acutely aware of the tragedy abroad, and Niven "announced to Goldwyn that he had been called to the colors and had to leave immediately." However, Goldwyn contacted the British embassy in Washington and learned that no one outside of Britain had been called up yet. Nevertheless, Niven soon returned home to join the RAF.[19]

My Love Came Back, a spritely comedy, followed. Olivia's part "had been turned down by Priscilla Lane," one of the three Iowa-born Lane sisters (the others Lola and Rosemary) and an up-and-coming Warner starlet.[20] Accepting a role that had been rejected by the blonde Priscilla (who would work with Hitchcock in 1942's *Saboteur*) couldn't have been pleasant for Olivia, despite receiving top billing. Clearly, the film is a B-tier programmer for the bottom half of a double bill. It's sweet and energetic, and at least Olivia got to work with an excellent cast of supporting players, including the charming Eddie Albert, future Oscar winner (and fellow nominee for 1948) Jane Wyman, previous *Hard to Get* costar Charles Winninger, and the always delightfully spiky Spring Byington, with whom Olivia had worked in *The Charge of the Light Brigade* and *It's Love I'm After.* But Jeffrey Lynn as her romantic costar? Lynn—who tested for Ashley Wilkes (poorly) opposite Vivien Leigh—is one of those pallid actors who seems like a perfectly nice man who should be selling insurance rather than acting in Hollywood films, let alone opposite the divine Olivia. There were plenty of pretty, interchangeable actors available, battling for recognition, and Lynn is simply not leading-man material.

Warner Brothers wasn't afraid to exploit Olivia's appearance in *GWTW.* In the trailer, a young, handsome viewer is diagnosed as suffering from "the 1940 blues." What does the doctor suggest? Go see Olivia in *My Love Came Back!* Next, an attractive young couple is depressed by listening to news of the war. What do they decide? "Let's go relax with Olivia," suggests the husband. "And Jeffrey!" pipes the wife. The trailer advises, "Relax with Olivia de Havilland in Her First Picture since 'Gone with the Wind,'" which is not quite true, but it's an effective allusion used to market the film and Olivia. She has a flattering close-up in the trailer, and at age twenty-three, she seems a bit more grown up, a bit more angular. The film actually looks like fun, with its "rollicking cast of cheerer-uppers," and if it were as delightful as the trailer, it would be much more important to Olivia's canon.[21]

Hal Wallis produced, Kurt Bernhardt directed, and Olivia wore lovely Orry-Kelly creations. The film has a youthful energy and was clearly made with a great deal of gumption. Its musical aspect adds vibrancy to the rather pedestrian script. But the film is still distinctly unmemorable. If Olivia had been given a worthy costar—including Flynn, who was always eager to show his comedic chops—this film would have had more life.

This time, Olivia is violinist Amelia Cornell, attending the Brissac Academy of Music. The always jovial S. Z. Sakall is directing the orchestra, but there's an empty chair! Jane Wyman is worried, Eddie Albert is worried, and Olivia is engaging in her trademark lip biting as she anxiously rides the subway. She manages to sneak into her place, and a profile shot shows her playing very prettily—of course, she'll be a great violinist someday. But her constant tardiness is a problem. She is always late for her lessons because she must supplement her scholarship by giving lessons herself. She cries breathlessly and violently as Sakall chastises her, but she needs the money to meet her familial responsibilities: her mother and brother have a farm, and her sister is ill. But there are rules attached to her scholarship; she can't be permitted to give private lessons and continue her tardiness. What will she do? Will she have to abandon her dreams of Carnegie Hall to play in a swing band with her pals Albert and Wyman? Will Jeffrey Lynn help her? Will they get engaged at the end of the film?

My Love Came Back is like a black-and-white, 1930s *High School Musical,* with fresh moments and very good music, both classical and swing. Olivia had trouble fingering the violin, so she did the bowing onscreen while an off-camera professional did the rest, but those scenes still play well. Though not as adept at comedy as her costars, Olivia offers a winsome heroine. She's very feisty in the film, such as when she gets angry with Sakall and throws a book across the room, breaking the glass in a door. Her interactions with Wyman and Albert are lively, and her comedic timing is more assured than in previous roles. She's also very pretty, which is part of the plot: Wealthy Julius Millette (Winninger) sees her play and is charmed. He learns of her financial difficulties, fancies her, and decides to secretly write a check to support her income. He agrees to be president of the music academy if this indiscretion is kept quiet, and this allows him to work behind the scenes to help her achieve her goal of becoming a classical violinist. In the meantime, her fellow students need her to play fiddle in their band. *My Love Came Back* was successful enough to be broadcast as a thirty-minute radio adaptation on *The Screen Guild Theater* on March 16, 1941, with Olivia and Winninger. Even so, the film is essentially a run-of-the-mill pleasantry.[22]

Olivia followed this film with *Santa Fe Trail* (see chapter 3), "yet another Civil War–era production cashing in on *Gone with the Wind.*"[23] It's certainly memorable for Raymond Massey's barnstorming performance as abolitionist John Brown and Ronald Reagan's ingratiating role as George Armstrong Custer. Olivia plays heroine Kit Carson Halliday with a "provocative, slightly tongue-in-cheek manner."[24] Her character's romance with Errol Flynn's Jeb Stuart is flirtatious and sincere, as always. She could play the role sleepwalking, and it's to her credit that she didn't.

Olivia was still trying to make peace with what was happening and not happening for her at Warner Brothers. She had been loaned out to Selznick for *GWTW* and to Goldwyn for *Raffles,* so she knew there might be other opportunities at other studios. She was only twenty-four years old, and she was just two years away from completing her seven-year contract. Stress had made her ill in the past, and she didn't want to repeat those breakdowns. She knew that *Santa Fe Trail* would at least be a box office hit; audiences loved Livvie and Errol, and by this time, they were a beloved screen couple.

Interestingly, Flynn was jealous of their costar Ronald Reagan, for "day after day de Havilland is seen to be chummy with Ronnie."[25] He became convinced that they were having an affair. This was paradoxical, given Flynn's track record. Besides, Reagan had married fellow Warner contract player Jane Wyman in January 1940. But he was quite handsome, and both he and Olivia were quite interested in the Screen Actors Guild; they got on well during filming and became very friendly. Olivia explained later that "Ronnie Reagan was a very sociable creature. . . . [He was] already interested in the Guild and [he] would sit beside me on the set to chat about SAG and other things."[26] This piqued Flynn's outrage; regardless of his reputation or his marital status, he truly loved Olivia. This had to be satisfying to the young actress, but at the same time, Flynn was behaving badly on the set, and retakes were needed; there was "enmity between the stars."[27] After a sitting for publicity stills, they were furious with each other and didn't want to work together again.

Thankfully for Olivia, her next project was a lighthearted comedy that reteamed her with James Cagney. Another thorn in Jack Warner's side, Cagney had been battling the mogul for several years over roles and contract terms. To find the role, Olivia "sneaked the script out of the makeup department."[28] Then she persuaded Cagney's brother William, who was the associate producer, to cast her in the lively, pleasant film.[29] Directed by Raoul Walsh—usually known for his action films (including the upcoming *They Died with Their Boots On*) but equally adept at lively comedy—and photographed beautifully by the great James Wong Howe, *The Strawberry Blonde* is a charming romp. It offers Olivia excellent costars—Jack Carson and a seductive but distinctly unsympathetic Rita Hayworth as the local flirt—and a role that is both feisty and endearing.

The Strawberry Blonde is a romance set during America's idealized Gilded Age, but in typical Warner Brothers fashion, it also offers a commentary on social class, pitting the hardworking middle class against the money-grubbing upper class. Cagney plays Biff Grimes, a rather hapless dentist whose business isn't going terribly well. He's got a past—he's a jailbird—and has had to move from two other neighborhoods. As he plays horseshoes in his Willy Loman-esque backyard, he gets into a shouting match with his annoying next-door neighbor George Reeves (former Tarleton twin from *GWTW* and future Superman), who portrays a guitar-playing Yale man in a mustache and a letter sweater. Out comes Biff's wife Amy, played by Olivia in no-nonsense mode, who chastises her husband by saying, "Biff Grimes, you're worse than a child."[30] Amy, a nurse, is a thoroughly modern, professional, free-speaking woman. Olivia's got her hair up, and at twenty-five, she's maturing into her own beauty and confidence. Her ability to boss around tough-guy Cagney is completely believable.

A telephone call about a toothache sets the film's plot and conflict into motion. The guest of the local bank president is suffering, and Biff is the only dentist available. And who should that guest be but Biff's old rival Hugo, a rich alderman who is now married to the strawberry blonde both men fancied! Played with his trademark gusto by the sturdily comic Jack Carson, Hugo is pompous and a dreadful blowhard. Biff seems justified when he contemplates giving Hugo too much gas and maybe killing him. As he dreams of revenge, the film goes into a flashback of youth, ambition, competition, and adoration for a strawberry blonde—prim and seemingly proper, her trim ankles and spats showing—who is not as delicious as she appears to be.

Just as Carson and Cagney represent the proper and the improper, Hayworth and de Havilland represent the silly and the substantial, and their portrayals are perfect parts of the ensemble. As Virginia, Hayworth wears a white dress with frilly puffed sleeves and a little hat. Olivia's Amy, in contrast, wears a nurse's uniform. "It's a sign to the men," she explains, that she won't stand "the tyranny of man over woman." She's a saucy suffragette, proud of her uniform, and more honest than the faux feminine Virginia. One of Amy's delightful qualities, in addition to her feminist stance, is her flirtatiousness. Amy winks at men and has great fun shocking Virginia: "That's the way men behave toward women. . . . Don't be a hypocrite, Virginia. Spiritually, you winked!" Olivia's Amy is a tough cookie, even asserting, "A little kiss is harmless if it's all in fun." "Even if it isn't," Biff replies. "'Zactly," she says as she winks at him, scaring him off with her rebelliousness.[31] Being in an A-picture with an outstanding cast, crew, and script seems to energize Olivia. A fan magazine noted, "The part throws new light on Olivia's talents, and opens up immense possibilities for her future. . . . The way Miss de Havilland handles the comedy . . . is extraordinary."[32]

Meanwhile, Virginia and Hugo have married, and Amy must break the news to Biff. In a sweet gingham gown, Olivia's Amy is meltingly sincere and loving, and as they talk, they both confess to being lonely. So why doesn't she have a date? "Free thinkers have a lot of time on their hands," Amy explains. When Biff finally sees—really sees—how good Amy is, he takes his hat off and asks, "Can I be your steady?" She cries, he smiles, and then, taking the bull by the horns, Amy asks, "Biff, would you like to kiss me?"[33]

As the plot unwinds, Hugo has become rich, but when the poor folks dine with the rich folks, we see that money doesn't buy taste, manners, class, or happiness. Hugo offers to take Biff into the firm with him, and Amy is thrilled for the man she loves. Biff, however, is merely a tool for Hugo. For six months he has done nothing but sit in his huge office and sign the papers Hugo thrusts at him. Noblesse oblige, the film reminds viewers, doesn't guarantee honor. Hugo is accused of running an unethical and unsafe operation, and when one of his buildings collapses on Biff's father and kills him, the metaphor of being hit by a ton of bricks wasn't lost on an audience still suffering from the effects of the Depression. Because Biff has been signing the documents, he is implicated in Hugo's dirty dealings and winds up serving five years in prison for the firm's illegal business practices. Amy, of course, stands by her man and goes back to nursing. In these scenes, Olivia and Cagney demonstrate the camaraderie and solidity they've shown in their previous two films together. Their reunion scene, after Biff's release from prison, is extremely tender and memorable. Amy is waiting for him in the park where they first met, wearing a pretty floral dress and hat. As Amy's tears glisten, Biff humbly says, "I want to thank you for all your goodness and kindness." Then Biff finally tells her what he should have seen from the start: "I think you're the loveliest lady in the whole world."[34]

These two actors worked well together in terms of energy, reactions, physical balance, and wit. They were both able to play comedy and drama, period pieces and contemporary stories. They were united in their disapproval of the way the studio ran their careers. However, there was "a reported rift between Olivia and Cagney during the filming of this vehicle, when he accused her of upstaging the less-experienced Hayworth."[35] It's difficult to conceive of Olivia behaving this way, but if she felt Hayworth was getting more attention, she might have been willing to assert herself in a scene. The rumored disagreement blew over, in any case, and Olivia described Cagney as "wonderful . . . generous, fair—so was Henry Fonda—exquisitely fair. They have a kind of morality about their work . . . and it's just heaven to work with someone like that. . . . Jimmy was marvellous. I learned many things from him."[36] Elsewhere she remarked, "And he knows how to tell stories so well! He knows how to make the smallest scene richer with a personal contribution."[37] When she asked Cagney what acting is, in his opinion, he told her, "'Well, whatever you say, just mean it.' I can't think of anything more pertinent as a reply to that question. . . . It is *the* statement and it helped me all my life."[38] That's the same advice Victor Fleming gave her when she played Melanie. Warner Brothers missed an opportunity when it failed to team James Cagney and Olivia de Havilland in other films.

The Strawberry Blonde ends on a comic note, returning to Hugo's present need of a dentist. Biff pulls out the tooth with no gas—"I wouldn't be quite human if I didn't take a little revenge." He and Amy go for a walk, and when she whispers in his ear about an impending baby, he says, "You mean?" She winks and replies, "'Zactly!" Before "The End," a title card announces, "One Moment Please!" Cornily but charmingly, the audience is invited to follow the bouncing ball and sing along with "The Band Played On."[39] It is a sweet conclusion to a lively film in which Olivia has an excellent role for a change.

Critics were beginning to take a closer look at Olivia. She had the Flynn films, of course, she had the *GWTW* nomination, and now she had a hit comedy. Her maturing beauty was also gaining more attention, as were her relationships with men like Howard Hughes and Jimmy Stewart. I asked her whether she was conscious of her looks and figure at the time:

> The film business does impose upon one the discipline of appearing at one's best in public and on film, and maintaining a suitable and becoming weight. . . . As far as my features were concerned, only my eyebrows received special attention from the make-up man and . . . [I wore] porcelain caps to cover, on each side of my upper row of front teeth, my pointed canines. To speak . . . of the matter of weight: incredibly, after an appendectomy in January of 1941, I gained weight in the hospital. . . . From then on it was a struggle to return to, and then maintain, the 110 or 112 pounds which was for years my normal and photogenic weight. Later, I found that I could becomingly weigh 115 pounds.[40]

While recovering from that surgery, Olivia's lucky streak continued. She learned that screenwriter Charles Brackett, along with Billy Wilder, had written the role of Emmy Brown for her in the film *Hold Back the Dawn,* based on a semiautobiographical tale by Ketti Frings.[41] In another stroke of luck, the film would be made at Paramount Studios.

Paramount valued Olivia in the 1940s, and the first indication of that fortuitous relationship was *Hold Back,* filmed and released in 1941. Charles Boyer and Paulette Goddard were Olivia's costars, with Olivia earning second billing behind the accomplished Boyer. It was based on a treatment by Frings entitled "Memo to a Movie Producer," which would be developed into a novel after the film was released.[42] The project also facilitated several personal and professional relationships. Olivia and the Bracketts would become lifelong friends. Edith Head designed the costumes, and she and Olivia established a happy association. Ketti Frings's husband, Kurt, was an agent, and Olivia would sign with him in the future. Even more important, Olivia worked with director Mitchell Leisen for the first time, and their collaboration and friendship would be valuable for both. Earning six Oscar nominations, including Olivia's first for best actress, *Hold Back the Dawn* signaled to Hollywood—if not to Jack Warner—that the young actress was a talent to be reckoned with.

The producer of *Hold Back,* Arthur Hornblow Jr., showed Olivia the script at a luncheon at Charlie Brackett's. She was still recovering from her appendectomy and had to be carried into Brackett's house. She remembered, "It was a miracle I ever got to do *Hold Back the Dawn* at all . . . because Jack Warner hated to loan anybody out, especially if it was a role you were well-suited for that might help your career. . . . I read [the script] and loved it . . . then the long days of waiting began."[43] Olivia left it to Hornblow to negotiate with Warner, who wasn't necessarily interested in building Olivia's career at other studios but was anxious to secure Fred MacMurray for *Dive Bomber.* Feigning indifference about who would be swapped for MacMurray, Hornblow offered to take Olivia off Warner's hands, and none the wiser, Warner accepted.[44] A copy of her contract for the film, dated February 17, 1941, noted that she had two months without compensation beyond her usual salary, but $1,500 per week if the shoot ran longer.[45] Warner Brothers would profit, but Olivia would not. However, with such a good script, "flawlessly cast, from the smallest bit parts right up to the leads," Olivia was thrilled with the project.[46]

The film addresses an issue with which the United States is still dealing: immigration. The film's immigrants are refugees from Europe during World War II, however. The film's timing was particularly poignant, given the widespread emigration to escape Hitler and the war in Europe, and one of those refugees was screenwriter Billy Wilder himself. To intensify the autobiographical element of the film, and perhaps as an effort by these expatriate filmmakers to urge a reluctant America to aid Britain and France, *Hold Back* begins with the protagonist relating his story to a director on the Paramount set. It is an intriguing meta-film, a film within a film that makes the larger international issue more relatable for an isolationist American audience; it tells the story of one small group of people who are not just desperate émigrés but also sympathetic characters.

In a kind of preview for Wilder's *Sunset Boulevard* ten years later, the film uses a framework of present and past to establish its parameters and to demonstrate that although the audience is watching a film, a fiction, the story within the story is reality for millions. By opening with a voice-over, the structure of *Hold Back the Dawn* reiterates the peculiarly vivid alternative universe that cinema can establish.

The man telling his tale on the movie set is Charles Boyer, portraying Romanian dancer and louche gigolo Georges Iscovescu. He has bluffed his way past the security guards and onto the set where, in another meta-moment, director Mitchell Leisen portrays director Dwight Saxon, rehearsing a scene from *I Wanted Wings* with Veronica Lake. Iscovescu met Saxon a few years earlier in Nice, and he asks for $500.00 in exchange for the story he has to tell. In the real world, he would have been thrown off the lot. In this meta-world, however, the director listens to his story, explaining in his narration, "Perhaps the best way to begin this story is to tell you how it came to us. One day last August into the Paramount Studios in Hollywood walked a man."[47]

Iscovescu, along with a colorful group of European refugees, lives in penury in a small Mexican town across the border from California, at the ironically named Esperanza Hotel. He is waiting for a quota number so that he can enter the United States. An advance person for the film working in Mexicali and Calexico in January 1941 noted that "between six and seven thousand people, both American and Mexican, pass through the Border Gates each day," and "it is very easy to jump the fence and get into the United States, but once you get across you will have to avoid twenty-five men on motor cycles and in automobiles."[48] (At that time there were no plans to build a wall.) With a waiting period of between five and eight years, however, the chances of Iscovescu getting into the United States are slim. Fortuitously, the professional charmer meets his former dance partner Anita Dixon, played with ruthless vigor by Paulette Goddard, and learns that she has become a US citizen through a quickie marriage and divorce to an American. Anita still carries a torch for her former partner and lover, and together they scheme to get Georges married off to an unsuspecting citizen as well.

Even more fortuitously, driving a van full of rowdy children on a field trip across the border is schoolteacher Emmy Brown, played without glamorous makeup and with innocent enthusiasm by Olivia, looking as sweet and all-American as her character's name. Georges ascertains that she is single, and she becomes the immediate target of his green-card marriage plan. He removes a part from her car, forcing her and the children to spend the night at his hotel as he plays the hero and comes to their rescue. She awakens early the next morning to find Georges gazing dreamily at her, and he tells the young woman, "We are like two trains halted for a moment at the same station, but we are going in different directions. We can't change our course any more than we can hold back the dawn."[49] What a line! And there's more: he has slipped his "mother's" wedding ring on her finger—actually, it's Anita's ring from *her* green-card marriage. Emmy has no hope in the face of the trademark Boyer charm, and they marry immediately.

Emmy has to take the children home, and the local consular officer, Mr. Hammock (played with tremendous world-weariness and irony by Walter Abel), is certainly suspicious of the marriage; he has seen these tricks before. However, Emmy demonstrates her initiative and her loving heart when she arrives unexpectedly a few days later with a car, a cake, and a week off so she and Georges can have a honeymoon. This is problematic for Georges—who must go away with his young wife and appease Anita—and he is slowly coming to the realization that he may be more ethical than desperate where Emmy Brown is concerned.

Paulette Goddard plays the heartless and practical gold digger with aplomb, in a performance reminiscent of her role as divorced showgirl Miriam Aarons in *The Women* (1939). What redeems Anita's ruthlessness is her genuine love for Georges, and she tells him, "All those years with all the others, I've shut my eyes and thought of you."[50] In one of those synchronistic Hollywood intersections, Olivia and Goddard share Boyer onscreen, and they would both date Burgess Meredith offscreen. And if Vivien Leigh hadn't made a last-minute, dark-horse grab at the part of Scarlett O'Hara, they would have made *GWTW* together.

In addition to the love triangle, tension is provided by the situations of the many supporting characters. These include a radiant Rosemary DeCamp as the pregnant German refugee Berta Kurz, who very cleverly manages to get herself across the border and is waiting in Hammock's office when the first stages of labor begin, thereby guaranteeing that at least her child will be an American citizen.

But it is the relationship between Olivia's Emmy and Boyer's Georges that gives the film its complex and moving core. With Leisen's sensitive direction, Olivia's performance explores her character's awakening maturity and sexuality. Emmy may be gullible and naïve, but she represents the best of American womanhood. If Emmy were simpering or fluttery, one might think, "Good on you, Georges." But Emmy Brown is a responsible career woman who is loyal to her family. And when she loves, she loves. That Georges is a refugee without a visa and without means is unimportant to her; Emmy represents a kind of Lady Liberty who willingly facilitates a better life for a tired, hungry, poor refugee.

The chemistry between Olivia and Boyer is palpable. He is dreamy, charming, and utterly irresistible, and her pliable romanticism provides a believable counterpoint. He was one of her favorite costars, and she noted years later, "I loved working with Charles Boyer: a true professional! And what excellent manners!"[51] Olivia sparks off Boyer, who in turn acts as her gentle guide both in the role and as a more confident ensemble player. Finally, one of Hollywood's leading men (and Bette Davis's former leading man in *All This and Heaven Too*) is Olivia's romantic interest.

There is a particular scene in the film that might be identified as the moment when the actress transitions from ingenue Livvie to adult Olivia. While on their honeymoon, Georges finds himself falling for Emmy, and he fakes a shoulder injury to keep her purity intact. However, after a week together, Georges is overwhelmed by his feelings for her. As Emmy emerges from the sea, he "falls fully in love, his duplicity turned to truth. Never before has Emmy looked more pure and beautiful. She is honest as the ocean, true as the waves, and his own arrival in America is now a wholesome tide."[52] Their kiss, Boyer's desire, and Olivia's sensuality offer an authentically passionate moment. Director Leisen "filled the picture with lyrically beautiful close-ups of de Havilland. . . . That Emmy was so beautiful and intelligent yet had reached her mid-twenties apparently unaware of sex, implied a very protected rural upbringing and created an ambiguity which made the part more complex and difficult for de Havilland," but Olivia rose to the challenge.[53]

Emmy finds out from Anita that she has been manipulated, but she doesn't turn Georges in, maintaining her dignity. She is injured in a car accident on the way home from Mexico, and we learn that Georges needs the $500 from the film director so that he can repay Emmy money she had given him. At her bedside, Georges manages to bring the comatose Emmy back to consciousness, as befits a proper husband, but he's sent back to Mexico. However, as the film ends, we see Georges sitting on a bench and drawing with a stick in the dirt. Hammock sits beside him and gives him the news that Georges has gotten his visa: "You're the husband of an American wife, aren't you? Don't keep her waiting!"[54] The film ends emotionally and romantically, with Georges moving against a tide of people to be with Emmy, a perfect metaphor for the wave of immigrants who had come to America in the past and would be coming again during World War II.

Although this was a happy shoot for Olivia, she was still quite ill. Despite gaining twenty pounds on a diet her doctor had recommended after the appendectomy, she was frail when she returned to work. According to studio records, she missed six days of work and was in a very difficult physical and emotional state.[55] However, she's radiant in the movie, finally coming into her own in a role that's worthy of her. Reviews were laudatory, with Bosley Crowther stating, "Olivia de Havilland plays the school teacher as a woman with romantic fancies whose honesty and pride are her own—and the film's—chief support. Incidentally, she is excellent."[56]

Olivia's best actress Oscar nomination for Emmy Brown should have been exhilarating. However, her sister, Joan Fontaine, was also nominated as best actress for her role in *Suspicion,* and she had already won the New York Film Critics Award over Olivia. The press was watching both sisters with eagle eyes on the night of the Academy Awards. Although Joan's performance was competent, it was not career defining; her nomination was widely considered to be a consolation prize for losing the Oscar the year before (for her role in *Rebecca*) to Ginger Rogers. When Joan's name was announced as the winner, Olivia seemed outwardly delighted for her younger sister, but it must have been a painful, embarrassing loss.

Next for Olivia was her final pairing with Errol Flynn in *They Died with Their Boots On,* playing Libby and George Custer (see chapter 3). Although this western was fictionalized to a great extent, the real-life Custers' happy marriage was the basis for Olivia's Libby and Errol's George; their own off-screen romance had ended by this time. Raoul Walsh directed the film with great energy, humor, and commitment to the action scenes. Flynn referred to Walsh as "Uncle," and the set was a very friendly and enjoyable place.[57] Olivia was also reunited with Hattie McDaniel, and there were certainly no hard feelings about Hattie's best supporting actress Oscar for *GWTW.* That McDaniel was once again portraying a maid—this time, one who made comic owl noises, like the Nurse in *Romeo and Juliet*—spoke volumes about racism and misogyny in 1940s Hollywood.

The film finished shooting on September 22, 1941, ending with a farewell scene between the Custers. It was also Olivia and Errol's last screen moment together, and at a 1978 retrospective of her films in Los Angeles, Olivia "found it impossible to sit through the farewell scene of *Boots*. As it began she got up and walked into the lobby, and wept. It is easy to understand why."[58] According to Robert Matzen, however, after filming ended, Olivia and Errol were seen around town together. Flynn had finally left Lili Damita and had built a house on Mulholland Drive, and Olivia certainly visited that notorious love nest. But then something happened, according to Matzen, "something devastating that neither of them will speak nor write about."[59]

At least Olivia's assignments were becoming more interesting and notable. Her next movie was *The Male Animal*, a funny, thought-provoking film version of the 1940 Broadway play by Elliott Nugent and renowned *New Yorker* cartoonist and humorist James Thurber. Nugent was given the directing nod, and Henry Fonda starred as Tommy Turner, a self-effacing academic whose belief in intellectual freedom in the classroom is challenged. Olivia is very comely as the competent, supportive spouse of the typical absentminded professor, and her comedy scenes with former costars Jack Carson and Hattie McDaniel are pure pleasure.

Olivia relished working with Henry Fonda; happily for both, they would perform *A Gift of Time* on Broadway twenty years later and do a television miniseries together. She found him to be a supportive actor and a strong ensemble player. She remembered, "I found something interesting about actors (and, later, writers)—they seemed to be more compassionate than other people, and related easily to those less fortunate than themselves."[60] Olivia and Fonda also shared a political connection: both were Democrats and union supporters. Olivia had joined the Screen Actors Guild in 1936, when she was "still a minor under the law at that time."[61] After her naturalization on November 28, 1941, she was eligible to vote; she recalled, "Franklin Roosevelt had already begun his third term then, but when he ran for a fourth term in 1944, I voted for him. The Democratic Party seemed to me to be the Party of Humanity, profoundly interested in the welfare and wellbeing of mankind."[62] Their onscreen roles of a liberal thinker and his wife reflected the offscreen politics of Fonda and Olivia, and their affection for each other is certainly convincing.

The film's conflict comes when Tommy shares a letter written by Bartolomeo Vanzetti with his students. Vanzetti, along with Nicola Sacco, was convicted of murder in 1921 and executed in 1927 after a controversial trial that many believe was unduly influenced by their radical politics. One of Tommy's students, Michael Barnes (played with sweet intensity by future *Dennis the Menace* dad Herbert Anderson), publishes an essay in the school newspaper applauding Tommy's decision. This puts the professor in a difficult position with the administration of Midwestern University, which finds him seditious. Tommy insists on academic freedom in the classroom, and he declares in that earnestly comic Henry Fonda way, "I know I'm not a tiger, but I don't like to be thought of as a pussycat either."[63]

Tommy is up for promotion, which makes his dispute with the university a concern for his wife, Ellen. Compounding the problems between them is Ellen's flirtation with former college football star Joe Ferguson, played with hulking enthusiasm and humor by the great Jack Carson. Ellen was once engaged to Joe, "just for fun," and when he returns for homecoming in the midst of the fallout from Tommy's teaching methodology, marital misunderstanding gets entwined with university politics. Ellen must deal with the eccentric behavior of her husband, the flattering attentions of her former beau, and her recalcitrant maid Cleota (McDaniel). Olivia is energetic with her trim dresses and upswept hair, and the subtext of her performance represents the efficient young woman who can run a household (with help) and be an important member of her community as well; she is the prewar American wife.

Throughout the film, Olivia tries to infuse her underwritten role with conviction, which is helped by her affinity with both Fonda and Carson. Whether reliving the memories of college days with Joe Ferguson or fussing at her "house-wrecker" husband, she's amusing. One of her most delightful scenes takes place at the huge homecoming bonfire. In a trademark Warner Brothers trope, the names of the team's players are read; some sound eastern European, others Italian, Polish, and Welsh—this is the American melting pot. And then Joe introduces Ellen Turner as a former cheerleader, and she leads the crowd in a "big red team" cheer.[64] It's out of Olivia's comfort zone, and she's endearing.

The film also gives Henry Fonda a chance to do the physical comedy at which he excels, with his gangling physique and ingenuous delivery. Frustrated by his wife's flirtations and the brouhaha surrounding the Vanzetti letter, he gets drunk with Michael and declares, "All animals are the same . . . we're all male animals, too." That animalistic tendency inspires him—"You do something! You don't just sit there!"[65] And that's exactly what he does the next day.

There has been so much controversy about the letter that the university has moved Tommy's class to the auditorium. Campus bigwig Ed Keller (played by the divinely grumpy Eugene Pallette) informs Tommy that he'll be asked to resign, but the professor takes a stand and insists, "I'm fighting for a teacher's rights—and a student's rights." He fumbles for the letter and fears he has forgotten it, but then he finds it in a book in his pocket and observes, "My wife must've put it there." As Fonda reads the letter—quietly and subtly and movingly—a tearful Olivia gets a close-up and declares, "He used to be just nice, but now he's wonderful! When he read that letter, that's when he was the real male animal!"[66] The crowd is now completely transformed by the situation (only in the movies, alas), and the students carry the Turners on their shoulders. Ellen fixes Tommy's hat, he lays a huge kiss on her, and they all cry hurray for free speech. It's a storybook ending to a still-relevant comedy. Olivia's role as a university wife isn't particularly challenging, but she seems to be having fun. The *New York Times* observed, "Olivia de Havilland concocts a delightfully pliant and saucy character as the wife. . . . See 'The Male Animal' if you are interested in one of the funniest sights extant."[67]

Olivia was maturing at this point both as an actress and as a woman. She was finally living on her own at 2337 Nella Vista Avenue in Los Angeles. Sister Joan was living with her husband Brian Aherne, and mother Lilian visited only occasionally. It wasn't terribly posh, but it was a beautiful home and, more important, it was her very own. It was during this time that Olivia met the man who would become one of the great passions of her life and certainly her most profound romance: John Huston.

In an interview with Anjelica Huston in December 2013, I mentioned her father's relationship to the actress, and she replied, "I think they were crazy about each other; at least that's how it looks in a short film of them which you've undoubtedly seen of them romping around a swimming pool in Tarzana."[68] Anjelica met Olivia in 2003 at the seventy-fifth anniversary of the Oscars, and they chatted for a few minutes in a very warm and friendly way. Allegra Huston, Anjelica's younger sister, also knew that her father and Olivia had once been in love, and she recalled home movies that showed them together.[69] Rather poignantly, in both the John Huston papers at the Margaret Herrick Library and Huston's 1980 memoir *An Open Book,* there is a small photograph, about two by two inches, of him and Olivia in a fishing boat on the water. They are intimate, heads together, looking rather scruffy and perfectly content.

Huston was definitely Olivia's kind of man—tall, lean, a few years older, strong, intellectual, a bit of an iconoclast, and committed to cinema. Although he was married to his second wife, Lesley Black, at the time, things were not happy between them. Huston and Olivia were inexorably drawn together for the next twenty years, off and on, a peripatetic passion. Well into the 1960s, Huston invited Olivia to visit his home, St. Clerans, in Galway, Ireland. She stayed only three days, but clearly their romantic feelings remained.

The project that brought them together was *In This Our Life,* filmed at the end of 1941. Huston wasn't mad for Howard Koch's screenplay, an adaptation of Virginia novelist Ellen Glasgow's 1942 Pulitzer Prize winner. Koch altered much of Glasgow's grit and created another melodramatic women's picture. Nevertheless, *In This Our Life* was Warner Brothers' highest grossing film for 1942 and Bette Davis's biggest hit to date, earning over $1.7 million.[70] However, it wasn't nominated for any major awards, and the reviews were mixed. Interestingly, John Huston wrote about the film, "I never cared for *In This Our Life,* although there were some good things about it." It was his second directorial effort at Warner Brothers and his first after *The Maltese Falcon,* yet he gave it only three paragraphs in his memoir—perhaps to avoid discussing his affair with Olivia. Huston admitted, however, that "it was very flattering for me . . . to be given a picture with Warners' top stars."[71]

The film was a major career opportunity for Olivia because it reteamed her with Bette Davis in the third of their four pairings. Finally, the frost between the two actresses melted, despite Olivia's romance with the director. They played sisters, and as Olivia recalled, "I was the good sister and she was the bad sister and that pleased Bette—she likes that sort of thing." Davis was wary of Olivia's youthful beauty, and having clashed with other female costars, including Miriam Hopkins, she was determined not to be upstaged by Olivia. Olivia remembered, "I had the first scene to shoot. I glanced up and I saw, sitting under the camera, Miss Davis and she was watching me, and the challenge was unmistakable. And I thought, 'I just can't be Miriam Hopkins.' . . . What I said through my eyes was, 'I can't pick up the gauntlet. I just want to be your friend.'"[72] Miraculously, the telepathy worked.

Olivia has an excellent role as Roy Timberlake, the calmer sister in a Virginia family. Her crazy, wild sister Stanley, played with manic energy by Davis, not only steals Roy's husband (the luscious Dennis Morgan) but also drives him to suicide, dumps her own fiancé (the stolid George Brent), exploits her dying uncle (the lascivious Charles Coburn), and runs down a mother and her child and tries to pin the accident on African American law clerk Parry Clay (the admirable Ernest Anderson). While Davis enjoys striding through the action with riveting histrionics, it is Olivia's calm characterization that holds the film together. She is loving, tough, forgiving, steadfast—attributes we have come to expect from her roles. But she's also sexy in her scenes with George Brent (in their third film pairing), tough when she leaves her marriage and comforts her horrid sister, and competent at work. Olivia's affect is thoroughly contemporary.

While the film is a melodrama, it also reiterates the sociopolitical tenor of so many Warner Brothers films, and so many of Olivia's and Huston's films as well. The mixture of messages is not incompatible; one critical view of the genre suggests that "melodramas open space prohibited by the so-called classical realist film text, which is restricted to oppressive patriarchal norms."[73] *In This Our Life* addresses the racism endemic in American society, with Davis's Stanley thinking nothing of accusing young Parry Clay, whose mother, Minerva (Hattie McDaniel), works for the Timberlake family. Huston was particularly proud that the film "was the first time, I'm certain, that a black man had ever been treated other than as comedy relief."[74]

Even though Hattie McDaniel portrays yet another maid, some studio advisers objected to casting her as Minerva Clay because they felt she "was suited only for comedy."[75] McDaniel knew this was an important role, and she desperately wanted to demonstrate her acting abilities as well as to reinforce the film's terribly personal message. Fortunately, Jack Warner stepped in to advocate for the actress with producer Hal Wallis, and "at his insistence, McDaniel was hired. It was an encouraging sign."[76] Throughout the 1930s and 1940s, Warner Brothers was consistently proactive in its employment of black actors, albeit in stereotypical roles. Although McDaniel has only three scenes, her Minerva is clearly central to the Timberlake family; she uses her gift for both irony and sorrow, demonstrated in *Gone with the Wind,* in her scenes with Olivia. Alternately humorous and poignantly dignified, McDaniel makes the most of her screen time.

The studio system promoted a kind of paternalism, and working repeatedly with the same people in a creative environment built unique connections. Family feeling was central to the plot of *In This Our Life,* and it extended to the players. Huston cast his father, Walter, in a brief, unbilled role as a bartender deeply annoyed with Davis's Stanley. Davis herself missed several production days because her husband Arthur Farnsworth was ill with pneumonia in a Minneapolis hospital. George Brent, Davis's costar in eleven films, was also her longtime on-and-off lover, and Olivia had worked with and briefly dated Brent, too. Meanwhile, Olivia was engaged in one of her many battles with the pater familias of the studio, Jack Warner, over her contract and even her costumes.[77]

In This Our Life was most important to Olivia's life and career because of her love affair with Huston. They had first met in the mid-1930s, "when we were both assigned to play an episode in a radio broadcast [of Max Reinhardt's *The Miracle* with Miriam Hopkins[78]]. . . . It was quite clear then that he was an unusually brilliant person and a superb actor."[79] They met again while she was filming *The Male Animal,* but his assignment to direct *In This Our Life* brought them into close contact, and Huston "became strongly attracted to de Havilland." He had had an affair with Mary Astor during *The Maltese Falcon,* "but this time it was more serious."[80] One Friday night, Huston told Olivia that "he would like to take me to dinner at Chasen's to talk about my performance. I was in my work clothes: a brown pair of slacks, a brown sweater, and was still wearing my makeup—he said that it didn't matter." Ever cautious and independent, Olivia drove herself to the restaurant, and there were sparks: "We found, to my surprise, a great deal to talk about which had no connection to my performance. We talked about a range of things, all very spontaneously and engrossingly. Our minds were not dissimilar. Neither were our interests, and it was that which, first of all, brought us together, and which nourished a dawning attraction between us."[81]

However, as there had been with her first great romance, Errol Flynn, there was a hitch—her love interest was hitched. Huston and Lesley Black were still living together, although he was unhappy and "he told Olivia they were estranged from one another. Huston asked his wife for a divorce in the spring of 1942, but she soon afterward suffered a nervous breakdown."[82] Olivia knew all about unkept promises from Flynn, and she had just broken up with Jimmy Stewart because the relationship had stalled. But after twenty-five years of good behavior, Olivia was ready to explore her passionate nature. For once, the restrained young woman threw caution to the wind: "'John was a very great love of mine. . . . He's capable of tremendous love of a very intense order. . . . He's very sensitive.'"[83] Huston, in turn, "loved the euphonious sound of her multisyllable names," as well as her energy, her athleticism, her humor, her fire, and her intelligence.[84]

They began a full-on love affair. That certainly wasn't unusual for two people working together on a film project, but this relationship was particularly dynamic. Both fell hard. They were filming on December 7, 1941, when the Japanese attacked Pearl Harbor, and the United States' declaration of war certainly contributed to the vibrancy of their passion. During filming, it became obvious, particularly in the daily rushes, that Olivia "was getting the bulk of Huston's lavish photographic attention, and [Jack] Warner warned him that he'd better 'get back on track.'" It wasn't surprising, given that they were "having a torrid affair. They were openly living together at the time."[85]

What was surprising was Olivia's openness about their situation. Although she was always careful "to protect her chaste screen image," Olivia was affected by what was happening in the world.[86] The country was at war, and so many of the societal strictures about purity seemed specious. As related in the introduction, Olivia wrote to me about biographer Charles Higham's tale that during filming, Bette Davis would visit Olivia's home and read to her from the Bible "while the two of us shared a hot tub," which would have "appalled" both actresses. In her typically sardonic way, she continued, "On the other hand, John Huston did, indeed, cross the threshold of that small vine-covered house, but he certainly did not read the Bible while there."[87]

During wartime, many couples had to deal with separation, and both Olivia and Huston understood duty. He enlisted in the Signal Corps and went overseas to shoot documentaries, while she did her bit for service members at home and abroad. Huston gave Olivia an Airedale dog, Shadrach, to keep her company.[88] A photograph taken years later, after both Olivia and Huston had married other people, shows Olivia with her new husband Marcus Goodrich and her beloved Shadrach.

Olivia's next project—*Princess O'Rourke*—won director and screenwriter Norman Krasna an Oscar for best original screenplay. This film was clearly a prototype for *Roman Holiday,* with Audrey Hepburn (which Krasna refashioned for Olivia in 1956 as *The Ambassador's Daughter*). Olivia portrays a European evacuee—albeit a princess—who finds a safe haven as well as a husband in the United States. A Cinderella-in-reverse tale, with the woman's magical kiss having the power, *Princess O'Rourke* has a happier ending than the more sophisticated Audrey Hepburn vehicle and manages to be romantically comic as well as patriotic.

Jane Wyman and Jack Carson costar, so the ensemble chemistry was already well established. Photographed by the great Ernest Haller, Olivia is very elegant in her Orry-Kelly costumes. She also gets top billing. At twenty-seven, the ingenue has grown up, and this is one of Olivia's best roles at Warner Brothers. The production itself was bumpy, however, and although the film was completed in 1942, distribution was delayed for almost a year. Olivia initially rejected the script and was still dissatisfied with Jack Warner's helming of her career. She was suffering from anxiety and exhaustion as well. Meanwhile, leading man Robert Cummings was shooting another film at another studio and was sometimes absent from the set. None of that tension shows onscreen.

Olivia's maturity and growing confidence are obvious in the opening scene in New York City. A delivery man comes to the apartment of Miss Williams (the pseudonym of Olivia's Princess Maria), and her plainclothes bodyguard enters the elevator and listens to the box—which contains a hat with flowers. In our first view of Olivia, we see her sitting cross-legged while reading, wearing horn-rimmed glasses and a simple skirt and blouse, with her hair down—an appealingly simple people's princess. Olivia's secretary, Miss Haskell, is played by Gladys Cooper, and her uncle is played by Charles Coburn (also her uncle in *In This Our Life*). They insist that she must marry someone suitable soon, but she feistily declines and says, "Then I'll be an old maid." Like millions of others, they are refugees, but they hope to return home one day and restore the princess to her throne, so they believe she should be birthing boys to carry on the royal line. Olivia refuses to be a brood mare for her country, explaining, "I don't ask for any wild and passionate mating. Only for a man with whom I have something in common. I have to spend a lifetime with him. Is that too much to ask?" The sad response she receives—"It might be, Maria"—adds poignancy to the plight of expatriates during wartime.[89] As in *Hold Back the Dawn,* Olivia expresses her liberal political conscience in this film role, even though it is a comic one.

Maria wants to escape the inexorable matchmaking of her uncle, who has come to the conclusion that a healthy young American is just the ticket to restock their country with an heir and several spares. As a respite, she plans to travel incognito, as "Mary Williams," to Ambassador Harrison's ranch by airplane. However, she's afraid of flying (ironic for Olivia), so Miss Haskell gives her a sleeping pill and tells her that if she wakes up, she can ask the stewardess for another. Maria/Mary curls up in her berth, but she's still nervous, so she calls out to the stewardess and gets a second pill. Still not sleepy, she asks the copilot for another pill. By the time the pilot walks by, she's goofy, so she takes the pill he offers and passes out (exactly like Audrey Hepburn's princess).

The plane must return to New York City because of fog, but the princess won't wake up. Fortunately for Maria/Mary, her plane is piloted by the handsome, all-American Eddie O'Rourke, played with affable ingenuousness by Robert Cummings. Cummings found real success a decade later on television, but at this point in his career, he was a competent leading man; he had already made *Saboteur* (1942) with Alfred Hitchcock and would work with him again in *Dial M for Murder* (1954). Eddie's attraction to Princess Maria is believably sweet as he takes her to his apartment to sleep it off. There she meets his copilot, Dave, and Dave's fiancée, Jean—Jack Carson and Jane Wyman.

Maria returns to her hotel after enjoying the pleasures of the lower classes (a typical Warner trope in defense of American values). In a rather daring scene, Olivia takes a bubble bath. Although she had posed in swimsuits quite often during her starlet days, the actress had matured. Today's ingenue might agree to do a nude scene to show the world she's become a woman, and this was the 1940s equivalent for Olivia. She looks pretty with her hair up, and her cleavage is impressive.

Of course, New York City is the perfect place to fall in love, so after spending the day with Eddie, their destiny is realized. He proposes; she demurs: "Thank you for asking me to marry you. I'll remember it the rest of my life."[90] He's insistent, and as they kiss and embrace in the cab, she's compliant and romantic. And unlike the tragic parting of Audrey Hepburn and Gregory Peck, this princess will be allowed to marry her commoner. What follows in the second half of the film is a comedic statement about the difficulties of merging cultures and peoples.

One of the funniest moments in the film is when the princess's uncle gets the results of the background check he's run on the young flier. Not only is he a good, clean American boy who "has all his teeth," but he is one of nine brothers, all living, and his father is one of eleven boys. So it makes sense for Maria to marry this commoner, as the bloodlines are getting thin in Europe—"Everybody's bleeding." And as Maria says, just to make an obvious point to the audience, but a rather feminist one: "You know what this is? A Cinderella story, only the boy is Cinderella. It's just turned about."[91]

Olivia's diction, posture, and poise make her a believable princess. Cummings is appropriately disoriented and earnest when it becomes clear to egalitarian Eddie that he can't be a mere consort to Maria, and he certainly can't waive his US citizenship. After a series of events indicating that the marriage seems to be doomed, the princess has a brainstorm. Maria goes to the White House (as one does), writes a note, and gives it to Franklin Roosevelt's Scottish terrier Fala, who grabs it, growls, and runs off to deliver it to the president. Of course, FDR fixes everything. Harry Davenport (Dr. Meade from *GWTW* and here a Supreme Court justice) shows up at 1600 Pennsylvania Avenue and marries the princess and the pauper. In a great closing line, Eddie suddenly realizes the identity of the man guarding the door and says, "The president? Holy mackerel, I tipped him a buck. And he took it!"[92]

Olivia made the film under duress: "'I wanted to do complex roles, like Melanie for example . . . and Jack Warner saw me as an ingénue. I was really restless to portray more developed human beings. Jack never understood this, and . . . he would give me roles that really had no character or quality in them. I knew I wouldn't even be effective.'"[93] Still, unlike her usual assignments, *Princess O'Rourke* offered Olivia an excellent script, talented costars, and a character who possessed some seriousness along with her prettiness. A genuine delight for Olivia was Whiskers, who portrayed Fala; always an animal lover, Olivia employed her famous dog bark in her scenes with Fala. When I met her new pug puppy, Oscar, in December 2017 and mentioned Olivia's well-known animal impersonations, she immediately sat up in her club chair and barked!

Despite the cachet of Krasna's Oscar for *Princess O'Rourke*, Olivia's next film unceremoniously put her back on the studio treadmill. *Government Girl* (1943) is another wartime comedy, featuring Olivia as a feisty female fighting for the cause. This was an RKO loan-out, so at least she was able to work on a different lot. She began shooting only a week after completing *Princess O'Rourke,* demoted from princess to secretary.[94] Unfortunately, her costar was Sonny Tufts. The poor man was a walking block of earnest awkwardness, and how Olivia ended up making *two* films with this nonactor is inexplicable. *Government Girl* could have been a delight with an adept comedic actor like Joel McCrea or Henry Fonda or James Stewart. Originally, the debonair Joseph Cotten was cast, but he later withdrew from the project (although he and Olivia would work together years later).[95] Paramount loaned Tufts to RKO in return for Maureen O'Hara's services; clearly, Paramount got the better deal.[96] Despite his familial link to the founder of Tufts University, his operatic background, and his Yale education, Tufts was a B-level leading man who was far below Olivia's status and ability. In fact, in the notorious book *The Golden Turkey Awards* by Harry and Michael Medved, Tufts's role in *Government Girl* was recognized as worst performance by an actor.[97]

This loan-out was flattering to Olivia at first. Screenwriter Dudley Nichols had requested her for his first outing as producer and director. Nichols, who had proved himself as a writer with such classics as *Bringing Up Baby* and *Stagecoach,* was less successful in this film, based on a story by journalist Adela Rogers St. John. *Government Girl* should have been breezy, but instead, it has been described as "an uneasy cross between *The More the Merrier* and *Mr. Smith Goes to Washington.*"[98]

Set in bustling, wartime Washington, DC, the film offers a long prologue involving the difficulties of getting a hotel room. Tufts, as new government employee Ed Browne, appropriates the suite that Olivia, as secretary Smokey Allard (a great nickname for an edgy girl, if the script had given her any real character), has reserved for the wedding night of her friend Mary (Anne Shirley) and Mary's soldier fiancé Joe (James Dunn)—Mary and Joseph, the future of the free world. Their inability to find a place to consummate the nuptials provides a rather embarrassing subplot.

In true screwball romance style, Olivia and Tufts dislike each other on sight, and when she learns that she is to be his secretary, she is outraged in a spritely way. However, their difficult relationship slowly unthaws as she comes to respect his efforts to increase the production of bomber airplanes by getting around the bureaucracy of a manic, war-focused Washington. There are some fine moments for Olivia, including a madcap ride on a motorcycle behind the hapless Tufts, and she has real chemistry with gal-pal Shirley. She also has a second love interest—Jess Barker as a Washington player who thinks she's swell—and their thwarted romance seems more believable than her attraction to Tufts. Her intelligence and efficiency in the office scenes make her position as the assistant to an important man completely believable.

Tufts, whose character does things his own way and with a huge helping of American ingenuity, is accused of stealing a large shipment of steel destined for Delaware that ended up in Wisconsin instead, to build a fleet of bombers. When he is grilled by a Senate committee (led by Harry Davenport), Olivia offers a very strong speech in defense of her boss—a star moment in a better film. In a lengthy monologue, Olivia's Smokey admits that he "made mistakes" and that "he gets things done in a funny way, but he gets them done. The way George Washington did." Then, as the planes fly overhead, she challenges, "Look at the results—please. Will you? Look? And listen, will you please?" Olivia gets a flattering close-up. "Listen! Who built those bombers?" She has made her point. Davenport says, "Thank you, Miss Government Girl . . . you've been very eloquent."[99] She gets applause as she leaves the hearing room.

At the film's end, Smokey is sure she's lost her job, but her friend Branch (Paul Stewart), a savvy journalist, tells her, "You're a government girl! Why, it's your life!" Unbeknownst to the weeping woman, Branch leaves the room and Browne comes in. Her speech has helped save him; they've called off the investigation. She turns to him with tears running down her face and joyfully exclaims, "Oh, Mr. Browne!" He warns her that if she ever calls him that again, "I'm gonna grab you and—and . . . I'm gonna kiss you!"[100] As the film closes, Olivia kisses Tufts in a two-shot and does a rather fey twirl with her hand—which apparently means it's a good smooch.

As always, Olivia gives the film her all, although this kind of over-the-top, dizzy comedy isn't really her forte. She has enormous energy and looks very pretty with her upswept hair, stockinged feet (Smokey frequently takes off her shoes, apparently in some sort of bohemian gesture), and bright eyes, reflecting the spirit of working women during World War II. This may be why, when she weeps foolishly and tells Shirley that she actually likes Tufts, it doesn't ring true; Olivia's Smokey is fiercer than that. Still, *Government Girl* was a box office success, showing that Olivia could open a film, and she was prominently featured on the advertising posters.

At age twenty-seven, Olivia's status in Hollywood was secure if static. She was counting the days until her contract was up, but in the meantime, she was trying to be accommodating to the studio, which included participating in a musical revue. Given that the war had finally come to the United States, Warner Brothers released an entertaining diversion for the public and the troops, enlisting all its contract players: *Thank Your Lucky Stars* (1943). The same year, United Artists distributed *Stage Door Canteen,* about Broadway performers doing their part. Warners followed up in 1944 with *Hollywood Canteen,* about the Hollywood USO club opened by Bette Davis and others.

Thank Your Lucky Stars is a revue hung on a rather loose plot featuring Dennis Morgan and Joan Leslie as a singer and a songwriter who are trying to break into show business and manage to fall in love during a gala performance. With songs by Arthur Schwartz and Frank Loesser, the film is a lively tribute to America at war. It is most memorable for Bette Davis singing "They're either too young or too old." Bette's a bit flat, but she looks great wearing a long sequined dinner suit and waving a hankie.

Olivia appears as part of a goofy trio with Ida Lupino and George Tobias (who went on to play Abner Kravitz on TV's *Bewitched*), performing "The Dreamer." Their sequence is introduced by Edward Everett Horton: "Ladies and gentlemen, leaving the field of lighter entertainment for just a few moments, we now present a more serious interlude. It is with genuine pride we bring you three of the screen's foremost dramatic stars. Miss Olivia de Havilland, Miss Ida Lupino, and Mr. George Tobias." The audience applauds, and then the curtain opens. The number begins with the trio's backs to the camera, shaking it like there's no tomorrow. Olivia and Lupino are clad alike in large gingham-print, circle-skirt pinafores, dreadfully puffed short sleeves, and huge hair ribbons. The two bobby-soxers plus the zoot-suiter Tobias perform to a brassy big-band number, and Olivia gives it the old college try. This is particularly impressive, given the opening lyrics (according to the subtitles): "Tye ah ta ree tau, Tye ah ta ree tau, Tye ah ta ree tau / Tye frutilli eye tye tye."[101] It's a silly song and a wide-stanced dance, but Olivia is genuinely funny and throws dignity to the wind, winking, chewing gum, and even being yanked back onstage after leaving at one point. Once, she pulls her arm back and knuckles Ida. They all do forward neck bobs, and Olivia snaps her fingers, gets a comically determined look, squints with one eye closed, and swirls in a circle in one part of the dance when Ida doesn't, stealing the scene. Olivia was dubbed by Lynn Martin, and she had some trouble lip-synching with the playback.[102] However, only once does she forget to lip-synch, and she sparkles in all her dance moves. When the curtain closes, she looks like she's about to fall over with exhaustion.

Thank Your Lucky Stars was filmed while Olivia was completing her final role for Warner Brothers, and not a moment too soon. After getting top billing in her two previous films, the demotion to third place in *Devotion* signaled to the actress that her time at the studio had truly reached an end. Filming for *Devotion* was completed in February 1943, when Olivia's contract was due to end. However, it was not released until 1946, not only because it wasn't particularly strong but also because the delay kept the actress offscreen during her battle with Jack Warner.

Devotion is a highly romanticized story of the Brontës. It had been planned for years, and "the studio believed [it] would be in the same league with their successful biographies about Emile Zola, [and] Louis Pasteur."[103] But by the time production began in November 1942, Bette Davis and Miriam Hopkins were out as the stars, and Ida Lupino and Olivia were in, with Lupino given the lead as the sensitive and dreamy Emily over Olivia's pushy, unsympathetic Charlotte. Arthur Kennedy plays the doomed, drunken Branwell; contract player Nancy Coleman is a pallid Anne; and Paul Henreid appears as Arthur Nichols, the curate who eventually marries Charlotte. In this version, Emily and Charlotte are fighting for Arthur's affections, a radical departure from the truth.

Olivia was given what should have been the plum role of *Jane Eyre*'s author, but she disliked the screenplay by Theodore Reeves, Keith Winter, and Edward Chodorov, as well as the supporting nature of the role (she got third billing behind Lupino and Henreid). The trailer for the film declared, "They called them free souls!" and that irony could not have been lost on the unhappy actress.[104] Adding insult to injury, her sister, Joan Fontaine, was about to portray the eponymous heroine of *Jane Eyre* in a prestigious production with Orson Welles.

This version of the Brontës makes Charlotte a bully, an "unscrupulous ruler of the Bronte ambitions," despite her sisters' retiring nature.[105] Although she wrote in a recent email, "I do not remember that any of the characters in this film were dark or enigmatic," her Charlotte was certainly on the dark side, given her unsympathetic badgering of her siblings.[106] Olivia was extremely contentious during the making of the film, and costar Henreid mentioned her behavior in his autobiography: "Stars are not vulnerable women," he wrote. "To get to the top you must have an aggressive nature. But of all the women I worked with, Ida Lupino seemed the most vulnerable. She was a soft person with a great sense of sweetness about her, but anything that might have developed between us was destroyed by Olivia's machinations."[107]

The director, Curtis Bernhardt, was also frustrated by the actress's attitude on the set. Jeremy Arnold notes, "Bernhardt found Olivia de Havilland (Charlotte Brontë) much more difficult to work with, describing how she fought him on the simplest staging instructions. "'Lupino,' he said, 'was more accessible artistically than de Havilland during the making of the film. De Havilland became really obnoxious.'"[108] In defense of Olivia, despite her two Oscar nominations, eight box office successes with Errol Flynn, and top billing in her last two films, Ida Lupino was considered the greater star and the better dramatic actress at Warner Brothers. Additionally, the script turned *Devotion* into a weak women's picture that "purported to show how the sisters had become involved in an unhappy romantic triangle with the Reverend Arthur Nichols (Paul Henreid, badly miscast)."[109] Olivia's ongoing love affair with John Huston may have contributed to her frustrations; the maverick director was still married, and getting him to make a commitment was proving difficult. All this contributed to the creation of a disagreeable actress who was about to sue her employer, whom she privately referred to as "'Jack the Warden.'"[110]

By this time, Olivia was known for becoming ill whenever she was frustrated. During the wardrobe and makeup tests for *Devotion,* she was "afflicted with an odd sickness in her legs, which broke out in large swellings that made it almost impossible for her to walk."[111] It is difficult to ignore the metaphor of being unable to walk away from the studio and the film.

To Jack Warner's credit, he revised the script to give Olivia the closing shot with Henreid after the death of Lupino's character: "He wanted to have de Havilland end up with Henreid at the film's climax because winning the leading man's heart would help build de Havilland's stardom, and her future box office power."[112] However, Lupino had been told that *she* would have the closing shot, and when she learned the truth, she cried to her costar Henreid, who pronounced, "'Olivia is a troublemaker.'"[113] It is ironic that in a scene with Olivia, Henreid intones with complete sincerity, "There are two ways of dealing with young ladies of your perverse temperament, Miss Brontë. It is fortunate for you that I am not a woman beater!"[114] The kiss that follows is not only unromantic; it looks as if the actor wants to shatter Olivia's mouth with his teeth.

Olivia may not have had top billing, and the role of Charlotte may have been written—and acted—bitchily, but the actress is believable. Although the film is disparaged by most scholars because of its Hollywood view of the Brontë family, Olivia's Charlotte evolves from harpy to heroine. Abandoning her usual persona of rational bemusement, she is strident, needy, bossy, and deliciously unpleasant.

By 1943, Olivia's soft prettiness is settling into more interesting angles and planes. The ringlets she wears, thanks to Perc Westmore, do not mirror the simple, smooth style worn by the real Charlotte in portraits we have of her, but they frame the actress's face becomingly. Her flowing, hoop-skirted costumes, designed by Milo Anderson, flatter her figure. Vocally, Olivia explores a lower register in the romantic scenes with Henreid, further contributing to Charlotte's dark edge. The great Ernie Haller photographs Olivia flatteringly, so if she must be cast as a perverse Becky Sharp–type heroine, she certainly commands her scenes. In fact, one of her best moments features the fabled meeting between Charlotte and William Makepeace Thackeray, the author of *Vanity Fair.* As portrayed by Sydney Greenstreet, Warner's contract star and fabled "Fat Man" from *The Maltese Falcon,* Thackeray is like Father Christmas. He shows great appreciation for the young writer, and their exchange is spirited and lively, with both enjoying their witty repartee.

The reason for Charlotte's unpleasantness is never clearly articulated in the script. She seems flighty: one minute she wants to publish, and the next she wants to pursue the legendary M. Heger, the Brussels school principal who oversaw the real Charlotte and Emily's training as governesses. Charlotte's motivations aren't clearly developed, yet Olivia makes something of her. Charlotte's desires are built on a need to see the world, just as Emily's are built on a need to enclose herself in her own world. Charlotte feels the weight of her siblings' fortunes on her shoulders, particularly given Branwell's tragic failures. There is a fierceness in Olivia's portrait of Charlotte, and the actress's steel backbone shows through in the character she plays.

The film was not particularly well received. However, those reviews would not appear until three years after *Devotion* was filmed, due to the delay in the film's release. Bosley Crowther wrote in the *New York Times*, "Olivia de Havilland plays Charlotte with a vast deal of pretty arrogance," but to accept that the film presents the real "story of the Brontës . . . is a ridiculous tax upon reason and an insult to plain intelligence."[115] Today, we can appreciate the film as a romanticized and occasionally intriguing view of a mythic family, told through the black-and-white lens of 1940s studio filmmaking and featuring some of Warner Brothers' finest contract players.

Olivia was ready to leave Warner Brothers in May 1943 and take her career in a new direction. She had been with the studio since 1935, and despite her frustrations, she had learned her craft there and readily acknowledged the training she received. She remembered, "There was marvelous discipline about it. It was splendid training. Everything was so concentrated and condensed that careers were built throughout that system. . . . It [Warner Brothers] was a hard-working lot and it was technically beautiful . . . it was *so* efficient."[116] Olivia was respected in Hollywood as a hard worker, and she had an international profile. She owned her own home and had had relationships with some of the brightest talents in Hollywood. The world was hers.

And then Olivia learned that the head of Warner Brothers was refusing to release her from her contract on its designated end date. She had been on suspension five times during that seven-year period, either for illness or for her refusal to accept certain projects. It was standard procedure for studios to tack on that time to a performer's contract, making actors a highly paid species of indentured servant.[117] Olivia remembered, "This was the sword of Damocles . . . the great black Dragon that rested over all of us."[118] She was informed that she still owed the studio twenty-five weeks of work because of those suspensions. This was after she had agreed to make the frenetic *Government Girl*, believing "it would use up the time accumulated during her suspensions."[119]

Then, in August 1943, Jack Warner "wanted me to go to Columbia . . . for a film that had only 20 pages of script. He said, 'Oh, we'll write it on the set.' Well, I had heard that story before so I thought there's nothing I can do, I'll have to take another suspension. I didn't see my contract ever ending with Jack Warner."[120] "Olivia took a voluntary suspension [her sixth] and left the picture on August 13, 1943—an action hardly appreciated at Warners and certainly not tolerated. It was now clear that completing the extended contract would be difficult and that her unhappy involvement with Warners was likely to stretch into additional months or years."[121] Angry, frustrated, and physically and emotionally exhausted, and "at the risk of committing career suicide," Olivia took action.[122] Calling on her reserves of courage and intelligence, as well as the discretion she'd learned in the Hollywood fishbowl, she took her agent's suggestion and consulted a lawyer, Martin Gang, a respected professional with many clients in the film industry.[123] He informed Olivia that California had an anti-peonage law on the books that limited the length of time an employer could enforce a contract against an employee to seven years. In Gang's opinion, that meant seven calendar years, with no provision for additional time due to suspensions. On November 4, 1943, Olivia de Havilland took Jack Warner to court, and her lawyer "asked . . . for declaratory relief."[124]

Others had taken on Jack Warner in the past. James Cagney continually went on suspension, and when his contract with Warner Brothers ran out, he became one of the first Hollywood stars to secure roles as a free agent, negotiating for each film rather than signing with a major studio. Unwilling to wait out her seven years, Bette Davis had gone to court over this issue in 1936, after receiving a number of Academy Award write-in votes for 1934's *Of Human Bondage* and winning an Oscar in 1935 for *Dangerous*. Davis shared Olivia's frustration at being cast as a type rather than recognized as an artist, and she too chose to go on suspension rather than appear in weak films. Davis, who tried her case in the London courts in the hope of obtaining a fairer hearing, had failed. But fortunately for her, Jack Warner recognized her value to the studio. After Davis's attempt at rebellion, she was given better roles and began a ten-year run as the queen of the studio, winning a second Oscar for *Jezebel* in 1938.

Olivia's dissatisfaction didn't result in the same kind of palliative projects. Instead, the studio styled her as the sweet heroine of the Errol Flynn epics. Molly Haskell described her as one of a group of actresses who were "the sunny side of a decade."[125] She was a star "whose delicacy and daintiness were enormously winning."[126] Olivia was a lady—a lady who hauled Jack Warner's butt into court.

Olivia and Gang took her case to the California Superior Court, and it was a risky move. Troublesome actresses had come and gone in Hollywood. Olivia was challenging the studio system itself, which developed its product, distributed it, and exhibited it in studio-owned theaters (antitrust laws would put an end to this practice in 1948). There was also the financial element. Hollywood was a small town, and given her support of the Screen Actors Guild, Olivia could not hope to find work even at an independent studio. The lawsuit would cost her $13,000 (almost $200,000 today), and there would be no studio income during the trial. The risk was worth it, however. After a brief hearing, the court decided in Olivia's favor, ruling that "contracts in the State of California could not exceed seven *calendar* years."[127] The result? Warner Brothers immediately filed an appeal, "prepar[ing] a case that attempted to move the court's attention away from a simple interpretation of the law to an accusation against an uncooperative actress."[128]

The appeal was not heard until September 10, 1944. What was particularly galling was that Warner Brothers sent a letter to seventy-seven studios and production companies, effectively blacklisting Olivia and preventing her from appearing in vehicles at other studios.[129] Jack Warner also delayed the release of *Devotion,* determined to keep Olivia's face off the screen. However, the resourceful Olivia did several productions for *Lux Radio Theatre,* as Warner's injunction didn't include radio.[130] She also did her bit for the war effort and appeared regularly at the Hollywood Canteen. "I felt comfortable serving coffee and went to the Canteen often to fulfill this task," she recalled. Also, "in the winter of 1943, the U.S.O. asked me if I would make a tour of middle-western military hospitals during the Christmas season. I said yes. . . . I visited military hospitals in the continental U.S.A., Alaska, and the Aleutians, and otherwise spent my time constructively."[131] "After a jungle showing of the picture 'Princess O'Roarke [*sic*],'" a company of troops in New Guinea dedicated the front page of the base newspaper, *The Cockatoo,* to her, printing a fan letter in which they proclaimed, "'Olivia, to us, you are the American woman. You are our girl, whether you like it or not.'"[132] Olivia traveled to Fiji as well, where she was hospitalized for six weeks with pneumonia.[133] She also participated in a war bond rally at Madison Square Garden in New York City.[134]

During her travels, Olivia never quite crossed paths with John Huston. He had shot *Report from the Aleutians,* a documentary about the offensive there narrated by his father, but he flew to Italy just before she arrived. As Olivia remembered, "John Huston was overseas. However, on the very day I left Washington State for Alaska, and unknown to me, John returned to the U.S.A. Following my return home from my Alaskan assignment, John's orders eventually brought him to the Los Angeles area."[135] Those missed opportunities seemed to be a cosmic sign of the peripatetic nature of their affair.

Olivia's passion for Huston was still blazing, however, and when he returned to Hollywood, he was "in pursuit of Olivia and a quick divorce."[136] Olivia adored Huston and even went to the press in May 1944, "telling Louella Parsons she was in love with John and that they would marry as soon as he was free."[137] They lived together on and off for more than two years, despite their various travels during the war, and it was because of their affair that his marriage to Lesley Black ended.[138] Olivia hadn't been willing to risk public ire with Errol Flynn over Lili Damita, but she risked it all for John Huston. This certainly wasn't in keeping with the virginal persona the studio had crafted for her, and Huston wouldn't have been interested if she were really that chaste, although he loved a challenge and relished the chase. He was a brilliant man capable of great tenderness, and Olivia responded in kind, even taking care of Huston's grandmother, Adelia, while he was in Italy.

Huston engaged in a fabled fistfight with Flynn in 1944 at David O. Selznick's house, in defense of Olivia's honor. It has been recounted in various Hollywood histories, but in his notes for his autobiography, Huston recalled the big night in delightful, true raconteur detail:

> Errol must have been spoiling for trouble . . . for he very quickly got around to saying something wretched about Olivia de Havilland. It was common knowledge that Olivia and I were quite close friends. I was furious at his remark, and I said, "That's a lie! Even if it weren't a lie, only a sonofabitch would repeat it." Errol asked if I'd like to make anything out of it, and I decided that I did. . . . We reached a place secluded enough to preclude interruptions, took off our coats, and went at it. . . . I don't think my head was all that clear when we first started, but it cleared up after a few punches, and then I began to get my licks in. . . . And those were the days when "motherfucker" was not a term of endearment. . . . Errol went on to a hospital that evening, and I . . . checked into a different hospital the next morning, where I received a call from Errol wanting to know how I was. . . . I said that I had thoroughly enjoyed the fight and suggested we do it again sometime.[139]

It was just like a movie. Who could resist one's two great loves battling it out?

Olivia and Huston were a great match, theoretically. However, her ardor was more intense than his. Although there was no doubt he loved her, "she was more passionate than he was and understood his emotional makeup. . . . Olivia's intense nature inevitably came into conflict with John's moody defensiveness."[140] Whether caused by Huston's difficult relationship with his mother, his overt masculinity, or the culture of manly stoicism prevalent at the time, he sometimes felt overwhelmed by her desire for him and seemed driven to sabotage their romance. Subsequently, "things John did to undermine his relationship with Olivia were often very public. He sent for Doris Lilly [an attractive newspaper columnist] and took her to parties at [film producer] Sam Spiegel's."[141] Olivia, unrealistically, wanted fidelity from Huston; he, jealously, expected fidelity from her but couldn't reciprocate. Still, Olivia was a great sport and a cool girl, and even after she discovered he had been unfaithful, they tried to make things work.

It has been suggested that, partly in revenge for Huston's cavalier attitude about monogamy, Olivia had a romance with another man who loved airplanes and the freedom of the skies. Major Joseph McKeon of the Army Air Corps was a fighter pilot stationed in California when Olivia met him in 1944. Olivia recalled in 2013, "The U.S.O. organized a small dancing party at the Beverly Wilshire Hotel for a few officers and a sprinkling of stars. One of the former was an Air Force officer . . . Joseph McKeon, who later named his plane Olivia, and with the aid of the Red Cross sent letters to me. He flew on missions over Germany, was shot down at 40,000 ft., broke his ankle on landing, was captured by German farmers, and placed in a prison camp for American captives. . . . He became a candidate for care packages which I regularly sent him."[142] Olivia and the tall, handsome McKeon were constant companions; he was tremendously fond of the actress, and the fan magazines predicted marriage.[143] Although their romance was interrupted when he was called to active duty, she saw him after he returned to California, "scarred and limping, following [his] midair collision over Germany and a stint in a Nazi prison camp."[144] However, Olivia ended the relationship in 1945; perhaps the love wasn't strong enough, or perhaps she needed to make her career a priority, or perhaps McKeon just wasn't John Huston.

By the time Huston secured a divorce in Las Vegas in April 1945, he and Olivia had grown apart. He had had other relationships, and she had been with McKeon. Although they still loved each other, Olivia could see that, in some ways, she had fallen in love with another Errol Flynn. Huston married Evelyn Keyes (who had played Scarlett O'Hara's younger sister) in 1946 but still pursued Olivia. Huston and Olivia's relationship heated up again in 1952, but that too ended. In 1964, Olivia wrote to Huston on behalf of Robert Fiz, an assistant director on *Light in the Piazza* (1962), who wanted to work on *The Bible.* She told Huston she'd gone to see *Freud,* which he had narrated, and it stunned her: "It was an extraordinary experience . . . with the first word I knew it was you speaking. It brought back, with a rush, the year of 1942 and the Aleutians, and the film you made there, that beautiful film . . . and your voice on the soundtrack for that picture, and, well, many things. I hope all goes well with you—I always have, I always will."[145]

In the background of war and romance, Olivia's court case was looming. The appeal required "lengthy testimony on Olivia's part. . . . She answered time and again during the long hours of the cross-examination that the parts offered were not suited to her and that in her best judgment . . . participation in the films she rejected would have hurt not only her career, but also the film and the studio."[146] It was a difficult time for Olivia, personally and professionally. She lost weight, and the press was sometimes unkind. However, on September 10, 1944, "the three judges of the Appellate Court voted for her unanimously, and on February 3, 1945," after Warner tried one last move, "the Supreme Court of California ruled that there was no reason to review her case."[147] The state supreme court, "in refusing to review, tacitly upheld the decision of Superior Judge Charles S. Burnell, later affirmed by the District Court of Appeals, that such additions, or extensions, are forbidden by the State Labor Code, which sets a seven-year calendar limit on employment contracts."[148] Olivia was finally free.

This ruling, known as the "de Havilland decision," contributed to the end of the contract system and the rise of the actor-agent relationship, and it remains an important precedent in entertainment law. "California's seven-year rule, also known as Labor Code Section 2855, is such an accepted tenet of entertainment law that it's hard to imagine the business before it existed. . . . Today, film and television lawyers say the seven-year rule is such a given in negotiations that serious disputes rarely arise. Still, the law remains a sharp arrow in the quiver of disgruntled talent, especially in the music industry, where such artists as Courtney Love and Smashing Pumpkins have cited the rule in challenging open-ended deals that require delivery of several albums."[149]

The ladylike Olivia had conquered the only mountain the tough Bette Davis, nicknamed the fifth Warner brother, couldn't climb.[150] Davis paid homage to Olivia's triumph in the foreword to Tony Thomas's *The Films of Olivia de Havilland*. She wrote of her friend: "Olivia should be thanked by every actor today. She won the court battle that no contract should ever have to continue more than seven years. Years ago, our contracts could have been indefinite. A sort of potential contract for life."[151] David Niven, whose career was subject to the whims of Sam Goldwyn, also saluted Olivia in *The Moon's a Balloon:* "Players were sometimes trapped for twelve or fifteen years working off a seven-year contract. . . . Olivia de Havilland fought this and . . . won, and thereafter, if someone refused to work, he didn't get paid, but it became illegal for the length of his contract to be altered without his consent. Olivia struck a great blow for freedom and everyone in the industry should bless her."[152]

Olivia was triumphant. She was free of Jack Warner. She was the mistress of her own destiny and her own career. The war was winding down, and peace—at least temporarily—was on the way for the world. But in 1945, Olivia was on the verge of her twenty-ninth birthday, she was single again, and she had not been onscreen for two years. Ever resilient, what Olivia did next was remarkable, inspiring, and life-changing—almost like a movie.

7

THREE GOLDEN YEARS

By February 1945, Olivia's battle with "'Jack the warden,' as she referred to her boss," was over.[1] She had risked everything for artistic freedom, and she had been released from her contract with Warner Brothers. As her good friend Robert Osborne noted, "She was really flirting with career suicide doing that, because if she'd lost the case she probably wouldn't have worked in Hollywood again. But it is in the law books today, the 'de Havilland decision.' And as Bette Davis always said, every actor in the business owes a great debt of gratitude for Olivia de Havilland for doing that."[2] Hollywood journalist Bob Thomas added, "Olivia remains a patron saint of the Screen Actors Guild because she had the guts to challenge Jack Warner and win."[3]

Olivia was in a unique position for any actor, but particularly for a young woman in the mid-1940s. She had Hollywood's respect and the freedom to direct her career on her own terms. She was intelligent and resolved, and although she had been offscreen for two years, she had been working steadily on *Lux Radio Theatre* and traveling with the USO in the United States, Alaska, and the South Pacific. She observed, "It was a way I could serve my country and contribute to the war effort. . . . These were endeavors which I might not have been able to engage in had I not been on suspension.'"[4] Thus, Olivia's public and professional profile was still viable. The real challenge professionally—and it was enormous—was to make the most of this hard-won freedom and land roles that would demonstrate her talent.

Olivia was an anomaly in many ways. She had two Oscar nominations and a highly successful run of films with Errol Flynn that were great fun but presented no particular acting challenge. She had shown her versatility over many genres and periods in more than twenty films. She had taken on Jack Warner and the studio and won. She was now a freelancer like Cary Grant and James Cagney, managing her own career without the safety net of a studio contract, prefiguring contemporary contract negotiations. Also, she had never been married, and at the time, a twenty-nine-year-old single female was a rarity. Osborne commented, "In the '40s she was known as the Bachelor Girl of Hollywood. Men like Jimmy Stewart, Burgess Meredith and John Huston were all in love with her, and who could blame them. She was—and is still—very attractive, very feminine."[5] Olivia was poised to assert herself as an authentic Hollywood heroine.

It would have been wonderful if Olivia had walked right into a hugely successful film and immediately won an Oscar. There was a precedent for that kind of luck. Like Olivia, Joan Crawford was being given inferior scripts by her studio boss, Louis B. Mayer, and after eighteen years at MGM, it was clear that she was considered old news. Her contemporaries Greta Garbo and Norma Shearer had retired at the advanced ages of thirty-six and forty-two, respectively. (Hollywood's misogynistic view of women over forty has been ingrained for decades.) Joan knew she was being marginalized with weak scripts and costars. Bravely, she bought out her contract rather than accept the B-level projects she was being given. Ironically, Jack Warner offered her a deal, in part to threaten a recalcitrant Bette Davis, one of the many reasons for the bad blood between the two actresses. Joan waited two years until the right script came along—*Mildred Pierce* (1945)—and it won her a best actress Oscar.

Alas, Olivia's first film after her two-year hiatus wasn't that kind of project. Paramount offered her *The Well-Groomed Bride*—an absurd title and odd adjectival choice, as every bride is well groomed—when Paulette Goddard withdrew due to pregnancy. Even though the Supreme Court of California hadn't yet made its decision on her legal status relative to Warner Brothers, Paramount clearly had faith in her potential and her box office appeal. Her agent, Bert Allenberg, "convinced her that if Paramount was willing to risk a lawsuit . . . it would be a good chance to establish a precedent so other studios would thereafter hire her."[6] In a case of bad timing, on the first day of filming in early February 1945, Olivia's lawyer Martin Gang informed her that the court had rejected Warner's appeal two days earlier.[7] If she had known that, she never would have agreed to do the film, and in fact, she "sued the agent who brought it to her."[8] Clearly, Olivia wasn't intimidated by the courts. She still isn't.

Paramount believed in Olivia and had, in fact, given her a three-picture deal. Paramount also gave Olivia an excellent collaborative partner in Edith Head. The renowned costume designer had created Olivia's wardrobe for *Hold Back the Dawn* (for which she received her first best actress nomination), and Head would go on to design the costumes for *To Each His Own* and

The Heiress (Olivia's two Oscar wins for best actress). In 1945, Head was in negotiations with *Look* magazine to prepare a book of "fashion advice for the modern woman" titled *What Are You Going to Wear?*[9] Olivia was supposed to be featured in the book, and Head's archival papers include several photographs of Olivia (taken by *Look* photographer Dorothy Taylor) wearing various Head creations, with penciled edits drawn on them. She wears picture hats, day dresses, shantung silk suits, and a particularly stunning "flower-trimmed black organza dance frock." Head's text states, Olivia "represents the romantic type" in a dinner gown of "black crepe and flower trimmed organza [which] emphasize[s] her femininity."[10] Unfortunately, the project was never realized.

The Well-Groomed Bride, set in San Francisco, proved to be a tepid romantic comedy. It was directed rather unimaginatively by Sidney Lanfield, who at least had the delightful *You'll Never Get Rich* (1941) and *My Favorite Blonde* (1942) to his credit. Olivia got top billing, and her costar was Ray Milland, who had just won an Oscar for *The Lost Weekend* (in which Olivia's mother, Lilian, had a small role). The stolid Sonny Tufts, her romantic lead in *Government Girl,* was a supporting player this time. The film is strained and predictable, another military romantic comedy in which Olivia is pretty and spirited but not much more.[11]

The plot, rather flimsy at best, revolves around a magnum of champagne—perhaps an attempt to put the fizz back into filmmaking as the war was coming to an end. Milland plays navy lieutenant Dudley Briggs, who is promised a promotion by Captain Hornby (the always droll James Gleason) if he can locate a magnum of champagne by the next day in order to christen the battleship USS *Vengeance*—a metaphorical message to the United States' enemies. But the only magnum he can find has been purchased by a beautiful, lively, independent woman named Margie—Olivia, of course. She is engaged to army lieutenant and former Oregon football star Torchy McNeil (the earnest, wooden Tufts). Even though she hasn't seen him in two years, she is foolishly planning to marry him immediately. After trying to steal the magnum and following Margie to her nuptials, Dudley arranges for Torchy to meet his ex-girlfriend Rita (Constance Dowling). Margie catches them in a clinch, and she runs off with Dudley, who tells her that he has fallen in love with her. But she's wary—does he really love her, or does he just want the champagne? It's much ado about nothing, and happily, all's well that ends well.[12] It's not Shakespeare, but at least Olivia was back to work, and at a studio that had her back.

This film, released in February 1946, wasn't going to propel her back to her prior status with the public or the studios. Meanwhile, now that the war was over, Joseph Stalin and the socioeconomic theories of communism and socialism became the next threats to American democracy, and the red scare infiltrated Hollywood. When I asked Olivia whether she had any fears of blacklisting, she responded coolly, "Having no reason whatsoever to be worried, I wasn't."[13] Olivia was, in fact, a Roosevelt Democrat, and she took that privilege of being a US citizen seriously, as evidenced by her USO tours. Inspired by her patriotism and her commitment to her craft, Olivia joined the Hollywood Independent Citizens Committee of the Arts, Sciences and Professions (HICCASP). Its "Statement of Policy" delineated its interests in a powerful opening paragraph: "The Hollywood Independent Citizens Committee of the Arts, Sciences and Professions is a non-partisan organization devoted to an action program to ensure, implement and extend the ideals of Franklin Delano Roosevelt and to help make the four freedoms—freedom of speech, freedom of worship, freedom from want, and freedom from fear—a living reality for all people."[14] There were more than 3,000 members in the Hollywood chapter, and Olivia was in good company: the letterhead included the names of Lena Horne, Linus Pauling, Dore Schary, Artie Shaw, and Vice Chairman Frank Sinatra. Olivia was happy to participate and thought, "'I'll join and try to be a good citizen.'"[15]

Olivia's problems began in June 1946, when she was asked to attend a Seattle rally and deliver a speech written for her by renowned screenwriter Dalton Trumbo, a member of the Communist Party. Trumbo's speech was supportive of the Soviet Union and highly critical of the Truman administration. Olivia rewrote the speech and "underlined the significant differences between those she termed genuine liberals and Hollywood Communists."[16] Trumbo was furious, and the discord began. Olivia wanted to resign from HICCASP, but "producer Dore Schary, another FDR loyalist, persuaded her to stay by arguing that her departure would be an embarrassment for Democrats and detrimental in the coming midterm elections."[17] Olivia reluctantly agreed but began to hold secret meetings in her home with a small group of members who were anticommunist liberals, including then-Democrat Ronald Reagan. They wrote a revised declaration that affirmed their position and tried to get HICCASP to accept it, but Olivia recalled that the meetings were so "'heated and contentious that I thought, "This is it." I had fought long enough, and as hard as I could, and I resigned.'"[18] Eventually, the group "deteriorated to a membership largely made up of hardcore Communists."[19]

Olivia had demonstrated her commitment to mainstream liberal Democratic ethics, and in May 1947, she agreed to headline "the galaxy of stars to participate actively in the *Examiner*-sponsored I Am an American Day observance in Hollywood Bowl."[20] She managed to escape investigation and blacklisting, despite being mentioned in the right-wing publication *Moscow over Hollywood* by Myron C. Fagan, appearing on a list of a hundred names that "by no means contained *all* the Reds and their palsy-walsies."[21] Writer and producer Art Arthur sent a letter to Arch Reeve of the Association of Motion Picture Producers in August 1949, and he included a photocopy from Fagan's book that listed Olivia as one of the Hollywood stars who had supposedly sent a cable to Stalin on November 16, 1944, offering their support. At the time, Olivia was in Fiji recovering from pneumonia. Arthur noted that this obvious falsehood "serve[d] to illustrate the dangers inherent in careless and irresponsible smear attacks."[22]

The matter reared its ugly head one last time on June 16, 1958, when Olivia gave secret testimony about HICCASP to a closed session of the House Un-American Activities Committee. When the testimony was made public in September, the *Los Angeles Examiner* printed the transcript in full. It revealed how the actress had been "duped into joining a Communist-front group . . . then resigned and set out to 'destroy' it when she learned it was dominated by communists."[23] The *Examiner* stood solidly behind Olivia, noting that "she dearly prized her American citizenship."[24] Olivia proved to be as fierce in this battle as she was in her fight with Jack Warner.

As a kind of karmic reward, Olivia's long-awaited break finally materialized. At last she found her star vehicle: *To Each His Own*. The role had been offered to Ginger Rogers, who turned it down and later commented, "'It seemed Olivia knew a good thing when she saw it. Perhaps Olivia should thank me for such poor judgment.'"[25] Olivia did indeed know a good thing. She was delighted to have such a challenging role and said, "'The script by Charley Brackett [and Jacques Théry] was one of the most perfect I'd ever read. The dialogue was tight . . . and the character of Jody Norris romantic and sentimental. I'm that way myself, and I felt I could play the part as I had played no other.'"[26] She also adored working with Mitchell Leisen again (he had guided her to her Oscar nomination for *Hold Back the Dawn*). After years of action films with directors like Michael Curtiz and Raoul Walsh, she was thrilled by Leisen's artistry. She acknowledged, "It was always Mitch. Whenever I needed help, he knew what to tell me. Then I could see it, then I could do it. *To Each His Own* could not have been made without Mitch."[27]

Olivia would receive her third Oscar nomination, and Brackett and Théry would be nominated for best original screenplay. Olivia's time had come.

Viewed now, the film is absolutely a woman's picture—a melodramatic weepie, a scandalous tale of unwed motherhood and female rivalry. What could be more delicious? In fact, it was adapted and refilmed as a Bollywood musical entitled *Aradhana* (1969). And like so many women's pictures of Hollywood's golden era, it affords its leading lady the opportunity to turn in the kind of tour de force that the Academy still adores and rewards. *Variety* gave the film an excellent review, noting that the "artistry of Olivia de Havilland as the mother is superb. From the eager, young girl whose first romance ends when her hero is killed before marriage, through to the cold, brusque business woman, her performance doesn't miss a beat."[28]

Olivia absolutely owns the role and the screen, proving that she can carry a big film. Sensitively guided by her good friend Leisen, she transforms from a frilly teenager to a successful businesswoman to an austere "spinster." As David Thomson notes, "Not only did she appear more beautiful than ever before, but the change to a world centered on the female disclosed a warmth and gentleness that Warners had never bothered about."[29] Aiding the film's success was the very popular song entitled "To Each His Own," which came out in 1946. It wasn't used in the film, although the song was inspired by it. Written by Livingston-Evans and recorded by Eddy Howard, the best-selling tune was of the saccharine crooner variety. It was subsequently recorded by other artists, and its popularity attests to the power of the picture.

To Each His Own is yet another wartime drama, and another film in Olivia's oeuvre, that features airplanes and pilots (particularly poignant, given that Olivia's cousin Geoffrey de Havilland Jr., son of the renowned aviation engineer, was killed in an air crash in 1946). Like *Hold Back the Dawn,* the film opens with Brackett's narrative framing device, written on the screen: "The most mysterious mysteries are people, and usually people who don't seem mysterious at all. Take Miss Norris, for instance. Here she is, a middle-aged American woman, walking down a London street on a blacked-out New Year's Eve."[30] In some ways, this opening statement about mystery encapsulates much of Olivia's persona—an outwardly sunny professional with depths and secrets.

Her story told in flashback from the World War II to World War I, Olivia plays the youthful, then twenty-something, and finally fortyish Jody Norris from Piersen Falls, New York. When shooting began on June 25, 1945, Olivia was "a scant ninety-seven pounds. This condition proved workable within the film, since the story was shot in sequence and Josephine 'Jody' Norris in the opening scenes . . . is a young girl. Olivia and her character gained weight" as her character aged.[31] Olivia noted that she "'deliberately gained weight. I drank malted milks and ate special foods . . . and actually put on fifteen pounds while the picture was in production.'"[32] That Leisen shot the film in chronological order proved to be a great help in terms of character development.

In her mature incarnation, she is a dour, heavy-browed, no-nonsense businesswoman whose London cosmetics factory, which employs 1,500 workers, has been recommissioned for munitions. Because she has no personal life, she is on fire watch on December 31, along with Lord Desham (Roland Culver), another lonely middle-aged person who volunteers on holidays. As she waits for a train, flashbacks supply us with Jody's long history.

In the best tradition of *Stella Dallas, Three on a Match,* and *Queen for a Day,* small-town-girl Jody works for her dad, the local pharmacist, in Piersen Falls. Local boy Alec Piersen likes her, and her friend Mac likes her, but Jody falls for a visiting World War I flying ace. Captain Bart Cosgrove, played by John Lund, tells her that love like hers is a lifetime job, "and I haven't any lifetime." In a beautifully lit scene of shadow and light, Jody declares, "How much time do you think I can be sure of? I've only got until dawn, too."[33] So they have one brief, shining night of passion together. Of course, he dies in a plane crash. Of course, she is pregnant.

Indicative of a postwar cinema that was still giving agency to women, Jody doesn't die for her sins, nor is she chucked into the street. Rather shockingly for the time, and demonstrating Olivia's embrace of socially relevant roles, the doctor she consults suggests that she have an abortion for health reasons. Instead, Jody goes to New York, gives birth to her son, and meets her friend, nurse Daisy, who agrees to take the baby for a while so Jody can return home without causing a scandal. The plan is that the baby will be left on the doorstep of an exceedingly fecund and comic family, Jody will appear to rescue the baby, and her little boy will be hers. If things went smoothly there would be no film, so of course, they don't. Alec has married Corinne, and their baby has just died. When they hear about the abandoned bundle from heaven, they adopt the baby before Jody can. In the meantime, she has moved to New York and started her Lady Vyvyan beauty line with Mac and Daisy, to enormous success.

When Jody finally reveals that she is the child's mother, Alec's business is in trouble, so Jody basically offers Alec a loan in exchange for her son. When she realizes the boy is unhappy, she returns him to Alec and Corinne and escapes to London to build her cosmetics empire. The last quarter of the film brings us back to the forty-something Jody, who unexpectedly meets her son, Gregory, now known as Griggsy, in London. He is a pilot and would like to marry his girlfriend but cannot due to wartime restrictions. Will they marry? Will he discover that Jody is his real mother? Will they dance together, happily reunited, at the end?

Olivia worked very closely with makeup man Bill Woods to make Jody Norris a completely realized character. Olivia recalled, "'Paramount's makeup department wasn't exactly sure how to turn me into a woman of forty or forty-five, until I found a series of pictures of Winston Churchill in a magazine. . . . These portraits showed him as a young man and as he grew older, wiser and more experienced.'"[34] Bill Woods studied those pictures as he worked on Olivia.

Olivia was always meticulous in her character preparation, so she also discussed with Edith Head how to handle Jody's transition from ingenue to aging businesswoman. Head enjoyed working closely with her actresses and directors (with the possible exception of Hubert de Givenchy on *Sabrina*). To age Olivia's character over twenty years, "Edith added padding to de Havilland's figure and then added a tightly laced corset and pulled in the padding. Edith felt this was the best way to suggest that Olivia's character was still a well-dressed wealthy woman, but that her youth had faded."[35] Olivia remembered, "The tea gown Edith made for the '20s segment was marvellous, smoke blue chiffon trimmed with chinchilla. . . . It gave me so many little things I could do, managing the train as I went around a corner and managing the chinchilla sleeves when I used my hands. . . . These are the things that enrich a characterization."[36]

Olivia's performance also benefits from an excellent ensemble cast: Philip Terry (Mr. Joan Crawford at the time) as her thwarted suitor Alec Piersen; the deliciously bitchy Mary Anderson (Maybelle Merriwether from *GWTW*) as Corinne, the woman who snags Alec on the rebound and adopts Olivia's baby; the elegant Roland Culver as smitten Englishman Lord Desham; Bill Goodwin as Olivia's good pal Mac; and the always reliable Virginia Welles as Olivia's friend and business partner Daisy. John Lund, an all-American but rather bland young beefcake actor, makes his debut as both Olivia's doomed lover and their son.

The entire experience was tremendously gratifying to Olivia. Director Leisen was so thrilled with her performance that "on the final day of production he and Brackett presented her with a live special Oscar—a bald man in a gold body stocking."[37] Leisen recalled that "Olivia was so stunned, all she could say was 'His eyes are blue, an Oscar with blue eyes.'"[38] Audiences liked the film enormously, and "by the end of 1946 the feature had grossed $3,500,000 against Paramount's cost of $1,600,000."[39]

Olivia was extremely happy with *To Each His Own.* She was also happy with Paramount. Her 1945 contract for the film paid her $8,333.33 per week for twelve weeks, and it gave her approval of the director if Leisen should be replaced, demonstrating the studio's respect for her as well as her tough negotiating skills.[40] She wrote in 1947 that it was her favorite role up to that point (although the passage of time would make Melanie Wilkes her favorite), observing, "I found Jody uniquely satisfying, for she not only was the most clearly drawn character I had ever played but the only one who, through experience, grew so much in the understanding of life."[41] This was Olivia's film, and it was a hit; "credit for the film's poignancy belongs almost entirely to Olivia."[42]

Within a month of the opening of *To Each His Own,* Warner Brothers released the Brontë biopic *Devotion,* filmed three years earlier. Some found the title "ironically applicable to Olivia's tenure at the studio. . . . For observers of the Hollywood scene, it was difficult to associate the shy, optimistic young actress who arrived on the [Warner] Burbank lot . . . with the experienced acting tyro who in 1946 could hold an audience's interest so rapturously" as Jody Norris.[43] Charlotte Brontë may not have been Olivia's greatest screen role, but the release of *Devotion* helped her regain the public's interest after her sabbatical. Whether Jack Warner was hoping to punish Olivia's critical triumph with this disappointing film is unclear, but this was her year, and nothing could stop her forward motion.

Also in 1946, Olivia made *The Dark Mirror* for Universal and received top billing. Although this was not a particularly huge box office success or an Oscar-winning opportunity, it offered her "the challenge of playing two roles in a film," something "no red-blooded actress can resist."[44] The same year, Bette Davis portrayed twins in *A Stolen Life* (brilliantly parodied on *The Carol Burnett Show* as *A Swiped Life,* complete with foghorn bellows), and she did it again in 1964's *Dead Ringer. The Dark Mirror* allowed Olivia to stretch her acting muscles with two roles in one film, portraying one good sister and one who is described by psychiatrist and shared love interest Lew Ayres as "completely insane."[45]

Psychological exploration was increasingly common in films after World War II, with the popularization of psychotherapy and the war's traumatic effect on individuals and cultures. Alfred Hitchcock's *Spellbound* (1945), with the dream sequence designed by Salvador Dali, established the template for such films. It was logical that Olivia's desire to establish herself as a serious actress would lead her to films that reflected Americans' growing interest in psychotherapy. In fact, the actress insisted that all the cast members meet with a psychiatrist. Vladimir Pozner's original story was nominated for an Oscar, and the script was written by Nunnally Johnson, a triple-threat screenwriter, director, and producer (and father of author Nora Johnson). Johnson would also write the screenplay for *My Cousin Rachel* and would direct *The Three Faces of Eve* (1957), based on the true story of multiple-personality sufferer Chris Costner Sizemore, which resulted in Joanne Woodward's best actress Oscar. *The Dark Mirror* was respectfully reviewed, and its impact on popular culture was strong enough to inspire a 1984 television remake with Jane Seymour.

Olivia plays twin sisters Terry and Ruth Collins, who refuse to incriminate each other when an acquaintance is found stabbed in the heart. One of the women was seen by neighbors at the crime scene, but neither will compromise the other's alibi. It is up to psychiatrist Lew Ayres, who happens to specialize in twins, and detective Thomas Mitchell (Gerald O'Hara in *GWTW*) to determine the true murderer. Ayres observes both sisters and falls for the good Ruth, while diagnosing Terry's madness through the use of Rorschach inkblots. Olivia reminisced about her preparation for the roles: "When the dialogue director and other members of the company joined me for an informal appointment with a psychiatrist to gain insight into Terry's psychotic condition . . . we asked her about the Rorschach test, to which Terry had submitted. . . . The doctor . . . swore us to secrecy and then divulged the key to that test. This secret . . . I have kept all this time."[46]

The subtle and growing differences between the sisters develop thanks to the artistry of Olivia and of director Robert Siodmak. Siodmak was a master of film noir. After a successful career in Germany, he came to Hollywood and produced a series of disturbing suspense films in the 1940s, including the southern Gothic *Son of Dracula* (1943) and *The Killers* (1946), starring the viscerally sensual Burt Lancaster and Ava Gardner. He also directed the great psychological thriller *The Spiral Staircase,* which is still chilling despite its now-primitive diagnosis of the mentally disturbed. Siodmak filmed *The Dark Mirror* in black and white, utilizing a "*film noir* technique . . . the nuances emphasized by Siodmak's lighting enable de Havilland's divided sisters to assume complexities not evident in their earlier scenes."[47] He brought the stylistic qualities of an A-list thriller to this B+ picture. He guided Olivia into a new persona—complex, sexual, and lethal.

While Olivia's Ruth is sweet and charmingly feminine and feisty, not unlike the Errol Flynn heroines of yore, she brings a new maturity to the role of Terry, the murderess. Her Terry is confrontational, manipulative, and ruthless (pun intended). When she is given the Rorschach test, she realizes that psychiatrist Ayres is analyzing her, so her responses are cold and clever. She wants to date the doctor and makes the first move: "Will we see each other outside of your office?"[48] Her posture is stronger and her figure shapelier (almost in anticipation of the transformation she will undergo as Catherine Sloper three years later in *The Heiress*), and there's a subtle sexuality in Terry's gaze. Olivia's shifts between the twins, who must be similar enough in appearance to fool a smart policeman, are effective and fun.

The role of Terry was Olivia's first "bad girl." She recalled in 1971, "That horrible Terry I had to play in that picture haunts me to this day."[49] Olivia's explanation for her reluctance to play dangerous women or femme fatales was interesting but ingenuous: "I think playing bad girls is a bore. I have always found more luck with good girl roles because they require more from an actress."[50] When I wrote to the actress and expressed my delight in her more devilish characters, she responded: "About your fascination with the roles of Terry, Miriam [*Hush . . . Hush, Sweet Charlotte*], Rachel [*My Cousin Rachel*] and the mature Catherine Sloper [*The Heiress*]—it is important not to confuse the persona of the roles with the character of the interpreter!"[51]

Bosley Crowther, the legendary and notoriously crotchety film critic for the *New York Times,* didn't enjoy the film. He particularly criticized Olivia's performance, writing, "De Havilland is the dual lady, and for the life of us we never were sure when she was being Ruth, the good sister, and Terry, the evil one. Or, was it the other way around?"[52] But to play them as extreme characters or with wildly different personalities would have been an absurd choice. Siodmak guides the actress to a very complex depiction of two sisters who are codependent yet too different to be truly sisterly. Olivia herself observed, "Terry . . . was so dark and so evil that playing her was an extremely painful experience for me—one I would never, ever, want to repeat."[53]

Jeanine Basinger, in her insightful book *A Woman's View,* notes that the bad sister, Terry, is a frightening portrayal of "a domineering menace, full of anger, and a murderess."[54] Terry portends the actress's graceful movement from one potentially malevolent manipulation to the next in her incarnation six years later as a nineteenth-century temptress in *My Cousin Rachel.* That

Olivia was interested in, but didn't secure, the lead role of Nancy, "a daring kleptomaniac whose criminal behavior drives numerous men to madness and suicide," in RKO's noir thriller *The Locket* signaled her willingness to cast off the good-girl persona, even though she later denied taking any pleasure in such roles.[55] Olivia was shrewd about her career, and in the 1940s, as now, the Academy loves an actress who breaks her own star persona stereotype.

Olivia turned thirty on July 1, 1946—a significant birthday for anyone. She was having a phenomenal year. She was back onscreen in a variety of period and contemporary roles. Her career was on the rise again, and this time not as a pretty ingenue or supporting player but as a real actress with the star power to open a film for a major studio. As James Agee noted in his review of *The Dark Mirror,* "I very much like Olivia de Havilland's performance. She has for a long time been one of the prettiest women in movies; lately she has not only become prettier than ever, but has started to act."[56] Perhaps now that her career was on track, she could focus on her personal life. However, the memory of John Huston lingered. She wrote in 2012:

> During those long years [of World War II], the man who meant the most to me was separated, but not yet divorced, and, as an officer in the US Signal Corps, was abroad most of the time, making stunning documentaries in battle conditions. By the time [the war] . . . was over and the divorce proceedings complete, our relationship had suffered so much stress and my freelance work . . . demanded so much of me—and his career as a director demanded so much of him—that there was no way for us to find each other again. Despite our profound mutual attraction and the many things we had in common, our circumstances had so altered that I was no longer eager to marry this unusually talented, intelligent, and interesting man who was never really replaced in my feelings in the years which followed.[57]

She had the reputation of being what the *Los Angeles Examiner* called "one of the film colony's last 'bachelor' holdouts who once headed a 'We Won't Wed Club' of starlets."[58]

There was a man waiting for her, however. They had first met at a party at producer Arthur Hornblow's house. Olivia remembered: "I'd just walked in when Arthur brought over a distinguished looking chap, tall, slim, with dark chestnut hair—a touch of gray at the temples, and gray-green eyes. . . . He had the kind of enormous vitality that impressed me even before he started to talk."[59] Although there was a mutual attraction, she missed his phone calls, and then the war interrupted their acquaintance. In August 1946, while she was doing summer stock at the Westport Country Playhouse in Connecticut—performing in J. M. Barrie's *What Every Woman Knows* (her first return to the stage since 1934's *A Midsummer Night's Dream*)—they were reacquainted through mutual friends Lawrence Langner, the renowned patent lawyer, playwright, director, cofounder of the Theatre Guild, and cocreator of the Westport theater, and his wife Phyllis.[60] They were intellectual equals, and he was the type of man to whom she was frequently drawn—older (by eighteen years), tall, masculine, accomplished, adventurous, something of a rebel, and very commanding. In fact, when they were first reunited, "He arrived about midnight and stayed till after 3. . . . He talked and we listened, fascinated."[61] The man was novelist Marcus Aurelius Goodrich.

Born in 1897, Goodrich left his Texas home in 1916 to join the navy. He used his World War I experience on a destroyer to inform his 1941 best-selling novel *Delilah.* Goodrich wrote frequently about the navy, and he served again during World War II as a lieutenant commander. After the war, he wrote for the drama department of the *New York Herald Tribune* and then went to Hollywood, where he wrote movie treatments, the most famous of which was for the 1947 holiday classic *It's a Wonderful Life.*[62]

Olivia may have disliked biographer Charles Higham enormously, but he rather accurately describes her hasty marriage to Goodrich. Goodrich swept the actress off her feet, taking charge of both her and the wedding plans—exhibiting a controlling nature that would cause difficulties later. On August 26, 1946, after a twenty-day courtship, they were married at the Langners' home in Westport.[63] Olivia wore a floral cap-sleeved day dress with a picture hat—not the garb one associates with the first marriage of a postwar movie queen, but reflecting a practical approach to the partnership. Goodrich had been divorced four times, which didn't bode well for the marriage. Presciently, the author had "advised [Olivia] to look for a businessman to marry. 'Beware of writers!' he said. 'Never get romantic about a writer.'"[64] More disturbingly, Olivia had requested "that the word 'obey' be retained in the wedding ceremony."[65]

Why did the careful, discreet actress marry so suddenly, and to a much older man with several marriages behind him? Was she just tired of dating, or did she feel that, at age thirty, she had wasted valuable time? No doubt marrying a writer was appealing; that had been part of her attraction to John Huston.

Her career was finally on track, so perhaps acquiring a husband seemed like the next logical step for Olivia. She said of marriage: "It was indeed the norm of that era, and I thought of it as a deeply romantic and desirable state of being. The vows exchanged were extraordinary and unmatchable. . . . It was . . . circumstances which delayed that much desired state from becoming a reality."[66] Marrying after a twenty-day courtship was certainly extraordinary and deeply romantic. The suddenness and inevitability of it were irresistible. It was the stuff of movies.

Though outwardly happy, there were some clues to potential problems in the early months of the couple's marriage. They were living in Olivia's flat in the Shoreham Apartments, which may have been convenient for her but seems like an unusual choice for a 1940s husband. Goodrich claimed they were waiting for house prices to come down, suggesting an inequality in income that would only grow in the next few years. That Goodrich didn't publish another novel suggests he was no F. Scott Fitzgerald. Hedda Hopper wrote a breathless puff piece about the newlyweds in December 1946 and noted, "Goodrich is boss of the family. Women haven't changed in 1000 years: they still want a master around the house, and that's what Livvy's got. Not that he does all the talking, but he does plenty." Moreover, because writing "enables him to work anywhere . . . he aims to stick closely around Olivia."[67]

A feature on Olivia's career in *Look* magazine in March 1947 certainly celebrated her "stature as a dramatic actress," but it also included a photograph of Olivia sitting on the floor, gazing adoringly up at her husband, who is seated on a chair. The caption read: "At tea-time, Olivia's husband Marcus Goodrich reads to her from books like *Don Quixote*."[68] Another profile in late 1946 recounted two very troubling anecdotes. The first claimed that Olivia "is a very jealous person and as soon as they were married she came across his list of telephone numbers. She wanted to know what women her husband used to go around with and she looked at the list. She saw her name there." Given his four previous marriages, it should have been clear that Goodrich was a player. The other anecdote, though presented comically, signaled a clash of personalities: "She learned that her husband is a Southerner and on the third day of their marriage she says they refought the Civil War. The battle went on for three hours and she finally surrendered. She went out immediately after finally conceding that the North really lost the war and bought a gray suit."[69]

Looking back, Olivia wrote, "Marc was a rather controlling person, and quite liked other people to think that he was very much in charge of anything to do with me. But of course, all major decisions regarding my work were made by me."[70] Perhaps that was true, but "Hollywood did not take to him, nor he to it, and a legend was soon built up that he was a Svengali who master-minded her every move."[71] The marriage seems an ironic choice for Olivia—to go from the control of Jack Warner to the control of Marcus Goodrich. We can attribute it to the misogyny of the culture and the era or to the pressure women felt (and still feel) to marry and heed the ticking of their biological clocks. Either way, it was out of character for Olivia.

By the end of 1946, though, Olivia had made some professional decisions. She left her former management team Berg-Allenberg, which had tried to force her to make *Ivy,* a rather interesting story about a murderous woman. Olivia disliked the script, and her sister, Joan, would later make the film. So she was offscreen again, this time for six months, due to entanglements with the agency and the film.[72] Olivia, however, claimed that it was "simply because [she'd] 'read script after script' without finding a good one, though she had wanted to do Theodore Dreiser's *Sister Carrie* but 'the price was prohibitive.'"[73] Then she signed with agent Kurt Frings, whose wife Ketti's tale had been the basis of *Hold Back the Dawn.* Frings would lead Olivia to *The Snake Pit,* a powerful work about mental illness and institutionalization that was in some ways a precursor to Sylvia Plath's *The Bell Jar.* Like *The Dark Mirror,* it reflected Olivia's and Hollywood's interest in psychiatry and would prove to be another triumphant role for her.

Olivia also received the thrilling news of her third Oscar nomination, for *To Each His Own.* It had been six years since her last nod, and she had worked very hard to position herself as a legitimate, serious, competitive actress. Hollywood was behind her, too. As one columnist noted in the aptly titled article "Scarlett O'Havilland": "Up to now, Hollywood's coveted Oscar has only winked at Olivia de Havilland. . . . Olivia is long overdue for an Academy Award. . . . This year, they say around town, she's a cinch for an Oscar."[74] According to a more recent writer: "MGM had both the largest number of popular stars in its stable and the strongest influence within the Academy from the beginning. . . . This had a curious 'delayed action' effect on the awards in the 40s when many of the winners were (non-MGM) 30s stars whose recognition was long overdue."[75]

On March 13, 1947, at the nineteenth Academy Awards, Olivia finally won the golden trophy. Ray Milland, the previous year's best actor winner and her costar in *The Well-Groomed Bride,* presented her with the Oscar. She had triumphed over a strong field of nominees—Jennifer Jones, Jane Wyman,

Celia Johnson, and Rosalind Russell. Wearing a strapless pale blue tulle gown with a full skirt of embroidered pink cabbage roses, covered by a net overlay, Olivia looked elegant and romantic.[76] Her acceptance speech garnered comments about the formality and staginess of the language, and there were rumors that Goodrich penned some of her comments: "Since I value highly the profession which has instructed me, rewarded me, and permitted me my share of the world's work, it will understand and forgive me, I know, for the very great pride I feel in receiving this symbol of its approbation, one of the Awards of Merit, for my part in this past year, what has been done."[77] It's stiff and grand and uncharacteristic, but at least she goes on to thank the team that made her Oscar possible.

And then came that moment between Olivia and her sister Joan Fontaine. Up until then, their relationship had been fairly calm for quite some time. Joan was a presenter that year and was standing backstage as Olivia walked off after her win. Joan extended her hand in congratulations, but Olivia turned away (a reaction to Joan's snide comments about Marcus Goodrich?), and of course, a photographer was there to capture the moment.

However, Olivia was too busy building her career to worry about it. In addition to the Oscar, she won the best feminine performance award from *Cine-Revue* magazine in Belgium, cementing her international appeal. She had even attracted a rather crazed stalker-fan named Paul Randall, who was convinced he had been advising her via mail for three years. Randall was arrested after coming to Los Angeles from Chicago "on a mission called 'Operations Everything'" and was referred to a psychiatrist.[78]

With her triumphant Oscar win, Olivia was ready to tackle the lead in *The Snake Pit* for 20th Century Fox, but she was not the first choice. Also under consideration was Fox contract actress Gene Tierney, who would experience her own mental health issues and institutionalization in later years. Ingrid Bergman, whose career Olivia admired enormously, wrote that producer-director Anatole Litvak had offered her the film, "but I didn't want to do it. Then Olivia de Havilland took the part and she got an Oscar for her performance which was marvelous."[79] Olivia may not have been the first choice, but she recognized a great role when she saw one. With exquisitely sensitive production and direction by Litvak; costumes by Bonnie Cashin; an excellent supporting cast of Mark Stevens, Leo Genn, and Celeste Holm; and a groundbreaking script by Millen Brand and Frank Partos, with Arthur Laurents offering structural help, Olivia had yet another memorable role in a remarkable film.

The title of the film came from "the ancient practice of tossing an insane person into a pit of snakes on the theory that the shock would return the afflicted human to normalcy."[80] That view of mental health treatment had evolved, of course, but Litvak, who had purchased the rights to Mary Jane Ward's novel for $75,000 in 1945, "spent more than a year shopping the project to the major studios. 'They all thought I was as crazy as the girl in the book,' Litvak quipped."[81] Finally, 20th Century Fox took the challenge, and so did Olivia. She visited, along with some of the cast and crew, several hospitals to observe treatments, staff, and patients, and that preparation invested the production with intensity and sometimes documentary-like realism.

Olivia portrays young newlywed Virginia Cunningham, who is committed to Juniper Hill State Hospital after a breakdown. We first see Virginia watching birds metaphorically flying away free. She looks extremely dowdy, exhausted, and tense; her brown eyes are huge, and her brown hair is straggly. She hears voices, and the voice-over of her own thoughts inserts an insecure, very high-timbred querulousness throughout the film.

Her doctor, Dr. Mark Kik, is portrayed wonderfully and compassionately by Leo Genn; Virginia fixates on him, understandably, for a while. Terrence Rafferty notes that the "kindly, pipe-smoking psychiatrist—of the sort played by Leo Genn in 'The Snake Pit'—became something of a fixture in the Freudianized women's pictures of the late '40s and '50s."[82] Genn's believability, idealized as it is, is one of many strengths in the film. *The Snake Pit* also illustrates the problems state hospitals were facing at the time—in Juniper Hill, there are 718 patients in a building that should hold only 300.

Virginia knows nothing about what happened to her, and she doesn't remember her husband, Robert Cunningham (the earnest Mark Stevens). We see in flashback how Robert and Virginia met. He was a clerk in a publishing house, and she was a writer. Despite her strange secrecy, they start dating, and then he moves to New York. He hears nothing from her for six months, and then she suddenly reappears. Too quickly, they get married (like Olivia and Goodrich?), making the viewer wonder who has the mental health issues. But obviously, Virginia is ill—she weeps, has headaches, screams, becomes hysterical, loses track of time, and yells, "You can't make me belong to you."[83] Virginia is out of control, and her hapless husband has no choice but to take her to the state hospital. Olivia handles the violent shifts in character vividly.

One of the film's most controversial elements is Virginia's receiving shock treatments, and these scenes are very realistic indeed. The nurses behave in a very matter-of-fact way as we see a close-up of the machine and the mouthpiece is inserted. When the power is switched on, Virginia moans and the camera pulls away, but the scene is still visceral. It takes several sessions for the treatments to take effect, and there are no quick fixes. But as the months pass, we slowly see Virginia improve. Olivia's gradual transformation is movingly effective. Virginia's grief when she realizes she's lost several months of the summer—"I don't even remember coming here. . . . I can't love anybody! I can't love anybody!"[84]—gives us a poignant vision of the slow return to mental health. Robert, however, mistakenly believes that a little progress means she's completely cured, and he wants to take her to his family farm, but Dr. Kik tells him she's not ready because she can't accept Robert's or anyone's love.

Through shock treatments and talk therapy and work therapy (Dr. Kik insists that Virginia write on a typewriter for an hour each day), Virginia finally remembers what happened to her former boyfriend, Gordon. He was terribly controlling—*he* had decided they would get married—and while they were on a date (Gordon had even picked out her clothing), Virginia started shaking, so he turned the car around to take her home. Then she remembers that it was raining and the car crashed—"If only I hadn't made him turn back, he wouldn't have died."[85] Virginia's guilt has led to her amnesia and her behavior—similar to the causes of Gregory Peck's character's illness in Hitchcock's *Spellbound* (1945).

Virginia is slowly brought back to health. In a tremendously moving scene, she looks after another patient, Hester, played with ragged dignity by Betsy Blair, saying, "Sometimes a sick animal knows better how another sick animal should be treated." As the film ends, Virginia calmly says good-bye to Ruth (Celeste Holm) and to Hester. She invites Dr. Kik to visit her and her husband, and as they shake hands, she says, "I'm not in love with you anymore." Robert greets her, puts her wedding ring on her finger, and happily declares, "Come on, darling, we're going home."[86] It's a heart-warming if sentimental ending to the troubling story of a lost woman who finds her way.

Even though, in hindsight, much of the film "ultimately displaces [the patients] into melodrama . . . *The Snake Pit* is important because it questions the profession's effectiveness from a more informed point of view. . . . Psychiatrists can heal the sick, but our society and the institutions it builds for troubled people do not always make psychiatric work easy."[87] This was Olivia's second film addressing mental health and psychiatry, and one can't help wondering how her performances might have been influenced by John Huston, who directed the 1946 documentary about postwar psychiatric trauma *Let There Be Light,* if their affair had continued.

The film was an enormous triumph for all the participants. It was "released on November 3, 1948, in New York and Chicago . . . [and] was a fast box-office success."[88] Olivia received her fourth Oscar nomination, her third for best actress, but Jane Wyman received the award for her moving performance in *Johnny Belinda. The Snake Pit* was also nominated for best picture, best director, best screenplay, and best score, and it won for best sound production. Olivia lost the Oscar that year, but she won many other awards: best foreign actress from the Italian National Syndicate of Film Journalists, the National Board of Review award, the Venice Film Festival Volpi Cup, and the New York Film Critics Circle Award.[89]

By mid-1948, Olivia was one of Hollywood's leading actresses, earning a salary of $200,000 per film.[90] She was thirty-two years old, lived in a new house in Brentwood with her writer husband, and had the respect of her peers. She would finish that year by filming her best screen performance in the remarkably acted, directed, and produced classic *The Heiress.*

The Heiress was adapted from the stage play by Ruth and Augustus Goetz, and their source material was Henry James's brilliant 1881 novella *Washington Square.* Terrence Rafferty posited in the *New York Times* that James's books are "ambiguous" and "elusive" in adaptation, and the film version worked so well because the Goetzes had "made the action considerably more dramatic, the conflicts sharper."[91] The play was a critical success and ran for almost a year, from September 1947 to September 1948, at the Biltmore Theatre in New York. It was directed by the legendary Jed Harris and starred Wendy Hiller as Catherine, a frigid Basil Rathbone as her father (for which he received a best actor Tony nomination), Patricia Collinge as Catherine's aunt, and Broadway actor (and husband of Oscar-winner Beatrice Straight) Peter Cookson as the caddish Morris Townsend. The play has been revived four times, most recently in 2013 with Jessica Chastain in the title role.[92] The work has proved to be a classic and was filmed in 1997 as *Washington Square,* starring Jennifer Jason Leigh, Albert Finney, and Ben Chaplin.

In his introduction to the DVD, Robert Osborne notes that the film "seems to grow in stature every day" and that her work in *The Heiress* "challenges the popularity of Olivia's performances as Melanie Hamilton in *GWTW.*" According to Osborne, it was "famed director Lewis Milestone who actually suggested to Olivia de Havilland that she should check out that Broadway play. In a conversation in Hollywood that Milestone had with Olivia at a party, he said, in essence, 'You must immediately get on a train, go to New York, and see this wonderful new play *The Heiress.* It would be a great story for you to do on the screen.' She did so, and by the first intermission she was on the phone with her agent." Olivia initially wanted George Cukor to direct, but he was busy, so she contacted the great director William Wyler, who called her after he saw the play: "'Let's do it,' he said. And they did it."[93]

Paramount bought the rights, offered Olivia the leading role, and was deeply fortunate to get Wyler as producer and director, a man who was "meticulous in all departments."[94] It was Wyler who commissioned a stirring score by renowned American composer Aaron Copland. Studio costume designer Edith Head contributed enormously, and the superb supporting cast included the great British actor Ralph Richardson as the imperious Austin Sloper, the delicious Miriam Hopkins as Aunt Pennimen, and the heartthrob of the moment, Montgomery Clift, as the ruthlessly charming Morris Townsend.

The story is a tale of misogyny and manipulation, but also of female agency and survival. Spinster and heiress Catherine Sloper is awkward, sweet, and unremarkable. She is described in *Washington Square* as "not ugly; she had simply a plain, dull, gentle countenance. . . . Catherine was decidedly not clever. . . . Doctor Sloper would have liked to be proud of his daughter; but there was nothing to be proud of in poor Catherine."[95] She finds herself caught between her arrogant father, Austin, a society doctor in New York City, and her gold-digging suitor, Morris Townsend. Austin forbids their marriage, as much out of his disdain for Catherine as his distrust of Morris. Catherine naïvely confides her willingness to be disinherited to Morris, who abandons her on the night they were to elope in pursuit of a greater fortune. Despite her betrayal by both her father and her husband-to-be, Catherine builds a life of her own and, in scenes that are profoundly, satisfyingly karmic, wreaks revenge on both men.

James's tale may carry such theatrical power because it is based on a real-life situation. Frances Anne Kemble, a London actress, "told James the story of her handsome brother's engagement to a dull, plain girl" with a private fortune. Like Catherine Sloper, the girl defied her father, and her suitor abandoned her out of greed; then he returned to woo her and was spurned.[96]

Olivia found the part challenging: "To play an ungainly girl and at the same time give undertones of color and excitement was difficult."[97] In her incarnation as Catherine, as she had for Melanie, Olivia deferred to the physical reality of the heroine, avoiding any glamorization and respecting the text. With her flat brown hair pulled back severely behind her ears and her eyes large and heavily browed, she offers a plain but pert homebody who is busy making chowder or embroidering; she is a shy girl and rather confused by her father. Vocally, Olivia plays the role in her upper register, sounding timid and breathless. However, with Miriam Hopkins, playing her giddy but wise Aunt Lavinia, she is funny and ironic, giving Catherine the saving grace of wit and self-awareness, which foreshadows her transformation.

Sometimes Wyler presents her as too girlish, so initially, she almost seems slow-witted rather than simply shy. But Catherine is also painfully earnest and desperate for affection and approbation. In one scene, the overly embellished party dress she wears to please her father draws his veiled criticism; the dress is cherry red (shades of Wyler and Bette Davis's *Jezebel*), and it was her mother's favorite, but "she dominated the color."[98]

Richardson's Dr. Sloper finds Catherine "an entirely mediocre and defenseless creature without an ounce of poise."[99] In turn, Catherine's pathetic need to please her father is palpable. Off camera, the two actors didn't like each other very much. It may have been a clash of egos. Before filming began, a journalist noted that at the party Paramount threw to welcome Sir Ralph, Olivia commented, "'I am delighted . . . to have Sir Ralph with me in this picture,'"[100] implying her dominance both onscreen and off. Olivia spoke about Richardson in 2006, and even "fifty-seven years later, her anger is genuine. 'He decided to treat me in just the way his character treats mine. It was low-down English cunning.'"[101] He also tried to steal a scene by "flapping his gloves. . . . I knew from just working with him it was a British theatre trick."[102] Fortunately for Olivia, Wyler was aware of the ruse and kept the gloves out of the frame.

This was the impossibly handsome Montgomery Clift's second film, and Paramount "decided to take advantage of his sudden fame and popularity by promoting him as their next big sex symbol." Clift chose the role to avoid typecasting as well as to work with Wyler, and he rather nervously asked the director not to "bawl me out . . . in front of the crew." Clift's desire to work with Wyler became "somewhat tainted however, as he was sure Wyler was favoring Olivia. Well, perhaps—she was the star, after all. He begrudged her reliance on Wyler and complained that her 'performance is being totally shaped by Wyler.'"[103]

Olivia's method of working was meticulous and intellectual, formed by years in the studio system. It was true that she relied on the director, but Clift—the newest young thing—didn't understand what she had riding on this film. She had sacrificed enormously to get to this point. She knew about Wyler's blowups with Bette Davis, but she also knew that he had guided Davis to the Oscar. Ironically, Clift ended up relying on his acting coach Mira Rostova,

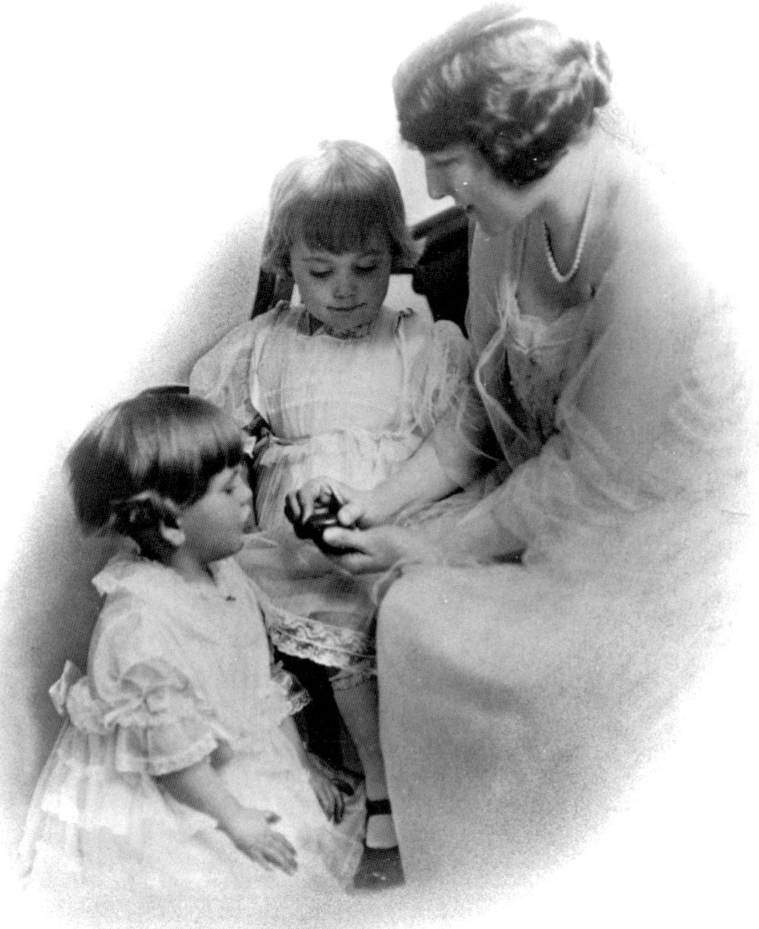

A tender portrait of mother Lilian Ruse, sister Joan, and wee Olivia at their feet, circa 1918.

Olivia resplendent in an elaborate headdress from her 1934 triumph *A Midsummer Night's Dream* at the Hollywood Bowl. (From the core collection biography, production, and non-film [performing arts] photographs, Academy Awards show photographs, Hattie and Sam McDaniel papers, and the Bison Archive photographs collected by Marc Wanamaker of the Margaret Herrick Library, Academy of Motion Pictures. Hereafter credited as "Margaret Herrick Library.")

Re-creating the role of Hermia in *Midsummer* for her first film role, 1935. (Margaret Herrick Library)

Olivia's first film with her idol and future friend Bette Davis (left)—*It's Love I'm After* (1937), costarring Patric Knowles.

Olivia on horseback for *Dodge City* (1939); she adored riding. (Margaret Herrick Library)

In costume as Melanie Hamilton Wilkes in *Gone with the Wind* (1939), the film that secured Olivia's film legend status.

Arriving in Atlanta for the *Gone with the Wind* premiere in December 1939 are (from left) Olivia, David O. Selznick, Vivien Leigh, and Irene Mayer Selznick. (Margaret Herrick Library)

Olivia with James Stewart, circa 1940. He was one of her favorite beaus.

Between a rock and a hard place—Olivia with Burgess Meredith (left) and Jimmy Stewart (right). She dated the former after the latter. (Margaret Herrick Library)

Her last screen moment with Errol Flynn in *They Died with Their Boots On* (1941). After eight films and years of unfulfilled passion, they parted.

Olivia loved working with Charles Boyer in Paramount's *Hold Back the Dawn* (1941), for which she received her first Oscar nomination for best actress.

The fateful night in 1942 when sister Joan Fontaine won the Oscar for best actress over Olivia. Despite the positive show for the press, it was an awkward moment, as Burgess Meredith looks on. (Margaret Herrick Library)

Olivia was growing more sophisticated, onscreen and off, as the 1940s commenced. (Margaret Herrick Library)

James Cagney and Olivia made three films together, including *The Strawberry Blonde* (1941).

Olivia enjoyed making the James Thurber comedy *The Male Animal* (1942) with Henry Fonda.

Olivia on the set of *In This Our Life* (1942) with director John Huston and her friend Bette Davis.

Olivia reunited with Hattie McDaniel in *In This Our Life*. (Margaret Herrick Library)

Olivia on a date with her great romance, John Huston (standing), circa 1942.
(Margaret Herrick Library)

Olivia (left) with her Airedale, Shadrach, a gift from beau John Huston, and her sister, Joan Fontaine (right), circa 1944.

All in a good cause—Olivia with fellow Warner Brothers contract players George Tobias and Ida Lupino in a bebop number from *Thank Your Lucky Stars* (1943).

Olivia conferring with Warner Brothers designer Orry-Kelly.

By 1945, Olivia had become a sultry leading lady and was poised to break free from Warner Brothers.

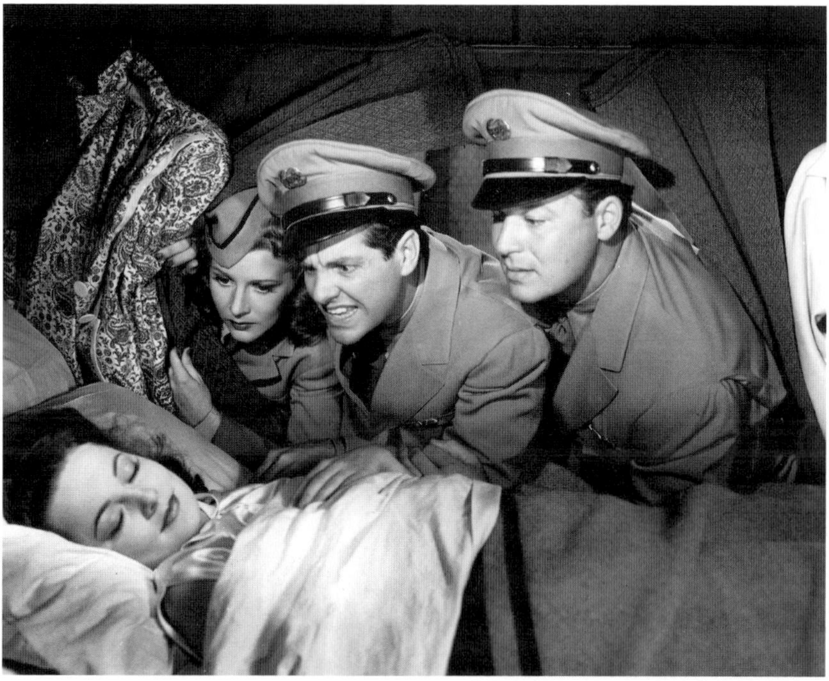

A rare comedy for Olivia, *Princess O'Rourke* (with Robert Cummings, in the middle) won an Oscar for best screenplay in 1943.

Olivia's last film at Warner Brothers was *Devotion* (1946), a romanticized biopic about the Brontës. Ida Lupino (middle) and Nancy Coleman (right) costarred.

Every actor enjoys the challenge of portraying twins. Shown here are good and bad Olivias in *The Dark Mirror* (1946). (Margaret Herrick Library)

Olivia with her first husband, Marcus Goodrich. (Margaret Herrick Library)

Olivia's breakthrough role as a freelancing star—*To Each His Own* (1946), with John Lund.

Olivia in 1947 with her best actress Oscar for *To Each His Own*. Her dress was blue net with pink roses. (Margaret Herrick Library)

Another happy photograph from Oscar night 1947 with Jean Hersholt and Hattie McDaniel.

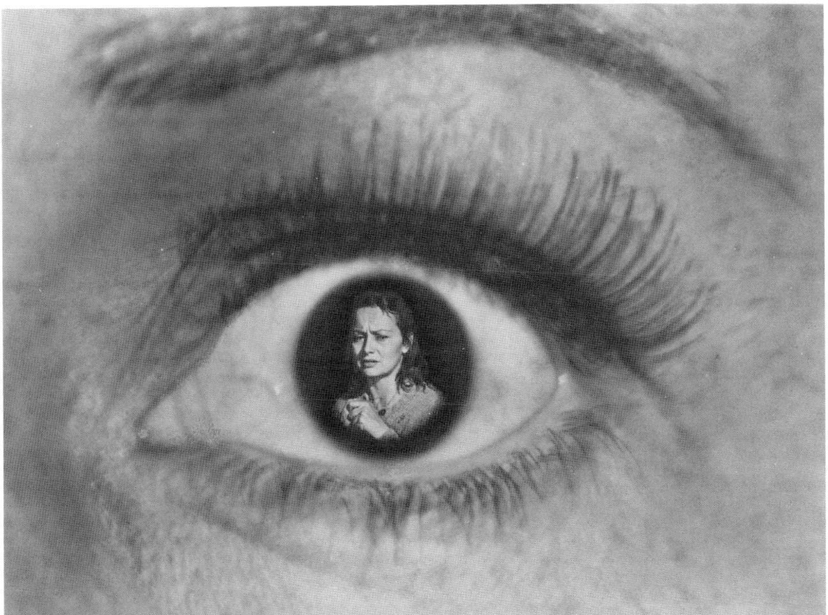

The Snake Pit (1948) offered an illuminating look at the treatment of patients with mental illness. Olivia relished the role. (Margaret Herrick Library)

Olivia's rejection of Montgomery Clift at the end of *The Heiress* (1949) prompted thousands of Monty's fans to send her hate mail.

Olivia as Catherine Sloper in *The Heiress*—possibly her greatest role and best film. (Margaret Herrick Library)

Olivia at the Oscars in 1950, when she received her second award. With her is best actor winner Broderick Crawford. (Margaret Herrick Library)

Olivia and her beloved son, Benjamin Briggs Goodrich. (Wiki Commons)

The mark of stardom—Olivia leaves her hand- and footprints at Grauman's Chinese Theatre, 1952. (Margaret Herrick Library)

Olivia's first Broadway role as Juliet (with Evelyn Varden as the Nurse) garnered mixed reviews but provided excellent experience.

Olivia's costar in *My Cousin Rachel* (1952) was Richard Burton in his first American film.

Olivia with Frank Sinatra playing young health professionals in Stanley Kramer's serious study of hospitals and interns, *Not as a Stranger* (1955).

Olivia in demure bridal wear for *The Ambassador's Daughter* (1956). With her is her favorite couturier, Christian Dior; he designed both her professional and private wardrobes.

Olivia with second husband Pierre Galante in the mid-1950s.

Olivia, soignée in Dior, with Dirk Bogarde in the postwar identity thriller *Libel* (1959), shot in England.

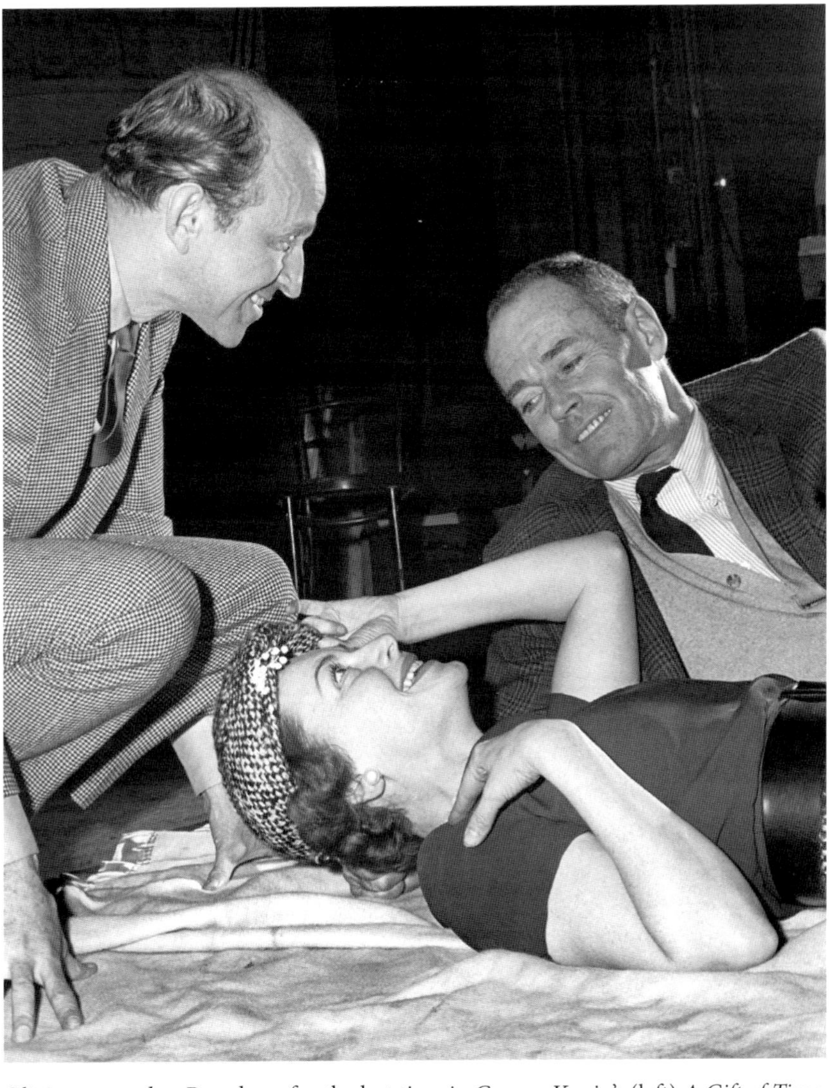

Olivia returned to Broadway for the last time in Garson Kanin's (left) *A Gift of Time* (1962), happy to be working again with Henry Fonda (right).

The closing moments between Olivia and Yvette Mimieux in 1962's *Light in the Piazza,* adapted for the Broadway stage in 2005.

Visual depiction of the dehumanization endured by Olivia's character in the grim *Lady in a Cage* (1964).

Olivia and Joseph Cotten loved working together later in their careers. This clinch is from *Hush . . . Hush, Sweet Charlotte* (1964).

Two good friends—Bette Davis and Olivia, circa 1964. (Margaret Herrick Library)

Olivia appeared in the film version of Katherine Anne Porter's novella *Noon Wine* (1966), with Jason Robards Jr. Sam Peckinpah directed.

Olivia in a steamy clinch with Bekim Fehmiu, a player for hire, in the 1970 misfire *The Adventurers.*

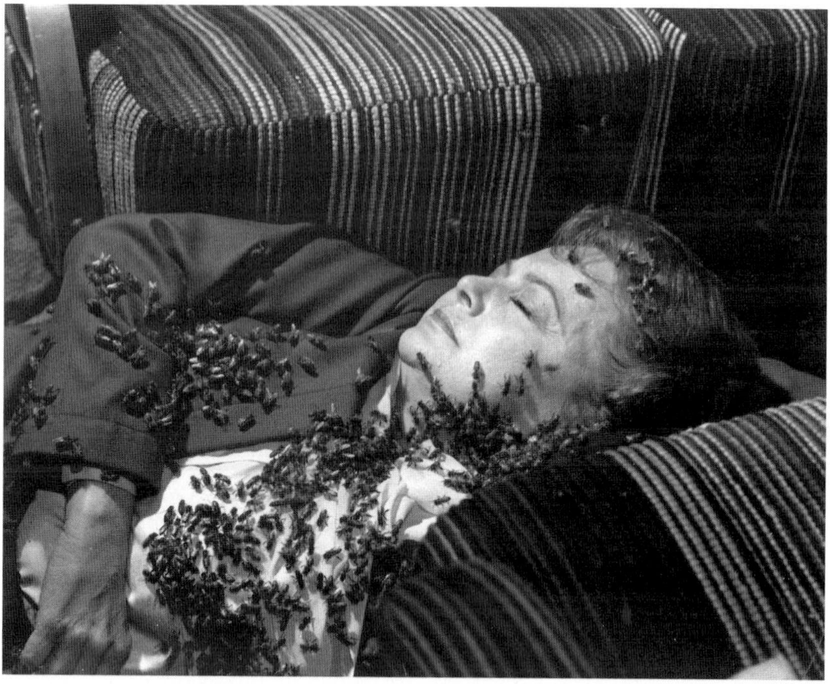

Always a good sport about physical challenges on the set, Olivia allowed herself to be draped in bees in the 1978 disaster flick *The Swarm*.

Olivia as a chiffon-draped muse in a late 1930s publicity shot. (Margaret Herrick Library)

Olivia once again displayed her penchant for flowing garments in this elegant caftan gown worn for the seventy-fifth anniversary of the Academy Awards in 2003. (Margaret Herrick Library)

The author's first visit with Olivia, at 3 rue Benouville, August 2012. (Author's collection)

When I met with Olivia the third time, she was living in the Saint James Hotel. The champagne flowed, and I crawled to my Metro stop. (Author's collection)

With Dame Olivia and her pug Oscar in Paris, December 2017 (note the champagne flutes). (Author's collection)

utilizing Method techniques to develop the charming, caddish, tragic Morris. Rather than clashing in the film, his youthful spontaneity provides a wonderful counterpoint to Richardson's theatricality and Olivia's carefully modulated growth from innocent girl to wise woman. Despite Clift's concerns, "he was so effective . . . that after the film's release, he, de Havilland, and the studio were deluged with mail from young girls in shock that plain Catherine could have let gorgeous Monty pound vainly on her door."[104]

Olivia's clothes are also tremendously effective in creating the character of Catherine Sloper, resulting in Edith Head's first Oscar win for costume design. Head's designs are severe yet sumptuous; they would be lovely on a beautiful woman but seem appropriately wasted on a plain one. Head "travelled to New York to do research for the film at the Brooklyn Museum. Every detail, whether viewed on screen, or made on an undergarment and seen only to the actors and wardrobe personnel, had to be correct down to the smallest detail." Olivia accompanied Head, "examining original clothing of the mid-nineteenth century. Olivia practiced how to move in the cumbersome costumes . . . because the authentic undergarments were very restricting." Although the garments Catherine wears in the early part of the film had to look costly, Head "made the clothes fit awkwardly with gaps and wrinkles . . . or by adding too many ruffles."[105] The beautiful dress she wears in the final scene of the film, after her father has died and Morris has come crawling back, is utterly feminine, fitted and gossamer. Interestingly, one of the hats Olivia wore in the film—a "tan silk bonnet adorned with olive green piping, ruffles and bows"—was purchased for $777 in December 2002 at a Christie's sale in New York.[106]

In the closing act of the film, Catherine's hair is fashionably styled in a braid, crowning her new confidence. Her cool French gown of lavender silk reveals a lace décolletage and is light, feminine, and floating. Her horror at her aunt and her mixed feelings about Morris, who has returned after several years, demonstrate a Catherine who has matured. She no longer bends backward but stands straight. She moves with sternness and grandeur, and as Morris babbles, simultaneously desperate to be saved yet impressed by her transformation, Catherine becomes more beautiful by the second. Olivia's entire being resonates with disgust and revenge: "He came back with the same lies, the same silly phrases. . . . He has grown greedier with the years. The first time he only wanted my money. Now he wants my love, too. Well, he came to the wrong house." Her face is as frozen as a Kabuki mask. Aunt Lavinia questions pitifully, "Can you be so cruel?" And Catherine answers, "Yes, I can be very cruel. I have been taught by masters."[107]

The closing scene, in which Catherine bolts the door against the desperately pounding Morris, is reminiscent of Greta Garbo in *Queen Christina*—a close-up of the actress's inscrutable thoughts. Catherine listens to the doorbell and to the fists banging for admittance; she breathes and sets her mouth; and as she walks up the stairs, holding her own light, there is a subtle elevation on her face and in her eyes as Copland's score crashes. She climbs to the dark at the top of the stairs her own woman. Montgomery Clift has the last shot, but Olivia de Havilland has the last word.

The trailer for *The Heiress* certainly affirms Olivia's standing in Hollywood in 1949. The lengthy preview emphasizes her status and the importance of the production with its use of the repeated question (against Copland's sweeping score), "What makes a motion picture great?" The first answer is "The Stars." Immediately following is footage of Olivia receiving the Oscar for *To Each His Own* from Ray Milland. The announcer says, "Olivia de Havilland, winner of the Academy Award for *To Each His Own,* acclaimed for her arresting performance in *The Snake Pit,* now confirms her position as dramatic queen of the screen with her poignant and unforgettable portrayal of 'The Heiress.'" Olivia is indeed the dramatic queen of the screen. The trailer then affirms the greatness of Clift, Richardson, and Hopkins, as well as "The Director" William Wyler (shown smoking in his office beneath a shelf with two Oscars) and "The Story." Yes, it's Paramount touting its own production, but for once, all the sound and fury are true.[108]

The Heiress premiered at Radio City Music Hall, and reviews were unanimously celebratory. Bosley Crowther, writing for the *New York Times,* was flattering about Olivia's performance and the entire production. His reservations were directed more toward Wyler than Olivia:

> The soft and pliant nature that Miss de Havilland gives to the shy and colorless daughter is much less shatterable by shock, and her ecstasies and her frustrations are much more open than they appeared on the stage, where Wendy Hiller performed her with significant restraint. Thus her emotional reactions are more fluent and evident, which has forced Mr. Wyler to abandon her poignant breakdown at the shock of being deceived. On the whole, however, her portrayal of the poor girl has dignity and strength.[109]

More joyous than the wonderful reception of the film was news of Olivia's pregnancy. Both she and Goodrich were thrilled; gossip maven Louella Parsons quoted him as saying, "'This is the most wonderful thing that has ever happened to either of us and we're both delighted.'"[110] However, Olivia was ill throughout the pregnancy; Parsons reported that she was "a very sick girl" and confined to bed.[111] It was during this time that she lost the Oscar to Jane Wyman, but Olivia's focus was on her health and her baby's well-being. Parsons noted, "No woman I know ever wanted to have a baby as much as Olivia."[112] She had to have a caesarean delivery, but on September 28, 1949, she gave birth to a nine-pound son, Benjamin Briggs Goodrich, named for his father's ancestors.

Olivia was, at last, exactly where she wanted to be. She had a husband, a son, and a stable home, and she had success. *The Heiress* was the "apex of Olivia's screen career and marked the end of her glory years in Hollywood."[113] The actress was nominated for her fifth Oscar, won her second New York Film Critics Circle Award, and received the Women's National Press Club Distinguished Achievement Award, presented to her by President Harry Truman. She won the Independent Theatre Owners Association's award as the top-grossing actress of 1949–1950 and the best actress gong at the International Film Festival in Venice, Italy.[114] The Brazilian film critics also honored her performance in *The Snake Pit*.[115]

Olivia's professional and personal dreams had come true. Her three golden years were beautifully wrapped up on March 23, 1950, at the RKO Pantages Theatre when she won her second best actress Oscar. Her ex-lover Jimmy Stewart handed her the trophy, and although their onstage interaction was quite cool and professional, she wrote later, "'Jimmy, Jimmy, Jimmy! . . . How extraordinary that, almost exactly 10 years after we first met . . . it should be you who presented me with that second Oscar.'"[116] Stewart had just married, but one can't help wondering how different Olivia's career might have been if they had stayed together. Hitchcock had always wanted to work with her. What if she and Jimmy had done *The Man Who Knew Too Much* (with all respect to Doris Day)?

Olivia looked lovely on Oscar night "in a pretty Orry-Kelly sequined, white organdy dress."[117] In a weirdly synchronistic and prescient moment, "there were signs of a sea change on her winning night. As she swept into the Pantages Theatre amid a fusillade of flashbulbs, the word PARIS was emblazoned in neon on a marquee high above."[118] Bronwyn Cosgrave, in her book on Oscar fashions, meant that French fashion was going to reemerge after World War II, but of course, this signaled Olivia's future as well.

Once again, Olivia's acceptance speech was very cold and grande dame-ish. She is normally quite formal in her discourse, which comes from her mother's influence and her schooling in the 1920s and 1930s, but it also comes from her intelligence and her delight in language. Also, sensitivity about the lack of a college degree can sometimes lead to a greater complexity of syntax and vocabulary. Nevertheless, the speech was stiff and officious, as was her delivery: "Your award for 'To Each His Own' I took as an incentive to venture forward. Thank you for this very generous assurance that I have not entirely failed to do so."[119] A photograph taken on the morning after the ceremony shows Olivia seated with her two Oscars before her, smiling quietly, while her husband, who "had to stir her from her revelry," offers her a glass of orange juice and places it between the Oscars, as he looms behind her.[120] Goodrich had to be in the frame, whether he belonged there or not.

Professionally, Olivia had tied Bette Davis's record for two best actress Oscars, and she was the most well-regarded actress in Hollywood. Personally, she was married to a respected author and mother to a beloved son. In March 1950 she was beautiful, talented, wealthy, and only thirty-three years old. She seemed to have it all. Surely she would continue to make films and maintain her position as the reigning queen of Hollywood. However, great actresses and great life stories don't always follow smooth paths. Her three golden years had ended.

8

EVERY FRENCHWOMAN HAS ONE

In a photograph taken after the Academy Awards ceremony in March 1950, Olivia is poised between two of the golden totems, beaming and looking youthfully joyous. Her brown eyes seem positively glistening and glitteringly intense. She had won her second Oscar, matching her career idol and friend Bette Davis (although Davis would end up with ten nominations to Olivia's five). She had won other awards and was the top moneymaking actress of 1949–1950, according to the Independent Theatre Owners' Association.[1] She was married to the well-known author Marcus Goodrich and had her first child, her beloved Benjamin. At thirty-four, she had everything a woman and an actress could want. Her next move seemed obvious—capitalize on her two Oscars, make another film or two in rapid succession, choose prestige projects, bank some healthy paychecks, and follow in Davis's footsteps as one of Hollywood's most respected dramatic actresses. But Olivia's nature wouldn't allow her to take the obvious route in anything. She wasn't cantankerous or particularly difficult (compared with other professionals in the industry), but she was ambitious and sensitive, and she never shied away from a challenge. Sue Warner? Sure. Stand up to communist sympathizers? No problem. Fend off attractive wolves? She was like a ninja Red Riding Hood. Olivia had secured her place in Hollywood, and she thought that now was the time for self-improvement as well as professional achievements. So she made some very interesting choices—based on enthusiasm, confidence, and just a smidgen of contrariness.

One interesting and rather unfortunate choice was her refusal of the role of Blanche DuBois in Elia Kazan's film version of *A Streetcar Named Desire,* written by the brilliant Tennessee Williams (along with Arthur Miller, one of the premier American dramatists at the time). She was "the first choice of Marlon Brando as his co-star," and Blanche is one of the greatest roles in history for an actress.[2] Olivia had "attended the premiere on Broadway in which Jessica Tandy interpreted Blanche DuBois. That night I was suffering acutely from a bad cold and my judgment of the play was so gravely affected thereby that, after the curtain fell, I commented that 'the play had everything in it including the kitchen sink!'"[3] Imagine what her career might have been had she said yes to the film version! Given that the cast and the director were immersed in the Method, one wonders what kind of impact this training would have had on her talent. How could she possibly decline this opportunity?

Olivia told John Meroney of the *Wall Street Journal* the reason: she had just had Benjamin and was so happy and so besotted by her son that she couldn't possibly imagine taking on such a dark role. "'I couldn't relate to it,'" she said.[4] I asked her for more details a few years later, and she replied:

> I had given birth to Benjamin and was in such a special spiritual state that I could neither relate to the character of Blanche . . . nor to the drama itself—and so I declined the offer. A year later . . . I realized that this marvellous little child of mine was going to require sustenance beyond milk and purees in the years ahead; by then I was up to returning to work . . . only to learn that [Elia Kazan] had decided to cast Vivien Leigh in the role. Her performance in the London stage presentation had not been well received either by the critics or by Kazan himself . . . but evidently he finally realized that Vivien had been badly directed (by Larry Olivier!) and that he, Kazan, could draw from her a very different performance, which he did. I thought Vivien absolutely marvellous in the part. . . . I did not, of course, see Vivien during the shooting and so never discussed the role with her. I never regretted that I did not play Blanche.[5]

The closest Olivia came to *Streetcar* was when she appeared in *A Gift of Time* in 1962 at the Ethel Barrymore Theatre, where Williams's play had opened.[6] Ultimately, Vivien Leigh was a better choice for Blanche, but imagine if Olivia had played Stella—Scarlett and Melanie in the twentieth century. It might have been wonderful.

Although she hadn't done a play since summer stock in Westport, Connecticut, in 1946, Olivia had loved performing in high school theater productions, and her big break had been in Max Reinhardt's stage production of *A Midsummer Night's Dream*. Reinhardt always believed that Olivia had great potential as a stage actress. She remembered, "Having begun my career in Shakespeare in the Hollywood Bowl under the direction of the greatest theatrical genius of that time . . . during the years that followed I always wanted to do more theatre. Furthermore, Reinhardt had said to me that I must promise him that one day I would play Juliet. I took that promise very seriously and this is why I chose to return to the theatre in *Romeo and Juliet*."[7]

The Broadway initiation is often attempted by Hollywood actresses who are at the peak of their film careers, to demonstrate their seriousness, or by those in their thirties who fear a decline in their careers as they careen toward the dreaded forty (in theater parlance, "They'll never see it from the house"—"it" being age). Olivia was in the former category. Her terms for playing Juliet were "reportedly the steepest on record. [The] film actress' representatives are understood [to be] demanding 15% of the gross, plus 50% of the profits, with a $3,000 guarantee."[8] In September 1950, Olivia and her family moved to a New York City apartment (with a rumored three tons of possessions), and rehearsals began.[9] After a two-month out-of-town tour, the play opened on March 11, 1951, at the Broadhurst Theatre.

The role she chose was a huge challenge for Olivia, despite her prior experience with Shakespearean blank verse. Portraying the ideal of nubile, sensual, suicidal love is an enormous task. Until the 1968 Franco Zeffirelli film, Juliet was often played by women more than double the fourteen-year-old heroine's age. Norma Shearer was, like Olivia, thirty-four when she made the 1936 MGM version with forty-three-year-old Leslie Howard (*GWTW*'s Ashley Wilkes) as Romeo. In another *GWTW* intersection, Vivien Leigh tackled the role in 1940, after her triumph as Scarlett. Leigh was twenty-seven, only twice Juliet's age, and had far more theatrical experience than Olivia. Also, Leigh's Romeo was her new husband, Laurence Olivier. Unfortunately for the couple, who invested all their savings in the production, the response to their performance was almost universally unenthusiastic. Olivia must have been aware of all this, as well as Leslie Howard's 1936 crash and burn as Hamlet on Broadway during the same season as John Gielgud's monumental triumph. Shakespeare is tough, to put it mildly, and *Romeo and Juliet* was not an easy or logical choice for Olivia's first Broadway play. Why not portray the witty Beatrice in *Much Ado about Nothing* or the elegant Portia in *The Merchant of Venice*? Instead, Olivia was trying to turn back the clock fifteen years, portraying a character she would have been perfect for in 1935, when Reinhardt first spoke to her about it.

Overall, her gamble paid off, but more on a personal than a professional level. On opening night in Detroit, "Katharine Cornell, whom Olivia remembered vividly as Juliet many years earlier, sent Olivia a good-luck telegram which said, 'Hie to high fortune!'—Juliet's line to her nurse just before the girl rushes off to meet Romeo."[10] Olivia recalled the 1951 production in 2015: "It was also an extraordinarily distinguished and beautiful production with wonderful performances by the other players, among them: Douglas Watson as Romeo, Jack Hawkins as Mercutio, James Hayter as the Priest, Evelyn Varden as the Nurse, together with others. Furthermore, it was produced by Dwight Deere Wiman, the sets (and costumes) were designed by Oliver Messel, and it was directed by Peter Glenville."[11]

Photographs of the production show a demurely youthful Olivia as Juliet, with long flowing locks and delicately lovely gowns; Messel's sets and costumes were sumptuous. Overall, her Broadway debut was a respectable success—but not a triumph. Owing to high production costs and a short run of forty-nine performances (100 total, including the tour), the play was "badly in the red."[12] Additionally, Olivia's reviews were mixed. Some critics applauded her efforts. *Variety* wrote of her Detroit appearance, "Olivia de Havilland endows Juliet with the winsomeness of a 14-year-old enmeshed in the joy of first love and the heartbreak of a child grown to maturity. . . . [She] enacts the two sides of the heroine to perfection."[13] William Hawkins of the *New York World Telegram and Sun* trumpeted, "There were 16 curtain calls at the Broadhurst Saturday night. . . . The dominant characteristic of this production springs from Miss de Havilland's performance. . . . There is never for one instant a suggestion of a star. . . . There is a young girl . . . caught up in swift wild doom."[14]

Other critics were less kind. One "opin[ed] that no matter how big a star she was in the movies she came to the stage unequipped to face live audiences, and that it was especially forward of her to make her debut in the role of Juliet."[15] One strongly negative voice, and it was a powerful one, belonged to George Jean Nathan. One of the great men of American theater, he was harshly dismissive of "these screen girls" who believed that doing a play for eight shows a week was like shooting a film and that they would automatically be fantastic. Nathan spared Olivia none of his ire, asserting, "She gives absolutely no evidence of any real dramatic acting talent. . . . Her Juliet in the current production of the Shakespeare classic is completely and utterly inept."[16] And those were not his harshest comments. Nathan was so cruel, in fact, that the attack almost seemed personal. Olivia's response in an interview a year later showed her intrepidness: "'George Jean Nathan didn't like it, but he doesn't like anything. . . . And we closed only because our operating expense was fantastically high.'"[17] All in all, it was a modest success, and a prestigious one.

Doing the play allowed Olivia to be with Benjamin during the day, once the run started. And being back on the East Coast was stimulating for her as well as for her husband. She was building a reputation as a dramatic actress, and by gaining more theater experience both on Broadway and on the road, her talent was maturing.

Olivia's next play was far more appropriate for her—George Bernard Shaw's *Candida,* produced by the Westport Country Playhouse, her old summer stock theater. She ended up doing *Candida* at the playhouse for eleven weeks and then on a transcontinental tour for another eight months. This too was a brave move, given Katharine Cornell's success in the role fifteen years earlier. Cornell was a role model for Olivia, however, and her kind message at the opening of *Romeo and Juliet* may have seemed like a sign. Olivia remembered Cornell's influence on her acting career years afterward: "I had been brought up at a time when Katharine Cornell annually toured with her Broadway productions, and my high school English teacher arranged for our English class to see these plays. We took the bus ride all the way up to San Francisco under her guidance and sat high in the top balcony of the San Francisco theatres where Katharine Cornell presented . . . *Romeo and Juliet* . . . Shaw's *Candida.* . . . Cornell's touring with these plays seemed so glamorous to me that I dreamed of one day doing the same."[18]

The cover of the program for *Candida* is sea green, forming an oval, patterned-edge mat framing a large black-and-white image by fashion photographer Francesco Scavullo of Olivia in a fin-de-siècle costume by Motley. Her open, smiling stance as she leans forward is beautifully welcoming. The program mentions Olivia's many awards and her love of the theater, and it throws subtle shade at Warner Brothers: "She had set her heart on the stage rather than the motion pictures as a career. But as soon as the termination of her studio contract permitted, she began making plans for a return to the stage."[19]

Olivia toured the United States for months, taking Benjamin with her on the road. One journalist wrote that she was "as wildly stage struck [as a girl] who has just been lauded for her performance in the senior class play. . . . [She is] a woman who seeks an audience, and yet she is so shy that she is intimidated by the butcher and the baker. . . . [She] carries with her a picture of the immortal actress, Eleonora Duse, which she tore out of a newspaper when she was a schoolgirl."[20] Olivia was on a mission to prove herself as an actress—to herself and to the world. That she was willing to take the show on the road for a reduced salary compared with what she could make for one film and expose herself to the critics again showed her determination.

Her reviews were polite and generally positive but failed to approach the accolades she received for her films. When the tour finished with a short run in New York City, the comments by Brooks Atkinson encapsulated what most critics had to say about her performance: "Miss de Havilland is a beautiful, modest and sincere lady whose enthusiasm for the stage is much appreciated in this neighborhood. For all her grace and sweetness, [she] does not reach down either into the comedy or the wisdom of Shaw's most beloved heroine. . . . For she is a lovely lady with good motives who unfortunately lacks experience in acting on the stage."[21] She was damned with faint praise, but at least the effort was appreciated.

Never one to give up, Olivia followed *Candida* with a brief run at the La Jolla Playhouse in *The Dazzling Hour,* directed by Jose Ferrer. The playhouse, which opened in 1947 in San Diego and is still in existence, is a significant regional theater and a fine testing ground for the Hollywood and Broadway communities. Her experience here was more positive, and she would have even better luck in 1962, when she returned to Broadway with her *Male Animal* costar Henry Fonda in Garson Kanin's *A Gift of Time*, a moving play about a couple dealing with the husband's imminent death from cancer.

The wisdom of Olivia's three-year break from Hollywood to pursue work in the theater was questionable. There were rumblings that she was becoming a bit of a grande dame. Olivia was rumored to be "turning into a temperamental star of the the-a-tuh."[22] Many placed the blame on Marcus Goodrich. During the *Candida* tour, the trade papers "snickered that the two-time Oscar winner meekly acts under her husband's thumb since she left Filmville to become a stage queen. Her mate, the gossips scribble, wants her name up in lights as 'Mrs. Marcus Goodrich.' They say he insists the cast call her that, too."[23] Her marriage to the older, much-married author "blew up a storm of speculative comment. . . . He is scornful of Hollywood pretense. . . . If Olivia is a Trilby she is an obviously happy one. She shows her adoration of her husband as openly as a schoolgirl."[24] Except that Olivia wasn't a schoolgirl, making that description disturbingly paternal. Her future costar Richard Burton remarked, "'[Olivia] was married to a very eccentric man, very forgettable, who thought that his wife was the mid-century Duse and had a notice put on the board that all members of the crew and cast were no longer to call Olivia "Livvy" which was her long-established diminutive in the industry, but as Miss de Havilland at all times.'"[25]

As a sort of mini-analysis, there are these points to consider: Olivia's marriage to Goodrich just as she freed herself from Jack Warner suggests the need for some kind of support and control, and Goodrich's age and physical stature could signify another father figure. Her mother, Lilian, was present to offer advice, but she had her own life and career, and her laissez-faire marriage to George Fontaine gave her considerable freedom. Like her daughters, Lilian was quite self-sufficient, and she expected them to be the same. Maybe Olivia was just tired and needed a place to rest her head. She also wanted to have children, and thirty years old is a turning point for career women, then as now. Finally, and this cannot be underestimated, she was on the rebound from John Huston. There had been others, but Huston was Olivia's great love, and their inability to stay together even after he divorced was a painful loss. In terms of both fidelity and charm, John was another Errol. Perhaps she had settled for the next best thing.

Olivia had married in haste and was repenting at leisure. Goodrich had taken over her career, or at least he was trying to. The gossip columns and even her own sister reported that Olivia had changed, becoming demanding and uncooperative. The couple fought. Olivia was unhappy, tired from touring, and desperate for quiet. She said of Goodrich years later:

> Marc was a rather controlling person, and quite liked other people to think that he was very much in charge of anything to do with me. But, of course, all major decisions regarding my work were made by me. Alas, Marcus was not free of the psychological reaction which many men who endure war and violence undergo, and was, himself, subject to episodes of violence. To protect our small son, Benjamin, from exposure to these occurrences was one of the reasons moving to France turned out to be so beneficial to my son's life and to my own.[26]

Although Olivia insisted that she was in complete control of her career, there were some disturbing developments that indicated an attitude of recalcitrance. She was voted "the 'most uncooperative actress of 1950.'"[27] That same year, her contract with Paramount was terminated. Initially, the three-year contract, which commenced in January 1946, called for her to appear in three films, but she made only *The Heiress* in 1948–1949. Amendments to the contract indicated that Olivia had rejected or disapproved a number of scripts, until "her employment agreement of 9-4-45 is Terminated by mutual consent as of 8-4-50."[28] Given her willingness to go on suspension when she was at Warner Brothers, this attitude wasn't surprising. However, she had been offscreen for a long time, and building her career was vital. This termination may have been influenced by her return to the theater, as well as by her and Goodrich's expectations of her talent. According to Hedda Hopper, she had "a very well preserved will of her own . . . it's made of iron."[29] But there was a grandeur and *froideur* to her behavior at this time that was unusual.

On May 18, 1952, Olivia's lawyer, Roland Rich Woolley, announced that she had separated from Goodrich, and "'unless differences are reconciled, Miss de Havilland will file divorce papers in the near future.'"[30] In a statement to the *New York Daily News* a few days later, Olivia refuted rumors that she was relinquishing custody of three-year-old Benjamin: "'I was confined to my bed for seven months to bring that boy into this world. . . . The very idea of being separated from him is terrifying. I'd never stand for it.'" She was described as having "dark circles under [her] brown eyes and she twisted a handkerchief nervously as she spoke."[31] She and Benjamin left New York for California, ostensibly for a vacation.

Six weeks later, on July 4, 1952 (Independence Day—a symbolic gesture?), Olivia filed for divorce in Los Angeles, "alleging that Goodrich wrongly inflicted physical and mental suffering without any excuse or provocation."[32] The divorce wasn't cordial, and Olivia waved alimony and attorneys' fees to facilitate the final decree, asking only for the "return of a camera, books and a Mercator map book she claims as hers."[33] Goodrich didn't fight for custody, particularly after Olivia's testimony in superior court on August 27, 1952. She looked drawn and pale in photographs, and some of her accusations were shocking. In addition to "making decisions" for her, Goodrich was rude to fans and to film magazine representatives. Once he threw a beefsteak across the room because it wasn't to his liking, and another time he canceled dinner with producer Sam Goldwyn because Olivia was late getting home. He had beaten her, on one occasion leaving a bruise on her arm "'the size of a baseball. . . . He said he would kill me. . . . I got out of the car and ran down a driveway.'"[34] The divorce was granted. As one fan magazine succinctly noted, "It was on August 26th, 1946, that she married Marcus Goodrich, a scenario writer. She divorced him six years later on their wedding anniversary."[35]

At thirty-six years old, Olivia was a single mother. She declared that she would devote herself to Benjamin and her career, and she said, "'Right now it's impossible for me to imagine ever marrying again.'"[36] Her Hollywood career was still viable, but it had cooled. Had it been forty years later, she would have formed her own production company, but Olivia wasted no time landing herself a new project, noting that she had "wanted to get the divorce behind her before she report[ed] to work" in her next film.[37] Although her sister, Joan, had earned a reputation as a Daphne du Maurier screen heroine for her work in *Rebecca* (1940) and *Frenchman's Creek* (1944), Olivia took the lead in 1952's *My Cousin Rachel* for 20th Century Fox. This return to the screen "is notable for providing de Havilland with one of the few interesting roles she would have in the next three decades and as Richard Burton's American film debut."[38] It is one of her last powerful, star-worthy roles, and she makes the most of it.

Daphne du Maurier's novel was something of a comeback for the author, just as the film adaptation would be for Olivia. Du Maurier had been inspired by her unrequited love for and complicated relationship with Ellen Doubleday, widow of publisher Nelson Doubleday. The two women had vacationed together in Florence, Italy, in 1950, and their friendship became fraught due to Daphne's rejected desires. She began to imagine a novel about a widow "she decided to call Rachel—'a cold-blooded bitch.'" Perhaps reflecting her frequent depression as well as her unrequited love for Ellen, she said the book would be "'rather sinister and a bit creepy and you will never really know whether the woman is an angel or a devil.'" Upon its publication in July 1951, the novel was a huge success in Britain, and it was "even more rapturously received" in America.[39] Given the success of previous du Maurier adaptations, it was inevitable that the novel would be made into a film.

Olivia first heard about the property from a newspaper interview given by du Maurier: "'Miss du Maurier was quoted as saying she wanted any one of four women to play Rachel in the film . . . and I was one of them. (The others were Greta Garbo, Vivien Leigh and Alida Valli.) I decided I must get the book at once—and did, from England. It fascinated me.'"[40] Olivia's competition was stiff, and getting the film made was a challenge.

George Cukor, Olivia's great friend, had read Nunnally Johnson's adaptation of du Maurier's novel and thought it would be a good opportunity to lure Greta Garbo out of retirement. But Garbo wasn't interested. Adding to Cukor's disappointment, Vivien Leigh turned it down as well. However, Cukor was delighted when Olivia secured the part, and she was thrilled at the prospect of working with the great director again. Cukor was enthusiastic about the project and visited du Maurier in Cornwall—a landscape that informed much of her writing. Cukor realized that a truly exceptional adaptation of the novel had to be filmed in that beautiful English countryside. Studio head Darryl F. Zanuck refused to authorize this expense, unfortunately. Hollywood filmmakers were reluctant to leave the back lots and shoot on location, resulting in many contemporary films that look extremely old-fashioned (MGM's misbegotten *Brigadoon* [1954] and Hitchcock's *Marnie* [1964] are two examples of obvious soundstage shoots). Cukor's dissatisfaction with the sets, the script, and the concept of the film eventually led him to drop out of the project, "leaving the picture with another puzzle hanging over its head. Would it have been a greater film had it been directed by Cukor?"[41]

Mitchell Leisen, whom Olivia adored and who had guided her to her 1946 Oscar for *To Each His Own,* was supposed to replace Cukor, but Paramount wouldn't loan him out. Then Carol Reed was "chosen to direct," but he "was unable to fulfill the assignment because of a conflict of dates."[42] Finally, contract director Henry Koster took over. Although Koster provided "sympathetic direction," one can't help but wonder what the film would have been like with Cukor or Leisen or Reed in charge.[43]

Johnson's screenplay successfully condensed the highlights of du Maurier's disturbing tale of a possibly lethal woman. Olivia appreciated the script as "'a precise transcription of the novel; all that is necessary is there. You'll never know . . . if Rachel poisoned her husband or whether she attempts to poison the boy. . . . The story is one of circumstantial evidence . . . so everything she does become[s] ambiguous.'"[44] Olivia always maintained that she preferred playing good girls over bad ones because it was more challenging to make them interesting, but she certainly embraced the ambiguity here.

Having another worthy male costar also contributed to Olivia's enthusiasm. The presence of Richard Burton, Fox's new rising star, electrified the film. He earned his first Oscar nomination, for best supporting actor (unfair, given his dominance in the film), as Philip Ashley, the young man who finds himself irresistibly drawn to Rachel, his uncle's widow. Olivia had seen Burton on Broadway in *The Lady's Not for Burning* and had tried to recruit him for *Romeo and Juliet:* "She offered Burton US$1000 a week to co-star opposite her. Burton didn't particularly take to her approach and turned her down flat."[45] Burton recounted years later that Olivia punished him for that rejection: "'I was merely a second-class citizen as far as Miss de Havilland was concerned. She refused to allow me to have co-starring billing with her. . . . I think Miss de Havilland wanted Gregory Peck for the part. . . . I never warmed to Miss de Havilland.'"[46] According to various accounts, Olivia didn't appreciate Burton making a pass at her, and she did everything she could to outshine him; he, in turn, claimed that he found her to be a snob and certainly did *not* hit on her. Another statement she made about Burton, reported by several sources, didn't help matters: "'He's a coarse-grained man with a course-grained charm, and a talent not completely developed, and a course-grained behavior which makes him not like anyone else.'"[47] She could have been describing Marcus Goodrich.

However, Olivia clearly recognized Burton's talent and told Hedda Hopper in September 1952, "I think he's very gifted. I saw him in 'The Lady's Not for Burning' on the stage. He was very fine. It was one of the finest productions I have ever seen. . . . He made a very vivid impression in that play. He has a great deal of talent. He is rather like the boy in the movie. Burton is 26; the boy is 25. I'm also the right age—10 years older (she said it with a sort of mock resignation)."[48] Olivia remembered in 2013: "Richard Burton was wildly talented and brilliantly cast. . . . He was a tempestuous sort of person, but then so was Philip Ashley! It was always a fulfilling experience to work with someone who is perfectly cast in the opposite role, and that was true with Richard in *My Cousin Rachel.*"[49] Whatever struggles they shared during filming, Olivia's view of Burton had mellowed with time, and she recognized his perfection in the role, which also won him a Golden Globe for new star of the year.

Playing Rachel created a new film image for Olivia, one of mystery and sensuality. In 2015, she discussed her preparation for the role:

> In preparation for *My Cousin Rachel,* I had to know whether Rachel was guilty or innocent before I could portray her. After reading the book twice, I still had no idea which she was. I read it a third time, and this time I thought I knew. It was now my task to play every scene so that she could be interpreted either way, thus fulfilling du Maurier's intention.
>
> Some years later I met du Maurier's great friend, Carol Reed, the brilliant British film director. . . . I asked Carol Reed if du Maurier had confided to him the secret of Rachel's guilt or innocence, saying that I had read the book three times before perceiving what I was sure was the truth, and was eager to know if I had guessed correctly. He swore me to secrecy and then let me know what du Maurier had told him. To my great delight it was the same as my conclusion. This is the secret I have kept all these years.[50]

As the title character, Olivia offers viewers an inscrutable "heroine." Is Rachel simply a sophisticated, continental widow, or is she a murderous black widow who kills one rich man and then seduces his heir? Jeanine Basinger, in her insightful book *A Woman's View,* comments, "Burton is Eyre to Olivia de Havilland's Rochester."[51] Her Rachel is a mysterious temptress who insinuates herself into the lonely young man's heart with her candor, her smiles, her flirtations, and her link to his dead uncle. She allows herself to be draped with jewels by her young lover while brewing a tisane for his health like a good auntie. And we never know whether that special tea is aphrodisiacal or arsenical.

Olivia is a changed actress in this film. And her costar is the new heartthrob of the screen. As Rachel, she wins his affection—believably—from the young, fresh Audrey Dalton as Louise, who is in love with Burton's Philip. In a wonderfully romantic dream sequence, when Philip is ill with fever (or did Rachel make him ill?), the young man dreams that he has married her, and Olivia is a beautiful bride in this soft-filter scene, desirable yet mature.

Olivia was particularly appreciative of the "glorious period wardrobe designed by Dorothy Jeakins."[52] She is dressed in black as a widow for most of the action, and her costumes are off-the-shoulder chiffon confections apropos for a woman of the world (which new divorcée Olivia was). Her dark eyes flash with a bright intelligence, and the actress emanates a soignée quality, offering her traditional warmth along with something else—an enigmatic sexual elegance. Her voice is still melodious, but as in *The Dark Mirror,* she uses a low register, incorporating a slight British intonation that adds "a further note of mystery to the woman who explains so little about herself, letting her actions speak for her."[53] Her hair is styled elaborately for Rachel's public appearances, but when it is long, loose, and flowing down her back as she kisses Burton passionately while clad in a white nightgown, we have an actress who is a true femme fatale. "This single kiss by one of the world's great *actors* was the most erotic she ever received on screen."[54]

The film is a melodrama and a mystery, a woman's film as well as a horror film, a romance and a Gothic tale in the feminine tradition that contributed to the reassessment of du Maurier's importance.[55] Although it doesn't rank alongside other adaptations, it "does have two perfect stars: Olivia de Havilland and Richard Burton."[56] Accompanied by Franz Waxman's beautiful score, the film offers "a profound understanding of fear, paranoia, and the way that a man's best impulses can be twisted by his worst, suspicion eating away at love."[57] Bosley Crowther applauded: "Olivia de Havilland does a dandy job of playing the soft and gracious Rachel with just a faint suggestion of the viper's tongue."[58] As Rachel Weisz said about the character Rachel Ashley, whom she incarnated in the 2017 remake (there was also a moody television version in 1983 with Geraldine Chaplin as a very Italian Rachel), "It has got this kind of modern streak to it, about a woman who is self-defining and transgressive. She's just got her own personal ideas about the way in which a woman should be allowed to live."[59] Weisz could have been describing Olivia herself.

Olivia was back onscreen, and the film was successful. But clearly, Hollywood was changing. Not only had the studio system been dismantled, but audiences were changing. The postwar world of cinema was far more European, far more socially conscious, far grittier. Olivia would not shy away from that trend, but she was associated with a more traditional, conservative Hollywood, and she was approaching the dreaded forty. Bette Davis had left Warner Brothers after the camp classic *Beyond the Forest* (1949) and had landed on her feet with *All About Eve,* but this was arguably her last great role, despite three more Oscar nominations. Joan Crawford was one of the few female stars of the golden era who managed to stay viable throughout the 1950s, but her films became increasingly melodramatic and formulaic. Television, too, was changing the industry. Olivia was astute enough to see that the Hollywood she had known no longer existed, and she was reconfiguring her career options.

One disappointment that may have influenced her opinion was her inability to attract interest in a film version of Graham Greene's novel *The End of the Affair.* She and producer David Lewis read a script they liked, although it was only a first draft, and Lewis had positive talks with Carl Laemmle Jr. at Universal about shooting the film in London. Lewis approached William Wyler several times, beginning in August 1952, to secure his interest in directing. Producer Ray Stark also tried to convince Wyler, and in an intriguing letter to the director he referred to "the person we were discussing" rather than naming Olivia, perhaps to protect the project from gossip or to prevent poaching of the idea. Wyler clearly had concerns about Olivia's willingness to play an adulterous woman, and Stark wrote, "I realize the restraint that you felt in this young lady, but I would like you to remember that during your last motion picture association she was playing a role that required restraint, and also that her own personal situation was one which, as you know only too well, forced her to restraint"—a reference to Marcus Goodrich's controlling influence.[60]

The project moved ahead to the point that the Breen office got involved with the script, and Wyler was clearly frustrated that the censors were trying to tone down the story's sexual passion. Wyler wrote to Lewis, "In the final analysis, this is a story about adultery and making a picture about adultery is what particularly interests me so there could be no question as to what this picture is about. . . . It would be a pity if our moral hypocrisy has carried us to a point where we wipe out adultery by taking it off the agenda."[61] Wyler also wanted $250,000, which Stark agreed to try to secure, although he noted that it was "a lot of dough in cash to dig up for an independent project these days."[62] Given Stark's later Hollywood successes, the financing difficulties are painfully ironic. By December 1952, the discussions between Wyler and Stark had slowed to pleasantries and a hope that everyone would be able to work together one day.

Meanwhile, Olivia remained steadfastly single. She said of that time, "Louella [Parsons] was unhappy, Hedda [Hopper] was unhappy, my agent was unhappy, and the publicity department at Fox, where I'd made *Rachel,* was unhappy. They wanted me to fall in love. . . . Louella, Hedda, my agent, and Fox just didn't understand; they wagged their heads and remarked sadly, 'There's only one male she loves, and that's Ben.'"[63] Fortuitously, she received an invitation from the French government to attend the Cannes Film Festival in April 1953 (she would be the first female jury president in 1965, followed the next year by Sophia Loren), which she happily agreed to attend with Benjamin, who was now almost four (this led to some misunderstanding about her need for a second plane ticket for the young man who would be traveling with her). In anticipation of the trip, Olivia wondered "what the very first Frenchman I would meet would be like" (she must have forgotten her passionate kisses with Charles Boyer in *Hold Back the Dawn*).[64] The man who greeted her when she landed in France was just her type—a bit older (forty-two to Olivia's thirty-seven), tall, powerfully built, intellectual, thoughtful, and successful. He was "handsome but hangdog. Clean-shaven and solemn. Didn't speak English, didn't even speak French. And did not kiss my hand."[65] He was Pierre Paul Galante—a wonderfully metaphorical surname—the *secrétaire général* of *Paris Match.*

Galante was a highly respected journalist who had worked tirelessly during World War II as a secret agent for the Allies. He was also one of Coco Chanel's biographers, having written *Les Années Chanel*—an irony, given Olivia's loyal association with Christian Dior.[66] Olivia and Pierre had a whirlwind courtship. Her divorce from Goodrich was finalized on August 26, 1953, and many press outlets speculated that she was now free to marry Galante, who had flown to California to be with her.[67] One claimed, "She plans to spend most of her time in Europe after the wedding."[68] In October 1953,

Olivia and Benjamin moved to France. She would never live full time in the United States again, although she retained her US passport.

Galante was a Roman Catholic and a French citizen, and under French law, they could not marry until Olivia had been divorced for one year. Her 1962 memoir *Every Frenchman Has One*—referring to a liver, of course—details this waiting period and presents a witty, bemused, stylish view of their first years together. Olivia was happy to be in Paris, where she would be able to explore her European heritage and share it with Benjamin. She remembered, "It was a very, very positive step to move to Paris, as Hollywood, its great Golden Era in ashes, was a most depressing place in which to dwell. Furthermore, it was no place to bring up my four-year-old son; Paris turned out to be a brilliant choice on his account alone."[69]

As she settled into her Parisian life, Olivia worked. Had she remained in California, with or without Galante, she might have done a television series, as did other stars of her era, including Loretta Young, Dick Powell, Ronald Reagan, and Robert Young. "Indeed," she commented, "very early on, I did receive such an offer which I declined."[70] Television was, at that time, definitely a step down for an aging generation of Hollywood stars, although it proved to be lucrative for people like Lucille Ball, Dick Powell, and Ozzie and Harriet Nelson. But Olivia didn't need the exposure; nor did she need the income. After almost twenty years, Olivia was ready for a complete change.

First, she made a film that is almost impossible to see now. It is not available on DVD, and just recently it appeared on YouTube dubbed in Spanish as *La Princesa de Eboli—That Lady* (1955). Clearly, it is still popular among some Spanish-speaking audiences. The screenplay was based on *That Lady,* a popular historical novel by Irish author Kate O'Brien. The author describes Olivia's character as follows:

> Ana de Mendoza y de las Cerda, Princess of Eboli and Duchess of Pastrana . . . heiress in her own right to the estates, privileges and titles of one of the greatest lines of . . . the leading family of Spain . . . was physically the expression of what that implied. Her beauty, for those who found her beautiful, was, paradoxically, of exaggeration and restraint. . . . Her left eye was full of light, but over the socket of the right one she wore, as has been said, a black silk eye-shade, cut in diamond shape. She had worn this since she was fourteen. At that age she fought a duel with a page in her father's house, and lost her right eye.[71]

In true heroine fashion, Olivia is "loved silently by King Philip II (Paul Scofield) and ardently by his advisor, Antonio Perez (Gilbert Roland). The plot involves a convoluted scheme to supplant Philip with his exiled brother."[72]

That Olivia looks utterly splendid in the period garments is a tribute to her maturing beauty as well as her long years of practice wearing such gowns. This was Paul Scofield's film debut, and the movie also features the wonderful British actor Dennis Price and the divine Christopher Lee, so it is not as weak as it might have been. Terence Young, who would gain fame just a few years later for his Hammer horror films, directs effectively if unimaginatively, but the script is weak, and ultimately, the movie feels like the bottom half of a double bill. On the plus side, *That Lady* is shot in luscious Technicolor. Paul Scofield brings elegance and gravitas to his role, and his chemistry with Olivia is solid. Despite her leather eye patch, Olivia overcomes the distraction, delivers her lines gracefully, and manages the scope of the action with spirit and ease, offering "a warm account of a troubled and thwarted beauty."[73] At times, she is almost too grand, despite her status in the story. Olivia is developing here her midlife persona of a sophisticated, witty woman capable of great feeling and great depth. Her performance is believable and gripping, but she doesn't take the chances she did in the 1940s. Nevertheless, *That Lady* is a competent historical melodrama, and Ana de Mendoza's sad end—prison and death—gives the film a genuinely tragic trajectory.

Olivia next returned to the United States to make a film with a director whose commitment to social cinema would grow over the years: Stanley Kramer, later known for his landmark comedy *Guess Who's Coming to Dinner* with Katharine Hepburn and Spencer Tracy. *Not as a Stranger* (1955) was, for the time, a realistic depiction of young interns in training and then establishing their first medical practices. It was based on Morton Thompson's bestselling 1954 novel, which was "948 pages of C sections, stitches, and sex. Not that it was a project without a socially relevant subtext . . . provok[ing] readers with its scathing exposé of the medical industry."[74]

Olivia told journalist Erskine Johnson that she had left Hollywood not only for Galante but also because there were few "'good stories with roles of stature for an actress. Hollywood went into a cycle of movies about brave men. The women roles were just decorative. I'd been decorative. I wanted to progress. . . . And when it was offered to me . . . I fled right back to Hollywood.'"[75] She had top billing in *Stranger* and was joined by Robert Mitchum, Frank Sinatra, Broderick Crawford, and Gloria Grahame. Kramer loved all-star casts, and this, his directorial debut, is no exception. It is also very earnest, which is one of the key elements in all of Kramer's films—an almost preternatural sincerity. *Stranger* also prefigures the popularity of doctor-based TV shows of the 1950s and 1960s such as *Ben Casey* and *Dr. Kildare.*

The film was an enormous popular success and "grossed what was an amazing figure in the 1950s—over $50 million."[76] Olivia brought her usual fervor to the role. She viewed real surgeries, spending "all day at a hospital while the film was in preparation and then go[ing] to the actors' rehearsals in the evening."[77] Cast as Swedish nurse Kristina Hedvigson from Minnesota, thirty-nine-year-old Olivia is beautifully petite, although her platinum-blonde hair is a bit jarring. Also jarring is her use of a "'yumpin yiminee' Swedish accent" that doesn't sound particularly authentic, despite dialect coaching from Swede Virginia Christine, who plays her sister.[78] Her role is underwritten, but Olivia appears believably competent in the surgery scenes.

Nurse Kristina meets and falls in love with Lucas Marsh (Robert Mitchum), a young doctor with a drunken father and enormous financial struggles as he tries to finish his medical studies. Attracted by Kristina's savings, he unscrupulously woos and weds her. His colleague Al (Frank Sinatra, returning to the screen after his Oscar win for *From Here to Eternity*) disapproves of Marsh's behavior, in a charming reversal of type. Marsh graduates, gets his first job in a small town, and has an affair with local femme fatale Harriet Lang (Gloria Grahame). He finally comes to his senses and returns to the long-suffering Kristina.

The black-and-white cinematography and Kramer's trademark insistence on authenticity, combined with the power of the ensemble and the cast's authentic camaraderie, give the film an almost documentary quality. *Not as a Stranger* is dated technically, of course, but it is still a highly watchable melodrama. This is a new kind of role for Mitchum, one with gravitas and understated grace. Sinatra plays a breezy rich kid, and his scenes with Olivia are warm and friendly. Olivia's Kristina is a mixture of brisk efficiency and the archetypically understanding doctor's wife who stops working after marriage, despite their money issues. Unfortunately, her frilly, uberfeminine costumes by Don Loper contradict her cool professionalism, and the steamy sexuality that should be apparent on her wedding night just isn't there. When I asked Olivia what it was like to kiss Mitchum, she confessed, "I don't remember."[79] They lack the kind of chemistry Mitchum has with bad-girl Grahame, but perhaps Marsh's exploitation of Kristina justifies the missing spark.

That may sum up the problem with the film. Everyone is pretending to be earnest, but no one is fully committed to it. The film set was very much a boys' club; all the leading actors were major boozers and brawlers. Sinatra and Crawford got into it so badly that Crawford ate Sinatra's toupee and almost choked on it.[80] Kramer recalled, "Mitchum, Sinatra, and Crawford constantly badgered Olivia de Havilland with their gags, leers, and suggestive remarks, they did not hesitate to squeeze or pinch her beautiful derriere. . . . Olivia was smart enough to fend them off without benefit of harassment laws. She told them they were just boys pretending to be sex symbols."[81]

Olivia held her own. She liked Sinatra and recalled that he had "an extraordinarily quick mind, was always on time, and perfectly prepared. He was so professional that it was unnerving. I admired him and his work very much but we had no contact with each other except during the scenes we played together."[82] She never complained about her adolescent, arrested-development castmates, telling screenplay author Edward Anhalt, "'They don't bother me. I've been around drunks.'"[83] Overall, *Stranger* was a good experience for Olivia, maintaining her career profile in Hollywood as she awaited permission to marry Galante.

Finally, on April 2, 1955, two years after they met, Olivia and Pierre Galante were married in a civil ceremony in the village of Yvon-Le-Marron in central France, at the hunting lodge belonging to the mayor. Like her wedding to Goodrich, the ceremony was small and private (except for the press afterward), without much pomp and circumstance, although the impressive guest list included film director Lewis Milestone, author Marcel Pagnol, and Princess Niloufer of Turkey.[84] Olivia's witness was *Look* magazine editor Fleur Cowles, who remembered, "I gave her away as her 'temoin' as she and her mother and sister, Joan Fontaine, were not on speaking terms at that time."[85] Cowles remained a close friend of Olivia's.

Five-year-old Benjamin wore a French sailor suit, complete with a jaunty beanie and red pom-pom. Olivia looked very chic in "a gray flannel suit by Christian Dior [also a wedding guest] named with the single letter 'A.' The name derives from the shape of the skirt which spreads out broadly with many pleats on either side. She also had a small white hat with a veil and shoes and purse in gray suede to match her suit. The bridegroom wore a blue suit."[86] Photos show a joyous Olivia and Pierre, with Benjamin beside them, walking through the village after the ceremony, followed by a crowd of local well-wishers, and beaming as they cut their four-tiered cake. After a two-week honeymoon in Ischia, off Naples, they resumed their lives in Paris.

Shortly after their wedding, Olivia and Galante helped engineer another fairy-tale romance, albeit unintentionally. Grace Kelly had been invited to

Cannes in the spring of 1955 but was not interested in attending, preferring to stay in New York. However, when it turned out that her new romantic interest, Jean-Pierre Aumont, had business in Cannes and then in Paris, Grace suddenly *was* interested. Meanwhile, *Paris Match*'s managing editor, Gaston Bonheur, had learned of Grace's impending visit and asked Galante whether he might arrange a photo opportunity with the actress and Prince Rainier of Monaco, which would be of international interest and a coup for the magazine. Galante told him that he "doubted such a meeting would be possible. . . . Galante and his wife . . . departed from the Gare de Lyon and headed for Cannes. By sheer coincidence, Grace held a reservation on the same train."[87] Olivia shared with me the story of how she and Galante arranged the encounter that changed Grace Kelly's life:

> In the restaurant car of the train bound from Paris to Cannes, I was dining with . . . Gaston Bonheur, his assistant, and my French husband . . . when Grace Kelly entered the car, passed by our table, and seated herself out of sight. . . . This prompted my dinner companions to urge me to seek her out and ask if she would be willing to be presented to Prince Rainier. . . . I immediately replied that I did not know Grace Kelly and would not think of disturbing her while she was dining. . . . Grace Kelly finished her dinner and passed by our table once again. This time all three dinner companions insisted that I follow her and present their proposal.
>
> Ever cooperative, I followed her to the end of the car. . . . I introduced myself with an apology for doing so, and posed the essential question. Grace Kelly replied that she would be willing, but the appointment had to be approved of by Metro Goldwyn Mayer, the studio sponsoring her visit to the Festival. This was the message I took back to my dinner companions.
>
> The next morning, somebody staged and photographed a meeting between Grace Kelly and me on the station's platform as if we were meeting for the first time, which I didn't like because it was contrived, and which I don't think she liked either for the same reason.
>
> A few days later, my husband . . . arranged the appointment with Rainier and Grace Kelly. He obtained the counsel of an expert on the protocol . . . and on the appointed afternoon, called for Grace and her advisor in a limousine to effect this very special meeting.

Both Prince Rainier and Grace Kelly seemed very much affected by this meeting and, in due time, a Monacan priest visited the Kelly family in Philadelphia as Rainier's emissary, and was soon followed by a visit from Prince Rainier, himself.

The marriage took place in Monaco the following year (April 1956). My husband attended, but I could not do so because I was, as they say, "big with child," expecting my darling daughter, Gisèle.[88]

Olivia's life in Paris was joyous. After the long wait to marry Galante, she wrote a charming piece for the *Los Angeles Times* about her new world:

> Now I am a French wife. My husband, son and I live in an apartment I like to think is very French indeed. Its chandeliers are so low you run a risk of bumping your head. . . . With us is my 14-year-old three-legged Airedale, Shadrach [John Huston's gift], whose infirmity is owing to an accident he had when he was only a few weeks old. It does not stop him from being happy. . . . My son is completely taken with Pierre. . . . By the time we returned from our honeymoon in Italy . . . [Benjamin] presented to me, obtained we will never know how, a French book entitled "Guide to Newlyweds."
>
> "Read this," he ordered. "It will tell you all about how to take care of the baby. . . ."
>
> I am getting reading practice in French. I am busy with "Guide to Newlyweds." For Ben is going to have his wish in July—but it mustn't be a baby sister because he wants a brother to box with![89]

On July 18, 1956, just two weeks after Olivia's fortieth birthday, Gisèle was born. Adored by Olivia, she would grow up to earn a law degree and also be a journalist like her father. Despite his stated preference for a brother, Ben and Gisèle had a strong relationship. Soon, they would all move to their house at 3 rue Benouville, in the sixteenth arrondisement in Paris, which is still owned by Olivia.

Life was delicious at long last. Olivia had an elegant home, a happy marriage, two beautiful children, and the luxury of choosing projects that interested her. Unlike so many of her contemporaries, she wasn't possessed by the mad need to earn a living or maintain her star status. She wrote the occasional article, indulging an interest she had had for years. She often wrote with humor, noting in *McCall's* magazine, "By golly, I'm alive, all right, and I do live in France. Furthermore, I speak first-class foreign French."[90] In an interview in 1958, she discussed her love of yoga and sparred happily with Galante (wearing his Legion d'Honneur ribbon). She declared, "'That is what I like about Frenchmen. They are courteous, attentive, mature, protective towards women,' . . . [a]nd *stroked his grey hair.*"[91]

Olivia balanced her private and public lives extremely well. While her public persona was one of sophisticated comportment, privately, she could be tough. Another article from 1958, entitled "Olivia—The Bellicose Belle," captured the essence of that dichotomy: "A chit of a woman . . . Miss de Havilland at 42 looks as lovely, as fragile and innocent as a bit of Dresden bric-a-brac. But anyone who tries to fool with her deep-seated sense of moral integrity feels as though he has grabbed a high-voltage wire." She explained that curious yin and yang of her personality: "'I think it may be because I have a man's mind in a woman's body.'"[92]

She used that sangfroid to positive effect in 1958, when she was "secretly called to Washington by the House Committee on Un-American Activities" to defend her association with the Hollywood Independent Citizens Committee of the Arts, Sciences and Professions. She effectively explained her 1946 activities, but with characteristic rebellious wit, she recalled, "'I wore a red suit and I said, "Please don't think that the color explains my political opinion." The staff investigator was infuriated with the line and roared, "Strike that from the record."'"[93] Olivia returned to Paris unscathed.

She engaged with Congress again that year when she needed help with another issue. Under the McCarran-Walter Immigration Act, the citizenship of naturalized Americans who lived abroad for more than five years could be revoked. Olivia had lived in Paris since 1953 and was in danger of losing her US citizenship unless she returned to the States and took up permanent residence for at least twelve months. However, as reported by the *Los Angeles Times,* the "State Department can waive the requirement of returning to this country if it finds that a naturalized citizen abroad is performing duties that contribute to the welfare and security of the country. It has refused to waive the requirements for Miss de Havilland."[94] Once again demonstrating her perspicacity, she "found a champion in Rep. Francis Walter (D., Pa.) who . . . introduced a bill which would permit her to remain in France. . . . His bill, introduced simply as 'bill for relief of Olivia Mary Galante,' is expected to pass Congress without any trouble."[95] It did.

Back in Paris, Olivia was happy. Although she had always enjoyed wearing beautiful clothes in her films and for special events such as Hollywood premieres, Olivia had never been a fashionista. With the move to Paris, however, she became a devoted client of Christian Dior. Olivia chose a Dior creation for her wedding to Galante, and he designed the maternity clothes she wore during her pregnancy with Gisèle; her "fragrance of choice was Eau Fraiche, and later Diorissimo."[96] Her private life as a Dior client informed some of her film costumes over the next few years. For example, her wedding suit and the dresses she wore in the 1956 romantic comedy *The Ambassador's Daughter* were from the same collection. There are some wonderful photos of her posing with Dior at fittings for her costumes, and their affection for each other is obvious. One photo of Olivia in the wedding dress from the film seems to prefigure Helen Rose's design for Grace Kelly the following year; Kelly, another transplanted American, became a loyal patron of the design house. Olivia was also dressed in Dior by Yves Saint Laurent in *Libel* (1959) and Marc Bohan in *Light in the Piazza* (1962). Other Dior creations for Olivia included "evening gowns for the big movie events: a taffeta-print Nuit de Grenade for the Academy Awards ceremony in 1960, a *Soirée* à Rio for the *Gone with the Wind* Civil War centennial in Atlanta in 1961 . . . and a Framboisine for the London premiere of Walter Grauman's *Lady in a Cage* (1964)."[97]

The Ambassador's Daughter was "an offer that Olivia de Havilland could not resist: a light-hearted comedy to be filmed in Technicolor in her new hometown, Paris, and concocted by writer-director-producer Norman Krasna, who had been responsible for her delightful *Princess O'Rourke* a dozen years earlier." Olivia's radiance, "plus the excellent CinemaScope photography by Michael Kelber of the magnificent city, almost compensates for the rather weak scenario."[98] Olivia's wardrobe is elegant, her hair is done by Carita-Alexandre in bangs and a flip, and she looks petite and fresh at thirty-nine. The ensemble is delightful, including handsome John Forsythe, personable sidekick Tommy Noonan, the divine Myrna Loy as her aunt, and Adolphe Menjou as her ambassador father. Norman Krasna, who won an Oscar for the *Princess O'Rourke* screenplay, creates a breezy and bubbly bit of froth. The only problem: everyone is fifteen years too old.

The sophisticated Joan Fisk (Olivia) is bored with her duties as her father's hostess in Paris. However, life becomes interesting when she attends a charity Dior fashion show, where she will be modeling the glorious gowns. There, she meets two GIs—Danny Sullivan (John Forsythe) and his pal Al (Tommy Noonan), who bluff their way into the venue. Olivia swirls and bows past the two lads like a pro, and she fakes a good French accent as she says flirtatiously, "*Je vous aime.* I love you. *Je vous aime.*" This intrigues Danny, who replies, "She knew how to say it, too." On a bet, she accepts a date with Danny, in defiance of her father and her fiancé, who think of her as a sheltered girl who can't handle these wolves. She decides to go out for an hour with Danny and then return to prove that "the American enlisted man is not a mucker, though I'm not sure what a mucker is."[99] Of course, love and romance ensue, and there are misunderstandings, but American amour conquers all.

The film is dated, but it serves a purpose. Olivia "leads viewers, foremost among them the American viewer, into that Paris of fantasies where all (or almost all) women are wearing Dior, and where even the little neighborhood bistro has a doorman . . . and Baccarat crystal [is] on the tables. . . . One drinks only champagne."[100] Ten years after the end of World War II, the travelogue film was very popular with Americans (think 1954's *Three Coins in the Fountain*), and it was a patriotic way to encourage European tourism. It's well intentioned and pretty and pleasant, and the Belgian Film Critics gave Olivia the Prix Femina for the best comedy performance by an actress that year.[101]

Olivia was back in Hollywood in July 1957, with baby Gisèle and eight-year-old Ben, filming *The Proud Rebel* (1958) for Buena Vista—a wonderful, underrated western directed by Michael Curtiz and starring Alan Ladd. In the film, for which she received $175,000, Olivia "portrays a mannish Western pioneer-type woman who plows, harnesses horses, jumps spraddle-legged onto mules, and in the end is softened into femininity by her love for Alan Ladd," a bit of a caricatured summary of her role as Linnett Moore.[102] She "negotiated her own contract, which is the kind of forthright thing the no-nonsense lady in this particular story would have done."[103] Olivia, "looking ten years younger than she should, . . . has returned to work, bursting with self-sufficient enterprise . . . and outspoken comments."[104]

Producer Sam Goldwyn Jr. was very interested in Olivia, and when he called to talk to her about the role, he said, "Mike [Curtiz] says he wants *you* for the part of Linnett." She noted that Curtiz "was *very* Hungarian but not always nice to me."[105] However, he certainly knew how to direct a western, and despite his terrible temper, Olivia felt comfortable with Curtiz and respected his expertise. Another plus: the role of Linnett would put her back on a horse, which was something she loved. The film also introduced her to Alan Ladd's young son David, who was around the same age as Olivia's Benjamin. David turns in a memorable performance as a traumatized lad who finds comfort and friendship with Olivia's character. He grew up to become a Hollywood producer, and they remained close; David Ladd attended Olivia's 100th birthday celebration in Paris.

The film is a tribute to the brave pioneers who settled the western territories as America expanded after the Civil War. Set in Aberdeen, Illinois, but partially filmed in Utah, the film offers lush panoramic views as the Ladds, playing John and son David Chandler, ride past lakes and rivers, along fields and country roads, and across pastoral prairies. Father and son have moved north to make a new life after the South's defeat, as well as to find a doctor for David, who is mute (his condition induced by the horrors of war). Chandler's bridle gives him away as a Confederate to a traveling salesman (aquiline character actor and bad man John Carradine), who hates these southern refugees. Chandler is defensive, saying, "The war's over, Mister."[106] Therein lies the film's tension—the residual anger and mistrust in America after the Civil War, the toll the war took on children and parents, and the hope for redemption and a more united country. Once again, Olivia chose a film with a social message.

Olivia's role is a supporting one, but it was a very smart move for the actress. Now forty-one, Olivia recognized the trajectory of "aging" actresses in Hollywood; character roles offered a way to keep working and stay visible. Rather than attempting to hold on to her youthful beauty in every role, she followed her Dior-clad sophisticate in *The Ambassador's Daughter* with a prairie woman, sans makeup and airs, in *The Proud Rebel.*

Olivia's lifelong love of canines was gratified on this shoot. King, a border collie, adds a sweet touch to this family picture as David's dog, Lance. This is, after all, a Buena Vista film, a branch of Walt Disney Productions, and it maintains a balance between sentimentality and action throughout. There is also a terrific supporting cast, including the gentle Cecil Kellaway as Quaker doctor Enos Davis, who tells Chandler that the boy's problem isn't merely physical "but up here," in his mind.[107] An operation by the right man could help, however, and the right man is at the Mayo Clinic in Rochester, Minnesota. Chandler's challenge is to raise the money. Young David Ladd's performance is very natural and winning, informed, no doubt, by working with his father. When they hold hands as they walk down the street, one is moved by the thought of Alan Ladd's early death only six years later.

A good western needs bad guys, and this film has two excellent villains. One is played by Dean Jagger, who watches young David's border collie herd sheep and decides that he wants the dog. John Chandler, who needs the money to pay for his son's operation, sells the dog—losing David's love in the process. The other evil critter is played by Harry Dean Stanton (billed as "Dean Stanton"), looking creepy, thin, and wasted. When a false charge of drunkenness and violence is leveled against Chandler by the two bad Deans,

Olivia's Linnett steps in. She offers to pay Chandler's fine and tells him that he can work it off at her place. Even though she has no husband and needs help on her farm, she declares, "I'm not a man-starved old maid."[108] So the Chandlers go to help Linnett with her 200 acres of barley. Then the two bad Deans cause more trouble, rampaging over Linnett's property, pulling down her fences, and allowing their sheep to trample her crops. They burn down her barn and destroy her harvest, yet the Chandlers don't desert her. Olivia, the Ladds, and three studio technicians "suffered minor but painful burns . . . when a gust of wind blew flames at them during a barn-burning scene."[109] Undeterred, they continued filming.

The tensions of the film are finally resolved with a successful operation for David, retribution for the bad men, and the reunion of the boy and his dog. At the end of the film, when Linnett sees John and David walking across the field, Curtiz gives them a clear-blue-sky close-up. David calls, "Linnett! Linnett! Linnett!"[110] They run toward each other, she embraces David in a sincerely tear-jerking moment, and she smiles lovingly at John. Then the three of them walk back to the farm, hand in hand and arm in arm.

Curtiz's direction offers a balance between action scenes and tender character development. This is a physical role for Olivia—she can unhitch the horses and wear a pretty dress—and she is beaming with health and joy. Without makeup, she looks pretty in the gorgeous sunset shots, and it seems clear that director Curtiz likes her. He and cinematographer Ted D. McCord know how to photograph Olivia to beautiful effect. In particular, her scenes with David Ladd radiate authentic affection. *The Proud Rebel* deserves more recognition as a moving family film and a classic of its kind, as well as a fine entry in Olivia's filmography.

Although Olivia was living a very respectable life, she couldn't escape a bit of Hollywood gossip. She managed to draw the ire of Jayne Mansfield, of all people. Olivia had commented on the trend in Hollywood films toward nudity, overt sexuality, and blonde bombshells, observing, "'With the aggressive bosom, American women risk losing their femininity.'"[111] On the one hand, Olivia's stereotyping of buxom women is a bit disappointing. On the other hand, the exploitation of women's sexuality in 1950s Hollywood cinema *is* stereotypical and misogynistic; Olivia preferred subtlety. She has clearly adopted the French approach to the female figure and to what constitutes femininity, asserting, "'There is no woman more clever with men than the French woman and more discreet. She knows that men consider the way a woman dresses as an expression of her taste and . . . to enhance her sex, not to exhibit it. If the average girl here would take away her platforms and padding . . . she would be much more charming, as is the Venus de Milo.'"[112] Jayne Mansfield didn't take kindly to Olivia's comments, saying, "'It's ridiculous to tell women of today to accept the Venus de Milo as a standard of beauty. . . . Her tummy sticks out and her waist is about the same size as her bosom.'"[113]

The specter of Olivia's feud with her sister, Joan, had also reappeared. She asserted to *Newsweek* in November 1957 that they were no longer angry with each other: "'I took a very English view of this. The English keep it inside, you know. But living in France has helped me this way.'"[114] However, gossip columnist Sheilah Graham (known for her love affair with F. Scott Fitzgerald and her memoir of that liaison, *Beloved Infidel*) chastised Olivia for refusing to meet with her mother, Lilian, and Joan when they were all in Hollywood, warning, "'One day it may be too late.'"[115] The source of the leak to Graham about the missed opportunity is unknown—but one can hypothesize.

Olivia's next project, *Libel* (1959), brought her to MGM in London to play an elegant society hostess whose husband may have a terrible secret. Directed by Anthony Asquith and based on a 1934 London and 1935 Broadway play, *Libel* also stars British actor Dirk Bogarde, who plays two roles: a noble lord and his scurrilous look-alike. Olivia again wears sumptuous Christian Dior couture, looking elegant and properly aristocratic throughout. Her role as lady of the manor is more decorative than dramatic, and she hasn't much to do until the climax of the film. Her chemistry with Bogarde is warm and authentic, and her kisses with him sizzle—tastefully, as befits the upper classes. She enjoyed working with Bogarde and told columnist Hedda Hopper, "He's very sweet to work with, very gallant and well mannered. I love making films—and you have to express your love."[116]

The plot revolves around the possibility that Sir Mark Loddon (Bogarde) may not be who he says he is. He has memory problems caused by trauma suffered during the war, and after he and his wife, Lady Margaret (Olivia), appear on a British television program, a former fellow soldier and friend of Mark's, Jeffrey Buckenham (played with conviction by Paul Massie), alerts the authorities to the possibility that Mark may really be con man Frank Welney. The men had been prisoners of war, and Welney bore a remarkable resemblance to Sir Mark. They committed a daring escape, but only one of them returned home—ostensibly, Mark Loddon. Or did he? The two roles offer a wonderful acting opportunity for Bogarde. Olivia had played good and evil twins in *The Dark Mirror*, so that aspect of the film likely appealed to her, although a richer role would have appealed much more.

The case goes to court, where the wonderfully watchable Robert Morley and Wilfred Hyde-White play dueling barristers, debating whether Mark is himself or Welney. The tension of the film comes not only from the possibility that Frank Welney has been impersonating an aristocrat but also that Margaret has allowed him into her bed and had a child with him. Her husband can't remember the full story of his imprisonment and escape, and he is missing fingers—exactly as Welney was.

The film is very 1950s British and very proper, but the acting is excellent. Bogarde is riveting to watch, as always, and as the film progresses, we see Olivia's Margaret start to have doubts about her husband, followed by guilt and anger about those doubts. Her demeanor is mature and confident throughout the film, yet she grows rather brusque as she begins to question the identity of the stranger beside her. At first, she has complete faith in "Mark," saying with sincerity, "Darling, I'm your wife, I know who you are, and I'll swear it in court if you'll let me."[117] Her romantic scenes with Bogarde, played in divine silk Dior nightgowns, are warm and womanly.

But as the plot twists and turns, Margaret comes to believe that her husband is Frank Welney after all. Every actress enjoys a courtroom scene, and Olivia gets hers in *Libel.* When a hideously scarred prisoner with no memory, known only as Number 15, is brought into court, Margaret realizes that *he* may be Mark Loddon after all. Olivia's confusion is palpable in the scene, and when Morley asks her if she still believes her husband is the real Sir Mark, she's silent. Then she looks at her husband with tears and says, "No. No he is not Mark Loddon."[118] She has that trademark de Havilland steel in her voice and her face. What made her change her mind? "What I have just seen and heard. . . . When I saw that he recognized Number 15 and that that poor creature recognized him. . . . No, I couldn't misinterpret the horror and the guilt I saw on my husband's face."[119] Olivia's building energy through the scene is profoundly moving, and when she rushes out of the courtroom, all seems lost.

However, in the film's final scene, Mark asks for the jacket Number 15 is wearing, and there he finds something he hid in the lining—a little silver and enamel medallion Margaret had given him. Finally, he remembers what happened. Jeffrey testifies that they were alone when Mark gave it to Welney. The trial is dismissed. And what of Margaret and Mark? With a kiss and a smile, they walk out of the courtroom arm in arm. Shot in gritty black and white, *Libel* is an interesting transitional film from traditional British drama to something more kitchen sinkish. The reviews weren't terribly positive, however, and they labeled the film a 1930s melodrama—which it was.

Olivia didn't make another film for three years, and the sabbatical suited her. Her interests were wide—she was involved with both Parisian and expatriate communities. Her daughter was growing up, and her son was in boarding school in Normandy. She also supervised the decorating of the house at 3 rue Benouville and was thoroughly involved in the process: "Then I will start a completely new life. I can't wait. This is the first house I've ever owned. I have always rented before. . . . Now I will be able to do all of the entertaining I've wanted to do."[120] In 1961, for the centenary of the beginning of the Civil War, she returned to Atlanta with David O. Selznick and Vivien Leigh for a poignant journey down memory lane and a screening of *Gone with the Wind.* Olivia wore Dior and looked chic and joyful, but Selznick was white-haired and heavier than ever, and Vivien's struggles with manic depression and the stress of her divorce from Laurence Olivier showed on her face. Selznick would die in 1965, and Vivien in 1967. The photographs and footage from that last meeting serve as a reminder of one value of cinema: it preserves beauty and youth and passion forever.

Throughout 1960 and into 1961, Olivia continued to write. Having published a few articles about her life in France, she embarked on a book project for Random House entitled *Every Frenchman Has One,* her suggestively titled memoir about her transplantation to Paris. In a 1961 interview with Hedda Hopper (with whom her relationship "was amicable—depending on whether or not Hedda got her facts straight!"[121]), she discussed the book and said, "I have five more chapters which I'll have to write in one week—how am I going to do it?"[122] She did finish it, and it appeared to very positive reviews and sales in 1962. In 2016, in honor of Olivia's 100th birthday, the book was reissued by Random House. She poses saucily on the cover, smiling knowingly, and the story of her Parisian reinvention is equally delightful.

Then she was offered another wonderful role that would keep her in Europe—Florence and Rome, specifically—allow her to play her age (something many forty-something stars were loath to do), and wear Dior clothes again. She was quite excited and told Hedda Hopper, "I'm looking forward to it. It's about an attractive, handsome mother who goes with her daughter to Florence—they meet a Florentine family with completely different points of view. The young boy falls for the girl. The father . . . finds the mother attractive and would be willing to have a small adventure."[123] Olivia omitted the film's central issue in her summary, however—mainstreaming the mentally challenged. The film was the thoughtful comedy-drama *Light in the Piazza*

(1962), based on Elizabeth Spencer's novel; it was adapted as a successful Broadway musical by Craig Lucas and Adam Guettel in 2005.

Olivia had discovered the property, according to her friend Fleur Cowles, when she was in Switzerland waiting for the workmen at the Paris house to complete the façade—they seemed incapable of getting the color right (the house ended up a creamy white). While there, she read a story in the *New Yorker* that unfolded over several issues—Spencer's novel. Several months later, Benny Thau, who had worked at MGM for many years, approached Olivia about a role and wanted her to accept it immediately, without reading the script, as they were in a rush to go into production. She refused, but when Thau summarized the story for her, she recognized it as Spencer's novel and agreed.[124]

Again, Olivia chose a project that offered a socially significant narrative, something that isn't sufficiently appreciated in evaluations of her work. After breaking free from Warner Brothers—which was, ironically, the studio of social conscience in the 1930s and 1940s—Olivia chose her roles carefully, looking for opportunities to play *les femmes d'un certain âge* with brains and motivation as well as beauty. Olivia's seriousness, her intellectual interests, her liberal politics, and her self-determination made her selective about the roles she accepted. Her artistic integrity along with her viability in Hollywood afforded her the luxury of choice and patience. Even if the films weren't as successful as those she made during her three golden years, they were thoughtful, and they are still watchable. She wasn't averse to having fun or making money, and in later years, she worked in television and film projects that were beneath her talents but lucrative. However, in 1962, after almost twenty-five years in the business, Olivia could still open a good film.

In *Light in the Piazza,* Olivia portrays Meg Johnson, the wealthy wife of an American tobacco executive (Barry Sullivan). She is in Florence on an extended vacation with her daughter, Clara, played by a gorgeous and underrated Yvette Mimieux. Despite her ethereal beauty and high spirits, twenty-six-year-old Clara has the mind and maturity of a ten-year-old child, the result of a horseback riding accident. Clara has met Fabrizio (George Hamilton), a charmingly callow youth, and they have fallen for each other, but he is unaware of her condition.

Meg is clearly a woman on the run—running from her daughter's situation and from her husband, who wants to put Clara in a specialized school. In a tellingly rebellious moment, she offers Signor Naccarelli (a devastatingly dapper Rossano Brazzi)— Fabrizio's father—a cigarette. Brazzi asks, "Your husband's brand?" She replies insouciantly, "No, I don't like them so I don't smoke them." He says with amazement, "What independence! An Italian woman would never dare."[125] That coltish quality Olivia showed in the Flynn movies stands her in good stead these many years later.

Meg's dilemma is complex—wanting to give her daughter a normal life, while lying about her condition to the Naccarellis and trying to prevent her husband from institutionalizing Clara. She keeps trying to tell the Naccarellis about Clara, but something always comes up. As Meg watches her daughter with Fabrizio, a handsome boy but not the brightest bulb on the string, we see the idea of their union take shape in her mind. Clara wants to stay in Florence, and her desire for Fabrizio makes her increasingly independent. Could it work?

The script by Julius J. Epstein presents this complicated situation with a balance of humor and compassion. Meg's desperate desire to push Clara from the nest, hoping her childlike daughter might find a safe haven as a protected, indulged Italian housewife, is completely believable. Everyone in the film gives thoughtful performances. Director Guy Green uses the sumptuous Italian locations, shot in color, as backgrounds that are sometimes too confining and ancient and sometimes quite youthful and promising—just like Meg's and Clara's lives.

Olivia is sincerely affectionate with Yvette Mimieux, who walks the fine line between mental challenge and youthful charm with grace. Their mother-daughter chemistry is warmly loving, sometimes exasperating, and always completely familial. At the wedding of Clara and Fabrizio in a beautiful Italian cathedral, we can almost believe that Clara and Meg have some very powerful guardian angels. However, as the couple leaves the church, the happy attendees are throwing candy, and Clara kneels down, picks up a piece of candy, and puts it in her mouth. The action stops for a moment—but then Fabrizio kneels down and does the same thing. The look on Olivia's face adds a sweet blessing to the film. Her closing line is tremendously encouraging: "I did the right thing. I know I did."[126] *Light in the Piazza* is another film in Olivia's oeuvre that deserves another look.

Olivia returned to Broadway one last time in January 1962 to perform in Garson Kanin's *A Gift of Time,* based on Lael Tucker Wertenbaker's *Death of a Man,* the story of her husband's passing. Olivia remembered that the play was "an irresistible opportunity to return to Broadway in a modern play written and directed by someone I greatly admired, and [to perform] opposite an actor [Henry Fonda] who was even more brilliant in the theatre than he was on screen. Furthermore, the play, itself, though it dealt with a tragic theme, was luminous."[127] The plot revolves around a controversial issue: assisted suicide. The husband has inoperable stomach cancer, and at the play's end he kills himself as his wife holds him, thereby making her an accessory.

The play ran for ninety-two performances, from February to May 1962, at the Ethel Barrymore Theatre in New York. Olivia and Fonda even did a scene from the play on *The Ed Sullivan Show.*[128] Despite the short run, the reviews were excellent. Howard Taubman of the *New York Times* said of the actors, "There are delicate, probing scenes between Mr. Fonda and Olivia de Havilland, whose Lael is quietly suffering and luminously courageous. With impressive refinement of acting styles they reveal a deep and comprehending love with humor and anguish and, praise be, without a trace of mawkishness."[129] *A Gift of Time* offered a compassionate statement about a subject that is still completely contemporary.

Olivia relished her return to the stage. She recalled, "It was not very difficult for me to adapt to the theatre again, in fact I never thought of the transition as a problem." Very confident in her skills, Olivia finally received the sort of universal critical acclaim she'd craved in the 1950s but had not consistently achieved. Still, she was open to learning about her craft: "While playing in *A Gift of Time,* Henry Fonda would sometimes take me to supper at the Drake Room after the performance. One evening as we were supping, I asked Henry, who was so brilliant in both mediums, what was the difference in his own technique. He startled the entire Drake Room by his reply: '*Instead of speaking like this, I just* SPEAK LIKE THIS.'"[130]

Sadly, after seven years of marriage, Olivia and Galante separated in 1962 but continued to share their home, a very modern conscious uncoupling. There was no public announcement, and although the gossips talked about their marriage, Olivia and Galante, the souls of discretion, remained quiet. There were rumblings that he hadn't been completely faithful, including a suggestion that he and Grace Kelly had had a fling.[131] If Olivia had her own private afternoons, she was so discreet that there was no gossip about her possible amours.

Olivia loved Paris, but the stresses of their two careers, their frequent travel, and their independent natures led the couple to grow in different directions. Olivia was always very positive about Galante in the press, and unlike Marcus Goodrich, there were no rumors that he tried to control his wife. It had been more of a practical than a passionate match, and both partners were ready for new horizons personally. Olivia was in her mid-forties, and Galante was in his early fifties. They adored parenting Gisèle and Ben, but they had fallen out of love and into friendship. Eventually, Galante moved across the street.

Olivia found herself traveling to the United States more frequently. She was a presenter at the 1963 Academy Awards (infamously portrayed in *Feud*) and appeared on the TV game shows *Password* and *What's My Line?* Although she still resisted doing television, she realized that it provided income and also helped maintain her visibility. She even cohosted the popular variety program *The Hollywood Palace* with Bette Davis.

Her next film was a controversial choice; it was refused a cinema certificate in the United Kingdom and remained unavailable until 2000. She recalled that she was "in Switzerland on a winter skiing holiday with my children and husband, when I read the script. I did not see it as a violent film but one of suspense, with an unusual situation, setting, and characters. It turned out to be much more violent than I anticipated—and, for some people, repellent."[132] *Lady in a Cage* (1964) is a sensationalized commentary on violence in society, the fine line between civility and madness, the superiority of the wealthy over the poor, and the desperate will to survive. That summary is far weightier than the film, which is very hard to watch due to the clichéd and unpleasant characters; the slow pace masquerades as building tension, and everyone overacts. It is a film with a message, though, which is something Olivia always sought.

Hollywood was excited about her return in early 1963, and although her sister, Joan, had left Los Angeles the day before, Olivia was welcomed by producer Luther Davis and pal Bette Davis. She dined with friends, including Bette Davis, *Lady in a Cage* costar Ann Sothern, and the Ray Millands, and was glad to be back in California.[133]

Olivia plays the caged lady of the title, wealthy and delicate poet Cornelia Hilyard. When the electricity goes out during a heat wave, she finds herself trapped alone in the elevator of her California home. Her son, whom she is smothering with love, is out of town. She rings an alarm, but rather than being saved, a series of events causes the house to be invaded by a homeless man (legendary acting coach Jeff Corey), a prostitute (Ann Sothern), and three juvenile delinquents (led by a young, feral James Caan). Proper Cornelia is gradually reduced to pure animality.

Shot in black and white at Paramount, the studio that had been so good to Olivia, the film looks like a low-budget television program. Its unending grimness is meant to function as a metaphor for a lawless society and the controlling Cornelia's loss of control. No one is redeemable, and when Cornelia finally manages to escape from her cage, stab Caan, and crawl into the street to flag down help, one is relieved as much by her rescue as by the end of the film. She screams at the invaders, "Murderers! Neanderthals! Monsters! Monsters"![134] Everyone is so dreadful, it is hard to care about the social context, but as a magnum opus of misery, it is thoroughly impressive. Author John Douglas Eames describes it aptly: "Director Walter Grauman maintained an unrelenting pressure on the audience, among whom a really good time was had only by sado-masochists."[135]

Olivia defended the film: "'People either hated it violently or thought it was brilliant—but in either case they didn't budge out of their seats until it was over. . . . I think someday it will be recognized as a depiction of the aimless violence of our era.'"[136] She asserted, "'I don't think I've ever played a more punishing role than I did in "Cage"—it was rougher than even "The Snake Pit." But I believe the women ticket buyers will be held fascinated.'"[137] In another interview to promote the film, 1950's most uncooperative actress spoke about the challenge of the role: "'In essence the part is a stunning tour-de-force, with real dimension. That's what appealed to me. You see this trapped woman, supposedly sensitive, educated and tasteful, finally exposed for what she is, a selfish mother who robbed her son of his young manhood. . . . She recognizes the truth about herself.'"[138] As the mother of a growing son, the role gave Olivia a vivid vision of what to avoid.

The film was supposed to be shown at the London Film Festival in November 1965, but after Olivia arrived, she "learned that [*Lady in a Cage*] ha[d] been banned by British censors as 'brutal and loathsome,'" although it was screened privately at the National Film Theatre.[139] Olivia was moved in March 1966 to do an interview for the British magazine *Films and Filming* that further clarified why she had been drawn to the project: "There is the isolation of the individual living in a city where there are millions of people. . . . That is a characteristic of modern urban life, this strange indifference of one human being toward another in distress in a city. . . . Thirty years ago people reacted much more instinctively . . . their spontaneous reaction would be to come to somebody's rescue. But that doesn't happen anymore."[140] The magazine chose her performance in *Lady in a Cage* as the best by an actress that year, but watching the film today requires determination and devotion to Olivia.

Olivia did a lot of press for *Lady in a Cage* that not only promoted the film but also defended it. She believed "it was prophetic, that film. It was prophetic. It was a warning. It really was ahead of its time. It was announcing its time and it scared people."[141] Viewed today, the violence is still disturbing, though too stylized and too beatnikish to sustain the terror. Olivia remains proud of it, however, and asserts, "It had its supporters: the drama editor of one of Britain's most respected newspapers . . . saw the movie when it was running in Paris and . . . was so impressed by it that he . . . devoted the full front page of the Sunday entertainment section to his laudatory review of it."[142]

So, who better than Olivia to replace the ailing Joan Crawford in the 1964 shock horror movie *Hush . . . Hush, Sweet Charlotte*? Who better to costar with Bette Davis and almost drive her mad (as a character, *not* as a colleague) in this follow-up to the camp, grotesquely memorable *What Ever Happened to Baby Jane* (1962)?

The 2017 television miniseries *Feud* details quite thoroughly how the situation on the set of *Charlotte* deteriorated. It's deliriously fun to watch. In fact, there are many versions of the Davis-Crawford battles that led to Crawford being hospitalized with respiratory issues, causing delays in production, and being replaced by Olivia. Crawford claimed she heard about her replacement not from the studio but when she "received a telephone call in the hospital from Dorothy Manners. 'What do you think about Olivia de Havilland replacing you?'" Crawford said she wept "'for nine hours'" but then followed that vulnerable comment with a dart: "'I'm glad for Olivia; she needs a good picture.'"[143]

Olivia recounted her version of the story in 2014: "After Joan Crawford fell ill playing a dark character, Miriam, in *Hush* . . . , and it appeared she would never recover, the film's director, Robert Aldrich, brought the script to me in the Swiss Alps, where I was vacationing with my children. Once I had read it, I said to him that Miriam, like Terry [in *The Dark Mirror*], was all dark and that I could not submit myself again to playing a character so unremittingly malevolent."[144]

Olivia was interested in working with her friend Bette Davis again, but she'd taken critical heat for *Lady in a Cage*, which proved to be one of a series of 1960s shock, hag horror, Grand Guignol films that exploited the fading careers of once-great Hollywood actors and actresses. *Baby Jane* was included in that list, as was Crawford's *Strait-Jacket* and the Roger Corman adaptations of Edgar Allan Poe. Olivia didn't want to be identified with that genre and initially rejected the offer. Aldrich rather cattily commented later, "'I went off to Switzerland to try to convince de Havilland in person. It was terribly difficult. I'm not quite sure why, but I think it has to do with Miss de Havilland's opinion of what her image is vis a vis what it may be.'"[145]

Additionally, Olivia didn't like how the character of Miriam Deering was portrayed in the original script. As she recounted: "Undaunted, Aldrich then posed several questions which he knew would pique my curiosity: 'Weren't you attracted by the dichotomy? Intrigued by the ambiguity? By the ambivalence?' I replied that I saw no dichotomy, no ambiguity, no ambivalence whatsoever in Miriam's character, but that I would read the script again that night." After years of battling for her career and for better roles, Olivia was not about to accept a script she didn't like. She continued: "When I met him the next morning, I said, 'I still don't see any dichotomy, any ambiguity, or any ambivalence in Miriam; but I think I know how you can achieve this: give her perfect manners. As written, in her very first scene Miriam [is] abominably rude to Agnes Moorehead, a "slavey," leaving no doubt whatsoever as to Miriam's villainy. By giving her perfect manners the audience will be misled regarding her true character—which ought not to be revealed until the last possible moment.'" Fortunately, "Bette Davis . . . liked this idea; a re-write was arranged, and the script was altered accordingly."[146] Aldrich agreed to change Miriam from a patently evil woman to a "refined and charming and apparently sympathetic lady . . . [which] gave the character an ambivalence that no actress could resist."[147] Thus, Olivia enthusiastically accepted the role and said years later, "'I did it to please Bette and not disappoint her. Given the choice, I wouldn't have deprived Joan Crawford of the honor.'"[148] Aldrich had also offered her $100,000, which sweetened the deal.[149] Olivia flew to Los Angeles at the end of August 1964, with her children in tow, to begin filming immediately.

After the discord on the set between Davis and Crawford, the production took on a much lighter tone. Costar Joseph Cotten noted, "Olivia and I played lovers in *Hush . . . Hush, Sweet Charlotte.* She was a fine replacement. She and Bette worked beautifully together."[150] The result is an entertaining exploration of the duality of the divine and the dark; it earned seven Oscar nominations and generally good reviews. Rather than being a film in which Olivia and Bette are "turned into complete travesties of themselves,"[151] *Hush* offers two actresses having a grand time together.

Several critics recognized the film for what it is: a thriller whose notable cast raises the script to deliciously melodramatic heights. Arthur Knight called Olivia "properly oversweet as the solicitous Cousin Miriam."[152] *Time* captured the tone of the film in its review entitled "Dragon Ladies": "To make clear that the fright is all in fun, this monster rally offers not two but four seasoned movie queens—three of them ready to let down their hair. . . . The tidy one is actress de Havilland, who flings away her composure but retains her chic."[153]

Olivia's performance, however, is a bit subtler than that statement implies. Her ladylike Miriam Deering, sweetly named, substitutes charm for curare, tipping her intentions like poisoned arrows and delicately letting them fly at poor Charlotte. Olivia explained her approach to the character as follows: "'It's always the charming ones of evil intent who are the dangerous ones; the other ones you can see coming. But you can't see Miriam coming, and she's really dangerous.'"[154] She certainly is—blackmailer, killer, poseur, seducer, and avenger, all done with that honeyed de Havilland allure. Olivia's lethal sweetness had appeared in earlier films. Consider the last half hour of *The Heiress* and Olivia's cool, calculated revenge on gold-digging Montgomery Clift, culminating in that long walk up the dark stairs into permanent spinsterhood; it's bone-chilling.

Miriam Deering continues the elegant tightrope walk between satin and steel found in many of Olivia's performances. Her deceptive propriety as Miriam mirrors the spine of her famous Melanie: Scarlett gets everyone back home to Tara, but Melanie gives birth while the Yankees are storming Atlanta. Olivia's dainty belle–cum–ruthless avenger in *Hush* is as creamily menacing as a cyanide teacake. And let us not forget that she agreed to pose, along with Davis, Aldrich, and Cotten, holding bottles of Coca-Cola, a rather snide dig at Crawford, the queen of Pepsi-Cola.

What separates *Hush* from other William Castle–type genre classics, and what places it only slightly below *Baby Jane* in terms of pure camp delight, is the tone of the acting. Aldrich's directing style, informed in part by the uneven script of Henry Farrell and Lukas Heller, is wildly inconsistent in *Hush.* Is it a comedy? A tragedy? A tragicomedy? A parody? It's almost as if everyone wandered onto the same set at the same time to appear in their own strange southern Gothic film. Yet the veteran actors are riveting, and somehow it all works. The actors play off one another in true ensemble tradition, their collective years of studio training resulting in a delightfully broad, macabre entertainment. The film was parodied in a fantastically funny drag version entitled *Hush Up Sweet Charlotte* (2015), with Miriam portrayed menacingly but stylishly by drag performer Varla Jean Merman, cult actress Mink Stole playing Agnes Moorhead's trashy servant role, and Matthew Martin as the eponymous heroine.[155]

As the not-quite-mad Charlotte Hollis, Bette Davis careens from being wildly bitchy to disturbingly vulnerable, reminiscent of William Faulkner's southern belle–cum–murderer in "A Rose for Emily." Charlotte may or may not have cut off the hand and head of her married lover, John Mayhew, back in the 1920s, when he ended their affair. Bruce Dern resonates sleaziness as the unfortunate Mayhew in yet another incarnation of the creepy antagonist he plays in numerous 1960s films, including Hitchcock's *Marnie*. Noblesse oblige, thanks to Charlotte's rich Big Daddy (the menacing Victor Buono), kept her out of jail, but thirty-some years later, she is the local crazy woman. Charlotte's only "friend" is her hired woman, Velma Cruther (Agnes Moorehead), a raw but loyal servant. To make matters worse, the county plans to bulldoze Charlotte's ancient family home to make room for a bridge. If this happens, she will become a madwoman without an attic. Her doctor, Drew Bayliss (Joseph Cotten), advises her to leave, but she won't listen. Who can help Charlotte retain her refuge? Who else but her last remaining blood relative, cousin Miriam Deering? Who can help Bette but Olivia?

The Hollywood greats have a wonderful time in this spirited, spooky tale of revenge. Joseph Cotten portrays the manipulative Drew as an aging, slurring, drunken southern doctor and gigolo; his chemistry with Olivia is raffish and charming and slightly creepy. Mary Astor portrays Jewel Mayhew, John's widow and now a frail old lady, with poignant grande dame dignity. Cecil Kellaway invests his role as a compassionate insurance investigator with gentle English charm. Agnes Moorehead (who won a best supporting actress Oscar nomination and a Golden Globe for her efforts) is utterly hilarious and steals her scenes as the white trashy Velma Cruther, legendarily crass and crude, a Flannery O'Connor nightmare, the woman for whom the word "slattern" was invented.

In the center of these varied acting styles and personae stands the eye of the storm. Olivia plays Miriam as a cosmopolitan woman, an outsider to the rather extreme goings-on down south. Yet her poise gradually, impalpably becomes transparent, revealing a cool sociopath whose elegant restraint masks an empty heart and a desire for retaliation—a true femme fatale. As Olivia recalled, "Portraying Miriam became a game for me, thus saving me from undergoing the dark experience which had so profoundly and negatively affected me on *The Dark Mirror*."[156] Olivia plays the early scenes of the film with a kind of wide-eyed, gentle glissando. The delicate furrow between her eyes seems to express concern and amazement at Charlotte's condition. Her false eyelashes tilt up at the edges like wings. She wears the tailored day dresses and sexy chiffon evening gowns designed by Norma Koch with grace. Her voice is warm, her vowels long and soothing, her timbre young and light one moment, low and wise the next. But from her first appearance, there's the suggestion of a serpent in the garden. Miriam hasn't forgotten Drew's fickleness—he dumped her after Mayhew's murder to avoid the scandal—and she reminds him sibilantly, "You were always very quick with your compliments. It was just your inten—tions. They were sometimes . . . a little vague."[157] Olivia phrases that line by holding the *n,* by theatrically pausing between thoughts, signaling her seductive falseness.

Winning, control, and vengeance are key elements to Miriam Deering. We see these elements in the reunion between Miriam and Charlotte. The portrayals by Olivia and Bette are reminiscent of their characters in *In This Our Life.* Olivia is calm, poised, warm, and radiant; Bette is manic, ragged, imperious, and large. One by one, Miriam thwarts anyone who tries to interfere with her plan to drive Charlotte mad, shuttle her away, and take control of the Hollis fortune. However, there's one primary roadblock: Velma Cruther. The acting styles of Agnes Moorehead and Olivia are worlds apart, and that difference is wildly entertaining in their two major scenes together, culminating in Miriam's brutal murder of Velma by crashing a chair over her head and sending her down the staircase. Olivia's chic beauty and brisk efficiency could have been swallowed up by Moorehead's delicious *Tobacco Road* parody. Yet once more, Olivia uses Miriam's frozen heart to counterbalance Moorehead's juicy slices of ham. She is the still point, the eye of the storm, and in her brutal killing of Velma, we see the divine duality of murderous intent and ladylike comportment in all its Gothic glory.

Of course, there must be retribution, and it is divine. Believing that Charlotte has descended into babbling insanity, Miriam glides down the staircase (the same one she used to dispatch Velma) rather like Loretta Young. Dressed in a sleeveless, low-cut black evening gown, she pats her hair into place (a casually evil touch) and joins Drew in a champagne toast. With a jaunty air, mature sexuality on display, quaffing one glass and having another, she reveals to Drew the full force of her vengeful heart. But murder will out. While Miriam and Drew chatter mockingly about their plans, Charlotte creeps to the balcony above them and listens in. Miriam proclaims in a high, sugary voice, "All that lovely money that Big Sam sweated to get his hands on. While we're spendin' it like water, Charlotte will be weaving lots and lots of little baskets."[158] This line is delivered in a mocking soprano tone, singsonged almost too grandly, as though Aldrich directed Olivia to be as evil as possible so that Miriam deserves what she gets. That pushes Charlotte over the edge, and she pushes a concrete planter over the railing of the balcony. Miriam looks up just in time to shriek before she's smashed into the patio. Of course, Olivia looks glorious in death, laid out open-eyed in that glamorous gown and staring up at the woman who has triumphed over her one final time.

Olivia spoke of *Hush* as being "full of traps, it was a delicate tight-rope walking assignment. I found that very interesting. Aldrich gave it . . . a kind of dark glittering style which fascinated me."[159] She was pleased that the film was successful, given her "doubts about her current popularity, particularly with the younger generation."[160] She related that when she and Bette appeared in person in New York cinemas during the film's first run (it opened, rather diabolically, on Christmas Eve 1964), they were greeted by screaming fans who had to be held back by police. "'I learned they knew every picture I'd made—and some I'd forgotten. Through television, they knew Bette and me as well as their parents had. Oh, not in romantic terms but perhaps in more meaningful ones—respect and admiration.'"[161]

Olivia's opinion of television was slowly changing, although she still didn't want to work in "sustained television" at this time. "'Those commercials are unpardonable. They interrupt a performance every fifteen minutes. . . . Babies may be squalling or a convivial group may be distracted as their drinks are re-filled. . . . I wish pay television would arrive. So there wouldn't be any commercials,'" a prescient comment indeed.[162] As part of the promotion for *Hush* (her last great film role), Olivia and Bette appeared on *What's My Line?* and *The Hollywood Palace.* She also guest-starred on Barbara Stanwyck's popular television program *The Big Valley* in 1965. The times were changing, and Olivia recognized that.

The public learned in early 1965 that Olivia had been separated from Pierre Galante for more than two years. Galante told columnist Harrison Carroll, "'Olivia and I signed the separation papers two years ago . . . but we are on the friendliest of terms. We have children to consider. . . . I personally have no plans to seek a divorce.'"[163] They continued to share the same house and even gave "dinner parties and cocktail parties there."[164] Olivia laughingly told Earl Wilson, "'I am living in sin without the sin. . . . I have the front and he has the rear. . . . I consider myself a trail blazer . . . but the truth is, we're not the first to do it.'"[165] Olivia and Galante finally divorced in 1979, but they maintained a friendly relationship. He moved across the street, and they dined together regularly; he would even watch television in bed with her until she made him go home. When I asked how she managed to stay on such good terms with him, she told me, "I wasn't madly in love with my second husband."[166] Perhaps not, but their relationship was built on a true meeting of the minds, good timing, a desire for family, and a solid friendship that endured until his death. Olivia was personally and permanently settled in Paris, her children were growing up, and she had both the time and the desire to return to acting more regularly—in fact, for another twenty-plus years. Once an actress . . .

9

CLOSING A CAREER

Olivia was forty-nine years old in 1965, a separated woman with two children. Paris had become a real home to her, and the house on rue Benouville—with its walled garden, surrounding embassies, and chic restaurants and shops nearby—offered a perfect place for her to reconsider her life's journey and find new directions for her energy and intelligence. Her arrangement (better understood if pronounced in French) with Pierre Galante worked for both of them, professionally and personally, but more importantly, this thoroughly modern family created stability for Gisèle and Benjamin. This is a testimony to both Olivia and Galante, and it reflects Olivia's determination not to visit the difficulties of her own childhood on her children. Steel, practicality, protectiveness, dignity—those words have always been reflected in her personal life, but certainly in her relationship with Galante. He may not have been the grand passion of her life, but he was a grand friend. In fact, she helped promote his book *The Berlin Wall* in 1965, and in December 1966, columnist Earl Wilson wrote of their unique-for-the-time relationship, "There's little likelihood that you'll find a bigger rooter for Pierre than Olivia, or a better enthusiast for Olivia than Pierre. 'In fact,' as one friend of theirs remarked, 'they are just about to celebrate the 5th anniversary of their separation.' They will celebrate it, of course, together."[1]

Fifty can be a challenging age, bringing midlife crises and menopause, but Olivia was blessed with good health and energy, as well as a practical approach to life, and so she moved forward. One of the ways she did this was by serving as president of the jury for Cannes Film Festival in May 1965: "Selection of Miss de Havilland to head the jury marks the first time an actress has been so honored."[2] Cate Blanchett was the president at Cannes in 2018, but Olivia led the way. Olivia's reputation as a trailblazer is terribly underappreciated, and Katharine Hepburn wasn't the only free spirit of the era. Olivia led the way for women on many fronts—joining SAG in 1936, winning her lawsuit against Warner Brothers, and negotiating her own contracts, to name a few.

She also took a modern approach to child rearing. Olivia always encouraged both her children to be their own people. She said of Gisèle, "One of a mother's most sacred responsibilities toward a daughter is to help her to become psychologically independent of her maternal parent. I think Gisèle, as part of the growing up process, achieved this psychological independence on her own." The same went for Benjamin, who "in 1966, when he was only sixteen years of age . . . received the baccalaureate from a French educational institution, a degree equivalent to two years of university in the United States, when only 66% of the graduating population merited that honour."[3]

In other ways, however, she was rather old-fashioned. Olivia was comically unsentimental when she explained that children should not join the adults for dinner: "'They should be fed, bathed and ready for bed when the father arrives home. Then he sees them as little angels, instead of the hellions they can be at times.'"[4] She had also absorbed much of Lilian's independent approach to motherhood: "I'm well aware of the dangers of overwhelming love. . . . I feel parents run the constant risk of projecting their own faults and virtues on the children. It takes years to find out what they really are. They're something apart, absolutely themselves and no one else. The challenge parents face is to give proper training without stifling personality. . . . I believe essentially in discipline, fairness and affection, all administered with intelligent guidance. If the parents can do that, there is little danger that their children will grow up to represent an extreme type."[5] That approach worked for Olivia, and as author Jane Ardmore wrote, "Olivia de Havilland's parents may have been wrong in their ideas of raising children. Indeed they made the mistake of not trying to understand Livvy and help her through those trying, difficult teen-age years. But Olivia was lucky, she had the courage to fight for what she wanted and she is a better woman because of it. Olivia's children are lucky, too, because they have such an understanding and sympathetic parent to guide their growing up."[6] The proof of Olivia's child-rearing methods was the children themselves: both were successful and remained close to their parents, and neither wrote a tell-all autobiography.

It's a shame Olivia never made any French films. The nouvelle vague cinema movement in France would have been terrifically challenging for her, and there were many theatrical opportunities in Paris. However, she didn't pursue that course:

> I was not really interested in playing either in French films or in the French theatre, because doing so would have changed the strictly personal life I had made here, one for which I had a profound need.

> Furthermore, though I spoke fluent French in those earlier years, I had a slight accent which would have marked me as a foreigner. About this I have an amusing story to tell: One day, having been invited to lunch by Rene Julliard, Pierre and I arrived early at the great French publisher's apartment and were able to chat with our host and hostess before the other guests appeared. During the conversation, Madame Julliard remarked: "*Vous parlez parfaitement le français mais avec un accent légèrement Yougoslave*"!!!
>
> As you know, in the French theatre and French cinema, there are very few roles for Yougoslaves![7]

Instead, Olivia returned to Hollywood—and would do so regularly for the next twenty-plus years—to tackle television. She had often complained, "'I won't do television because they would interrupt me every fifteen minutes for a commercial. Can you imagine what would happen if somebody disturbed a movie every fifteen minutes in a theatre?'"[8] She was a practical woman, though, and in 1966 she was "signed by Talent Associates to co-star with Jason Robards, Jr. in [an] 'ABC Stage 67' presentation of 'Noon Wine' based on Katherine Anne Porter's novella."[9] Sam Peckinpah, one of the great rebels of Hollywood, directed the production and wrote the adaptation of this tale of tragedy and madness on a Texas farm—now considered a classic of American television. Olivia plays Ellie Thompson, whose husband Royal (Robards) brings about his own death through misplaced honor and possible hallucinations. She and Robards, one of the greatest actors of his generation, are excellent in this story of misunderstanding and loneliness. Peckinpah was nominated for both a Directors Guild of America award and a Writers Guild of America award.[10]

Olivia's next television assignment came in June 1967, when she signed with Danny Thomas and Aaron Spelling to appear on NBC-TV's *The Danny Thomas Hour.* She played a role in *The Last Hunters,* a tale about Nazi hunters that featured Dane Clark and Richard Todd. This production is virtually impossible to find now, which may be a commentary on its value; Olivia said, "'I didn't like [it] very much.'"[11] For the next few years, Olivia seemed to be set on a course of forgettable roles in mediocre productions. She was not alone. Neither cinema nor television used Hollywood's wealth of older talent intelligently during this era.

Olivia may have been working for the pleasure of performing, but she was also supporting two children. Her son Benjamin Goodrich, who was studying mathematics, attended the University of Texas at Austin and would become a statistical analyst. A tall, dark, handsome young man, Benjamin was as brilliant as his parents. However, when he was still a teenager, Benjamin was diagnosed with Hodgkin's lymphoma, and concerns about his health, not to mention the medical bills, weighed on Olivia. She stopped working to take care of him, when necessary; thankfully, the disease went into remission, and he was able to continue his studies.

In the meantime, Olivia attended a tribute to *Gone with the Wind* in Atlanta in October 1967. She was now the only living principal actor from the film; Vivien Leigh had died in July 1967. Although Evelyn Keyes, Ann Rutherford, and Victor Jory were in attendance, Olivia felt the loss of so many of her castmates. She also served on the Cannes Film Festival jury again in 1968, but there were no exciting film roles coming her way. Nevertheless, Olivia continued to work, and many of her choices reflected the trends at the time.

In the 1960s to the 1980s, international all-star casts were employed as a way to bring audiences back to the cinema. *The Adventurers* (1970) is one of those all-star nightmares, based on the novel by Harold Robbins. At three seemingly endless hours, the film is complete with orgy scenes and bare breasts galore, and it is directed clumsily by the usually sensitive Lewis Gilbert. South American playboy Dax Xenos (Bekim Fehmiu) is struggling to forget his troubled background; he is a player who beds everything that moves. Then, after a tragedy happens, he decides to avenge his father's death. The cast is astonishing—in addition to Olivia, there's Candice Bergen, Charles Aznavour, Rossano Brazzi (Olivia's costar from *Light in the Piazza*), Ernest Borgnine, Fernando Ray, John Ireland, and Leigh Taylor-Young. But like many of these overblown, star-studded films from the 1970s, there's not enough ballast to float this boat.

At least Olivia's role is brief, and she looks amazing at fifty-four years old. She portrays a variation on Vivien Leigh's role in Tennessee Williams's *The Roman Spring of Mrs. Stone.* A bored and lonely rich woman, Deborah Hadley, hires Dax as an escort while her husband is in America, drilling for oil. Olivia wears a beautiful low-cut, ice-blue satin dress with a sweetheart collar and a huge diamond necklace—it's a very *My Cousin Rachel* costume. Olivia saw in Deborah Hadley "someone that had grace in her," and "the entire company was illumined with hope" that the film would be better than the novel.[12] It wasn't.

Olivia and Dax have one rather amazing bedroom scene in which the side of her breast is showing a bit and he's resting his head on her bosom. She looks at him and says, "I've got a present for you."[13] When she stands, with her peignoir draped around her, she's nude underneath (or at least she appears to be). She gives Dax a check for $5,000—the camera zooms in on it—and a cigarette case. They kiss briefly, he hugs her and looks at his watch, and Olivia disappears. As one commentator noted, "Olivia de Havilland has discovered sex. . . . Sweet, simple Melanie of 'Gone with the Wind' has a torrid, week-long affair with a young South American playboy."[14] That unseemly description is an apt summary of her role in this melodramatic exploitation film. After the intermission—yes, there's an intermission—Dax is now in San Francisco, and he runs into Deborah again. He has become a revolutionary, and he hopes Deborah will help him secure a loan for his people. She tells him, "Maybe we both found happiness in Rome. But I was the lucky one. I brought my happiness back here. And kept it."[15] Dax pulls out the gold cigarette case she gave him long ago and kisses her palm; as she flies away on a helicopter, the camera zooms in and she smiles sweetly.

The Adventurers is one of the most tedious examples of the epic exploitation genre ever filmed. It seems impossible that Claude Renoir did the photography and Antonio Carlos Jobim did the music—just one of the many mysteries of a dying film industry from forty years ago. However, Olivia's moments are elegant, and she makes a beautiful cougar.

This was followed by an appearance at the National Film Theatre in London in 1971, where Olivia gave a lecture about her career for the British Film Institute. "The enthusiasm with which she was received by the usually staid and dignified British public was of such fervor as to seriously challenge the old adage about movie stars fading away."[16] However, it seemed "that a dinner date with [Prime Minister] Edward Heath would totally eclipse her achievements as an actress during thirty-five years of movies. She posed in rainbow chiffon [Dior, of course] on the Dorchester roof . . . while enraptured photographers of the national press rushed happily to their offices to pass off their film as a record of her leaving for Chequers that evening."[17] The press trumpeted that Olivia was dating Heath (interesting, given the speculation about his sexual orientation). Olivia offered the truth in 2012:

> On my way to New York . . . in the winter of 1961–62, my ship ran into the worst Atlantic storm in a hundred years. With few exceptions, the passengers took to their quarters and stayed there. Among those who remained upright were an American judge and his wife from the Middle West, cabinet member Edward Heath, and me.

> The judge and his wife invited Edward Heath to dine with them on New Year's Eve and . . . also invited me. There was a dance floor and an orchestra, so Edward Heath asked me to dance, an invitation I willingly accepted. We danced up the dance floor and down the dance floor, thoroughly enjoying ourselves.
>
> When I made a trip to London quite a long time later, Heath, by then the Prime Minister of England, invited me to lunch at Chequers, the Prime Minister's country residence. Ours was a pleasant acquaintanceship, which I valued, of course, and nothing more. Our paths did not cross in future years.[18]

More interesting than this faux romance was Olivia's appearance on American television that same year in *The Screaming Woman,* an ABC Movie of the Week based on a Ray Bradbury story, directed by Jack Smight, and with a score by John Williams. She was still "reluctant to act on TV—although she'[d] been rather visible in recent years as a talk show guest. . . . Olivia did few things on TV."[19] However, she found this film interesting. She had been out west on a lecture tour, something many actresses, including her sister, Joan, did to make money and keep themselves in the public eye. Olivia recalled:

> I received a call from my great friend, the producer Bill Frye, suggesting that I take the leading role in his TV production. . . . After reading the script, which I found extremely interesting . . . we started filming. The shooting took place in Santa Barbara at the Bliss Estate (supposedly owned by me), which was temporarily unoccupied. This locale and its name were not unfamiliar to me.
>
> On August 11th, 1934 . . . my two great friends, Frank Ingerson and George Dennison . . . drove me down to Hollywood to start my engagement as understudy . . . in . . . *A Midsummer Night's Dream.* Frank and George and I stopped off at the Santa Barbara Biltmore, where Mrs. Bliss entertained us at luncheon. Frank and George had assisted Mrs. Bliss with the décor of her house situated . . . above the Biltmore. . . . It was on this very estate that we shot some significant scenes for *The Screaming Woman*. The filming there was a wonderful experience evoking that day as it did.[20]

For this TV movie, Olivia was also reunited with her former artistic collaborator Edith Head. Although Head usually "wouldn't accept television assignments . . . work had been so slow, she agreed to design [Olivia's] wardrobe . . . [which] opened up a new avenue for Edith, and she went on to design TV specials for Raquel Welch and Debby Boone . . . as well as a television version of . . . *Little Women*."[21] Today, the television industry offers wonderful opportunities for actors of all ages, which is largely the result of these kinds of productions.

Olivia plays Mrs. Wynant, a plump, pretty, wealthy, middle-aged woman who takes her pony cart out to survey her property one Sunday. She comes across a stray dog digging, and then Mrs. Wynant hears someone calling. She kneels down, looks at where the dog had been digging, screams, and runs away down the road. Under the earth, a woman is buried alive and crying for help! Mrs. Wynant arrives home, but of course, no one believes her, including Olivia's *Hush* costar and good friend Joseph Cotten and MGM leading man Walter Pidgeon. As the plot unwinds, we learn that her family wants to have her committed, ostensibly for her own good.

Although this is a predictable thriller, Olivia's alternating moods of panic and imperiousness are reminiscent of her role in *The Snake Pit*. She gives as good as she gets, and when she declares to her tribe of disbelievers, "A sane person doesn't hear voices and see things that aren't there," we know that either she truly is insane or someone is in desperate trouble. The mockery of older women is certainly a theme in this teleplay, as is the greed of families. But after all the angst and struggle, Mrs. Wynant saves the woman's life and tells a policeman, "She saved mine."[22] Olivia is beatific, smiling and beaming in her last scene, as both the character and the actress have done their jobs well. Cotten remembered, "Olivia had a most physically exhausting part and she never flagged or faltered; she is such a hard worker and such a pleasure to work with."[23]

Her reviews were also good. Kevin Thomas of the *Los Angeles Times* wrote, "It is a wonderfully well-modulated, exquisitely timed performance, alternately calm and hysterical, created from within with superb technical finesse. It is altogether gratifying that a two-time Academy Award winner has made the switch to the small screen without any loss of stature."[24] Years later, Olivia recalled, "When the completed film aired . . . it was a smash hit, capturing 40% of the viewing audience. An altogether positive experience from first to last."[25]

In 1972, Olivia appeared in the Liv Ullmann vehicle *Pope Joan*, based on the possibly mythical, possibly historical ninth-century woman who briefly became the pope of the Catholic Church. Ullmann was at the apex of her stardom at the time, and the international cast—including Trevor Howard, Maximilian Schell, and Patrick Magee—at least looks good in the sumptuous settings and costumes. However, the drama lacks real intensity, and the script has no focus. Olivia plays a reverend mother superior and looks beautiful in her wimple, but her demise by crucifixion is horrific. Olivia was committed to the role, but the violence is gratuitous.

Olivia's performances in films and television in the 1970s and into the 1980s were not great works or great roles. Like many stars of her generation, she had a strong work ethic and was still in demand, but she did not appear in any significant productions. Olivia loved her profession, however, and the lecture tours she undertook twice a year throughout the 1970s fulfilled part of her need to perform; they also allowed her to reconnect with her loyal fan base and introduced her to new viewers as well. Her presentation was called "From the City of Stars to the City of Lights," and "her remarks condensed into 60 minutes 20 years of Hollywood living and 20 years of living in Paris."[26]

Olivia also loved writing. About this time, there were rumors that she was writing an autobiography; they have never ceased, and one day we may see that manuscript. She continued to write magazine articles occasionally; her charming tale for *Ladies' Home Journal* entitled "Bouboule," about the Boston bulldog that came to stay with the Galantes, is a delight to read. Her daughter wanted a dog, and Olivia recounts the decisions about which puppy to get, the discovery that the puppy had pneumonia, and how Olivia cared for him: "What Bouboule needed most, I concluded, was the warm comfort of a mother. I thereupon established him in my bed where, when I joined him, he promptly snuggled into my side and slept peacefully."[27] Olivia's Airedale Shadrach had gone to dog heaven, and it seems that Bouboule had found the right home.

Writing and acting also helped Olivia cope with loss. Her eighty-eight-year-old mother, Lilian, died of cancer on February 20, 1975, at her home in Santa Barbara, where she had lived for several years. Lilian had become a US citizen in 1948, and after George Fontaine died in 1956, she helped develop the Los Gatos Theater Workshop.[28] Olivia's father, Walter, had died in 1968 at age ninety-six; at the time of his death, he was still married to the Japanese woman for whom he had left Lilian. Olivia and Walter had found an uneasy truce, but they never truly reconnected. Her relationship with her mother, however, was extremely close.

Olivia flew back to California to be with her mother during the last weeks of her life. Sadly, Lilian's death precipitated the final schism between Olivia and her sister, Joan. Joan was touring with a play and could not leave the company because she was the star of the show. Joan claimed that Olivia didn't consult her about health care decisions for their mother. For instance, Olivia wanted Lilian to have an operation, but Joan didn't believe the additional stress was warranted at her age; Joan viewed this as one more usurpation of her mother's love. According to Joan, telegrams sent to her were either missed or late. Lilian was cremated, and the sisters scattered her ashes at Villa Montaibo in Saratoga, where the three of them had landed all those years ago from Tokyo. However, the bad feelings between Olivia and Joan were cemented. Although they both inherited the longevity gene from their parents, they shared little else for the next decades.

Olivia had always found solace in work, and over the next few years, she returned to the United States from her base in Paris to do a variety of projects. Gisèle was attending law school at the Université de Droit de Nanterre, and Benjamin was working in California, so Olivia enjoyed the commuter life: "When I lived here [Los Angeles], we were so impassioned with the movie business, that's all we would talk about. . . . Now I have several sets of friends, and when I'm in Paris, we never discuss movies; I don't think about work. I can think about other things. It's very rewarding to divide your life that way: it's gorgeous."[29] The films and miniseries she appeared in were of varying quality, and although she was always professional, they offered few acting challenges. Still, they provided income and an interesting transatlantic life for several years.

In the epic *Airport '77* (a follow-up to *Airport* and *Airport '75,* based on Alex Hailey's book), Olivia joins a number of old and new stars at the bottom of the ocean when a 747 jet crashes. At least Olivia was on trend—from the horror films of the 1960s to the disaster films of the 1970s. And she finally appeared onscreen with her former beau James Stewart, who plays the creator of a "prototype executive aircraft" who is bringing guests to the opening of his aeronautics museum when the plane goes down.[30] Olivia received fifth billing, but she is surrounded by a great cast, including former costars Joseph Cotten and Christopher Lee, as well as Jack Lemmon and Lee Grant. She also wears Edith Head's flattering costumes one last time.

Olivia's character, Emily Livingston, is a poker player. Olivia has a nice moment when she sits down to deal cards and says, "I declare a truce on all art critics, but only for the duration of the flight. Right now, the name of the game is poker. Five-card stud, ten-dollar ante, no ceiling on raises and nothing's wild. Any objections, boys?"[31] She's sassy and strong and positive, and her scenes are lively and enjoyable.

Of course, this is a disaster film, so the plane catches fire, crashes, and lands on the ocean floor; the passengers are running out of oxygen. Joseph Cotten remembered, "We picked up our screen romance . . . and again she had a most physical and exhausting role. So did I. We were in the Pacific off San Diego, battling the waves. On the stage at Universal, they kept us drenched in a tank after the 747 had supposedly crashed under the sea."[32]

Lee Grant was equally impressed by Olivia's physicality on the set. Grant was watching from an overhead grid as the soundstage plane was about to be deluged with tons of water. The producer wanted to know who volunteered to be the first one to be drenched. Grant recalled that at first, there was silence. "Then . . . 'Oh, me, me!' came a voice from the rafters. Olivia spent her days climbing the rafters, watching the action below, schmoozing with the stagehands high above. 'Me! I want to do it!' My jaw dropped as I watched Olivia, a seventyish daredevil heroine, perched eagerly on her seat in the plane while tons of water arched and fell on her, then shake her little head as she bobbed up to the surface, smiling."[33]

Olivia enjoyed the shoot and relished being with old friends. She was "clearly intrigued by the logistics of making this sort of disaster movie and want[ed] to watch every detail of stunt work and special effect." She was also secure in herself: "She would be merely matronly pretty if it wasn't for her expression, which is limelight. She is fully defined, a standout from any background. . . . Everything she says and does is designed to entrap and hold your attention. She manages to be theatrical without being outrageous."[34] Olivia declared, "I really loved this role a lot. I think this movie will be very successful. The script is well structured, there are a lot of special effects, drama, dramatic tension and, moreover, the numerous performers worked in an enthusiastic atmosphere."[35]

She was not so lucky with her next disaster film, the "stingingly bad flick" *The Swarm* (1978), directed by disaster king Irwin Allen.[36] The script, written by Stirling Silliphant and, according to the trailer, based on "scientific fact," is about killer African bees.[37] This was Olivia's "first time on the Warner Bros. lot now called the Burbank Studios—since 1943. Her look of horror and screams of anguish under the direction of Allen could well have described her feelings as she recalled her previous years under contract to Warner Brothers."[38] Again, we have a wonderful cast of actors who must have needed the work and the money: Michael Caine, Henry Fonda, Richard Widmark, Patty Duke Astin, Katharine Ross, and Richard Chamberlain. It must have been great fun to work with these pros, particularly in one scene when the bees destroy a town where the local cinema is showing Irwin Allen's *The Towering Inferno* (for which Olivia had declined a role).

Olivia's character, Maureen Schuester, is plump, matronly, and pleasant, and she has two suitors vying for her attention—Ben Johnson and Fred MacMurray. However, once again, no one listens to the warnings of this woman of a certain age: "But I can't shake this feelin' that somethin's closin' in on us."[39] That's too bad, because the bees take out most of the cast.

Olivia had quite an exciting moment with the deadly bees. "She had become something of an instant heroine on the set [one] day when given a choice of death by being thrown from a train window in a crash, as were her movie suitors . . . [but] she volunteered to die with the bees on her." As Olivia lay with her face and body covered by thousands of live bees, playing a dead woman, "'one of the bees broke loose from the rest and began to enter [Olivia's] nose.'" Fortunately, she recalled, "'the bee master was sending thoughts to it—the bee began to back out. . . . What made me proud when I went to the rushes . . . is that I didn't move . . . there was no sign of breathing.'"[40]

Olivia, always a professional and game for anything, enjoyed working on the picture, even though Irwin Allen is reminiscent of Ed Wood in the trailer as he calls out, "Cut! Sensational!" She said with great sincerity, "This kind of film I think has an awful lot of value, because people, the general public, all of us, run the risk of being threatened by these bees."[41] If only *The Swarm* were truly camp! Instead, it is gratuitous shock-schlock. At least Olivia got to spend time in her hometown of Saratoga, California, during a break in the filming, so it wasn't a complete waste. Olivia declared proudly, however, "'It made $5 million in three days, achieving exactly what it set out to do—make a fortune.'"[42]

Next, Olivia appeared in the first two episodes of *Roots: The Next Generations* (1979). This sequel to the original adaptation of Alex Haley's landmark novel was a television event with an enormous cast. Olivia was delighted to work again with Henry Fonda, who was "'so kind and good to me. So caring and so generous. I wish we had more scenes but we don't. He looks out for me all the time. He knows all my lines.'"[43] Olivia enjoyed the experience, in part because they "shot on the Paramount lot, which always brought me fulfilment. . . . I loved being in this beautifully made, highly successful series. . . . I had already accepted the death of the Golden Era of Hollywood, brought on by television, and it was my job to adjust thereto and to do good work in the evolving new medium."[44]

Olivia plays a southern belle, the wife of local politician Colonel Frederick Warner (Fonda). They have two sons. One son, played by Richard Thomas, falls in love with a young black schoolteacher (Fay Hauser) and marries her rather than setting her up as a mistress, as Fonda suggests. Their other son, played by Marc Singer, is a racist who stands for office against his father and wins. Olivia's southern accent is fair enough, but she has nothing to do, and her hair and costumes are unflattering. She wears a morning dress with a bustle that looks like a train caboose, and a bad wig is elaborately piled on her head. When I mentioned this to her, she replied, "My costumes were rented or bought from a costume rental company, where genuine period clothing was also available. It took a bit of adapting to this very different system. The costumes I wore had been designed for some other actress playing in some other movie."[45] Always a trouper, Olivia adjusted.

In her first scene in episode one, she's in the carriage waiting to go to the train station and complains petulantly, "Won't the horses bolt? I'm not sure that a steam engine pouring out smoke is progress." She's quite plump at this point and simply clucks displeasure at her husband and sons. It's nice to see Olivia and Fonda together again, although there's no real opportunity for chemistry. In her one good scene in this first episode, she counsels her son (Richard Thomas) as they discuss "the colored." When she finally gets fed up at the arguments between her husband and her son, who dares to love a black girl, she declares with real anger and authority, "Don't be a fool, Frederick. Do you think I'm deaf and blind? . . . I've known about men and their Negresses since I was a little girl. My father, my brothers. I know that Andrew does not confine himself to that white slut he parades around town. . . . White men marry white women and hold them in such high esteem, they set them under glass jars on the parlor table to collect dust."[46] Olivia delivers this condemnation of white male hypocrisy and the exploitation of black women with sarcasm and irony.

More poignantly, in the second episode, we learn that Olivia's bad son is running with the Ku Klux Klan, and she has to visit her good son, married to a black woman, in secret. She arrives by night in a veiled hat, and she asks about her grandson, sadly saying, "I saw him last Tuesday in his schoolyard . . . I couldn't even ask the coachman to slow down." Olivia and Richard Thomas play the heartbreak of their positions realistically. She's sympathetic but constrained by her marriage, her generation, and her husband, saying, "Oh, it's very difficult, Jimmy. Your father would never forgive me if he knew I came at all." She represents that good-hearted white person who is too frightened to act on her convictions. Most movingly, she asks her grandson, "Frankie, would you like me to tuck you in?"[47] She smiles sweetly, but the child shakes his head no. Olivia's artistry allows us to see her character's confusion and sense of loss. It may have been a small role, but Olivia was choosing material that allowed her to demonstrate her principles.

The same year, Olivia appeared on the big screen in *The Fifth Musketeer,* based on *The Man in the Iron Mask* and photographed beautifully by the great Jack Cardiff in Austria. She was billed as a "guest star" and played the small role of Queen Anne. In keeping with the unfortunate 1970s trend of large casts in poorly scripted films, Olivia worked with Rex Harrison, Sylvia Kristel, Ursula Andress, Cornel Wilde, Ian McShane, Lloyd Bridges, and Beau Bridges, but "the impressive parts somehow do not add up to an impressive total."[48] Beau is the unlucky twin in the iron mask, and he simply lacks the acting chops and the physicality to play such a dashing role. Unfortunately, in this dire swashbuckler with bad costumes and worse dubbing, there are no Errol Flynns. However, it is rather sweet and poignant that Olivia got to work with Alan Hale Jr., the son of her costar in so many 1930s action films.

Olivia's Queen Anne is now Sister Anne. Having retreated to a convent, she is dressed in a simple brown robe and looks benignly beautiful. She has been released from her vow of silence so that she can return to Paris and sort out the power struggle between her sons: the hapless musketeer (Beau Bridges) and his twin, the bad king who has imprisoned him in the mask. She kneels deeply before the king, pale in her beige wimple. In a voice that is low and husky, as befits her vow of silence, she tells him, "He is your brother, Louis! You shall not harm him! Do you not know the invisible ties binding the lives of twins? By harming him, you will risk even greater danger to yourself. I shall not demand your word, when you have never felt obliged to keep it. But remember well my warning. It is the last thing you shall hear from me."[49] Her face is hard and set. Then she turns and walks away, taking the film's last element of dignity and interest with her.

Also in 1979, Olivia appeared at a fortieth anniversary screening of *Gone with the Wind* in Los Angeles. In an interview, she was very vocal about what the profession had done for her: "'Motion picture acting is a marvellous way for women to have careers. Without understanding what they were doing, they stood as a kind of symbol of women's liberation, I suppose. They were totally self-reliant, self-sustaining women. They were as well paid as men. They had identical problems to work out as men actors.'"[50]

At this time, Olivia found support through her church. She was active with the American Cathedral in Paris, where she was a lay reader and a member of the altar guild. She also traveled to the United States on frequent speaking engagements to various Episcopalian conventions.[51] In the late 1970s, she helped fund-raise for the church's Venture in Mission; the campaign raised $7 million to support black colleges as well as other projects. She loved this volunteer experience, which was inspired in part by Benjamin's illness and recovery: "'I find it thrilling. . . . It's so boring, this selfish life we lead to survive.'"[52]

It seemed that everyone who had ever worked in Hollywood guest-starred on *The Love Boat,* a popular TV series about a cruise ship and its crazy crew, and Olivia was no exception. She appeared in 1981 as the wealthy aunt of Captain Stubing (Gavin MacLeod) and said she liked the part because "'I have a glorious fantasy life.'"[53] It's a charming role for Olivia, and her interactions with young Jill Whelan, playing the captain's daughter Vicki, are authentically warm. Olivia was also reunited with old friend Joseph Cotten, about whom she said, "'It's as if we literally walked off the plane [*Airport '77*], took a shower and boarded the Love Boat.'"[54]

Olivia made two TV movies in 1982. The first, *Murder Is Easy,* was based on an Agatha Christie novel. It was shot in the English countryside and featured not only Helen Hayes but also the great actor Timothy West. Olivia plays local villager Honoria Waynflete, and Bill Bixby plays visiting academic Luke Williams, who writes about chance and probability theory. As he explains to her, "You see, the person in question is just the last person anyone would suspect. And as long as no one suspects you, murder is easy." Of course, this being an Agatha Christie tale, the body count rises quickly in the small village. And the least obvious person turns out to be the killer: none other than Olivia's cheerfully evil Honoria. As Bixby says, "She was so proud of her cleverness."[55]

Clearly, Olivia is having a ball wearing proper little gloves, pushing Helen Hayes under a taxi, and admitting that she once killed "my own pet canary just because it pecked me!"[56] She even has a cat named "Wonky Pooh." It's a lightweight but fun role—a precursor to the run of Miss Marple and Hercule Poirot mysteries that have been wildly popular for the last thirty-plus years. Olivia was certainly in control of her choices, and when I wrote to her in December 1981, she replied, "*Murder Is Easy*, an Agatha Christie movie I made in England last summer, will be aired by CBS on January 2nd, 1982. If you see it, I hope you will find it diverting."[57]

In Olivia's second TV movie that year, she appeared as the Queen Mother in *The Royal Romance of Charles and Diana.* By this time, Olivia was charmingly round, like the Queen Mum; her hair was white, and her smile was warm. At the time, Prince William had just been born, Diana's anorexia and bulimia were not public concerns, and no one knew about Camilla Parker Bowles. In hindsight, the movie is a frothy fairy tale, as much of a fantasy as a Disney film. Catherine Oxenberg, the daughter of Princess Elizabeth of Yugoslavia, is convincingly shy and sweet as Diana. Christopher Baines is a suitably diffident Charles. Olivia was reunited with Ray Milland, who plays Mr. Griffiths, a courtier. Olivia's scenes as a caring and compassionate grandmother-in-law guiding the young girl in the ways of royalty are far more loving than the real Diana's experiences, given what we now know about the truth behind the palace walls, but Olivia enjoyed the costumes, the pearls, and the chance to play royalty.

For the next four years, Olivia was occupied with her children. Gisèle had finished law school and practiced law for a while, but then she moved into journalism, like her father, writing for *Elle* and *Paris Match*. Gisèle was a lovely young woman, smart and socially active, with the same flashing dark eyes and independent spirit as her mother. She and Olivia shared the town house in Paris. Her relationship with Olivia "was a very close one and . . . they often travel[ed] together."[58] Gisèle briefly took the public stage when she was engaged to Johnny Hallyday, France's Elvis Presley, in 1987. Publicly, Olivia supported the match because "'he treats Gisèle beautifully, and because he's quite an exceptional man. I like him very much. . . . In a way . . . it's Melanie Hamilton marrying Rhett Butler.'"[59] She kept any reservations about the match to herself, saying, "'I am going to do what my mother did with me. . . . She kept silent. She didn't say a word. . . . I have decided that my mother was a very intelligent woman.'"[60] When I asked her many years later how she really felt about Gisèle and Johnny Hallyday, she replied succinctly: "Alarmed."[61] The marriage was postponed in August 1988, and eventually the relationship ended. In an ironic side note, I saw Olivia in Paris on December 5, 2017, the day Hallyday died. Olivia remembered him fondly.

Meanwhile, Benjamin was pursuing his career as a statistical mathematician in Austin, Texas, and then in California. Olivia was also close to her niece Debbie, Joan's daughter with producer William Dozier. She and Joan would not speak again—as far as anyone knows.

Olivia returned to television in 1986, appearing in several episodes of the popular miniseries *North and South, Book II*. The huge cast included young Patrick Swayze and Kirstie Alley, as well as veterans Lloyd Bridges and Hal Holbrook. James Stewart also appeared in some of the episodes. One wishes one could have eavesdropped on the two former lovers, but what we know is that "when she caught up with him for the final shot of the entire cast, she kissed him smack on the mouth."[62] Ah, Livvie.

Olivia's role of Mrs. Neal, the head nurse and director of a field hospital for the wounded, wasn't terribly demanding. However, "typical of de Havilland's attention to detail and research as an actress . . . [she arrived] in town early . . . [to] watch a tape of all 12 hours of that first 'North and South,' since her new character will be interacting with people established in Part One."[63] Her character insists that all soldiers be treated equally, no matter which side they are on, reflecting Olivia's sense of social justice.

Her second role of 1986 was much more successful. She appeared in the TV movie *Anastasia: The Mystery of Anna,* which reteamed her with *Fifth Musketeer* costar Rex Harrison (in his last television role). Amy Irving was excellent in the lead, and this was the first film for a young Christian Bale. The production is based on the legend of Anastasia, the daughter of Czar Nicholas II and Queen Alexandra. It was rumored and fervently believed that Anastasia had escaped execution during the Russian Revolution and made her way to the West, until DNA evidence at the Romanov burial site proved that Anastasia died with her family. The title role in the 1956 movie had won Ingrid Bergman her second Oscar, and Olivia's role was good for her, too—she received an Emmy nomination for best supporting actress and won a Golden Globe.

Anna Anderson has been institutionalized in a mental institution in Berlin, but she believes she is Princess Anastasia. Amy Irving's delicate beauty and portrayal of her character's instability help to drive the film's intensity. Wearing a dark, curly wig, a corseted black dress (costume designer Jane Robinson won a well-deserved Emmy), and impressive Russian pearls, Olivia is both intimidating and sympathetic as Dowager Empress Maria. The flashbacks to the revolution and the executions are handled smoothly by director Marvin J. Chomsky, and the screenplay by James Goldman and Peter Kurth (who wrote the book *Anastasia: The Riddle of Anna Anderson*) is intelligent.

As time passes, some believe that Anna is Anastasia, and some do not. However, Dowager Empress Maria resolves to find out for herself. Prince Erich (Jan Niklas) has met Anna and is convinced of her identity, but Maria must be sure. Olivia's voice is deep and firm as she admits the possibility of Anastasia's escape. She argues with the skeptical Grand Duke Cyril (Rex Harrison) about meeting the young woman and says, "I will consider what you said, of course. Then I shall do what I think best."[64] Maria is the matriarch, and Olivia is completely comfortable in that role.

Anastasia/Anna becomes a huge media sensation and travels the world, but the Dowager Empress, who is ill in bed, is still wary. Bravely, Olivia plays the scene with no makeup, and her double chin isn't attractive. We learn that Anastasia was always her special favorite. She would like to receive her, but the painful decision to allow the past to stay in the past is heartbreaking: "But life gets smaller every day. And I did love her so."[65] Maria dies before she can see poor Anna. As for the real Anna Anderson, a trial began in August 1939 to prove that she was Anastasia, and it took until the spring of 1970 for a verdict, which held that Anastasia's death had never been established as a fact. Anna lived in Charlottesville, Virginia, until she died in 1984, and it wasn't until the Romanov bones were unearthed that her sad, delusional existence was revealed.

Olivia gives a very poignant performance, and she deserved the Golden Globe. When she heard about the nomination, she exclaimed, "'It's wonderful news! . . . The show just aired on Dec. 7 and now, one month later to the day, I received this very nice honor.'"[66] Footage of her at the banquet receiving the award shows an energetic and delighted actress, happy to receive this acknowledgment of her work at the age of seventy.

Olivia's final film was another TV movie about royalty. Given her own status as a Hollywood legend, it was perhaps appropriate that she played Wallis Warfield Simpson's beloved Aunt Bessie in *The Woman He Loved* (1988). The story of that "evil" woman from Baltimore and King Edward VIII has been filmed countless times, but this version, while romanticized, is eminently watchable. The cast includes Anthony Andrews, Jane Seymour, Julie Harris, and Tom Wilkinson. The costumes by Robin Fraser-Paye resonate with the elegance of the era, and the performances hit the right balance of melodrama and sincerity. While it's clearly a movie of the week, with neither a wonderful script nor a particularly effective director, it's great fun.

Olivia had actually known the duke and duchess, and she told Robert Osborne, "'They were quite an extraordinary couple, you know, and I liked them both very much. The Duchess was always very gracious and warm toward me. . . . I always felt very shy with the Duke. But it feels quite unusual to have known them socially, and now to be appearing in a story about their lives.'"[67]

As Wallis's chaperone, Olivia is plump and pretty, white haired, and welcoming, with a rather suspect southern accent. Olivia said at the time, "'I am always attracted to portray Southern women. Perhaps "Gone with the Wind" gave me a Confederate heart.'"[68] She has wonderful chemistry with Jane

Seymour. In one scene, while reclining on a deck chair on the royal yacht, Olivia sports a white straw picture hat with a black bow. She warns her dear niece that although she's "no prude about modern morality," Wallis should watch her step. She's loving and witty, and she owns the moments she's onscreen; there is a lot of Olivia in Aunt Bessie. Later, after the love affair has become international news and Bessie must leave Wallis to her fate, there is a comic moment when she tells her distraught niece, "There are always blessings to these things. . . . You put Baltimore on the map!"[69] It's a funny exchange, underplayed and delivered in Olivia's typically dry fashion.

This was Olivia's last acting job, although she would have been happy to accept a good role if one came up. She returned to her life in Paris, where she kept busy with interviews, friends, and her still-unseen memoir, while enjoying regular visits with Gisèle and Benjamin in the States.

The 1990s, however, brought Olivia several profound personal crises. Her daughter, Gisèle, struggled with depression for several years, and Olivia supported her as much as possible. Gisèle eventually improved and relocated to Malibu after marrying renowned art collector Edward Broida, who was twenty years her senior—rather like Olivia's first marriage, but much happier.

There was no happy ending for her son, Benjamin. Diagnosed with Hodgkin's lymphoma as a teenager, he battled the illness for many years, and Olivia cared for him, devoting her time and energy to her son while giving him his independence. The cancer treatments weakened him, and tragically, Benjamin Briggs Goodrich died in Paris on September 29, 1991. He was only forty-one years old. Olivia's grief was unimaginable, and I didn't hear from her for some time. Later, she was kind enough to share some of the details: "Alas, I lost him. . . . He returned to Paris June 1st greatly depleted, was thrice hospitalized during the summer, and finally his long struggle against the long-term effects of the over-radiation he received 20 years previously came to an end. He died of progressive constrictive pericarditis."[70] His father, Marcus Goodrich, died three weeks later.

Years later, Olivia told me more about Ben: "He was also lots of fun and could imitate people with great accuracy and wit (one of his favourite characters was an 'encrusted Englishman'). Benjamin was over-radiated at an American institution in Paris, a therapy that burned his heart, burned his diaphragm and led to his premature death. . . . I was told by a brilliant French doctor after he had seen Benjamin's x-rays early in his therapy that Ben had only ten years to live. Through exercise and other efforts Benjamin extended his life for another twenty years, and only the last five years were hard for him."[71]

Then, in February 1998, Pierre Galante was diagnosed with lung cancer. Although they had been divorced for almost twenty years, he and Olivia had remained close, and he moved back into 3 rue Benouville, where she and Gisèle cared for him until his death. He stayed in the master bedroom, while Olivia slept in a nearby room. Robert Osborne remembered her explanation of her compassion for her ex-husband: "'She knew how much he meant to her daughter. . . . She also said to me, "Even though we're no longer married and I'm not in love with him anymore, I did make a commitment to love, honor and cherish him. I like to keep my commitments." That's just the way Olivia is.'"[72]

But with her characteristic strength, Olivia once again emerged into the world. She still had Gisèle, her faith, her health, her home in Paris, her friends, her church, and her books—her life. She would face the new millennium, as well as her advancing years, with bravery, grace, and joy.

10

SISTER JOAN

When Joan Fontaine died in her sleep on December 15, 2013, at the age of ninety-six, one couldn't help but recall her comment about her renowned "feud" with her sister Olivia: "I married first, won the Oscar before Olivia, and if I die first, she'll undoubtedly be livid because I beat her to it!"[1] Leave it to the *Daily Mail* to pick up on that rivalry at Joan's death, ghoulishly reporting, "Fontaine has trumped her nemesis once again."[2] As the decades rolled along, it seemed that both actresses would live forever, and columnist Michael Musto noted, "I just know neither will *ever* die."[3] Christopher Hitchens, estranged from his own brother Peter, wrote in an essay about sibling rivalry of the "glacial relationship" the actresses shared. He even added to the mythology of their feud by relating a false anecdote about the 1946 Oscars: "Olivia refused to accept the Oscar for *To Each His Own* when she found out that Joan would be presenting it. She turned her back and flounced off the stage, leaving her sister standing all alone with the statuette."[4] Pure fiction, but great press.

One would think that the intensity of their disagreement would fade over the decades, but it was too delicious. The estrangement between "these two extraordinarily beautiful and remarkably talented young women . . . for over seventy years [was] a Hollywood mystery that has never been solved."[5] They were both "grandes dames from a vanished era," and perhaps because of that, "theirs [was] no petulant exchange of talcum powder, forgiven or forgotten the next morning. For seven decades, maybe nine decades, it . . . separated two of the leading actresses of their generation."[6] The feud even reentered the popular culture of the film industry itself when Laura Dern offered a tribute to her father, Bruce (who had worked with Olivia in *Hush . . . Hush, Sweet Charlotte*), at an Academy Awards luncheon in December 2013. Dern responded humorously to a "voluminous round of applause" in appreciation of her obvious adoration of her father by saying, "'It's a lie. We're actually like Olivia de Havilland and Joan Fontaine—we don't speak.'"[7]

In their responses to a *Vanity Fair* Proust questionnaire, the sisters offered interesting comments about their own mortality. Each was asked: How would you like to die? Olivia's answer in March 2005 reflected her elegance, her love of language, and her favorite tipple: "I would prefer to live forever in perfect health, but if I must at some time leave this life I would like to do so ensconced on a chaise longue, with a flute of champagne beside me and having just discovered the answer to the last problem in a British cryptic crossword." Joan's answer in March 2008 was far more succinct and, as it turned out, close to her actual end: "In bed—alone."[8] Olivia's poetic demise presents a stark contrast to her sister's vision, offering a metaphor of sorts for the difficulties they experienced in their careers and their relationship.

Ironically, one of the major triggers for Olivia's lawsuit against Ryan Murphy Productions in June 2017 was the scene in *Feud* in which Catherine Zeta-Jones (as Olivia) refers to Joan as "my bitch sister."[9] Olivia even issued a statement through her lawyers admitting that she called Joan "Dragon Lady" but never "bitch."[10] Other than an occasional reference to "my sister," Olivia usually refers to Joan as "my sibling," although in some of our conversations, she has rather sardonically used the "Dragon Lady" appellation. Throughout her career, and certainly since Lilian's death in 1975, Olivia has steadfastly refused to discuss her relationship with Joan in any detail, although those refusals have sometimes been tantalizing. For example, she told *Interview* magazine in 1987, "I have always had a feeling of tremendous responsibility and affection for Joan. Her feelings toward me are extremely mixed, and that's where the trouble lies. There is really nothing more to be said. . . . Everything about us is off-limits. I just wish that you and everyone else would forget that she is my sister."[11] Joan's 1978 autobiography, *No Bed of Roses,* a lively and seemingly candid account, essentially accuses Olivia of the same ambivalence toward her.

In a story related by Charles Higham (and elsewhere), both Olivia and Joan happened to be staying at the Beverly Hills Hotel for the 1988 Academy Awards: "It seems . . . management had no idea Fontaine and de Havilland were sisters, much less that they don't talk to each other. After a short conference, it was determined that since de Havilland had checked in first, Fontaine would be moved to another room on a lower floor."[12]

Olivia had remained a visible if discreet celebrity with her occasional performances through 1988 and her frequent interviews with the media, often coinciding with anniversary screenings of *Gone with the Wind.* She very skillfully avoided discussions of anything too personal for years, perhaps partly in deference to her children, but as she reached her eighties and then nineties, she began to reveal a bit more. For example, breaking a long silence in terms of videoed interviews, she participated in *Melanie Remembers* in 2004 for Turner Classic Movies, in recognition of the sixty-fifth anniversary of *Gone with the Wind.* She also talked sweetly and rather saucily about her beloved costar for another TCM documentary, *The Adventures of Errol Flynn.* But she had never commented in any significant way about Joan Fontaine. When Olivia was awarded the Légion d'Honneur by the French government in 2010, one reporter noted that "her only sibling . . . was conspicuous by her absence from the ceremony."[13] However, neither sister commented about no-show Joan. Joan's name occasionally appeared in the press, often in discussions of Hitchcock's blondes, but she was retired, living in California with her menagerie of animals, and enjoying a quiet, happy life in her beautiful Carmel home.

Upon learning of Joan's death, Olivia issued a statement through her manager, saying that she was "shocked and saddened" and grateful for "the many kind expressions of sympathies."[14] She didn't comment about their famous feud, and only later in 2016, in an exclusive email interview with *People* magazine, did Olivia directly address her relationship with Joan, calling her "'a brilliant person, very gifted, and alas, [with] an astigmatism in her perception of people, which could cause great distress in others.'"[15]

Joan's death surprised Olivia. According to her assistant, Mimi, she had no idea her sister had been ill, and whether Olivia's subsequent battles with pneumonia and lung infections (to which she has always been prone), as well as troublesome back and leg pain, could somehow be connected to Joan's death is pure speculation. But they were, after all, antipodes linked by blood and genetics, by talent and drive, by independence and privacy, by career choice and success. They were witty and elegant, celebrated beauties and Oscar winners; each had been profoundly influenced by their powerful mother. They had even dated some of the same men and shared directors and costars. They had been movie stars in the greatest era of Hollywood and had seen their careers wind down in the 1950s and 1960s.

Sadly, Olivia's son, Benjamin, had died, and Joan had become estranged from her adopted daughter, Martita. She had met the young girl in Peru and, perhaps foolishly, had brought her to the United States to raise with her biological daughter, Deborah (with producer William Dozier). It didn't work out, and Martita eventually went to live with another family. Deborah remained close to her aunt Olivia, and Gisèle lived just down the road from Joan in Malibu, although it is doubtful they shared regular aunt-niece lunches.

At the time of Joan's death, the two sisters were in their nineties, living alone with the help of personal assistants, comfortably and contentedly divorced—Olivia in Paris, and Joan in California. Both had been off the screen, large and small, for several years, but they emerged occasionally as two of the last remaining stars of Hollywood's golden era. The two women had not seen each other since their mother's funeral. Clearly, they had a great deal in common. Which was always the problem.

In her autobiography, Joan shows Olivia no sisterly understanding. She claims that Olivia resented having a baby sister and never relished the competition. They were given Stanford-Binet IQ tests when they were young, and according to Joan, her IQ was so high that she was called back; she magnanimously attributes Olivia's lower score to having had a fever on the day of the test. "Olivia was told the results of both our tests. Joan [writing about herself in the third person here] was undeniably her enemy. Besides the inexcusable intrusion into her life—that of Joan's birth—this latest display of arrogance was the last straw for the older sister. I regret that I remember not one act of kindness from her all through my childhood."[16] Joan reiterated that sentiment in 1987, when she affirmed, "My mother told me that Olivia would not even look into the crib after I arrived. She has always felt I was an intruder . . . usurping her position all the time."[17] Joan, the younger child, felt like an outsider, unwanted.

That grim statement is all the more poignant, given that both girls had to deal with their parents' divorce and remarriage to people to whom the sisters weren't close. Their father, Walter de Havilland, played no part in their upbringing past their toddler years. In fact, he showed up alone in the United States in November 1940, after "the effects of war in the Orient had wrecked the business he carried on in Tokyo for 47 years." He claimed to be impoverished and was looking for an inexpensive place to live. He was also looking for a handout from his daughters, but, he said, "My pleas were ignored." Lilian felt compelled to remark that she had heard from Walter only once since 1919.[18] His Japanese mistress-turned-wife had established no kind of stepmotherly relationship with the sisters. Even the fan magazines of the day acknowledged that Walter's treatment of his family and his "unwanted return" was "casting them unwillingly together in an off-stage production," although "these two long ago informed their studios that they would rather do almost anything than appear in the same production. That is one of the few points on which they have ever agreed. . . . Fate has given them something else to agree on."[19]

Joan and Olivia finally consented to a reunion with their father, who ended up in Victoria, British Columbia. Olivia reconnected with him in 1949 and Joan in 1950, but both meetings were, in Olivia's words, "'an act of love to make an old man happy.'"[20] Olivia saw him again in 1951 when she was touring with *Candida,* and in 1952, when Walter was eighty-one, she welcomed him for a week's visit. Tellingly, Olivia signed an autograph at the train station where they met, and Walter suddenly chimed in, "'Wait a moment. . . . After all, my name's more important than hers. . . . She's only one. I'm the father of two movie stars.' He signed his name with a flourish."[21] That the sisters agreed to see him at all qualifies them for sainthood.

As related earlier, Lilian's move to Saratoga, California, and her remarriage to department store manager George Fontaine also proved to be an unhappy development for Olivia and Joan. They disliked their stepfather, and Joan claimed that he attempted sexual impropriety with both of them: "Olivia and I, never given to confidences, did agree that something was odd. We were to have the same discussion eight years later, this time joined by Mother, with more serious consequences [presumably, Lilian's estrangement from her husband]. Fathers and daughters, stepfathers and stepdaughters. The story is not new."[22]

These familial upheavals weren't helped by Joan's view that Olivia was the favored child, while she was an afterthought. Olivia was close to her mother, and her vitality was the direct opposite of Joan's fragility and frequent illnesses. Although Olivia moved out of the house as a teenager to escape her stepfather's controlling behavior, Joan committed an act that might have seemed like a betrayal to Lilian—she returned to Tokyo to live with her father and stepmother. That relationship fell apart, according to Joan, due to Walter's incestuous intentions toward her. Joan's return to California didn't strengthen her ties to Lilian.

By that time, Olivia was already at Warner Brothers, and Joan was exhibiting a burgeoning interest in becoming an actress. Here again, the sisters were in opposition to each other. Rather than embrace the notion of a family business, like the Barrymores, the Hustons, and the Fondas, Joan and Olivia and Lilian used three different surnames. Lilian used her maiden name, Ruse, and Olivia, of course, used her real last name, de Havilland. According to Joan, Olivia and Lilian forced her to adopt her loathed stepfather's last name as her stage name. She said, "Olivia and my mother felt that we should have different names, so as not to be like the Andrews sisters, I guess. . . . But I would have liked to have been Joan de Havilland. That one is going to be on my tombstone."[23] Thus Joan de Beauvoir de Havilland became Joan Fontaine. How much of this name game is true is anyone's guess. However, there is no denying that Olivia and Joan were competitors in the same cutthroat industry. Although the media—both celebrity gossip publications and more legitimate news sources—made much of their feud, where there's smoke, there's fire.

They were two talented, driven women whose temperaments and dreams were similar. Olivia, the older sister, had already begun her career when along came Joan, the beautiful younger sister whose blonde hair and blue eyes made her yet another ideal ingenue in a business where ingenues were as plentiful as rabbits. After her unexpected theatrical triumph, Olivia was rewarded with a contract from Warner Brothers during the Depression. But at eighteen, she had to help support her mother as well as her younger sister. (In many ways, Olivia's situation was comparable to that of Bette Davis, who also had a divorced mother and a sister to care for.)

The sisters' competition extended to men. Olivia briefly dated the gifted Irish actor Brian Aherne, but Joan married him. According to Olivia, "I hadn't gone with him for some months when she started going out with him."[24] Yet at age twenty-one, Joan was married to a tall, handsome, up-and-coming actor that Olivia had dated (and worked with) first. As recently as 2012, the *New York Post* revealed that "the night before the wedding, de Havilland's beau at the time, billionaire Howard Hughes, flirted with Fontaine—something her sister was none too happy about."[25] Joan confirmed that Hughes had indeed "slipped me his private telephone number." When she told Olivia about it, instead of being grateful, "sparks flew. Hell hath no fury like a woman scorned . . . especially in favor of her sister. This, plus my engagement to Brian, was very hard for her to take."[26]

In the meantime, Joan had become a film actress, and although her early efforts are completely unremarkable—*A Damsel in Distress* with Fred Astaire is particularly excruciating—by 1939, she was costarring with Cary Grant in *Gunga Din* and appearing in the MGM comedy classic *The Women.* To add insult to injury, by 1940, she had a contract with David O. Selznick, one of the most respected producers in Hollywood and, of course, the mad genius behind *Gone with the Wind.* What a painful "common thread" this must have been for Olivia.[27] How could she not envy her sister? Olivia was still at Warner Brothers, battling Jack Warner for decent scripts and roles, while Joan was cast in *Rebecca.* It was a miracle they didn't enact a *Baby Jane* scenario and try to run each other over with a Packard.

Then there were the Academy Awards. Olivia had lost her first nomination for best supporting actress in *GWTW* to Hattie McDaniel. Olivia admitted being upset until she realized how important McDaniel's landmark win was to the American artistic and racial landscape. Olivia had waged an enormous battle just to get the role of Melanie, and Joan's supposed contribution added intrigue to the sisters' competition. Joan told journalist Scott Feinberg that George Cukor (the original director) had invited her to discuss the role of Melanie, but because she had mistakenly worn "rather chic clothes," she was discounted by the director. So she said, "'Well, what about my sister?'"[28]

Joan's Oscar nomination for best actress the next year (1940) for *Rebecca*—Alfred Hitchcock's first American picture, based on Daphne du Maurier's best seller, and produced by Selznick—had to be difficult for Olivia to accept. Then, in 1941, both sisters were nominated for the best actress Oscar: Joan for Hitchcock's *Suspicion,* and Olivia for Paramount's *Hold Back the Dawn.* They were seated at the same table at the Academy Awards banquet, and when Joan won the Oscar—awarded to her, most agree, as compensation for losing the previous year to an undeserving Ginger Rogers—how did Olivia feel? She had been generous earlier that day, sending a crew and gowns from I. Magnin to Joan's dressing room (she was shooting *The Constant Nymph* at the time) when she confessed she had nothing to wear to the Oscars that evening.[29] She also behaved beautifully that evening in public, proud that one of the de Havillands had accomplished this feat, but conflicted, conflicted, conflicted. Seated at the table with her new beau Burgess Meredith, Olivia put on a brave face and a good show. She even took Joan's hand after the win and lifted it up in the air, exclaiming, "'We've got it!'"[30] Yet Joan claimed to be frozen with fear at Olivia's response to her win and recalled that Olivia brusquely ordered her, "'Get up there, get up there.' . . . Now what had I done!"[31]

It took Olivia five more years and several mediocre films before she received another best actress nomination in 1946 for *To Each His Own*—and won. In those same five years, Joan would go on to make *Jane Eyre* in 1944 with Orson Welles, who reportedly took over from director Robert Stevenson whenever possible. Nevertheless, Joan's venture into Brontë territory was much more successful than Olivia's portrayal of Charlotte Brontë in the oddly entertaining *Devotion.* Joan played Jane Eyre, and Olivia played Jane's creator—the metaphor isn't a particularly complicated one. In the mid-1940s, Joan seemed to be besting Olivia at every turn.

The gossip magazines kept an eye on their relationship during these years. In 1942, columnist Sidney Skolsky claimed, "Livvy has a recurring dream that she is standing on a high cliff, and, down below her, in the sand nearer the ocean, is Joan. Then suddenly she sees a tidal wave approaching. . . . She never knows whether to save herself or go to Joan, and she always wakes up before she decides."[32] A 1947 article entitled "Fighting Sisters," illustrated with two little girls tearing each other to bits in a fight, suggested that "if they could get Olivia and Joan, both Academy Award winners, to play their real life parts, the picture should take every Oscar the manufacturer can turn out. . . . After all, it takes good acting to make a good picture. And the two sisters wouldn't be acting!"[33] In 1949, Joan told Hedda Hopper, "'Olivia was always the breadwinner, and I the no-talent, no-future little sister not good for much more than paying her share of the rent.'"[34] Even in 1954, when Olivia was living in Paris, gossip magazine *Inside Story* trumpeted that "the blazing war between the sisters is hotter than ever," noting that they tried to hide their mutual dislike to prevent "giving the public a look at a feud that makes the Hatfield-McCoy affair look like a class reunion at Vassar."[35]

However, while Olivia's career skyrocketed from 1946 to 1949, Joan's was beginning to quiet. She couldn't compete with Olivia's three Oscar nominations and two wins in those years. In fact, Joan's last great role was in Max Ophuls's romantic tragedy *Letter to an Unknown Woman* in 1948. So, on the night of the 1946 Oscars, when Olivia won for *To Each His Own,* she came offstage to find Joan's hand extended toward her in congratulations. Olivia turned away, in no mood to play nice for the cameras. She was reportedly angry about Joan's admitted crack about her husband, the much-married Marcus Goodrich: "'All I know about him is that he has had four wives and written one book. Too bad it's not the other way around.'"[36] Olivia was angry and "very shocked by it. I didn't understand that kind of behavior, and I expected her to apologize." Joan didn't apologize, and according to Olivia, the backstage meeting had been arranged: "I knew right then that it was all a setup. I turned away, and she started toward me, knowing how I felt. It was an unthinkable situation."[37] Naturally a photographer, Hymie Fink from *Photoplay,* was standing by to record the awkward moment. And *Daily Variety* "reported at the time that Olivia then muttered to her press agent, Henry Rogers, 'I don't know why she does that when she knows how I feel.'"[38] The rumored feud now had photographic proof.

In a 2012 article in the *New York Post,* author Lou Lumenick quotes from a 1957 interview Olivia gave to gossip maven Hedda Hopper in which she discusses that difficult evening. Lumenick acquired this from Robert Matzen (author of *Errol & Olivia*), who in turn found the transcript at the Margaret

Herrick Library in Beverly Hills and suspected it had never been printed because it might be "bad for business."[39] In response to Hopper's question whether she and Joan were friends, Olivia's reply was a terse "Yes." Then, when Hopper asked about their relationship, Olivia explained in more detail:

> The reason I felt so estranged for so long was because she hurt me very much. I knew in advance when we were both to appear at the Academy there would be difficulty. I said in advance, "If you don't see us together there is a reason—if I happen to win, I won't acknowledge any gesture on her part in public unless she comes to me privately first." I was very English. [Publicist Henry Rogers] didn't believe me—and it did happen. I never explained it and have been criticized ever since. I was married [for the first time] to Marcus Goodrich—it was not an easy marriage as you well know. But I was married to him, he was my husband and I felt a very keen loyalty. I had committed myself to him—that means something to me. Joan, who is very witty and clever, as you know, made some remarks about Marc which got into the papers. This cut me to the heart. Under the circumstances I expected her to at least say something about being sorry it happened—or that she shouldn't have said it and was sorry it was printed. But I never got any kind of apology and wasn't going to say how do you do to her until I did get it. I wanted an explanation or apology in private not a public thing. . . . I didn't see her for a long time—about five years—not until after I got a divorce. Then it seemed ridiculous to demand this apology after I'd separated from the man about whom the issue arose. She asked me to dinner and I accepted, and so we resumed diplomatic relations.[40]

Olivia went on to explain how their antagonism began. Interestingly, Olivia felt that Joan was the favorite and that *she* was the misunderstood child: "I've been trying to analyze Joan—she's only 15 months younger than I am—when she was little she was treated well and spoiled by Mother. When Joan got sick it was an immense drama—and for an imaginative, hysterical child that was bad. If she got chickenpox, it was a drama of state. When I had it, I went to bed and was told to keep still and not scratch."[41]

Perhaps their birth order led Olivia to be more controlling and to feel exploited, whereas Joan felt subordinate in the family. Had they been able to see, objectively, how much they shared—beauty, physical grace, wit, talent, determination, insouciance, and a willingness to be iconoclastic when necessary—they might have written a different kind of history for themselves. But every family has its own dynamics, and siblings often have different versions of a shared childhood. In Olivia's view, "She seems to need what I have. She needs what another woman has."[42]

So, as the 1950s arrived, the sisters seemed to be living parallel lives they couldn't share with each other. Olivia divorced, moved to Paris, remarried, and had a daughter; she left Hollywood at the right time, making occasional appearances on film, on television, on lecture tours, on talk shows, and at the Oscars. Joan divorced and remarried two more times, gave birth to one daughter and adopted a second, and moved to New York; she left Hollywood at the right time, with occasional appearances on film, on television, on lecture tours, on talk shows, and at the Oscars. Both sisters enjoyed the good health and longevity of the de Havillands, and life settled into a comfortable routine into the mid-1970s. Olivia metamorphosed into an elegant matron and a charming character actress in a series of occasional roles. Joan glittered privately on the international political and artistic scenes.

And then came the event that would bring them together and break them apart for the last time. Lilian Augusta Ruse de Havilland Fontaine died on February 20, 1975, at the age of eighty-eight in Santa Barbara. Joan was touring with *Cactus Flower* on the East Coast that January when she learned from her mother's doctor that Lilian had terminal cancer. Joan couldn't get released from her contract to rush to her dying mother's bedside, so after cabling Olivia in Paris, she continued with the play. A few weeks later, Olivia called from California and suggested that their mother have "'an exploratory operation.'" Joan was vehemently against inflicting further "pain and indignity" but insisted that it was their mother's decision. In the end, Lilian's heart was too weak, and a few weeks later, she "died in her own bed and in her sleep."[43] Olivia hasn't spoken publicly about this exchange, although I have heard (from an admittedly dubious source) that her version is quite different—although they disagreed over Lilian's treatment, Joan was recalcitrant and disinterested.

Joan got the news of Lilian's death from her daughter Deborah. Two weeks later, she received a letter from a family friend and executor of Lilian's will informing her that her mother been cremated and the memorial service would be held in two weeks near Villa Montalvo, a theater Lilian had helped found; there would be readings by Olivia and by Joan's ex-husband Brian

Aherne. In Joan's view, Olivia had co-opted all the decisions and taken charge of the funeral arrangements, rather than discussing them with her. Joan accused Olivia of taking center stage.

Joan flew to California in time to scatter her mother's ashes. She wrote, "Thus I said good-bye forever to my mother. As for Olivia, I had no words at all."[44] Joan walked away and never spoke to her sister again, as far as we know. Joan dedicated her autobiography's last pages, entitled "Epilogue," to her mother. It is poignantly clear that Joan wished things had been different between them and that she didn't feel the love from Lilian that she needed: "I do not remember one time when you said I was pretty, that my figure was acceptable, that my clothes were well chosen. . . . Of your three grandchildren, only Olivia's daughter, Gisèle . . . captured your heart. When her son, Benjamin, became seriously ill . . . you remembered him generously in your will. You left not a trinket to Deborah."[45] How could Joan be close to Olivia, feeling that their mother loved her sister more? Yet how could Joan not regret their distance?

One thing is certain: Olivia was very close to her mother and admired her enormously. In our email correspondence, she wrote of Lilian, "I experienced her exclusively as a mother who was always there. . . . As I have said, I knew her as a constant, devoted mother."[46] When we met in November 2015 in Paris, we talked for more than an hour about Olivia's affection and respect for Lilian. Whatever the truths of this triangulated theatrical family, both sisters reflected the strong personality of their mother.

Joan observed later in her life, "By the way, we may not get along personally, but I am absolutely thrilled that my sister has accomplished what she has. . . . Imagine what we could have done if we had gotten together. We could have selected the right scripts, the right directors, the right producers—we could have built our own empire. But it was not to be."[47] One cannot help but be reminded of the final exchange in *What Ever Happened to Baby Jane* between Jane (Bette Davis) and Blanche (Joan Crawford): The dying, sand-covered Blanche confesses to crippling herself and blaming Jane for it. A poignant, keening Jane questions, "You mean all this time we could have been friends?"[48] The echoes among the actresses are undeniably similar in the extreme.

And now it is finished. Joan's end was peaceful. She died of natural causes at home, according to her assistant, Susan Pfeiffer.[49] Joan's ashes were scattered in the Pacific Ocean off Carmel Beach in California, where she resided with her beloved animals. Both Lilian and Joan, such forces of nature, returned to nature at the end; neither could be kept in one place for all eternity. In her will, Joan left a large legacy from the sale of her home (valued at more than $3 million) and her Oscar for *Suspicion* to the Society for the Prevention of Cruelty to Animals in Monterey County.[50]

Joan's death inevitably led to headlines about her estrangement from Olivia, in addition to her Oscar win and her Hitchcock roles. Someday, Olivia's obituaries will mention her Oscars, her role as Melanie Wilkes in *Gone with the Wind,* and her famous feud with Joan Fontaine. The sisters were, ultimately, sisters; "like the two sides of a coin, they are very different, yet strangely the same."[51] Which was always the problem.

At least there will be peace and closure between them with that final curtain—unless Ryan Murphy gets a bright idea. . . .

11

THE TIME IS NOW

In 2009, and then again in 2010, a title appeared on the Amazon website—*Now Is the Time* by Olivia de Havilland. It was billed (erroneously) as her long-awaited autobiography. This would not be Olivia's first book. Her 1962 memoir about her move to France and marriage to Pierre Galante, *Every Frenchman Has One,* is a charming, frothy romp—very consciously so. Olivia shares many amusing details about her life in Paris, making her seem tantalizingly candid. But Olivia is discreet, so the extent of revelation is deceptive; she is nothing if not careful about her public image and the language she uses.

A rather interesting profile of her handwriting by graphologist Muriel Stafford, written in 1950, noted that she had "a gifted, creative mind." When Stafford commented that Olivia's handwriting reflected that of "many authors and journalists," the actress replied, "'I've always wanted to be a writer.'"[1] However, Olivia has not yet produced an autobiography. That's lucky for me, of course, but one hopes she will publish another memoir at some point. She has been planning to do so for more than forty years, and she has had a remarkable life.

In 1977, in an interview for *Family Scene* magazine (the article was rather appropriately entitled "Olivia de Havilland . . . Too Busy Living Her Life to Write about It"), Olivia revealed she had commenced work on her autobiography the year before. She said, "'I started writing it, but I didn't like the way it was going so I tore the pages up. I found the very act of writing an autobiography was self-defeating because it's like saying it's all over, when for me, life is still full of wonderful things. . . . I still want to write that book, but every day that goes by is providing me with newer, fresher, and more exciting chapters.'"[2] An article in the *Los Angeles Times* at the end of 1980 noted that Olivia had a contract with Dutton and was due to deliver a manuscript for her memoir at that time, but it was going to be delayed. She said, "'I had to write them and say I needed at least another year . . . I said it was a far bigger project than I had realized, and it is.'"[3]

Over the years, I wrote to Olivia several times asking for quotes or information for various academic and conference papers. In 1983, she charmingly refused one such request in a letter: "As to your questions: I shall delay replying to them now—so that you will have the entertainment of finding the answers in the autobiography I will one day write!"[4] Not to be deterred, I requested an interview in 1986 and once again encountered the gentle stone wall: "About doing an interview with me: I presently have under consideration an agreement which will very much limit my freedom in this regard, and so I am afraid I shall have to disappoint you in this respect. However, this should not really discourage you . . . and you will soon think of other subjects . . . which will have appeal for the magazines you have in mind."[5]

I was not discouraged. I tried again a few years later, and again, the iron fist in the velvet glove wrote beautifully to deny me: "I . . . greatly regret that I am unable to provide you with the information you seek for a commentary on my work as Miriam in 'Hush . . . Hush, Sweet Charlotte.' You see, I am obliged to reserve all such material for my autobiography, to the writing of which, after many interruptions, I am at last able to return."[6]

When I inquired in 2002 about the progress of her memoir, she mentioned "three projects which Roger Mayer [a renowned film preservationist who passed away in March 2015] has proposed [which] I cannot begin to consider until the autobiography is at last completed. When the typewritten copy (triple-spaced) is finally in the hands of the publisher then, of course, I shall give the proposals serious thought." She went on to say humorously, "God will determine the date when I shall have written the final word of the book—and He has not so far hinted when that will be. I am reassured by the fact that Shirley Temple took 8 years to finish her life story."[7]

Then, without fanfare, there was that surprising announcement on Amazon in 2009. I wrote a letter to Olivia, congratulating her on the publication of her autobiography. Over the last almost fifty years, there have been gaps in our correspondence—sometimes months, sometimes years. That wasn't the case this time. Within a month of my note, Olivia responded, voicing her "great dismay" at the Amazon announcement, "misinformation which my nice young assistant, Emily, has made every effort to correct; this she has also done with my so-called 'mini-biography' on the Internet Movie Data Base, a resumé rife with errors. Alas, I think that very little which has been printed about me is accurate."[8]

Following the second announcement of her memoir in 2010, she wrote: "The report that my autobiography is soon to be published . . . is quite incorrect, as one thing after another has impeded its progress. Patience is required of everyone—especially of me! I have made every effort to remove from the internet this error, to no avail; perhaps only a lawyer can bring about a change. I am sorry to say that the internet, including Wikipedia's entries thereon, is a mine of misinformation."[9]

In early 2015, she mentioned in an interview that she "hopes to make progress on the autobiography she began a few years ago. She's written five chapters. . . . A lover of words, she is enjoying mining her rich, long life remembrances."[10] This project would be fascinating, particularly if Olivia allows herself to be as candid in print as she is in person and off the record. She is very quick, however, when it comes to defending her reputation.

When I first told Olivia back in 2009 that I wanted to write a critical study of her work and her life, she was very wary and self-protective: "I'm a bit concerned about the book which you [will write for] the University of Kentucky Press [*sic*]. Your letter tells me that it is about my life and career—yet almost nothing accurate is known about my life, and therefore whatever sources you may have turned to for information are bound to have been unreliable."[11] Not exactly a vote of confidence. But in November 2011, she shared "felicitations re the book contract" and asserted, "I understand that many questions will occur to you to which only I can provide the answers. I find that the very best method to follow in serious enterprises such as yours is for the author to send me written questions upon which I can reflect and, subsequently, provide accurate written replies. Once you will have in hand this vital material by correspondence, then it would be logical for us to meet."[12] That is what we did for several years, with numerous emails and meetings. I finally gained Olivia's trust, for the most part. As she wrote in February 2015, "I wish you infinite good luck with 'The Project'—every word of which you and I hope will be accurate!"[13]

Olivia has been the subject of, or an important part of, a variety of books, including publications on the actresses of Hollywood's golden era. She loathed Charles Higham's book *Sisters* (published in Britain as *Olivia and Joan*), as well as his book on Errol Flynn in which he claims that Flynn was a Nazi spy. Joan Fontaine's 1978 *No Bed of Roses* is ultimately her own story, and Olivia told me in a conversation in February 2015 that she hadn't bothered to read the book written by "Miss Fontaine."[14] Biographies about Errol Flynn feature Olivia as his costar and real-life romantic interest, including a lively publication by Robert Matzen entitled *Errol & Olivia*. Judith M. Kass and Tony Thomas have written tributes to Olivia's work (his has an introduction by Bette Davis). In February 2018, Ellis Amburn's book about Olivia's career and the golden age of Hollywood was published. She may not be a Crawford or a Davis in terms of the number of studies, but Olivia retains her place in contemporary popular culture.

Olivia hasn't written her autobiography as of spring 2019; she is still too busy living. *Now Is the Time* may not exist, but it perfectly captures Olivia's zest for life. If her memoir ever appears, it will be strictly managed by Olivia, her publisher, her trusted agent (for more than thirty years) Jim Wilhelm of DGRW Talent Agency, and whichever media outlets she chooses to favor with interviews. Olivia will definitely be in charge of every detail. She didn't battle Jack Warner for nothing.

She may not have written an autobiography (yet), but she does still write creatively, and not only answers to her voluminous letters. When she was in Hollywood in 2003 for the Oscar telecast, she regaled me with her decision to do a little rewrite of her speech for the night:

> I boarded the waiting limousine ahead of schedule and set out for the rehearsal at the Kodak Theatre at Highland and Hollywood Boulevard. Having only just received the text of what I was to say, and having also called Gil Cates, the producer, to tell him that (the war [the invasion of Iraq] having broken out) I felt it was not appropriate in tone or content, I wanted to arrive early so as to revise the speech with his and the writer's aid. The progress of the limousine was unexpectedly hampered by roadblocks and heavy traffic. . . . This turned out, however, to be the greatest of blessings as Bob [Osborne], Jim [Wilhelm] and I took advantage of the delay by revising the text ourselves—in the limousine.
>
> Eventually arriving at the Theatre and Cates' office, I showed the new text to the producer (and to the writer, when he appeared a bit later) and onto the teleprompter it was transcribed in . . . an illegible script. . . . I realized that it would be foolhardy to depend upon the little box and asked permission to address the whole audience when I spoke, for I intended to memorize the speech and ignore the teleprompter. To my surprise, Cates assented—I say "to my surprise" because other producers on previous occasions have firmly restricted my attention to the little box.[15]

Her appearance was a huge success, and she received a standing ovation as she glided onto the stage in one of her trademark chiffon caftans.

In 2007, she wrote the foreword for Axel Nissen's *Actresses of a Certain Character* and commended him for "his encyclopedic knowledge of, and his love for, the films of the Golden Era and the supporting actresses whose performances embellished them."[16] She wrote to me in 2010 that for "four special showings of *GWTW,* one at the Academy in May of last year, two others held later in Georgia, and another in New York City, I composed and recorded messages which were heard just before the screenings of the film, each message fashioned to suit the particular occasion."[17]

Another recent publication was the April 10, 2014, tribute in *Time* to Mickey Rooney (Olivia's Puck in *A Midsummer Night's Dream*). Her farewell provided a poignant punctuation to his troubled life:

> Mickey, Mickey, Mickey. They say that you have died, but I find this hard to believe for you are so alive in my memory.
>
> There you are, in the big room of the Chamber of Commerce building on Sunset Boulevard in the summer of 1934, a little boy passing easily as a nine-year-old when you are really thirteen. . . .
>
> Seven decades later there you are, in the rehearsal room of the Kodak Theater on Hollywood Boulevard where 59 Oscar winners are gathering to rehearse their appearance at the Academy's 75th anniversary broadcast.
>
> I silently turn toward you, waiting for the moment I know will come. You sense something and glance briefly my way. Then you look again, recognition illuminating your face and tears springing to your eyes as you bound across the aisle, fling your arms around my waist, and pour forth lines of Shakespeare which are new to me but which come spontaneously to your lips as words meant for meetings like this one.[18]

Olivia has explored a variety of creative outlets since her last screen role in *The Woman He Loved* (1988), choosing her public statements and appearances carefully. It is unfortunate she hasn't appeared in a film since then, especially because she has mentioned in several interviews over the years that she would be happy to return to moviemaking if a good role came along. When François Ozon's delightful murder mystery *8 femmes* was released in 2002, Danielle Darrieux played the matriarch of that madhouse of Machiavellian women. I wrote to Olivia that she would have been equally wonderful in that part; the French view of women aging onscreen seems so much more intelligent and sophisticated than Hollywood's. Olivia's reply cited the same explanation she had given many years earlier: "French films are not really a possibility for me as my spoken French . . . marks me as a foreigner—and very few roles for ladies of advanced years with foreign accents can be found in French scenarios."[19] This was a missed opportunity by French filmmakers, sadly. She would have brought a wit and mature beauty to any role—in Dior, *mais bien sur!*

Olivia is now rather petite—just above five feet tall, down from her youthful five feet four inches—and beautifully full figured. She moves gracefully, vigorously. There's something lively and pert about her, like her character in *The Strawberry Blonde,* and there's always a naughty wink waiting. Thankfully, she has managed to stay in the public's consciousness, and she has done this with the same care and control she exercised over her career. Unlike other golden era stars, no trashy secrets or whispered love affairs have come to light.

The only major issue to appear somewhat regularly, usually on slow news days, was the feud with Joan Fontaine. Every few years, a piece would appear about the sisters, touting their unwillingness to stay in adjacent hotel rooms for one of the Oscar reunions and speculating about the reasons for their refusal to make up. In one of those omnipresent "100 best" lists, *Entertainment Weekly* did "The 100 Greatest Stars of All Time" in 1998. As the article noted, "Consternation sets in below the top 10. Almost 40 of the remaining 90 are still starring in films, creating an odd imbalance that will enrage film buffs (but cater to the youth market). . . . Olivia de Havilland [is included] but not her sister Joan Fontaine."[20] These kinds of slights did nothing to heal the rift between the siblings.

However, even after Fontaine's death in December 2013, their names still come up whenever someone writes about sibling rivalry. In April 2015, in honor of National Siblings Day (one of those silly Hallmark holidays), *Time* published yet another article about Olivia and Joan's estrangement. Recalling a 1942 *Life* magazine profile of the women, the feature included several photographs by Bob Landry of the two beauties, although "they appeared in only seven photographs together out of the more than hundred he shot."[21] One of those images was a very sexy, very fetching photograph of Olivia perched sideways in a comfortable chair, her lovely legs draped over the arm, the actress smoking and staring flirtatiously into the camera lens. *Vanity Fair* reprinted that photograph in its May 2016 tribute to Olivia's 100th birthday; however, the article was part of its "Sisters: A Love Story" issue, and of course, it addressed the "vicious, relentlessly competitive sniping" inflicted on Olivia by Joan.[22]

But there is so much more to her life than old news. Her energy and vigor are remarkable, as is her love of Paris. She reiterated that love in a 2000 interview: "The city's cleaner now than it was in the past, and it's still so beautiful, so elegant. The lack of elegance elsewhere is dismaying, but the French have such marvellous style, and I love them for their independence. . . . I love the Île de la Cité. Notre Dame's so lovely since it was cleaned, too. And the Tuileries and my favorite restaurant, which is L'Ambroisie in the Marais district."[23]

Interestingly, she might have moved to California to be near her daughter, Gisèle; she had considered such a move in the late 1970s, when both children were still in university. However, she chose to stay in Paris, which has been her home for sixty years. She remarked, "One of a mother's most sacred responsibilities toward a daughter is to help her to become psychologically independent of her maternal parent. I think Gisèle, as part of the growing up process, achieved this psychological independence on her own. It would have been most unsuitable for me to have moved to the U.S. when Gisèle became engaged to her first husband."[24] But Olivia isn't alone. For the last few years, she has employed a series of bright young women—undergraduate and postgraduate students who are in Paris for a gap year or a fellowship—to serve as her personal assistants. Obtained through friends and other trustworthy connections, these young women serve as companions as well as archivists and clerical wizards, assisting Olivia as she catalogs her personal and professional belongings, maintains an active correspondence, and, presumably, continues to work on her long-awaited memoir.

In August 2013, Olivia had the charming, high-walled garden in the rear of her Paris town house redesigned; a modern, Japanese-style aluminum fountain now burbles beneath a beautiful chestnut tree, with flower beds along the stone walls. In 2014, Olivia continued renovations on the town house and moved into the nearby Saint James Hotel, aided by her assistant at the time, Mimi (a charming Canadian graduate student and Joan Cusack look-alike). In true romantic fashion, Olivia was trying to fix Mimi up with one of her doctors. When we met in April 2014 near Olivia's home, Mimi told me that the actress "wanted all [my] news" and that despite her recent health challenges, "she still has so much to do!" At the sight of some savory crackers I had brought for the actress from Dubai, Mimi laughed, "Oh, good! She's been looking for something new to nibble with champagne."[25] Olivia is quite fond of champagne, in fact, and favors pink Taittinger; we have shared it several times, and curiously, I always end up cross-eyed, while she is more sparkling than ever.

At our next meeting, in February 2015, Olivia was still resplendent at the Saint James Hotel while her home was being refurbished, but she was now attended by Stefanie and Philippa. At our most recent meeting, in December 2017, Olivia remained in her comfortable suite at the Saint James, where she is beloved by the staff and well attended to by Stefanie, other assistants, and friends.

Olivia has always been athletic, although her age has kept her from practicing her beloved yoga. A 1958 article about her then-happy marriage to Pierre Galante was entitled "It Isn't Yoga, It's Love," referring to the fact that her "secret" to personal joy wasn't the ability to "stand on her head" but her French husband.[26] An article from 1961, written while she was shooting *Light in the Piazza,* revealed how she maintained her figure, given the delights of French cuisine: "'Yoga. . . . It tones the body and relaxes it at the same time. . . . You have to concentrate to perfect it, but it's a wonderful way to refuel and break tension.'"[27] A publicity photo from the mid-1980s showed her doing a headstand in a leotard. Yoga certainly helped her retain her limberness and vigor all these years, and despite back and leg pain, she has until recently maintained a very active physical schedule.

There have been some other health issues as well. Olivia deals with "annual battles with bronchitis which strike [her] without fail during the Christmas season."[28] The American Academy of Ophthalmology issued an announcement in 2008 when Olivia had cataract surgery: "In Ms. de Havilland's case, outpatient surgery to remove her cataracts and insert intraocular lenses have restored her vision. Because she had cataracts in both eyes, her ophthalmologist, James Salz, MD, performed surgery on one eye and then waited until the first eye had healed before performing the second surgery. The results were dramatic. Ms. de Havilland's vision is now 20/40."[29] It was only as she approached 100 that her vision began to weaken.

One of her pleasures over the years has always been beautiful clothes, usually accompanied by her favorite string of pearls. Olivia was an early couture client of Christian Dior himself and then Yves Saint Laurent and Marc Bohan after Dior's death. While she was always beautifully attired in her Hollywood films, her move to Paris led to a more sophisticated personal style. In 1958, during an interview for the *Sunday Dispatch,* she was described as "chic (*she is dressed by Dior*)"; she was wearing a "subtle perfume" and "looked dreamy."[30] She wore

Dior again as an elegant lady of the realm in *Libel* (1959) with Dirk Bogarde. During a 1961 interview with Hedda Hopper, the gossip queen described Olivia as "dressed in a Dior vivid green woollen suit—it was St. Patrick's Day."[31] That same year, while filming *Light in the Piazza* (in which she also wore Dior), she met interviewer Lydia Lane for lunch "wearing a two-piece linen Dior dress." When Lane asked why she was intrigued by French clothes, Olivia replied, "'There is a fundamental difference between American and French tastes. . . . We like to see the body line—bust, hips and waist—but the French think that emphasis on parts of the body is vulgar. . . . I don't think the effect is masculine. They like a flowing line instead of obviously following the contour. To the French, all accessories are secondary to the dress—even hats.'"[32]

Olivia kept her Dior fashions for many years, but in June 1993, she sold her collection at Christie's in London, for which she received more than $43,000. The Dior Museum paid $7,400 for the A-line gray flannel suit she wore at her wedding to Pierre Galante.[33] "All labelled the House of Dior, some of the garments were done by the designer's protégés. . . . Said Marc Bohan of Olivia, 'Her choice of outfits was consistent with her personal style. She was never led by fashion; her image was one of classic elegance.'"[34] When we spoke about the auction in August 2012, Olivia expressed regret about selling the collection, but she was glad she had kept one suit from *Light in the Piazza.*

Her elegance has always included a minimalist approach to jewelry. Unlike many stars of her generation, her taste in jewelry is simple, and her preference for pearls has been part of her style for many years. When I asked about her jewelry choices, she wrote a lovely, detailed response:

> I was brought up in the countryside of Northern California by a conservative English mother and at a time when it was considered bad taste for young women to wear any sort of jewelry until they were into their 20s—and then only something very discreet. Furthermore, the depression meant that emphasizing anything superfluous like jewelry was of no interest and really grossly bad judgement.
>
> Eventually, when (at 23) I was well-established in my profession, and a costume for a great occasion (*Gone with the Wind*'s three premieres) required some sort of jewelry to set it off, I chose only what would look well with the gown in question. So jewelry was interesting only as an accessory to an ensemble, and costume jewelry usually served the purpose.[35]

Olivia's elegant yet practical approach to jewelry, and her attention to detail, ensured that the image she projected was precise. She continued in that 2002 letter:

> Once, however, when I ordered some ensembles from Bernard Newman, Magnin's resident designer, and he and I found that they needed some sort of jewelry to set them off, I bought a pair of matching brooches from Laykin, the shop's resident jeweler: two leaves, made in gold, with jade grasshoppers poised upon them, and a pair of plain gold earrings to go with them. These I wore with all three of the suits and the dress which were part of the wardrobe made by Newman. I still have the brooches, I still have my sister's three-strand pearl necklace. I have no idea what happened to the cyclamen necklace and earrings.[36]

She also wore pearls with a beautiful royal-blue chiffon gown at the 2003 Oscar telecast. When I inquired about them, she replied:

> About the pearls: I have a pair of almost identical 2-strand necklaces and one single-strand pearl necklace, and all three are, of course, costume jewelry. The three-strand necklace of small cultured pearls which, as a bridesmaid, I received from my sister in 1939, I do not wear as one of the strands is broken and I am told there is almost no jeweler that one can trust to do the necessary work without his replacing a real pearl with a false one![37]

Olivia's life in Paris has been enriched by her connections to her church. Long a member of the American Cathedral on the Avenue George V in Paris, she commented, "Once I pick up the Bible, I find it extremely hard to put it down again."[38] She wrote in a letter that her chronic bronchitis sometimes keeps her from "fulfilling a task which I greatly treasure—reading the Lessons at the American Cathedral's Christmas Eve service."[39] A friend of mine contributed some information about Olivia's participation at this Episcopal church: "Our friend's son is the Director of Music in Paris at the church she attends . . . and often she is the reader at the Sunday services. . . . Zach is her friend . . . and often she will sit in his office until just before the service starts."[40]

The last twenty years have finally brought Olivia the recognition she so richly deserves, so it's a good thing she enjoys such longevity. In 1998, at

St. Albans Cathedral, Olivia received an honorary doctor of letters degree from the University of Hertfordshire; the university has a de Havilland campus in honor of her cousin Geoffrey's accomplishments in aviation. In 1997, Olivia helped the Duke of Edinburgh unveil a statue of Sir Geoffrey and said, "'We owe our peace to men like Sir Geoffrey and his associates and to aircraft like the Mosquito.'"[41] Both events reiterated Olivia's lifelong love of flying.

In June 2006, the Academy of Motion Picture Arts and Sciences offered a tribute to Olivia at the Samuel Goldwyn Theatre in Beverly Hills. With good friend Robert Osborne as her escort, Olivia appeared in person, elegantly dressed in a white shantung silk suit, to the delight of everyone at the sold-out event. Olivia discussed her career, and the audience enjoyed a number of her film clips. It was a long-overdue celebration of her artistry and her commitment to her craft, as well as to the changes wrought by the de Havilland decision. When host Bill Higgins extended a hand to help the actress up from her chair at the end of the evening, Olivia "graciously accepted his hand and rose, thanking him. But she added, 'You know, I really don't need help getting up,' and promptly sat back down, then rose to her feet in a flash, demonstrating remarkable agility."[42]

In 2008, Olivia received the Presidential Medal of Freedom from George W. Bush; despite being a lifelong Democrat, she accepted this honor gracefully in Washington, DC. On September 9, 2010, she was awarded—at long last—the Legion d'Honneur at the Elysee Palace. Her daughter was in attendance, as well as her great friends Robert Osborne, Lee and Berna Huebner (the latter an Alzheimer's advocate), and David Ladd. Olivia wore a chic black dress with a double strand of pearls at the ceremony where she received the medal from French president Nicolas Sarkozy (a rare honor). Recognized not only for her career and her long residence in Paris but also for her patronage of the American Cathedral, American Library, and American University of Paris, Olivia looks pleased in photographs of the event, along with fellow recipient Jacqueline Bisset. An article in *Washington Social Diary* noted that Sarkozy "opened his tribute with a line from Miss O de H's comically amusing 1962 best-seller, 'Every Frenchman Has One,' that ensconced in family life in Paris as she was at age 56, people were surprised she was still alive. Sarko wryly observed that 'apparently very much alive she still is some 40 years on, and still claimed among Paris' great treasures.'"[43] He went on to say, "'You honor France for having chosen us.'"[44]

At the thirty-sixth annual Cesar Awards in February 2011, host Jodie Foster, in perfect French, graciously pointed out Olivia's presence in the audience. The actress, who attended the awards with Frederic Mitterrand, received an unexpected standing ovation, and she was surprised by and appreciative of the warm tribute. On September 27, 2014, Olivia received a very special honor from the union she had joined in 1936: "I was presented with a Baccarat vase bearing the following inscription: Olivia de Havilland / The SAG AFTRA Founders Award / For her legendary service to actors and her union."[45] In May 2015, the Cannes Film Festival presented Olivia, actress Jane Fonda, and producer Megan Ellison the first Women in Motion awards at the presidential dinner, recognizing both influential women in the film industry and newcomers.[46] One of the most delightful recognitions came from *Oldie* magazine for "Oldie of the Year 2016." Olivia accepted that award with humor and delight.

Olivia's portrayal of Melanie Wilkes in *Gone with the Wind* gave her not only her favorite role but also recognition among generation after generation of moviegoers. Although Olivia was unable to attend, she taped a greeting for the Cherry Blossom Festival in Marshfield, Missouri, in 2012, which honored the four surviving cast members of *Gone with the Wind.* They included Alicia Rhett (India Wilkes—her only onscreen credit), who made an appearance; she passed away in 2014 at age ninety-eight.[47] In low, mellifluous tones, Olivia spoke wistfully of her love for Melanie Wilkes and for the classic film and spoke lovingly of "her fellow cast mates who have gone to that 'great plantation in the sky.'"[48]

Sadly, Olivia's health forced her to cancel plans for a personal appearance at an event honoring *GWTW*'s seventy-fifth anniversary in 2014, sponsored by Turner Classic Movies and hosted by Robert Osborne. She has actively promoted *GWTW* whenever possible, and as Osborne noted, "'She is very proud of it; this is her legacy.'"[49] At a Christie's sale in New York in July 2012, a hand-knitted sweater Olivia wore as Melanie was estimated to be worth \$4,000 to \$6,000. Gratifyingly, the sweater sold for \$16,730.[50] Clearly, people's love for the film continues through the decades, as does their love for Olivia's Melanie.

Olivia's visibility in the twenty-first century has remained high. She has given several interviews that always touch on *GWTW,* her two Oscars, and Jack Warner, but they also address her current interests. *ES Magazine* in London showed her photographed (by pop singer–photographer Bryan Adams), like the grande dame of cinema that she is, wearing a long black gown and a zebra evening jacket. The article notes, "Meeting Miss de Havilland restores one's faith in film stars."[51] She allowed a reporter from *Paris* magazine to enter the inner sanctum, ascend the red-carpeted staircase to her boudoir/office, and photograph her with a cup of tea and her Oscars beside her. She even granted an interview to *Garden and Gun* magazine, and when she was asked which she valued more—her many awards or appearing in *GWTW*—she answered fetchingly, "Must I choose between a sapphire and an emerald?"[52]

She even participated in three documentaries: *Melanie Remembers*, produced in 2004 for inclusion in the boxed DVD set celebrating *GWTW*'s sixty-fifth anniversary; *The Adventures of Errol Flynn* in 2005, in which she reminisces about their partnership with pride, humor, and melancholy; and *I Remember Better When I Paint* (2009), about the use of art therapy for those suffering with Alzheimer's disease and dementia. Olivia narrates this last film, which was written and directed by Eric Ellena and Berna Huebner and presented by French Connection Films and the Hilgos Foundation. It also features Rita Hayworth's daughter, Princess Yasmin Ali Khan, discussing her mother's struggles with Alzheimer's. Olivia's sharp, perceptive narration about those her age and younger who have lost their memories and themselves is poignant and profound, but there's no pity in her voice. She's too practical for that.

Gisèle's husband, art collector Edward Broida, died in 2006, and she later suffered "a health crisis brought about by the mismanagement of her medication."[53] Happily, however, Gisèle married Andy Chulack in 2011, and Olivia takes great joy in getting to know his grown children—her new step-grandchildren. Gisèle resides in Santa Fe, New Mexico, and while Olivia no longer travels such distances, Gisèle visits her mother in Paris twice a year, staying for a month at a time, and is delighted by her happiness.

Sadly, her beloved friend Robert Osborne, with whom she enjoyed "weekly telephone chats to talk about everything and nothing," died in March 2017.[54] At a "celebration of life" held in Osborne's honor in New York two months later, Gisèle represented her mother, who sent a recorded message. Columnist Liz Smith wrote:

> Olivia's voice was immediately recognizable, husky but silky, hardly the tones of a woman who has seen a century of living. She said she wanted to inject something "light-hearted" and so she related the tale of knowing Robert for years, as he became more and more well known. She always referred to him as "Bob."
>
> One day, Robert "gently asked me if I could call him 'Robert' which he preferred. And I did, ever after. Now, I'll admit, once or

twice or even thrice, I might have slipped and called him 'Bob.' But I never made the ultimate error and called him 'Bobby'!"[55]

Chic and soignée in her now-trademark snowy white chignon, double strand of pearls, and tailored suit with pencil skirt or flowing caftans, Olivia's public appearances and statements echo her private self. Her attire and home suggest a woman of her history and position, and she is charming enough to tell delightful stories without talking badly about anyone—even Jack Warner. She even made friends with Jared Leto, whose fights with his record company over his band Thirty Minutes to Mars led his lawyers to successfully invoke the de Havilland decision. He invited the actress to participate in a documentary as well as attend one of his band's concerts, but she gracefully demurred. Still, "Leto was so grateful that he made a trip to Paris . . . to personally thank her for her ground-breaking legal battle and support."[56]

The double issue of *Entertainment Weekly* in honor of the 2015 Oscars featured an article about Olivia entitled "The Last Star," which is almost true—Kirk Douglas is still with us. Photographed wearing her trademark pearls, she told the interviewer that she "has every intention of celebrating her 100th birthday come July 1, 2016. 'Oh, I can't wait for it,' she says. 'I'm certainly relishing the idea of living a century. Can you imagine that? What an *achievement*.'"[57] Then, in the month before her 101st birthday, she was made a dame of the British Empire by Queen Elizabeth II, the presentation made by the British ambassador to France in May 2018. Making more of a splash in the press, on the day before her 102nd birthday, she filed a lawsuit against Ryan Murphy Productions for undisclosed damages due to the unauthorized depiction of her in *Feud*. Olivia has never shied away from a lawsuit, and she is proving to be a formidable opponent.

When *Feud* was first televised in March 2017, I watched with delight. When I asked whether she had seen the show or knew that Catherine Zeta-Jones was portraying her, Olivia's answer was a resounding no. In April 2017, in response to the *Hollywood Reporter*'s inquiry as to her opinion of the program, she replied, "'Having not seen the show, I cannot make a valid comment about it. However, in principle, I am opposed to any representation of personages who are no longer alive to judge the accuracy of any incident depict[ed] as involving themselves.'"[58] Clearly, Olivia also opposed the inaccurate representation of personages who are still alive—particularly herself—and she filed a defamation suit on June 30, 2017, against Ryan Murphy Productions.

She was displeased with both the dialogue and the situations depicted in *Feud,* and she had not been consulted about the accuracy of either. Given the competence of Murphy's research team, one would have expected them to know that Olivia is of sound mind and body and not averse to a legal battle. Olivia had the support of SAG and AFTRA, and because of her age, the court granted her a hearing more expeditiously than usual, set for March 2018. However, the case did not go her way, and a three-judge panel of the California appeals court threw out her argument. Had she won, the obstacles to depicting nonfictional characters in creative productions would have been enormous; several articles commented that current films such as *I, Tonya* might be impossible to make, given the potential script complications, the need to secure permissions from real persons, and the resultant libel suits. The decision was not a surprise; predictably, the judges sided with the industry rather than Olivia. They also concurred with Murphy's defense of Catherine Zeta-Jones's use of the word "bitch" to describe Joan Fontaine to Susan Sarandon's Bette Davis. Rather than seeing that word as damaging to Olivia's reputation, they considered its usage as equivalent to Olivia's own descriptions of Joan as "Dragon Lady." Semantically, the argument was weak, as was the defense's use of a 1940s blooper reel from Warner Brothers showing Olivia blowing a line and swearing like a sailor.

When I sent her flowers in sympathy for the ruling, she responded in an email, "My counsellors and I will soon decide what course we will now take."[59] A month later, in May 2018, Olivia and her lawyers asked the California Supreme Court to review the lower court's ruling. As Suzelle Smith argued in a public statement about that request:

> The Court of Appeal opinion, if allowed to stand, will infringe on the Constitutional right to a trial by jury not only of Miss de Havilland, but for any person in a similar situation, whether a celebrity or not. This puts everyone at the mercy of the media and entertainment industry, which may find that false statements and fake news sell better than the truth. . . . No filmmaker, biographer, or reporter with integrity can support the Court of Appeal decision. It rewards the unscrupulous and will put those who investigate and seek to tell the public the truth at an economic disadvantage.[60]

That Olivia refused to accept defeat said a great deal about her insistence on telling her own truth and protecting her own legacy. The court, however, ruled against her. In August 2018, Olivia's lawyers announced their intention to file a petition with the US Supreme Court. In January 2019, her suit, asserting that Ryan Murphy Productions intended to defame the actress, was not accepted by the justices for consideration. Despite the outcome, Olivia's pursuit of the case was awe-inspiring.

In the meantime, Olivia continues to reside in Paris with her adoring assistants. Loving friends and family keep in contact from around the world. Despite failing hearing and eyesight, Olivia maintains a vigorous correspondence and a delight in champagne, now limited to one glass a day. She greets visitors wearing caftans and pearls, her white chignon meticulously swirled atop her head, a welcoming and witty hostess.

We met most recently at the Saint James Hotel in December 2017, where she has lived for more than four years. With its services and comforts, the hotel has become her permanent residence, although she still owns 3 rue B., as she affectionately refers to her house. A Relais & Chateaux hotel, "with its five thousand square metres, fifty guest rooms, lounges, library, restaurant, spa by Gemology, venerable gardens and its history, the Saint James hotel has what it takes to raise fear among the boldest."[61] Her charming assistant Stefanie, whom I first met two years ago, greeted me in the foyer at 5:30 p.m. Squirming in her arms was a lovely pug puppy, Oscar. All the staff knew Oscar, and Stefanie told me that Gisèle and some friends had suggested that the wee pug would be a good companion for the actress, known for her love of dogs.

We went upstairs, and it was wonderful to be back in the now-familiar hotel. A bottle of pink Taittinger in one hand and an embroidered cashmere shawl in the other, I entered the foyer of the elegant blue suite and then walked into the sitting room. There sat Olivia ensconced in a comfortable chair, offering more champagne on ice, canapés, and a warm welcome: "There you are at last. Tell me all about you."[62] I did, and she did, for the next two hours. She was funny, kind, and welcoming, and it was like spending time with a saner Auntie Mame, but just as elegant and loving.

Dame Olivia continues to lead a fascinating life, seeing friends and family, maintaining her voluminous correspondence, reading, staying up-to-date on contemporary issues, and relishing every moment. When I wrote to wish her well on her 100th birthday (and sent an appropriately fabulous bouquet), she responded by email: "I'm both delighted and touched that you should have watched *Captain Blood* in celebration of that special day and wish you to know that I like being 100 years old! Furthermore, I look forward to achieving at least the age of 110!"[63] And why not? If anyone can achieve that goal, it is she. Olivia de Havilland is the lady triumphant.

ACKNOWLEDGMENTS

There are many people who help bring a book to life. My thanks go out to the following people, in no particular order, who assisted me with this project:

- At the University Press of Kentucky, Anne Dean Dotson, my patient editor, and Natalie O'Neal, who helped so much with the design elements. Thanks also to copyeditor Linda Lotz.
- The British Film Institute Library staff in London.
- The Margaret Herrick Library staff in Beverly Hills.
- The Duke University Library staff in Durham, NC.
- The American University of Sharjah Library staff in Sharjah, United Arab Emirates.
- Stefanie Rodriguez and all the assistants working with Dame Olivia who have been so kind to me.
- Anne-Marie Keighan and Kelly Fennema for their translations.
- Allegra Huston, a wonderful writer and pal.
- The Right Honourable The Lord Smith of Kelvin, K.T., C.H., for his friendship and encouragement.
- My colleagues at the American University of Sharjah who encouraged my research interests.
- My students, who did the same.
- Patrick McGilligan, a fellow Wisconsinite, who helped me write the original book proposal.
- Nancy McCrary, Barbara Griffin, and Michael Kedzlie for their suggestions about photographs.
- Kristine Krueger at the Margaret Herrick Library and Buddy Weiss at Photofest for their patience as I chose photos.
- Dame Olivia de Havilland for, well, everything.
- Above all, to my dear friends Steven LaVigne, Gene Downs, Kitti Carriker, Jane Queenan, Robbie Mochrie, and everyone else who kept faith with me over the years about this project and everything else.

NOTES

Introduction

1. Margaret Mitchell, *Gone with the Wind* (1936; reprint, New York: Pocket Books, 1964), 142.

2. Ibid., 143.

3. Olivia de Havilland, letter to the author, August 13, 1969.

4. Ibid., January 20, 1973.

5. Ibid., December 16, 1981.

6. Ibid., May 19, 1986.

7. Peter Mikelbank, "Olivia de Havilland: A Star Turns 100," *People,* July 18, 2016, 66.

8. Olivia de Havilland, letter to the author, June 27, 1985.

9. Ibid., June 14, 2010.

10. Ibid., November 20, 2011.

11. Ibid., July 27, 2005.

12. Lee Server, *Robert Mitchum: "Baby, I Don't Care"* (London: Faber & Faber, 2002), 267.

13. Philippe Trétiack, "Saint James Paris: A Crazy Chic State of Mind," *Elle Decoration,* n.d., 3.

14. Olivia de Havilland, email to the author, February 4, 2015.

15. Missy Schwartz, "The Last Star," *Entertainment Weekly: Special Oscars Guide 2015,* January 30–February 6, 2015, 93.

16. William Stadiem, "De Havilland's Bumpy Flight," *Vanity Fair,* May 2016, 148.

17. Olivia de Havilland, letter to the author, July 27, 2009.

18. Ibid., September 22, 2009.

19. Peter Mikelbank, "Olivia de Havilland on Becoming the Oldest Person to Be Named a Dame: I'm Extremely Proud," *People,* June 17, 2017, accessed June 21, 2017, http://people.com/royals/olivia-de-havilland-oldest-to-be-named-a-dame/.

20. Olivia de Havilland, email to the author, February 11, 2017.

21. Jackson McHenry, "Olivia de Havilland Sent a Gorgeous Email about How She Doesn't Watch *Feud,*" *Vulture,* April 18, 2017, accessed April 19, 2017, http://www.vulture.com/2017/04/olivia-de-havilland-emails-about-how-she-doesnt-watch-feud.html.

22. "And the Winner Is . . . (the Oscars of 1963)," episode of *Feud,* directed by Ryan Murphy (FX, 2017).

23. Dominic Patten, "Ryan Murphy & FX in Legal Feud with Olivia de Havilland, Who Is Suing over 'Feud,'" *Deadline,* June 30, 2017, accessed July 1, 2017, http://deadline.com/2017/06/ryan-murphy-fx-sued-olivia-de-havilland-feud-catherine-zeta-jones-1202122984/.

1. An Englishwoman Abroad

1. James Robert Parish and Don E. Stanke, *The Leading Ladies* (New Rochelle, NY: Arlington House, 1977), 272.
2. Daniel Bubbeo, *The Women of Warner Brothers* (Jefferson, NC: McFarland, 2002), 54.
3. Olivia de Havilland, email to the author, October 11, 2012.
4. Bubbeo, *Women of Warner Brothers,* 54.
5. Charles Higham, *Sisters: The Story of Olivia de Havilland and Joan Fontaine* (New York: Dell, 1986), 15–16.
6. Olivia de Havilland, email to the author, October 11, 2012.
7. Joan Fontaine, *No Bed of Roses: An Autobiography* (New York: William Morrow, 1978), 23.
8. Olivia de Havilland, email to the author, October 16, 2013.
9. Ibid., September 17, 2013.
10. "Actress Pays Flying Visit to Honour Pioneer," *Times* (London), July 31, 1997, 5.
11. Bubbeo, *Women of Warner Brothers,* 55.
12. Olivia de Havilland, email to the author, March 20, 2012.
13. Ibid., November 1, 2014.
14. Ibid.
15. Judith M. Kass, *Olivia de Havilland* (New York: Pyramid Books, 1976), 17.
16. Olivia de Havilland, email to the author, March 20, 2012.
17. Higham, *Sisters,* 141.
18. Olivia de Havilland, email to the author, March 20, 2012.
19. Bubbeo, *Women of Warner Brothers,* 55; Higham, *Sisters,* 20.
20. Olivia de Havilland, email to the author, November 1, 2014.
21. Ibid.
22. Bubbeo, *Women of Warner Brothers,* 55.
23. Olivia de Havilland, email to the author, March 12, 2012.
24. Ibid., March 11, 2012.
25. Ibid., March 12, 2012.
26. Ibid., March 20, 2013.
27. Ibid.
28. Ibid., October 16, 2013.
29. Ibid., March 20, 2013.
30. Tony Thomas, *The Films of Olivia de Havilland* (Secaucus, NJ: Citadel Press, 1983), 26.
31. Higham, *Sisters,* 27.
32. Thomas, *Films of Olivia de Havilland,* 24.

33. Ibid., 26.

34. Ibid., 25.

35. *Mrs. Bumpstead-Leigh, Playbill Vault,* n.d., accessed March 25, 2015, http://www.playbillvault.com/Show/Detail/6287/Mrs-Bumpstead-Leigh.

36. Parish and Stanke, *Leading Ladies,* 274.

37. Olivia de Havilland, email to the author, March 20, 2012.

38. Ibid.

39. Olivia de Havilland, letter to the author, October 14, 1977.

40. Parish and Stanke, *Leading Ladies,* 274.

2. From Starlet to Little Star

1. *Melanie Remembers: Reflections by Olivia de Havilland,* directed by John Rust (Turner Classic Movies, 2004; Warner Home Video, 2004), DVD.

2. British Film Institute, tape recording of lecture by Olivia de Havilland, London, August 28, 1971.

3. Ibid.

4. Robert S. Taplinger, "Life Story of Olivia de Havilland," n.d. (circa 1935), 5, Margaret Herrick Library, Beverly Hills, CA.

5. As quoted in ibid.

6. As quoted in J. V. Cottom, "Olivia de Havilland," trans. Anne-Marie Keighan, *Ciné-Revue* 56, no. 53 (December 30, 1976): 10.

7. Taplinger, "Life Story of Olivia de Havilland," 7.

8. "Olivia de Havilland Screen Test," *A Midsummer Night's Dream,* directed by Max Reinhardt (Warner Brothers, 1935; Warner Home Video, 2007), DVD.

9. Olivia de Havilland, email to the author, March 12, 2016.

10. Olivia de Havilland, letter to the author, May 22, 1995.

11. Olivia de Havilland, "Mickey Rooney: The Eternal Boy Wonder," *Time,* April 10, 2014, accessed December 11, 2017, http://time.com/57843/mickey-rooney-olivia-de-havilland/.

12. Thomas, *Films of Olivia de Havilland,* 54.

13. Trailer for *A Midsummer Night's Dream,* DVD.

14. "Presenting," *A Midsummer Night's Dream,* DVD.

15. Ibid.

16. Ted Sennett, *Warner Brothers Presents* (New Rochelle, NY: Arlington House, 1971), 34, 151.

17. *A Midsummer Night's Dream,* DVD.

18. Thomas, *Films of Olivia de Havilland,* 59.

19. Sennett, *Warner Brothers Presents,* 178.

20. British Film Institute lecture, 1971.

21. Thomas, *Films of Olivia de Havilland,* 59.

22. Ibid.

23. *Alibi Ike,* directed by Ray Enright (Warner Brothers, 1935; Warner Home Video, 2010), DVD.

24. Thomas, *Films of Olivia de Havilland,* 61.

25. Based on a 1985 cartoon by feminist-lesbian cartoonist Alison Bechdel in her "Dykes to Watch Out For" series, the test, when applied to fiction or film, is whether the work features at least two women who talk to each other about something other than a man.

26. Frank S. Nugent, "The Screen; Joe E. Brown Returns in a Merry Film Version of Ring Lardner's 'Alibi Ike,' at the Cameo," *New York Times,* July 17, 1935, accessed December 18, 2017, http://www.nytimes.com/movie/review?res=9407E2DB1E39E33ABC4F52DFB166838E629EDE.

27. Thomas, *Films of Olivia de Havilland,* 61.

28. *AFI Life Achievement Award: A Tribute to Bette Davis* (CBS, 1977; Loving the Classics, n.d.), DVD.

29. Trailer for *The Irish in Us,* directed by Lloyd Bacon (Warner Brothers, 1935; Warner Home Video, 2014), DVD.

30. Parish and Stanke, *Leading Ladies,* 275.

31. *The Irish in Us,* DVD.

32. "Strolling with Olivia," *New York Times,* November 8, 1936.

33. W. H. Mooring, "Hollywood's Normal Girl," *Film Weekly,* August 21, 1937.

3. Livvie and Errol

1. Emily Andrews, "Errol Flynn? He Never Had His Wicked Way with Me, Says *Gone with the Wind* star Olivia de Havilland," *Daily Mail,* June 17, 2009, accessed December 18, 2016, http://www.dailymail.co.uk/tvshowbiz/article-1193489/Errol-Flynn-He-wicked-way-says-Gone-With-The-Wind-star-Olivia-Havilland.html.

2. Quoted in Robert Osborne, "De Havilland: Caine Autobiography 'Untrue,'" *Hollywood Reporter,* December 15, 1992, 10.

3. Ibid.

4. Boze Hadleigh, *Hollywood and Whine* (Secaucus, NJ: Birch Lane Books, 1998), 221.

5. Olivia de Havilland, letter to the author, October 24, 1995.

6. David Niven, *Bring on the Empty Horses* (New York: G. P. Putnam's Sons, 1975), 114.

7. *Captain Blood: A Swashbuckler Is Born,* directed by Karen Hillhouse (Turner Classic Movies, 2005; Warner Home Video, 2005), DVD.

8. *The Adventures of Errol Flynn,* directed by David Heeley (Turner Classic Movies, 2005; Warner Home Video, 2006), DVD.

9. Olivia de Havilland, email to the author, August 20, 2016.

10. Errol Flynn, *My Wicked, Wicked Ways* (New York: G. P. Putnam's Sons, 1959), 200.

11. *Captain Blood: A Swashbuckler Is Born,* DVD.

12. Ibid.

13. Trailer for *Captain Blood,* directed by Michael Curtiz (Warner Brothers, 1935; Warner Home Video, 2005), DVD.

14. *Captain Blood,* DVD.

15. Ibid.

16. Ibid.

17. *The Adventures of Errol Flynn,* DVD.

18. "Dinah! And the Ladies Who Took Home Oscar," *The Dinah Shore Show,* 1977, accessed June 6, 2015, https://www.youtube.com/watch?v=14Q8tphR2xw.

19. Trailer for *The Charge of the Light Brigade,* directed by Michael Curtiz (Warner Brothers, 1936; Warner Home Video, 2007), DVD.

20. *Charge of the Light Brigade,* DVD.

21. Ibid.

22. Niven, *Bring on the Empty Horses,* 117.

23. David Niven, *The Moon's a Balloon* (New York: Dell, 1972), 202.

24. Bubbeo, *Women of Warner Brothers,* 58.

25. Flynn, *My Wicked, Wicked Ways,* 208.

26. Olivia de Havilland, email to the author, September 12, 2012.

27. Robert Matzen, *Errol & Olivia: Ego & Obsession in Golden Era Hollywood* (Pittsburgh: GoodKnight Books, 2010), 41.

28. Flynn, *My Wicked, Wicked Ways,* 208.

29. Matzen, *Errol & Olivia,* 81.

30. *Four's a Crowd,* directed by Michael Curtiz (Warner Brothers, 1938; Warner Home Video, 2009), DVD.

31. Bob Thomas, *Selznick: The Man Who Produced* Gone with the Wind (Los Angeles: New Millennium Entertainment, 2001), 147.

32. *Elizabeth and Essex: Battle Royal* (Taylor Made Entertainment and Warner Home Video, 2005), DVD.

33. American Film Institute, "Olivia de Havilland," *Dialogue on Film* 4, no. 3 (December 1974): 3–25.

34. *Elizabeth and Essex,* DVD.

35. *The Private Lives of Elizabeth and Essex,* directed by Michael Curtiz (Warner Brothers, 1939; Warner Home Video, 2005), DVD.

36. Ibid.

37. *This Is Your Life,* Ralph Edwards Productions, March 1971, accessed December 28, 2017, https://www.youtube.com/watch?v=jEkmS919cVM.

38. *The Private Lives of Elizabeth and Essex,* DVD.

39. Ibid.

40. *The Adventures of Errol Flynn,* DVD.

41. *Welcome to Sherwood! The Story of "The Adventures of Robin Hood,"* directed by Jeff Kurtti (Kurtti-Pellerin and Turner Classic Movies, 2003; Warner Home Video, 2003), DVD.

42. Ibid.

43. Ibid.

44. Ibid.

45. Internet Movie Data Base, *The Adventures of Robin Hood* (1938), accessed March 12, 2015, http://www.imdb.com/title/tt0029843/?ref_=nv_sr_1.

46. John K. Newman, "Straight out of a Story-Book," *Film Weekly,* May 13, 1939, 17.

47. Dorothy Spensley, "Victorian . . . with Variations," *Photoplay,* September 1938, 26.

48. As quoted in Cottom, "Olivia de Havilland," 11.

49. British Film Institute, tape recording of lecture by Olivia de Havilland, London, August 28, 1971.

50. *Welcome to Sherwood!* DVD.

51. Ibid.

52. Ina Rae Hark, "Errol Flynn and Olivia de Havilland: Romancing through History," in *Glamour in a Golden Age: Movie Stars of the 1930s,* ed. Adrienne L. McLean (New Brunswick, NJ: Rutgers University Press, 2011), 157–58.

53. Parish and Stanke, *Leading Ladies,* 283.

54. Rudy Behlmer, "Flynn on Target with *Robin Hood,*" *Journal of the Alex Film Society* 1, no. 3 (March 1995): 1.

55. *The Adventures of Robin Hood,* directed by Michael Curtiz and William Keighley (Warner Brothers, 1938; Warner Home Video, 2001), DVD.

56. Thomas McNulty, *Errol Flynn: The Life and Career* (Jefferson, NC: McFarland, 2014), 65.

57. Bubbeo, *Women of Warner Brothers,* 59.

58. *Welcome to Sherwood!* DVD.

59. Hark, "Errol Flynn and Olivia de Havilland," 164.

60. Ibid., 166.

61. Olivia de Havilland, email to the author, September 12, 2014.

62. Hark, "Errol Flynn and Olivia de Havilland," 167.

63. Olivia de Havilland, email to the author, September 12, 2014.

64. *Welcome to Sherwood!* DVD.

65. Ibid.

66. *The Adventures of Errol Flynn,* DVD.

67. Matzen, *Errol & Olivia,* 90.

68. Ibid., 90–91.

69. Thomas, *Selznick,* 134.

70. Matzen, *Errol & Olivia,* 95.

71. *Dodge City,* directed by Michael Curtiz (Warner Brothers, 1939; Warner Home Video, 2005), DVD.

72. *Dodge City: Go West, Errol Flynn* (Taylor Made Entertainment and Warner Home Video, 2005), DVD.

73. *Dodge City,* DVD.

74. Matzen, *Errol & Olivia,* 101.

75. Ibid., 99.

76. *Dodge City,* DVD.

77. Matzen, *Errol & Olivia,* 130.

78. *Santa Fe Trail,* directed by Michael Curtiz (Warner Brothers, 1940; Marengo Films, 2005), DVD.

79. Ibid.

80. Ibid.

81. Max Breen, "Olivia Comes out of Hiding," *Picturegoer Weekly,* May 28, 1938, 24.

82. McNulty, *Errol Flynn,* 109.

83. Ibid.

84. As quoted in John Lichfield, "Golden Girl: The Divine Olivia de Havilland," *Independent,* July 14, 2009, accessed July 15, 2009, http://www.independent.co.uk/arts-entertainment/films/features/golden-girl-the-divine-olivia-de-havilland-1744807.html.

85. McNulty, *Errol Flynn,* 109.

86. Niven, *Bring on the Empty Horses,* 24.

87. McNulty, *Errol Flynn,* 109.

88. Ibid., 122.

89. Hark, "Errol Flynn and Olivia de Havilland," 67.

90. Parish and Stanke, *Leading Ladies,* 296.

91. Laura Hillenbrand, *Unbroken* (New York: Random House, 2010), 45.

92. *They Died with Their Boots On,* directed by Raoul Walsh (Warner Brothers, 1941; Warner Home Video, 2005), DVD.

93. Ibid.

94. Ibid.

95. *The Adventures of Errol Flynn,* DVD.

96. Ibid.

97. Ibid.

98. Ibid.

99. Letters between Clifford McCarty and Olivia de Havilland, January–May 1969, Olivia de Havilland Collection, Margaret Herrick Library, Beverly Hills, CA.

100. As quoted in Lichfield, "Golden Girl."

4. Learning the Job

1. Olivia de Havilland, email to the author, August 20, 2016.

2. Ibid.

3. Trailer for *Anthony Adverse,* directed by Mervyn LeRoy (Warner Brothers, 1936; Warner Archive Collection, 2015), DVD.

4. *Anthony Adverse,* DVD.

5. Ibid.

6. Thomas, *Films of Olivia de Havilland,* 85.

7. *Call It a Day,* Internet Broadway Database, accessed May 27, 2014, http://www.ibdb.com/production.php?id=12066.

8. Thomas, *Films of Olivia de Havilland,* 89.

9. *Call It a Day,* directed by Archie Mayo (Warner Brothers, 1937; Warner Archive Collection, 2010), DVD.

10. Parish and Stanke, *Leading Ladies,* 281.

11. *Call It a Day,* DVD.

12. Ibid.

13. As quoted in Louella O. Parsons, "Louella O. Parsons in Hollywood: Olivia de Havilland," *Los Angeles Examiner,* May 26, 1946.

14. Thomas, *Films of Olivia de Havilland,* 96.

15. *The Great Garrick,* directed by James Whale (Warner Brothers, 1937; Warner Home Video, 2009), DVD.

16. Ibid.

17. Ibid.

18. Ibid.

19. Ibid.

20. Ibid.

21. Ibid.

22. Ibid.

23. Parish and Stanke, *Leading Ladies,* 282.

24. *It's Love I'm After,* directed by Archie Mayo (Warner Brothers, 1937; Warner Home Video, 2009), DVD.

25. Ibid.

26. Hark, "Errol Flynn and Olivia de Havilland," 163.

27. *It's Love I'm After,* DVD.

28. Ibid.

29. Hubert Cole, "Let Olivia Laugh It Off," *Picturegoer,* June 14, 1941, 9.

30. Thomas, *Films of Olivia de Havilland,* 103.

31. Trailer for *Gold Is Where You Find It,* directed by Michael Curtiz (Warner Brothers, 1938; Warner Home Video, 2014), DVD.

32. Frank S. Nugent, "The Screen; Technicolor Pretties Up a Feud in 'Gold Is Where You Find It,' at the Strand," *New York Times,* February 14, 1938, accessed March 3, 2015, http://query.nytimes.com/mem/archive/pdf?res=9A05E3D91F39EE3ABC4C52DFB466883629EE.

33. Olivia de Havilland, email to the author, August 12, 2013.

34. Thomas, *Films of Olivia de Havilland,* 104.

35. Nugent, "The Screen; Technicolor," 20.

36. Thomas, *Films of Olivia de Havilland,* 109.

37. Parish and Stanke, *Leading Ladies,* 284.

38. Bubbeo, *Women of Warner Brothers,* 59.

39. Spensley, "Victorian . . . with Variations," 26.

40. *Hard to Get,* directed by Ray Enright (Warner Brothers, 1938; Warner Home Video, 2014), DVD.

41. Ibid.

42. Parish and Stanke, *Leading Ladies,* 286.

43. *Hard to Get,* DVD.

44. As quoted in Spensley, "Victorian . . . with Variations," 27.

45. Ibid.

46. Thomas, *Films of Olivia de Havilland,* 127.

47. Trailer for *Wings of the Navy,* directed by Lloyd Bacon (Warner Brothers, 1939; Warner Home Video, 2014), DVD.

48. "The Screen; Audiences Learn about 'Wings of the Navy' at Strand—Three Offerings at Foreign Language House," *New York Times*, February 4, 1939, accessed March 10, 2015, http://www.nytimes.com/movie/review?res=9A02E6D91F3AE433A25757C0A9649C94894D6C.

5. Miss Melly

1. Armond White, "What the Wind Blew In," *New York Times Book Review*, March 1, 2009, 14.

2. Ben Nussbaum, ed., *Gone with the Wind* (Irvine, CA: 1–5 Publishing, 2014), 21–22.

3. Casey Kelly-Barton, "Frankly My Dear . . . The Ransom Center Remembers *Gone with the Wind*," *Texas Journey*, September–October 2014, 42.

4. Steve Wilson, *The Making of* Gone with the Wind (Austin: Harry Ransom Center, University of Texas Press, 2014), 131.

5. Robert Osborne, foreword to *The Making of* Gone with the Wind, by Steve Wilson (Austin: Harry Ransom Center, University of Texas Press, 2014), xi.

6. Andrew R. Chow, "Memphis Theatre Cancels 'Gone with the Wind' Screening," *New York Times*, August 27, 2017, accessed September 21, 2017, https://www.nytimes.com/2017/08/27/movies/memphis-theater-cancels-gone-with-the-wind-screening.html?emc=eta1&_r=0.

7. Olivia de Havilland, letter to the author, June 4, 2010.

8. Hedda Hopper, "Olivia de Havilland," March 17, 1961, 1–2, Hedda Hopper Collection, Margaret Herrick Library, Beverly Hills, CA.

9. Robert Lindsey, "Reunion Recalls Those Gone with the Wind," *New York Times*, December 31, 1979, accessed July 12, 2012, http://query.nytimes.com/gst/abstract.html?res=9405EFDD1538E732A25752C3A9649D946890D6CF.

10. *Melanie Remembers*, DVD.

11. Wilson, *Making of* Gone with the Wind, 3.

12. As quoted in Alexander Lobrano, "Catching Up with the Players," *TV Guide*, December 23–29, 2000, 16–18.

13. Olivia de Havilland, "The Dream That Never Died," *Look*, December 12, 1967, 113.

14. Ibid.

15. As quoted in Anita Gates, "The Good Girl Gets the Last Word," *New York Times*, November 7, 2004, 32.

16. William Pratt, *Scarlett Fever* (New York: Collier Books, 1977), 32, 79.

17. Rudy Behlmer, *Memo from David O. Selznick* (New York: Viking Press, 1972), 138.

18. *Melanie Remembers*, DVD.

19. Ibid.

20. Ibid.

21. Lindsey, "Reunion Recalls Those Gone with the Wind."

22. Molly Haskell, *Frankly, My Dear:* Gone with the Wind *Revisited* (New Haven, CT: Yale University Press, 2009), 60.

23. *Melanie Remembers,* DVD.

24. Pratt, *Scarlett Fever,* 80.

25. Jack Warner, *My First Hundred Years in Hollywood: An Autobiography* (New York: Random House, 1965), 127.

26. Matzen, *Errol & Olivia,* 104.

27. Wilson, *Making of* Gone with the Wind, 94.

28. Mitchell, *Gone with the Wind,* 29.

29. Ibid., 142–43.

30. *Melanie Remembers,* DVD.

31. Haskell, *Frankly, My Dear,* 177.

32. Mitchell, *Gone with the Wind,* 142–43.

33. *Melanie Remembers,* DVD.

34. Christie's, "Olivia de Havilland Sweater: 1939," lot 112/sale 114, 2002, accessed June 12, 2017, http://www.christies.com/lotfinder/LotDetailsPrintable.aspx?from+salesummary&intObjectID=3956526.

35. Atlanta Historical Society, Gone with the Wind: *The Facts about the Fiction* (Atlanta: Atlanta Historical Society, 1989), 3.

36. Haskell, *Frankly, My Dear,* 57.

37. *The Story of* Gone with the Wind (New York: National Publishers, 1969), 12.

38. Haskell, *Frankly, My Dear,* 177.

39. Kendra Bean, *Vivien Leigh: An Intimate Portrait* (Philadelphia: Running Press, 2013), 58, 60.

40. *Melanie Remembers,* DVD.

41. Ibid.

42. Ibid.

43. De Havilland, "Dream That Never Died," 114.

44. *Gone with the Wind,* directed by Victor Fleming (Selznick International Pictures, 1939; Warner Home Video, 2004), DVD.

45. Ibid.

46. Ibid.

47. Bean, *Vivien Leigh,* 58.

48. De Havilland, "Dream That Never Died," 114.

49. *Melanie Remembers,* DVD.

50. Ibid.

51. Ibid.

52. De Havilland, "Dream That Never Died," 114.

53. *Gone with the Wind,* DVD.

54. *Melanie Remembers,* DVD.

55. *Gone with the Wind,* DVD.

56. Obsorne, foreword, xi.

57. *Melanie Remembers,* DVD.

58. Anne Edwards, *Road to Tara: The Life of Margaret Mitchell* (New Haven, CT: Ticknor & Fields, 1983), 284, 290.

59. Olivia de Havilland, letter to the author, October 28, 2002.

60. Ibid.

61. *Melanie Remembers,* DVD.

62. Edwards, *Road to Tara,* 290.

63. Hedda Hopper, "Olivia de Havilland Interview," March 1959, 4, Hedda Hopper Collection, Margaret Herrick Library, Beverly Hills, CA.

64. Olivia de Havilland, email to the author, August 17, 2016.

65. Hopper, "Olivia de Havilland," 1959, 4.

66. Ibid.

67. Wilson, *Making of* Gone with the Wind, 277.

68. Pratt, *Scarlett Fever,* 226–27.

69. Ibid., 227, 228.

70. Haskell, *Frankly, My Dear,* 179.

71. As quoted in Gates, "Good Girl Gets the Last Word," 32.

72. *Melanie Remembers,* DVD.

73. Adam Withnall, "*Gone with the Wind* Actress Alicia Rhett Dies Aged 98," *Independent,* January 5, 2014, accessed September 12, 2017, http://www.independent.co.uk/news/people/news/gone-with-the-wind-actress-alicia-rhett-dies-aged-98-9039751.html.

74. Claire Noland and *LA Times,* "Mary Anderson Dies: She Played Maybelle Merriwether in 'Gone with the Wind,'" *Washington Post,* April 12, 2014, accessed August 9, 2015, https://www.washingtonpost.com/entertainment/mary-anderson-dies-she-played-maybelle-merriwether-in-gone-with-the-wind/2014/04/12/d986e3b8-c193-11e3-b574-f8748871856a_story.html?utm_term=.27d645b85328.

75. Bryan Alexander, "'Gone with the Wind' 75 Years; What Endures in This Movie Classic?" *USA Today,* September 25, 2014, Life 2D.

6. Leaving the Job

1. "The Life Story of Olivia de Havilland," *Picture Show,* May 6, 1944, 14.

2. Olivia de Havilland, email to the author, April 10, 2013.

3. Ibid.

4. Matzen, *Errol & Olivia,* 91.

5. Olivia de Havilland, email to the author, April 10, 2013.

6. *The Aviator,* directed by Martin Scorsese (Warner Brothers and Miramax, 2004; Warner Home Video, 2005), DVD.

7. Olivia de Havilland, email to the author, May 12, 2015.

8. Alexander Nemerov, *Wartime Kiss: Visions of the Moment in the 1940s* (Princeton, NJ: Princeton University Press, 2013), 23, 26–27, 37.

9. Ibid., 44.

10. Peter Mikelbank, "Olivia de Havilland Opens Up about Her Love for Married Errol Flynn—and Her Romance with Jimmy Stewart," *People,* July 7, 2016, accessed January 20, 2018, http://people.com/movies/olivia-de-havilland-on-romances-with-errol-flynn-and-jimmy-stewart/.

11. Parish and Stanke, *Leading Ladies,* 292.

12. As quoted in A. Scott Berg, *Goldwyn* (New York: Alfred A. Knopf, 1989), 335.
13. Ibid., 336.
14. Niven, *Moon's a Balloon,* 224, 225.
15. Berg, *Goldwyn,* 336.
16. Niven, *Bring on the Empty Horses,* 101.
17. Ibid., 102.
18. Thomas, *Films of Olivia de Havilland,* 155.
19. Berg, *Goldwyn,* 336, 337.
20. Bubbeo, *Women of Warner Brothers,* 61.
21. Trailer for *My Love Came Back,* directed by Curtis Bernhardt (Warner Brothers, 1940; Warner Home Video, 2011), DVD.
22. Internet Movie Data Base, *My Love Came Back,* accessed June 20, 2012, http://www.imdb.com/title/tt0032829/?ref_=fn_al_tt_1.
23. Matzen, *Errol & Olivia,* 156.
24. Thomas, *Films of Olivia de Havilland,* 165.
25. Matzen, *Errol & Olivia,* 139.
26. As quoted in ibid.
27. Ibid., 141.
28. Bubbeo, *Women of Warner Brothers,* 61.
29. Thomas, *Films of Olivia de Havilland,* 167.
30. *The Strawberry Blonde,* directed by Raoul Walsh (Warner Brothers, 1941; Warner Home Video, 2012), DVD.
31. Ibid.
32. "Let Olivia Laugh It Off," *Picturegoer,* June 14, 1941, 9.
33. *The Strawberry Blonde,* DVD.
34. Ibid.
35. Parish and Stanke, *Leading Ladies,* 297.
36. American Film Institute, "Olivia de Havilland," 9.
37. As quoted in Cottom, "Olivia de Havilland," 13.
38. American Film Institute, "Olivia de Havilland," 9.
39. *The Strawberry Blonde,* DVD.
40. Olivia de Havilland, email to the author, April 20, 2013.
41. Bubbeo, *Women of Warner Brothers,* 61.
42. Internet Movie Data Base, *Hold Back the Dawn,* accessed April 27, 2013, http://www.imdb.com/title/tt0033722/?ref_=nv_sr_1.
43. As quoted in David Chierichetti, *Mitchell Leisen: Hollywood Director* (Los Angeles: Photoventures Press, 1995), 154.
44. Parish and Stanke, *Leading Ladies,* 297.
45. "De Havilland, Olivia—Actress," contract, March 5, 1941, Olivia de Havilland Collection, Margaret Herrick Library, Beverly Hills, CA.
46. Chierichetti, *Mitchell Leisen,* 151.
47. *Hold Back the Dawn,* directed by Mitchell Leisen (Paramount, 1941; Universal, 2010), DVD.
48. *Hold Back the Dawn:* Notes Taken at Random while in Mexicali and Calexico, January 7, 1941, Margaret Herrick Library, Beverly Hills, CA.

49. *Hold Back the Dawn,* DVD.

50. Ibid.

51. As quoted in Cottom, "Olivia de Havilland," 13.

52. Nemerov, *Wartime Kiss,* 139.

53. Chierichetti, *Mitchell Leisen,* 151.

54. *Hold Back the Dawn,* DVD.

55. Nemerov, *Wartime Kiss,* 130.

56. Bosley Crowther, "'Hold Back the Dawn,' a Poignant Romance, at the Paramount—'Harmon of Michigan' at Criterion," *New York Times,* October 2, 1941, accessed January 23, 2018, http://www.nytimes.com/movie/review?res=9E06E3D8113FE13BBC4A53DFB667838A659EDE.

57. Matzen, *Errol & Olivia,* 167.

58. Thomas, *Films of Olivia de Havilland,* 186.

59. Matzen, *Errol & Olivia,* 173.

60. Olivia de Havilland, email to the author, April 20, 2013.

61. Ibid.

62. Ibid.

63. *The Male Animal,* directed by Elliott Nugent (Warner Brothers, 1942; Warner Archive Collection, 2012), DVD.

64. Ibid.

65. Ibid.

66. Ibid.

67. "'The Male Animal,' with Henry Fonda, Olivia de Havilland, at Strand—'Strange Case of Dr. Rx' Arrives at the Rialto," *New York Times,* March 28, 1942, accessed January 26, 2018, http://www.nytimes.com/movie/review?res=9B04E0DA143CE33BBC4051DFB5668389659EDE.

68. Anjelica Huston, interview with the author, December 15, 2013.

69. Allegra Huston, email to the author, July 10, 2012.

70. James Spada, *More than a Woman* (1993; reprint, London: Time Warner, 2005), 260.

71. John Huston, *An Open Book* (New York: Alfred A. Knopf, 1980), 81.

72. British Film Institute, tape recording of lecture by Olivia de Havilland, London, August 28, 1971.

73. E. A. Kaplan, "Classical Hollywood Film and Melodrama," in *American Cinema and Hollywood: Critical Approaches,* ed. John Hill and Pamela Church Gibson (Oxford: Oxford University Press, 2000), 52.

74. As quoted in Gerald Pratley, *The Cinema of John Huston* (Cranbury, NJ: A. S. Barnes, 1977), 42.

75. Jill Watts, *Hattie McDaniel: Black Ambition, White Hollywood* (New York: Amistad, 2007), 206.

76. Ibid.

77. Charles Higham, *Olivia and Joan* (Sevenoaks, UK: New English Library, 1986), 138–42.

78. Lawrence Grobel, *The Hustons: The Life and Times of a Hollywood Dynasty* (1989; reprint, New York: Cooper Square Press, 2000), 224.

79. Olivia de Havilland, email to the author, April 20, 2013.

80. Grobel, *Hustons,* 224.

81. Olivia de Havilland, email to the author, April 20, 2013.

82. Bubbeo, *Women of Warner Brothers,* 62.

83. William F. Nolan, *John Huston: King Rebel* (Los Angeles: Sherbourne Press, 1965), 18.

84. Jeffrey Meyers, *John Huston: Courage and Art* (New York: Crown, 2011), 89.

85. Ed Sikov, *Dark Victory: The Life of Bette Davis* (New York: Henry Holt, 2007), 190.

86. Meyers, *John Huston,* 85.

87. Olivia de Havilland, letter to the author, November 20, 2011.

88. Parish and Stanke, *Leading Ladies,* 302.

89. *Princess O'Rourke,* directed by Norman Krasna (Warner Brothers, 1943; Warner Home Video, 2011), DVD.

90. Ibid.

91. Ibid.

92. Ibid.

93. Kass, *Olivia de Havilland,* 77.

94. Thomas, *Films of Olivia de Havilland,* 202.

95. Higham, *Olivia and Joan,* 53.

96. "Screen News and in Hollywood; Paramount Lends Sonny Tufts to RKO Studios in Exchange for Maureen O'Hara," *New York Times,* June 9, 1943, accessed March 23, 2015, http://query.nytimes.com/gst/abstract.html?res=9D03E2D6173DE13BBC4153DFB066888659EDE.

97. Harry Medved and Michael Medved, *The Golden Turkey Awards: The Worst Achievements in Hollywood History* (New York: Perigee Trade, 1980).

98. Kass, *Olivia de Havilland,* 73.

99. *Government Girl,* directed by Dudley Nichols (RKO, 1943; Warner Home Video, 2014), DVD.

100. Ibid.

101. *Thank Your Lucky Stars,* directed by David Butler (Warner Brothers, 1943; Warner Home Video, 2008), DVD.

102. Thomas, *Films of Olivia de Havilland,* 198.

103. Ibid., 206.

104. Trailer for *Devotion,* directed by Curtis Bernhardt (Warner Brothers, 1946; Warner Home Video, 2011), DVD.

105. Kass, *Olivia de Havilland,* 82.

106. Olivia de Havilland, email to the author, January 8, 2015.

107. Quoted in Jeremy Arnold, *Devotion,* Turner Classic Movies, 2014, accessed April 20, 2014, http://www.tcm.com/this-month/article/159658|0/Devotion.html.

108. Ibid.

109. Sennett, *Warner Brothers Presents,* 287.

110. Kass, *Olivia de Havilland,* 77.

111. Higham, *Olivia and Joan,* 152.

112. Arnold, *Devotion.*

113. Ibid.

114. *Devotion,* DVD.

115. Bosley Crowther, "*Devotion,* a Fictionized Tale of Bronte Sisters, at Strand," *New York Times,* April 6, 1946, accessed October 12, 2014, http://www.nytimes.com/movie/review?res=9F03E7D81139E53ABC4E53DFB266838D659EDE.

116. British Film Institute lecture, 1971.

117. Higham, *Olivia and Joan,* 156.

118. British Film Institute lecture, 1971.

119. Neil Doyle, "Olivia de Havilland and Joan Fontaine: Oscar Winning Sisters," *Films of the Golden Age* 22 (Fall 2000): 21.

120. American Film Institute, "Olivia de Havilland," 9.

121. Joanne L. Yeck, "In the State of California: De Havilland, Plaintiff vs. Warner Bros., Defendant," in *American Classic Screen Features,* ed. John C. Tibbets and James M. Welsh (Lanham, MD: Rowman & Littlefield, 2010), 5.

122. Bubbeo, *Women of Warner Brothers,* 63.

123. Higham, *Olivia and Joan,* 157.

124. Kass, *Olivia de Havilland,* 78.

125. Molly Haskell, *From Reverence to Rape* (Harmondsworth, UK: Penguin Books, 1974), 193.

126. David Shipman, *The Great Movie Stars: The Golden Years* (New York: Crown, 1970), 151.

127. Yeck, "In the State of California," 6.

128. Ibid.

129. Thomas, *Films of Olivia de Havilland,* 36.

130. Kass, *Olivia de Havilland,* 78.

131. Olivia de Havilland, email to the author, April 20, 2013.

132. Frederick C. Othman, "Olivia Idol of South Pacific Boys," *Citizen News,* March 25, 1944.

133. Matzen, *Errol & Olivia,* 183.

134. Kass, *Olivia de Havilland,* 78.

135. Olivia de Havilland, email to the author, April 20, 2013.

136. Axel Madsen, *John Huston* (Garden City, NY: Doubleday, 1978), 66.

137. Ibid., 65.

138. Meyers, *John Huston,* 86.

139. John Huston, autobiographical notes, chap. VI, n.d., John Huston Collection, Margaret Herrick Library, Beverly Hills, CA.

140. Meyers, *John Huston,* 86.

141. Grobel, *Hustons,* 260.

142. Olivia de Havilland, email to the author, April 20, 2013.

143. Matzen, *Errol & Olivia,* 183.

144. Nemerov, *Wartime Kiss,* 41.

145. Olivia de Havilland to John Huston, January 20, 1964, John Huston Collection, Margaret Herrick Library, Beverly Hills, CA.

146. Yeck, "In the State of California," 6.

147. Kass, *Olivia de Havilland,* 78, 80.

148. "Olivia de Havilland Contract Ruling Upheld by High Court," *Los Angeles Examiner,* February 3, 1945.

149. Matthew Belloni, "De Havilland Lawsuit Resonates through Hollywood," Reuters, August 23, 2007, accessed April 20, 2014, http://www.reuters.com/article/2007/08/24/industry-lawsuit-dcidUSN2329585820070824.

150. *Here's Looking at You, Warner Bros,* directed by Robert Guenette (Robert Guenette Productions, TNT, and Warner Bros. Television, 1991; Warner Home Video, 2003), DVD.

151. Bette Davis, foreword to *The Films of Olivia de Havilland,* by Tony Thomas (Secaucus, NJ: Citadel Press, 1983), 9.

152. Niven, *Moon's a Balloon,* 207.

7. Three Golden Years

1. Bubbeo, *Women of Warner Brothers,* 63.

2. *Welcome to Sherwood!* DVD.

3. Ibid.

4. As quoted in Bubbeo, *Women of Warner Brothers,* 63.

5. As quoted in ibid., 54.

6. Parish and Stanke, *Leading Ladies,* 304.

7. Ibid.

8. Kass, *Olivia de Havilland,* 80.

9. Jay Jorgensen, *Edith Head: The Fifty-Year Career of Hollywood's Greatest Costume Designer* (Philadelphia: Running Press, 2010), 116.

10. Edith Head, "What Are You Going to Wear?" 1945, 2, 6, Edith Head Papers, Margaret Herrick Library, Beverly Hills, CA.

11. Thomas, *Films of Olivia de Havilland,* 204.

12. *The Well-Groomed Bride* (1946), Turner Classic Movies, accessed June 1, 2014, http://www.tcm.com/tcmdb/title/95302/The-Well-Groomed-Bride/original-print-info.html.

13. Olivia de Havilland, email to the author, April 20, 2013.

14. Hollywood Independent Citizens Committee of the Arts, Sciences and Professions, "Statement of Policy," n.d., 1, HICCASP file, Margaret Herrick Library, Beverly Hills, CA.

15. John Meroney, "Olivia de Havilland Recalls Her Role—in the Cold War," *Wall Street Journal,* September 7, 2006, accessed March 25, 2011, http://www.onlinewsj.com/article/SB115757993223555601.html#prin. . . .

16. Ronald Radosh, "How Olivia de Havilland Bucked Dalton Trumbo and Helped Save Hollywood from Itself," *Daily Beast,* July 7, 2017, accessed July 7, 2017, https://www.thedailybeast.com/how-olivia-de-havilland-bucked-dalton-trumbo-and-helped-save-hollywood-from-itself.

17. Meroney, "Olivia de Havilland Recalls Her Role—in the Cold War."

18. Ibid.

19. Radosh, "How Olivia de Havilland Bucked Dalton Trumbo."

20. "Olivia de Havilland Will Feature I Am American Fete," *Los Angeles Examiner*, April 20, 1947.

21. Myron C. Fagan, *Moscow over Hollywood* (Los Angeles: R. C. Cary, 1948), 7.

22. Art Arthur to Arch Reeve, August 8, 1949, HICCASP file, Margaret Herrick Library, Beverly Hills, CA.

23. "Leftists' Trickery Told by Olivia de Havilland," *Los Angeles Times*, September 6, 1958, 1.

24. "Olivia de Havilland Tells of Breaking L.A. Red Front," *Los Angeles Examiner*, September 6, 1958.

25. Jorgensen, *Edith Head*, 118.

26. Bubbeo, *Women of Warner Brothers*, 64.

27. As quoted in Chierichetti, *Mitchell Leisen*, 228.

28. "Review: 'To Each His Own,'" *Variety*, December 31, 1945, accessed June 25, 2015, http://variety.com/1945/film/reviews/to-each-his-own-1200414634/.

29. David Thomson, "Olivia de Havilland," in *The New Biographical Dictionary of Film* (New York: Alfred A. Knopf, 2003), 215.

30. *To Each His Own*, directed by Mitchell Leisen (Paramount, 1946; Universal, 2010), DVD.

31. Parish and Stanke, *Leading Ladies*, 304.

32. Jorgensen, *Edith Head*, 117.

33. *To Each His Own*, DVD.

34. Jorgensen, *Edith Head*, 117.

35. Ibid., 118.

36. As quoted in Chierichetti, *Mitchell Leisen*, 229.

37. Bubbeo, *Women of Warner Brothers*, 64.

38. Chierichetti, *Mitchell Leisen*, 232.

39. Parish and Stanke, *Leading Ladies*, 308.

40. De Havilland, Olivia—Actress, Paramount contract, May 24, 1945, Olivia de Havilland Collection, Margaret Herrick Library, Beverly Hills, CA.

41. Olivia de Havilland, "The Role I Liked Best," *Saturday Evening Post*, March 1, 1947.

42. Bubbeo, *Women of Warner Brothers*, 64.

43. Parish and Stanke, *Leading Ladies*, 308.

44. Thomas, *Films of Olivia de Havilland*, 212.

45. *The Dark Mirror*, directed by Robert Siodmak (International Pictures, 1946; Olive Films, 2012), DVD.

46. Olivia de Havilland, email to the author, January 7, 2015.

47. Kass, *Olivia de Havilland*, 93.

48. *The Dark Mirror*, DVD.

49. As quoted in Parish and Stanke, *Leading Ladies*, 309.

50. As quoted in Philip French, "Review: Critics: Philip French's Screen Legends: No. 73 Olivia de Havilland 1916–," *Observer*, November 1, 2009, 12.

51. Olivia de Havilland, email to the author, January 7, 2015.

52. Bosley Crowther, "The Screen; 'Deception,' Warner Film with Bette Davis and Claude Rains, at Hollywood—'Dark Mirror,' New Mystery, at the Criterion," *New York*

Times, October 19, 1946, accessed February 9, 2012, http://www.nytimes.com/movie/review?_r=2&res=9B05E1D61338E53ABC4152DFB667838D659EDE.

53. Olivia de Havilland, email to the author, January 7, 2015.

54. Jeanine Basinger, *A Woman's View* (London: Chatto & Windus, 1993), 90.

55. Server, *Robert Mitchum,* 127.

56. James Agee, "*The Dark Mirror* (1946 Film), by Robert Siodmak," *Nation*, November 9, 1946, 536, accessed October 24, 2017, http://www.unz.org/Pub/Nation-1946nov09-00536a02.

57. Olivia de Havilland, email to the author, March 20, 2012.

58. "Olivia de Havilland to Wed Writer Today," *Los Angeles Examiner*, August 26, 1946.

59. Olivia de Havilland as told to Alice Craig Greene, "How I Met My Husband," *Motion Picture Magazine*, March 1947.

60. Harry Ransom Center, *The Greenwich Village Bookshop Door: Lawrence Langner,* n.d., accessed June 23, 2015, http://norman.hrc.utexas.edu/bookshopdoor/signature.cfm?item=106#1; Kass, *Olivia de Havilland,* 83.

61. De Havilland as told to Greene, "How I Met My Husband."

62. William H. Honan, "Marcus Aurelius Goodrich, 93, Writer Known for Naval Stories," *New York Times*, October 22, 1991, accessed June 23, 2015, https://c01130.mail.live.com/?tid=cmgFENLtoZ5RG9GwAiZMF9dg2&fv=1&fid=flinbx.

63. Higham, *Sisters,* 172–76.

64. De Havilland as told to Greene, "How I Met My Husband."

65. "Olivia de Havilland Becomes Bride," *Los Angeles Times,* August 27, 1946.

66. Olivia de Havilland, email to the author, March 20, 2012.

67. Hedda Hopper, "Olivia de Havilland Enjoys Bride's Role," *Los Angeles Times*, December 1, 1946, pt. 3, 1.

68. Patricia Coffin, "Success Becomes Olivia," *Look*, March 18, 1947, 42, 44.

69. Sidney Skolsky, "A Practical Sentimentalist," *New York Post Week-end Magazine*, November 9, 1946, 18.

70. Olivia de Havilland, email to the author, March 20, 2012.

71. Neil Doyle, "Olivia de Havilland Was Not Content to Be Merely a Beautiful Costumed Prop," *Films in Review*, February 1962, 80.

72. Higham, *Sisters,* 179.

73. Mary Morris, "Lady Olivia," *PM's Sunday Picture News,* March 23, 1947, 7.

74. Elizabeth Wilson, "Scarlett O'Havilland," *Liberty*, March 15, 1947, 23.

75. Joel W. Finler, *The Hollywood Story* (New York: Crown, 1988), 62.

76. Academy of Motion Picture Arts and Sciences, "The 19th Academy Awards/1947," *Experience over Eight Decades of the Oscars from 1927 to 2015,* accessed June 27, 2015, https://www.oscars.org/oscars/ceremonies/1947.

77. Academy of Motion Picture Arts and Sciences, "Academy Awards Acceptance Speeches," 2009, accessed August 8, 2011, http://aaspeechesdb.oscars.org/results.aspx?AC=PREV_RECORD&XC=/results.aspx&B.

78. Dan Swinton, "Arrest Confuses Olivia's Admirer," *St. Louis Citizen-News*, May 31, 1947.

79. Ingrid Bergman and Alan Burgess, *Ingrid Bergman: My Story* (New York: Delacorte Press, 1980), 318–19.

80. Parish and Stanke, *Leading Ladies,* 312.

81. Bubbeo, *Women of Warner Brothers,* 65.

82. Terrence Rafferty, "Let's See What's Inside That Pretty Head," *New York Times,* November 27, 2011, Arts 10.

83. *The Snake Pit,* directed by Anatole Litvak (20th Century Fox, 1948; 20th Century Fox Studio Classics, 2004), DVD.

84. Ibid.

85. Ibid.

86. Ibid.

87. Glen O. Gabbard and Krin Gabbard, *Psychiatry and the Cinema,* 2nd ed. (Washington, DC: American Psychiatric Press, 1999), 61.

88. Parish and Stanke, *Leading Ladies,* 312.

89. Internet Movie Data Base, *The Snake Pit,* accessed June 28, 2015, http://www.imdb.com/title/tt0040806/awards?ref_=tt_awd.

90. Parish and Stanke, *Leading Ladies,* 312.

91. Terrence Rafferty, "A Heavy Lift onto the Screen," *New York Times,* April 28, 2013, 20.

92. Broadway League, *The Heiress, Internet Broadway Data Base, 2001–15,* accessed February 4, 2014, http://www.ibdb.com/production.php?id=1566.

93. Robert Osborne, introduction to *The Heiress,* directed by William Wyler (Paramount, 1949; Universal Cinema Classics, 2008), DVD.

94. John Douglas Eames, *The Paramount Story* (New York: Random House, 1987), 192.

95. Henry James, *Washington Square* (1881; reprint, Harmondsworth, UK: Penguin Books, 1968), 11–12.

96. Axel Madsen, *William Wyler* (New York: Thomas Y. Crowell, 1973), 291–92.

97. As quoted in ibid., 293.

98. *The Heiress,* DVD.

99. Ibid.

100. W. H. Mooring, "Will 'Livvy' Over-Do It?" *Picturegoer,* February 2, 1946, 8.

101. David Thomson, "Heiress Olivia," *LA Weekly,* June 9–15, 2006, 41.

102. Glenn Kenny, "Olivia de Havilland Remembers 'The Heiress,'" *Premiere.com,* February 2, 2007.

103. Patricia Bosworth, *Montgomery Clift: A Biography* (New York: Harcourt Brace Jovanovich, 1978), 139, 140.

104. Robert LaGuardia, *Monty: A Biography of Montgomery Clift* (New York: Arbor House, 1977), 69.

105. Jorgensen, *Edith Head,* 144, 145, 144.

106. Christie's, "Olivia de Havilland Bonnet from *The Heiress,*" December 20, 2012, accessed June 26, 2012, https://www.christies.com/lotfinder/Lot/olivia-de-havilland-bonnet-from-the-heiress-4040984-details.aspx.

107. *The Heiress,* DVD.

108. Trailer for *The Heiress*, DVD.

109. Bosley Crowther, "'The Heiress,' with Olivia de Havilland in Leading Role, Arrives at Music Hall," *New York Times*, October 7, 1949, accessed November 6, 2017, http://www.nytimes.com/movie/review?res=9400E7DC143BE23BBC4F53DFB6678382659EDE.

110. Louella Parsons, "Olivia de Havilland Dated for August Visit by Stork," *Los Angeles Examiner*, February 18, 1949.

111. Louella Parsons, "Actress Olivia de Havilland Falters in Fight for Health," *Los Angeles Examiner*, April 4, 1949.

112. Louella Parsons, "Olivia de Havilland Has Son," *Los Angeles Examiner*, September 28, 1949.

113. Bubbeo, *Women of Warner Brothers*, 67.

114. Parish and Stanke, *Leading Ladies*, 316.

115. "Olivia de Havilland Honored by Brazil," *Los Angeles Times*, March 13, 1950.

116. Schwartz, "The Last Star," 96.

117. Bronwyn Cosgrave, *Made for Each Other: Fashion and the Academy Awards* (London: Bloomsbury, 2008), 68.

118. Ibid.

119. Academy of Motion Picture Arts and Sciences, "Academy Awards Acceptance Speeches."

120. "Oscar Win Shocks Olivia; Crawford Says He's Numb," *Los Angeles Times*, March 25, 1950, pt. 1, 10.

8. Every Frenchwoman Has One

1. Parish and Stanke, *Leading Ladies*, 316.

2. Ibid.

3. Olivia de Havilland, email to the author, August 31, 2012.

4. Meroney, "Olivia de Havilland Recalls Her Role—in the Cold War."

5. Olivia de Havilland, email to the author, August 31, 2012.

6. Louis Botto, "At This Theatre: The Ethel Barrymore," *Playbill*, April 2016, 31.

7. Olivia de Havilland, email to the author, January 7, 2015.

8. "Olivia Asks Steepest Terms in History to Play Broadway 'Juliet,'" *Variety*, August 9, 1950.

9. Parish and Stanke, *Leading Ladies*, 316.

10. Bubbeo, *Women of Warner Brothers*, 67.

11. Olivia de Havilland, email to the author, January 7, 2015.

12. Jack Gaver, "Along the Great White Way," *Los Angeles Daily News*, August 25, 1951.

13. "Romeo and Juliet," *Variety*, January 24, 1951.

14. William Hawkins, "Olivia's 'Juliet' Grows Young Again," *New York World Telegram and Sun*, March 12, 1951.

15. Gaver, "Along the Great White Way."

16. George Jean Nathan, "Theatre Week," *Los Angeles Examiner*, March 26, 1951.

17. Bob Thomas, "Olivia Planning to Do Another Stage Vehicle," *Hollywood Citizen News*, June 9, 1952.

18. Olivia de Havilland, email to the author, August 31, 2012.

19. "Olivia de Havilland," *Candida* program, 1951.

20. James Poling, "Olivia's World Is the Stage," *Collier's Weekly*, January 13, 1951, 14.

21. Brooks Atkinson, "Olivia de Havilland Comes to Broadway in a Revival of Bernard Shaw's 'Candida,'" *New York Times*, April 23, 1952, 23, accessed February 11, 2018, https://timesmachine.nytimes.com/timesmachine/1952/04/23/93565852.html?action=click&contentCollection=Archives&module=ArticleEndCTA&region=ArchiveBody&pgtype=article&pageNumber=23.

22. Aline Mosby, "Leading Man Goes to Bat for Olivia," *Los Angeles Daily News*, December 22, 1951, 21.

23. Ibid.

24. Poling, "Olivia's World Is the Stage," 68.

25. As quoted in Richard Burton, *The Richard Burton Diaries*, ed. Chris Williams (New Haven, CT: Yale University Press, 2013), 573–74.

26. Olivia de Havilland, email to the author, January 7, 2015.

27. Muriel Stafford, "Olivia de Havilland's Script Reveals Gifted Mind," *New York Daily News*, December 28, 1950.

28. "De Havilland, Olivia—Actress," contract, November 29, 1945, Olivia de Havilland Collection, Margaret Herrick Library, Beverly Hills, CA.

29. Hedda Hopper, "The Goodriches," n.d. (circa 1950), 3, Olivia de Havilland Collection, Margaret Herrick Library, Beverly Hills, CA.

30. "Divorce Seen for Olivia de Havilland," *Los Angeles Times*, May 18, 1952.

31. Jay Breen, "Marriage Ends for Actress," *New York Daily News*, May 22, 1952.

32. Louella O. Parsons, "Decree Asked by Actress de Havilland," *Los Angeles Examiner*, July 4, 1952.

33. "Olivia Sues for Divorce, Wants Maps," *Mirror*, July 4, 1952.

34. "Actress Feared Death, Tells Court of Mate's Violence," *Los Angeles Examiner*, August 27, 1952.

35. "The Life Story of Olivia de Havilland," *Picture Show*, March 7, 1953, 12.

36. Aline Mosby, "Actress Says She Won't Remarry," *Los Angeles Daily News*, August 1, 1952.

37. Parsons, "Decree Asked by Actress de Havilland."

38. Kass, *Olivia de Havilland*, 104.

39. Margaret Forster, *Daphne du Maurier* (1993; reprint, London: Arrow Books, 2007), 251–53, 261, 252, 256, 261.

40. Philip K. Scheuer, "Olivia Seeks 'Interesting Ambiguity' in Rachel Role," *Los Angeles Times*, August 3, 1952, 1.

41. Thomas, *Films of Olivia de Havilland*, 223.

42. Olivia de Havilland, email to the author, January 7, 2015.

43. Higham, *Olivia and Joan*, 216.

44. Scheuer, "Olivia Seeks 'Interesting Ambiguity' in Rachel Role," 10.

45. Tom Rubython, *And God Created Burton* (London: Myrtle Press, 2011), 174–75.

46. Michael Munn, *Richard Burton: Prince of Players* (New York: Skyhorse, 2008), 72.

47. Rubython, *And God Created Burton,* 262.

48. Hedda Hopper, "Olivia de Havilland," September 10, 1952, 1, Hedda Hopper Collection, Margaret Herrick Library, Beverly Hills, CA.

49. Olivia de Havilland, email to the author, August 20, 2013.

50. Ibid., January 1, 2015.

51. Basinger, *A Woman's View,* 279.

52. Olivia de Havilland, email to the author, August 20, 2013.

53. Kass, *Olivia de Havilland,* 104.

54. Ibid., 105.

55. Mark Jancovich, "'Rebecca's Ghost': Horror, the Gothic and the du Maurier Film Adaptations," in *The Daphne du Maurier Companion,* ed. Helen Taylor (London: Virago Press, 2007), 312–13, 315–17.

56. Manohla Dargis, "Kiss Him Deadly," *New York Times,* June 9, 2017, C8.

57. Julie Kirgo, "My Cousin Rachel," DVD booklet essay, 5, *My Cousin Rachel* (Twilight Time, 2011), DVD.

58. Bosley Crowther, "'My Cousin Rachel' Presented at the Rivoli—'Ruby Gentry,' 'No Time for Flowers' Bow," *New York Times,* December 26, 1952, accessed February 15, 2014, http://www.nytimes.com/movie/review?res=9501EFDD1E3AE23BBC4E51DFB4678389649EDE.

59. "Daphne du Maurier," *My Cousin Rachel* (Fox Searchlight Pictures, 2017; 20th Century Fox Home Entertainment, 2017), DVD.

60. Ray Stark to William Wyler, November 5, 1952, David Lewis Collection, Margaret Herrick Library, Beverly Hills, CA.

61. William Wyler to David Lewis, December 2, 1952, David Lewis Collection, Margaret Herrick Library, Beverly Hills, CA.

62. Ray Stark to William Wyler, December 11, 1952, David Lewis Collection, Margaret Herrick Library, Beverly Hills, CA.

63. Olivia de Havilland, *Every Frenchman Has One* (New York: Random House, 1962), 13.

64. Ibid., 15.

65. Ibid., 15–16.

66. Justine Picardie, *Coco Chanel: The Legend and the Life* (2010; reprint, London: Harper, 2013), 107.

67. "Olivia de Havilland Free to Wed French Suitor," *Herald Express,* August 28, 1953, 1.

68. "Plan to Marry," *Los Angeles Times,* August 16, 1953.

69. Olivia de Havilland, email to the author, August 31, 2012.

70. Ibid.

71. Kate O'Brien, *That Lady* (1946; reprint, London: Virago Press, 1988), 4–5.

72. Kass, *Olivia de Havilland,* 107.

73. Thomas, *Films of Olivia de Havilland,* 226.

74. Server, *Robert Mitchum,* 274.

75. Erskine Johnson, "Big Role Lures de Havilland Home," *Los Angeles Daily News,* October 15, 1954.

76. Stanley Kramer and Thomas M. Coffey, *A Mad, Mad, Mad, Mad World: A Life in Hollywood* (New York: Harcourt Brace, 1997), 132.

77. Thomas, *Films of Olivia de Havilland,* 228.

78. Server, *Robert Mitchum,* 277.

79. Olivia de Havilland, conversation with the author, August 30, 2012.

80. Server, *Robert Mitchum,* 277.

81. Kramer and Coffey, *Mad, Mad, Mad, Mad World,* 132.

82. Olivia de Havilland, email to the author, January 7, 2015.

83. Quoted in Server, *Robert Mitchum,* 277.

84. "Olivia de Havilland Wed to French Film Reporter," *Los Angeles Times,* April 3, 1955, 1.

85. Fleur Cowles, *She Made Friends and Kept Them* (London: HarperCollins, 1996), 258.

86. "French Fete de Havilland at Her Wedding," *Daily Mirror,* April 2, 1955, 1.

87. Donald Spoto, *High Society: Grace Kelly and Hollywood* (London: Hutchinson, 2009), 156–57.

88. Olivia de Havilland, email to the author, January 7, 2016.

89. Olivia de Havilland, "I Married a Frenchman," *Los Angeles Times,* May 20, 1956, 11.

90. Olivia de Havilland, ". . . Where Am I? I'm in France, That's Where!" *McCall's,* August 1961, 54.

91. "It Isn't Yoga, It's Love," *Sunday Dispatch,* September 21, 1958.

92. Richard G. Hubler, "Olivia—The Bellicose Belle," *Coronet,* July 1958, 96.

93. Meroney, "Olivia de Havilland Recalls Her Role—in the Cold War."

94. "Congress Due to Aid Olivia and Romance," *Los Angeles Times,* June 3, 1958.

95. "A Law for Olivia," *Variety,* June 4, 1958.

96. Serge Toubiana, Florence Müller, and Jerome Hanover, *Stars in Dior* (New York: Rizzoli, 2012), 52.

97. Ibid.

98. Thomas, *Films of Olivia de Havilland,* 229.

99. *The Ambassador's Daughter,* directed by Norman Krasna (Norman Krasna Productions and United Artists, 1956; Education 2000, 2005), DVD.

100. Toubiana, Müller, and Hanover, *Stars in Dior,* 52.

101. Parish and Stanke, *Leading Ladies,* 321.

102. Hubler, "Olivia—The Bellicose Belle," 96.

103. Thomas, *Films of Olivia de Havilland,* 231.

104. "The 'New' Olivia de Havilland Says What She Thinks," *Newsweek,* November 4, 1957.

105. British Film Institute, tape recording of lecture by Olivia de Havilland, London, August 28, 1971.

106. *The Proud Rebel,* directed by Michael Curtiz (Buena Vista, 1958; HBO, 1999), DVD.

107. Ibid.

108. Ibid.

109. "Ladd, Olivia de Havilland Suffer Burns," *Los Angeles Times,* September 24, 1957.

110. *The Proud Rebel,* DVD.

111. "'New' Olivia de Havilland Says What She Thinks."

112. Lydia Lane, "U.S. Women Aggressive, Says Actress," *Los Angeles Times,* October 13, 1957, pt. IV, 14.

113. Ibid.

114. "'New' Olivia de Havilland Says What She Thinks."

115. Parish and Stanke, *Leading Ladies,* 324.

116. Hedda Hopper, "Olivia de Havilland," March 17, 1961, 4–5, Hedda Hopper Collection, Margaret Herrick Library, Beverly Hills, CA.

117. *Libel,* directed by Anthony Asquith (Metro Goldwyn Mayer, 1959; Warner Home Video, 2011), DVD.

118. Ibid.

119. Ibid.

120. Hopper, "Olivia de Havilland," 1961, 5.

121. Olivia de Havilland, email to the author, August 20, 2013.

122. Hopper, "Olivia de Havilland," 1961, 3.

123. Ibid.

124. Cowles, *She Made Friends and Kept Them,* 258.

125. *Light in the Piazza,* directed by Guy Green (Metro Goldwyn Mayer, 1962; Warner Home Video, 2011), DVD.

126. Ibid.

127. Olivia de Havilland, email to the author, January 7, 2015.

128. Parish and Stanke, *Leading Ladies,* 35.

129. Howard Taubman, "Theatre: 'A Gift of Time,'" *New York Times,* February 25, 1962, 34.

130. Olivia de Havilland, email to the author, August 31, 2013.

131. Vanessa Thorpe, "Grace Kelly: Screen Goddess, Princess and Enduring Source of Scandal," *Guardian,* May 10, 2014, accessed May 25, 2014, http://www.theguardian.com/film/2014/may/11/grace-kelly-grace-of-monaco-film-nicole-kidman-controversy.

132. Olivia de Havilland, email to the author, August 31, 2013.

133. Hedda Hopper, "Olivia de Havilland Here for Film Role," *Los Angeles Times,* January 23, 1963, pt. IV, 6.

134. *Lady in a Cage,* directed by Walter Grauman (Paramount, 1964; Warner Archive Collection, 2013), DVD.

135. Eames, *Paramount Story,* 246.

136. Kass, *Olivia de Havilland,* 127.

137. Dorothy Manners, "Ups and Downs," *Los Angeles Herald-Examiner,* June 7, 1964.

138. Howard Thompson, "Testament of a Roving 'Lady,'" *New York Times,* June 7, 1964.

139. "De Havilland Film out of London Film Fest," *Los Angeles Times,* November 5, 1965.

140. Olivia de Havilland, "Come out Fighting," *Films and Filming* 12, no. 6 (March 1966): 20–21.

141. American Film Institute, "Olivia de Havilland," 9.

142. Olivia de Havilland, email to the author, August 31, 2013.

143. Bob Thomas, *Joan Crawford* (New York: Simon & Schuster, 1978), 231.

144. Olivia de Havilland, email to the author, November 1, 2014.

145. Mark A. Vieira, *Hollywood Horror: From Gothic to Cosmic* (New York: Harry N. Abrams, 2003), 215.

146. Olivia de Havilland, email to the author, November 1, 2014.

147. Thomas, *Films of Olivia de Havilland,* 239.

148. Charlotte Chandler, *Not the Girl Next Door* (New York: Applause Theatre & Cinema Books, 2008), 131.

149. Vieira, *Hollywood Horror,* 215.

150. Joseph Cotten, *Vanity Will Get You Somewhere* (London: Columbus Books, 1987), 154.

151. Haskell, *From Reverence to Rape,* 328.

152. Arthur Knight, "Ghouls Rush In," *Saturday Review,* January 23, 1965, 56.

153. "Dragon Ladies," *Time,* March 19, 1965.

154. Thomas, *Films of Olivia de Havilland,* 241.

155. *Hush Up Sweet Charlotte,* directed by William Clift (Everything Is Going to Be Just Fine Productions, 2015; Amazon.com, 2018), streamed.

156. Olivia de Havilland, email to the author, November 1, 2014.

157. *Hush . . . Hush, Sweet Charlotte,* directed by Robert Aldrich (20th Century Fox, 1964; 20th Century Fox Home Entertainment, 2005), DVD.

158. Ibid.

159. As quoted in Thomas, *Films of Olivia de Havilland,* 241.

160. "The Star They Didn't Forget," *Family Weekly,* May 23, 1965, 19.

161. Ibid.

162. Joel Rose, "Tintype of Olivia de Havilland," Paramount Studios, 1964, 4, Olivia de Havilland Collection, Margaret Herrick Library, Beverly Hills, CA.

163. Harrison Carroll, "Olivia de Havilland Legally Separated," *Los Angeles Herald-Examiner,* March 15, 1965.

164. Earl Wilson, "Olivia, Mate Separated, Share Home," *Los Angeles Herald-Examiner,* June 28, 1965, A-8.

165. Earl Wilson, "Separated . . . but Together," *Los Angeles Herald-Examiner,* December 17, 1966.

166. Olivia de Havilland, conversation with the author, August 31, 2012.

9. Closing a Career

1. Wilson, "Separated . . . but Together."

2. "Olivia de Havilland Heads Cannes Jury," *Hollywood Reporter,* April 20, 1965.

3. Olivia de Havilland, email to the author, January 7, 2015.

4. Rose, "Tintype of Olivia de Havilland," 2.

5. As quoted in ibid.

6. Jane Ardmore, "Parents Can Be Wrong!" 1962, 55, Jane Ardmore Collection, Margaret Herrick Library, Beverly Hills, CA.

7. Olivia de Havilland, email to the author, March 20, 2012.

8. Parish and Stanke, *Leading Ladies,* 328.

9. "Olivia de Havilland to Make TV Dramatic Debut," *Hollywood Reporter,* May 25, 1966.

10. Internet Movie Data Base, *Noon Wine,* trivia, 2015.

11. Parish and Stanke, *Leading Ladies,* 329.

12. British Film Institute, tape recording of lecture by Olivia de Havilland, London, August 28, 1971.

13. *The Adventurers,* directed by Lewis Gilbert (Avco Embassy and Paramount, 1970; Warner Archive Collection, 2013), DVD.

14. Lucille Carroll, "Bekim Gets a Yes from Olivia," *Los Angeles Herald-Examiner,* December 13, 1968, D-3.

15. *The Adventurers,* DVD.

16. David Chierichetti, "Olivia in London," *Film Fan Monthly* 124 (October 1971): 3.

17. "Olivia de Havilland," *Films Illustrated* 1, no. 4 (October 1971): 3.

18. Olivia de Havilland, email to the author, March 20, 2012.

19. "Films on TV," *Films in Review,* February 1978, 107.

20. Olivia de Havilland, email to the author, January 7, 2015.

21. Jorgensen, *Edith Head,* 359.

22. *The Screaming Woman,* directed by Jack Smight (Universal Television, 1972), YouTube.

23. Cotten, *Vanity Will Get You Somewhere,* 154.

24. Kevin Thomas, "Miss de Havilland in Fright Film," *Los Angeles Times,* January 29, 1972.

25. Olivia de Havilland, email to the author, January 7, 2015.

26. "Olivia de Havilland Kicks Off Omaha Lecture Series," *Box Office,* October 21, 1974.

27. Olivia de Havilland, "Bouboule," *Ladies' Home Journal,* June 1975.

28. "Mother of Joan Fontaine, Olivia de Havilland Dies," *Los Angeles Times,* February 22, 1975.

29. As quoted in Robert Lindsey, "Olivia's Life Is Buzzing with Change," *New York Times,* November 16, 1977, 21.

30. *Airport '77,* directed by Jerry Jameson (Universal, 1977; Universal Pictures Home Entertainment, 2004), DVD.

31. Ibid.

32. Cotten, *Vanity Will Get You Somewhere,* 154.

33. Lee Grant, *I Said Yes to Everything* (New York: Penguin, 2014), 313.

34. Bridget Byrne, "Airborne with Olivia de Havilland," *Los Angeles Herald-Examiner,* September 2, 1976.

35. Cottom, "Olivia de Havilland," 11.

36. Bubbeo, *Women of Warner Brothers,* 70.

37. Trailer for *The Swarm,* directed by Irwin Allen (Warner Brothers, 1978; Warner Home Video, 2012), DVD.

38. James V. D'Árc, "'Perfect Manners': An Interview with Olivia de Havilland," in *American Classic Screen Interviews,* ed. John C. Tibbetts and James M. Welsh (1979; reprint, Lanham, MD: Scarecrow Press, 2010), 29.

39. *The Swarm,* DVD.

40. Lindsey, "Olivia's Life Is Buzzing with Change."

41. Trailer for *The Swarm,* DVD.

42. Dick Sheppard, "Olivia de Havilland—from Twelve Oaks to Henning, Tenn.," *Los Angeles Herald-Examiner,* November 5, 1978.

43. Ibid.

44. Olivia de Havilland, email to the author, January 7, 2015.

45. Ibid.

46. *Roots: The Next Generations,* directed by John Erman (David L. Wolper Productions and Warner Bros. Television, 1979; Warner Home Video, 2007), DVD.

47. Ibid.

48. Thomas, *Films of Olivia de Havilland,* 250.

49. *The Fifth Musketeer,* directed by Ken Annakin (S&T Films Berlin, 1979).

50. D'Árc, "'Perfect Manners,'" 29.

51. "De Havilland Active for Episcopalians," *Variety,* February 7, 1979.

52. Mary Vespa, "Amid Divorce, Disaster Movies and the Feud with Sister Joan, Olivia de Havilland Finds Solace Serving Her Church," *People,* March 5, 1979, 90.

53. Higham, *Olivia and Joan,* 269.

54. Betty Goodwin, "Olivia Sets Sail," *Los Angeles Times,* January 18, 1981.

55. *Murder Is Easy,* directed by Claude Whatham (CBS Entertainment Production, 1982; KNM Home Entertainment, 2017), DVD.

56. Ibid.

57. Olivia de Havilland, letter to the author, December 16, 1981.

58. Dotson Rader, "Rewards and Regrets," *Parade,* September 7, 1986, 4.

59. Robert Osborne, "Rambling Reporter," *Hollywood Reporter,* December 22, 1987.

60. "Parental Discretion Revised," *People,* October 19, 1987.

61. Olivia de Havilland, email to the author, January 7, 2015.

62. *Hollywood Reporter,* February 21, 1986, Olivia de Havilland Collection, Margaret Herrick Library, Beverly Hills, CA.

63. *Hollywood Reporter,* December 13, 1985, Olivia de Havilland Collection, Margaret Herrick Library, Beverly Hills, CA.

64. *Anastasia: The Mystery of Anna,* directed by Marvin J. Chomsky (Telecom Entertainment, 1998; Mill Creek Entertainment, 2011), DVD.

65. Ibid.

66. *Hollywood Reporter,* January 8, 1987, Olivia de Havilland Collection, Margaret Herrick Library, Beverly Hills, CA.

67. Robert Osborne, "Rambling Reporter," *Hollywood Reporter,* December 10, 1987.

68. "For Olivia, Paris Spells Home," *Variety,* March 16, 1988.

69. *The Woman He Loved,* directed by Charles Jarrott (Harlech Television [HTV], 1988).

70. Olivia de Havilland, letter to the author, May 18, 1993.

71. Olivia de Havilland, email to the author, January 7, 2015.

72. Bubbeo, *Women of Warner Brothers,* 71.

10. Sister Joan

1. Justin Ravitz, "Joan Fontaine, Oscar Winning Actress, Dies at 96," *Us Magazine* online, December 13, 2013, accessed December 22, 2016, http://www.usmagazine.com/celebrity-news/news/joan-fontaine-oscar-winning-actress-dies-at-96–20131612.

2. Tom Leonard, "Has There Ever Been a Sibling Rivalry More Venomous than This? Now Joan Fontaine Is Dead at 96, Her Sister Olivia de Havilland Will Be Livid She's Stolen the Headlines Again," *Mail Online,* December 17, 2013, accessed December 22, 2016, http://www.dailymail.co.uk/femail/article-2524952/Joan-Fontaines-d. . . .

3. Michael Musto, "Olivia de Havilland and Joan Fontaine Are Still Alive! My Thoughts," *Village Voice,* July 3, 2012, accessed July 9, 2012, http://blogs.villagevoice.com/dailymusto/2012/07/olivia_dehavil. . . .

4. Christopher Hitchens, "O Brother, Why Art Thou?" *Vanity Fair,* May 16, 2005, accessed July 21, 2017, http://www.vanityfair.com/culture/features/2008/03/proust_fontaine200803.

5. Philip Berk, "Hollywood's Most Bitter and Longest-Running Feud," Hollywood Foreign Press Association, October 21, 2013, accessed January 20, 2014, http://www.hfpa.org/2013/10/hollywoods-most-bitter-and-longest-ru. . . .

6. Rupert Cornwell, "Sibling Rivalry: Hollywood's Oldest Feud," *Independent,* May 15, 2008, accessed June 9, 2012, http://www.independent.co.uk/arts-entertainment/films/features/sibling-rivalry-hollywoods-oldest-feud-828301.html.

7. Scott Feinberg, "New Details about the Joan Fontaine–Olivia de Havilland Feud Revealed," *Hollywood Reporter,* December 17, 2013, accessed December 20, 2013, http://www.hollywoodreporter.com/race/joan-fontaine-olivia-de-havilland-666087.

8. Graydon Carter, ed., *Vanity Fair's Proust Questionnaire* (New York: Rodale, 2009), 65, 84.

9. "And the Winner Is . . . (the Oscars of 1963)," episode of *Feud,* directed by Ryan Murphy (FX, 2017).

10. Gene Maddaus, "Olivia de Havilland Says She Never Called Her Sister a 'Bitch,' Despite 'Feud' Scene," *Variety,* September 15, 2017, accessed September 15, 2017, http://variety.com/2017/tv/news/olivia-de-havilland-bitch-feud-lawsuit-fx-1202560454/.

11. Gregory Speck, "Olivia de Havilland," *Interview,* February 1987, 62, 67.

12. Higham, *Sisters,* 141.

13. Michael Thornton, "And the Oscar for Sibling Rivalry Goes to . . . the Nine-Decade Feud between Olivia de Havilland and Joan Fontaine That Is Still Raging," *Mail Online,* September 13, 2010, accessed March 9, 2015, http://www.dailymail.co.uk/femail/article-1311426/Olivia-Havilland-Joan-Fontaine-their. . . .

14. CBS News, "Olivia de Havilland 'Shocked and Saddened' by Sister Joan Fontaine's Death," http://www.cbsnews.com/news/olivia-de-havilland-shocked-and-saddened-by-sister-joan-fontaines-death/December 16, 2013, accessed December

17, 2013, http://www.cbsnews.com/news/olivia-de-havilland-shocked-and-saddened-by-sister-joan-fontaines-death/.

15. Mikelbank, "Olivia de Havilland: A Star Turns 100," 66.

16. Fontaine, *No Bed of Roses,* 30.

17. Gregory Speck, "Joan Fontaine," *Interview,* February 1987, 67.

18. "Stars' Father to Seek Haven in So. America," *Los Angeles Examiner,* November 16, 1940.

19. "Singular Dilemma of Papa de Havilland and His Japanese Wife," *American Weekly,* May 5, 1942, 4.

20. "Reunion Gladdens Dad, but Joan, Olivia Feud Goes On," *Los Angeles Examiner,* September 2, 1950.

21. "Man She Adores Met by Olivia de Havilland," *Los Angeles Times,* November 11, 1952.

22. Fontaine, *No Bed of Roses,* 304.

23. Speck, "Joan Fontaine," 64.

24. Lou Lumenick, "De Havilland on Fontaine, 1957: 'She Seems to Need What I Have,'" *New York Post,* August 20, 2012, accessed December 4, 2015, http://nypost.com/2012/08/20/dehavilland-on-fontaine-1957-she-seems-to-need-what-i-have/.

25. Lou Lumenick, "Sisters in Spite," *New York Post,* August 19, 2012, accessed July 4, 2014, http://nypost.com/2012/08/19/sisters-in-spite/.

26. Fontaine, *No Bed of Roses,* 103, 104.

27. Doyle, "Olivia de Havilland and Joan Fontaine: Oscar Winning Sisters," 21.

28. Feinberg, "New Details about the Joan Fontaine–Olivia de Havilland Feud Revealed."

29. Cosgrave, *Made for Each Other,* 55–56.

30. Bubbeo, *Women of Warner Brothers,* 62.

31. Fontaine, *No Bed of Roses,* 145.

32. Sidney Skolsky, "Tintypes," *Citizen News,* February 12, 1942.

33. Gene Coughlin, "Fighting Sisters," *American Weekly,* May 25, 1947, 4–5.

34. Hedda Hopper, "No Answer—So Olivia and Joan Still Feud," *Chicago Sunday Tribune,* April 10, 1947.

35. "Why Olivia de Havilland Hates Her Sister Joan," *Inside Story,* November 1954, 16–17.

36. Fontaine, *No Bed of Roses,* 187.

37. Speck, "Olivia de Havilland," 65.

38. Feinberg, "New Details about the Joan Fontaine–Olivia de Havilland Feud Revealed."

39. Lumenick, "De Havilland on Fontaine, 1957."

40. Ibid.

41. Ibid.

42. Ibid.

43. Fontaine, *No Bed of Roses,* 298, 299.

44. Ibid., 300.

45. Ibid., 304.

46. Olivia de Havilland, email to the author, August 17, 2016.

47. As quoted in Natalie Finn, "Joan Fontaine Dies, Olivia de Havilland 'Shocked and Saddened' by Sister's Death after Decades-Long Feud," *Eonline*, December 16, 2013, accessed December 17, 2013, http://www.eonline.com/news/491543/joan-fontaine-dies-olivia-de-havilland-shocked-and-saddened-by-sister-s-death-after-decades-long-feud.

48. *What Ever Happened to Baby Jane?* directed by Robert Aldrich (Warner Brothers, 1962; Amazon Video, 2017), DVD.

49. Claudia Luther, "Joan Fontaine, Star of 'Suspicion' and 'Rebecca,' Dies at 96," *latimes.com*, December 15, 2013, accessed December 17, 2013, http://www.latimes.com/obituaries/la-me-joan-fontaine-2013126,0,2145457.story.

50. Belinda Robinson, "Inside the $3 Million Mansion of Hollywood Starlet Joan Fontaine Which Has Been Left to an Animal Charity in Her Will—Along with Her Oscar," *Daily Mail Online*, October 20, 2014, accessed October 20, 2014, http://www.dailymail.co.uk/news/article-2800256/Sale-Joan-Fontaines-house-aid-animal-group.html#ixzz4qRLN4vvs.

51. Speck, "Olivia de Havilland," 62.

11. The Time Is Now

1. Stafford, "Olivia de Havilland's Script Reveals Gifted Mind."

2. Peter Genower, "Olivia de Havilland . . . Too Busy Living Her Life to Write about It," *Family Scene*, September 10–16, 1977.

3. Roderick Mann, "Olivia Keeps Publisher Waiting," *Los Angeles Times*, December 30, 1980.

4. Olivia de Havilland, letter to the author, August 2, 1983.

5. Ibid., May 2, 1986.

6. Ibid., July 11, 1994.

7. Ibid., October 28, 2002.

8. Ibid., July 27, 2009.

9. Ibid., June 4, 2010.

10. Schwartz, "Last Star," 96.

11. Olivia de Havilland, letter to the author, September 22, 2009.

12. Ibid., November 25, 2011.

13. Ibid., February 9, 2015.

14. Olivia de Havilland, conversation with the author, February 23, 2015.

15. Olivia de Havilland, letter to the author, June 9, 2003.

16. Olivia de Havilland, foreword to *Actresses of a Certain Character: Forty Familiar Hollywood Faces from the Thirties to the Fifties*, by Axel Nissen (Jefferson, NC: McFarland, 2007), 1.

17. Olivia de Havilland, letter to the author, June 4, 2010.

18. De Havilland, "Mickey Rooney: The Eternal Boy Wonder."

19. Olivia de Havilland, letter to the author, October 28, 2002.

20. "Olivia de Havilland," *Entertainment Weekly—The 100 Greatest Stars of All Time*, 1997, 96–97.

21. Elaine Berman, "Hollywood's Most Famous Sibling Rivalry," *Time*, April 10, 2015, accessed April 15, 2015, http://time.com/3768918/joan-fontaine-olivia-de-havilland/.

22. Stadiem, "De Havilland's Bumpy Flight," 148.

23. Lobrano, "Catching Up with the Players," 17.

24. Olivia de Havilland, email to the author, August 20, 2016.

25. Mimi, conversation with the author, April 5, 2014.

26. "It Isn't Yoga, It's Love."

27. Lydia Lane, "Yoga Helps Olivia Refuel," *Los Angeles Times*, August 27, 1961, 6.

28. Olivia de Havilland, letter to the author, July 27, 2009.

29. "A Screen Legend Now Sees Clearly," *Business Wire*, July 28, 2008, accessed August 9, 2015, https://www.businesswire.com/news/home/20080728005052/en/Screen-Legend-Sees.

30. "It Isn't Yoga, It's Love."

31. Hedda Hopper, "Olivia de Havilland," 1961, Hedda Hopper Collection, Margaret Herrick Library, Beverly Hills, CA.

32. Lane, "Yoga Helps Olivia Refuel," 6.

33. "Fine Costume and Needlework Including the Dior Wardrobe of Miss Olivia de Havilland," *Lodi News-Sentinel*, June 30, 1993, 4.

34. Maxine Mesinger, "De Havilland Sells Collection," *Houston Chronicle*, June 30, 1993. 1.

35. Olivia de Havilland, letter to the author, October 28, 2002.

36. Ibid.

37. Ibid., June 9, 2003.

38. As quoted in Genower, "Olivia de Havilland."

39. Olivia de Havilland, letter to the author, June 9, 2003.

40. Gary Polden, email to the author, September 12, 2012.

41. "Actress Pays Flying Visit to Honour Pioneer," 5.

42. "Olivia de Havilland Rises to the Occasion," *Los Angeles Times*, June 17, 2006, accessed July 12, 2012, http://stylescenes.latimes.com/fashion/2006/06/olivia_de_Havil.html.

43. Amy Bondurant and David Dunn, *Washington Social Diary*, September 2010, accessed October 20, 2010, http://www.newyorksocialdiary.com/node/1903613.

44. Associated Press, "Olivia de Havilland Honored by French President," NPR, September 9, 2010, accessed October 9, 2010, http://www.npr.org/termplates/story/story.php?storyId+1297557.

45. Olivia de Havilland, email to the author, September 7, 2016.

46. Nidhi Tehari, "Cannes Film Festival 2015: Producer Megan Ellison, Actresses Jane Fonda and Olivia de Havilland Honored as 'Women in Motion,'" *International Business Times*, May 18, 2015, accessed May 21, 2015, http://www.ibtimes.com/cannes-film-festival-2015-producer-megan-ellisonactresses-jane-fonda-olivia-de-1926968.

47. Withnall, "*Gone with the Wind* Actress Alicia Rhett Dies Aged 98."

48. Sally Tippett Raines, "*GWTW* Actors Olivia de Havilland, Alicia Rhett Heard from at Cherry Blossom Festival," *Gone with the Wind* booklet, May 4, 2012, accessed

May 6, 2012, http://gwtwbook.wordpress.com/2012/05/04/gwtw-actors-olivia-de-havilland-alicia-rhett-heard-from-at-cherry-blossom-festival/.

49. Alexander, "'Gone with the Wind' 75 Years," Life 2D.

50. Christie's, "Olivia de Havilland Sweater: 1939."

51. Hermione Eyre, "Hollywood's Sweetheart," *ES Magazine*, March 19, 2010.

52. John Meroney, "The Interview: Olivia de Havilland," *Garden and Gun*, December–January 2015, accessed March 12, 2015, http://gardenandgun.com/print/article/interview-olivia-de-havilland.

53. Olivia de Havilland, letter to the author, September 22, 2009.

54. Dan Barry, "Up Next, a Classic Who Loves Old Films," *New York Times*, November 23, 2014, Arts 14.

55. Liz Smith and Denis Ferrara, "Liz Smith: Celebration of Life," *New York Social Diary*, May 6, 2017, accessed December 9, 2017, http://www.newyorksocialdiary.com/guest-diary/2017/liz-smith-celebration-of-life.

56. Julie Miller, "How Jared Leto Charmed Hollywood Legend Olivia de Havilland," *Vanity Fair*, July 1, 2016, accessed September 6, 2016, https://www.vanityfair.com/hollywood/2016/07/jared-leto-olivia-de-havilland.

57. Schwartz, "Last Star," 96.

58. McHenry, "Olivia de Havilland Sent a Gorgeous Email about How She Doesn't Watch *Feud*."

59. Olivia de Havilland, email to the author, April 6, 2018.

60. Daniel Holloway, "Olivia de Havilland Looks to Revive 'Feud' Defamation Lawsuit," *Page Six*, May 4, 2018, accessed May 5, 2018, https://pagesix.com/2018/05/04/olivia-de-havilland-looks-to-revive-feud-defamation-lawsuit/?utm_source=email_sitebuttons&utm_medium=site%20buttons&utm_campaign=site%20buttons.

61. Trétiack, "Saint James Paris: A Crazy Chic State of Mind," 3.

62. Olivia de Havilland, conversation with the author, December 5, 2017.

63. Olivia de Havilland, email to the author, July 12, 2017.

BIBLIOGRAPHY

Academy of Motion Picture Arts and Sciences. "Academy Awards Acceptance Speeches." 2009. Accessed August 8, 2011. http://aaspeechesdb.oscars.org/results.aspx?AC=PREV_RECORD&XC=/results.aspx&.

———. "The 19th Academy Awards/1947." *Experience over Eight Decades of the Oscars from 1927 to 2015.* Accessed June 27, 2015. https://www.oscars.org/oscars/ceremonies/1947.

"Actress Feared Death, Tells Court of Mate's Violence." *Los Angeles Examiner,* August 27, 1952.

"Actress Pays Flying Visit to Honour Pioneer." *Times* (London), July 31, 1997.

The Adventurers. Directed by Lewis Gilbert. Avco Embassy and Paramount, 1970. Warner Archive Collection, 2013. DVD.

The Adventures of Errol Flynn. Directed by David Heeley. Turner Classic Movies, 2005. Warner Home Video, 2006. DVD.

The Adventures of Robin Hood. Directed by Michael Curtiz and William Keighley. Warner Brothers, 1938. Warner Home Video, 2001. DVD.

AFI Life Achievement Award: A Tribute to Bette Davis. CBS, 1977. Loving the Classics, n.d. DVD.

Agee, James. "*The Dark Mirror* (1946 Film), by Robert Siodmak." *Nation,* November 9, 1946. Accessed October 24, 2017. http://www.unz.org/Pub/Nation-1946nov09-00536a02.

Airport '77. Directed by Jerry Jameson. Universal, 1977. Universal Pictures Home Entertainment, 2004. DVD.

Alexander, Bryan. "'Gone with the Wind' 75 Years; What Endures in This Movie Classic?" *USA Today,* September 25, 2014.

Alibi Ike. Directed by Ray Enright. Warner Brothers, 1935. Warner Home Video, 2010. DVD.

The Ambassador's Daughter. Directed by Norman Krasna. Norman Krasna Productions and United Artists, 1956. Education 2000, 2005. DVD.

American Film Institute. "Olivia de Havilland." *Dialogue on Film* 4, no. 3 (December 1974): 3–25.

Anastasia: The Mystery of Anna. Directed by Marvin J. Chomsky. Telecom Entertainment, 1998. Mill Creek Entertainment, 2011. DVD.

Andrews, Emily. "Errol Flynn? He Never Had His Wicked Way with Me, Says *Gone with the Wind* Star Olivia de Havilland." *Daily Mail,* June 17, 2009. Accessed December

18, 2016. http://www.dailymail.co.uk/tvshowbiz/article-1193489/Errol-Flynn-He-wicked-way-says-Gone-With-The-Wind-star-Olivia-Havilland.html.

"And the Winner Is . . . (the Oscars of 1963)." Episode of *Feud.* Directed by Ryan Murphy. FX, 2017.

Anthony Adverse. Directed by Mervyn LeRoy. Warner Brothers, 1936. Warner Archive Collection, 2015. DVD.

Ardmore, Jane. "Parents Can Be Wrong!" 1962. Jane Ardmore Collection, Margaret Herrick Library, Beverly Hills, CA.

Arnold, Jeremy. *Devotion.* Turner Classic Movies, 2014. Accessed April 20, 2014. http://www.tcm.com/this-month/article/159658|0/Devotion.html.

Associated Press. "Olivia de Havilland Honored by French President." NPR, September 9, 2010. Accessed October 9, 2010. http://www.npr.org/termplates/story/story.php?storyId+1297557.

Atkinson, Brooks. "Olivia de Havilland Comes to Broadway in a Revival of Bernard Shaw's 'Candida.'" *New York Times,* April 23, 1952. Accessed February 11, 2018. https://timesmachine.nytimes.com/timesmachine/1952/04/23/93565852.html?action=click&contentCollection=Archives&module=ArticleEndCTA&region=ArchiveBody&pgtype=article&pageNumber=23.

Atlanta Historical Society. Gone with the Wind: *The Facts about the Fiction.* Atlanta: Atlanta Historical Society, 1989.

The Aviator. Directed by Martin Scorsese. Warner Brothers and Miramax, 2004. Warner Home Video, 2005. DVD.

Barry, Dan. "Up Next, a Classic Who Loves Old Films." *New York Times,* November 23, 2014.

Basinger, Jeanine. *The Star Machine.* New York: Alfred A. Knopf, 2007.

———. *A Woman's View.* London: Chatto & Windus, 1993.

Bean, Kendra. *Vivien Leigh: An Intimate Portrait.* Philadelphia: Running Press, 2013.

Behlmer, Rudy. "Flynn on Target with *Robin Hood.*" *Journal of the Alex Film Society* 1, no. 3 (March 1995): 1.

———. *Memo from David O. Selznick.* New York: Viking Press, 1972.

Belloni, Matthew. "De Havilland Lawsuit Resonates through Hollywood." Reuters, August 23, 2007. Accessed April 20, 2014. http://www.reuters.com/article/2007/08/24/industry-lawsuit-dcidUSN2329585820070824.

Berg, A. Scott. *Goldwyn.* New York: Alfred A. Knopf, 1989.

Bergman, Ingrid, and Alan Burgess. *Ingrid Bergman: My Story.* New York: Delacorte Press, 1980.

Berk, Philip. "Hollywood's Most Bitter and Longest-Running Feud." Hollywood Foreign Press Association, October 21, 2013. Accessed January 20, 2014. http://www.hfpa.org/2013/10/hollywoods-most-bitter-and-longest-ru. . . .

Berman, Elaine. "Hollywood's Most Famous Sibling Rivalry." *Time,* April 10, 2015. Accessed April 15, 2015. http://time.com/3768918/joan-fontaine-olivia-de-havilland/.

Bondurant, Amy, and David Dunn. *Washington Social Diary,* September 2010. Accessed October 20, 2010. http://www.newyorksocialdiary.com/node/1903613.

Bosworth, Patricia. *Montgomery Clift: A Biography.* New York: Harcourt Brace Jovanovich, 1978.

Botto, Louis. "At This Theatre: The Ethel Barrymore." *Playbill,* April 2016.

Breen, Jay. "Marriage Ends for Actress." *New York Daily News,* May 22, 1952.

Breen, Max. "Olivia Comes out of Hiding." *Picturegoer Weekly,* May 28, 1938.

British Film Institute. Tape recording of lecture by Olivia de Havilland, London, August 28, 1971.

Broadway League. *The Heiress. Internet Broadway Data Base, 2001–15.* Accessed February 4, 2014. http://www.ibdb.com/production.php?id=1566.

Bubbeo, Daniel. *The Women of Warner Brothers.* Jefferson, NC: McFarland, 2002.

Burton, Richard. *The Richard Burton Diaries.* Edited by Chris Williams. New Haven, CT: Yale University Press, 2013.

Byrne, Bridget. "Airborne with Olivia de Havilland." *Los Angeles Herald-Examiner,* September 2, 1976.

Call It a Day. Directed by Archie Mayo. Warner Brothers, 1937. Warner Archive Collection, 2010. DVD.

Call It a Day. Internet Broadway Database. Accessed May 27, 2014. http://www.ibdb.com/production.php?id=12066.

Captain Blood. Directed by Michael Curtiz. Warner Brothers, 1935. Warner Home Video, 2005. DVD.

Captain Blood: A Swashbuckler Is Born. Directed by Karen Hillhouse. Turner Classic Movies, 2005. Warner Home Video, 2005. DVD.

Carroll, Harrison. "Olivia de Havilland Legally Separated." *Los Angeles Herald-Examiner,* March 15, 1965.

Carroll, Lucille. "Bekim Gets a Yes from Olivia." *Los Angeles Herald-Examiner,* December 13, 1968.

Carter, Graydon, ed. *Vanity Fair's Proust Questionnaire.* New York: Rodale, 2009.

CBS News. "Olivia de Havilland 'Shocked and Saddened' by Sister Joan Fontaine's Death." December 16, 2013. Accessed December 17, 2013. http://www.cbsnews.com/news/olivia-de-havilland-shocked-and-saddened-by-sister-joan-fontaines-death/.

Chandler, Charlotte. *Not the Girl Next Door.* New York: Applause Theatre & Cinema Books, 2008.

The Charge of the Light Brigade. Directed by Michael Curtiz. Warner Brothers, 1936. Warner Home Video, 2007. DVD.

Chierichetti, David. *Mitchell Leisen: Hollywood Director.* Los Angeles: Photoventures Press, 1995.

———. "Olivia in London." *Film Fan Monthly* 124 (October 1971): 3.

Chow, Andrew R. "Memphis Theatre Cancels 'Gone with the Wind' Screening." *New York Times,* August 27, 2017. Accessed September 21, 2017. https://www.nytimes.com/2017/08/27/movies/memphis-theater-cancels-gone-with-the-wind-screening.html?emc=eta1&_r=0.

Christie's. "Olivia de Havilland Bonnet from *The Heiress.*" December 20, 2012. Accessed June 26, 2012. https://www.christies.com/lotfinder/Lot/olivia-de-havilland-bonnet-from-the-heiress-4040984-details.aspx.

———. "Olivia de Havilland Sweater: 1939." Lot 112/sale 114, 2002. Accessed June 12, 2017. http://www.christies.com/lotfinder/LotDetailsPrintable.aspx?from+salesummary&intObjectID=3956526.

Coffin, Patricia. "Success Becomes Olivia." *Look*, March 18, 1947.

Cole, Hubert. "Let Olivia Laugh It Off." *Picturegoer*, June 14, 1941.

"Congress Due to Aid Olivia and Romance." *Los Angeles Times*, June 3, 1958.

Cornwell, Rupert. "Sibling Rivalry: Hollywood's Oldest Feud." *Independent*, May 15, 2008. Accessed June 9, 2012. http://www.independent.co.uk/arts-entertainment/films/features/sibling-rivalry-hollywoods-oldest-feud-828301.html.

Cosgrave, Bronwyn. *Made for Each Other: Fashion and the Academy Awards*. London: Bloomsbury, 2008.

Cotten, Joseph. *Vanity Will Get You Somewhere*. London: Columbus Books, 1987.

Cottom, J. V. "Olivia de Havilland." Translated by Anne-Marie Keighan. *Ciné-Revue* 56, no. 53 (December 30, 1976): 10–13.

Coughlin, Gene. "Fighting Sisters." *American Weekly*, May 25, 1947.

Cowles, Fleur. *She Made Friends and Kept Them*. London: HarperCollins, 1996.

Crowther, Bosley. "*Devotion*, a Fictionized Tale of Bronte Sisters, at Strand." *New York Times*, April 6, 1946. Accessed October 12, 2014. http://www.nytimes.com/movie/review?res=9F03E7D81139E53ABC4E53DFB266838D659EDE.

———. "'The Heiress,' with Olivia de Havilland in Leading Role, Arrives at Music Hall." *New York Times*, October 7, 1949. Accessed November 6, 2017. http://www.nytimes.com/movie/review?res=9400E7DC143BE23BBC4F53DFB6678382659EDE.

———. "'Hold Back the Dawn,' a Poignant Romance, at the Paramount—'Harmon of Michigan' at Criterion." *New York Times*, October 2, 1941. Accessed January 23, 2018. http://www.nytimes.com/movie/review?res=9E06E3D8113FE13BBC4A53DFB667838A659EDE.

———. "'The Male Animal,' with Henry Fonda, Olivia de Havilland, at Strand—'Strange Case of Dr. Rx' Arrives at the Rialto." *New York Times*, March 28, 1942. Accessed January 26, 2018. http://www.nytimes.com/movie/review?res=9B04E0DA143CE33BBC4051DFB5668389659EDE.

———. "'My Cousin Rachel' Presented at the Rivoli—'Ruby Gentry,' 'No Time for Flowers' Bow." *New York Times*, December 26, 1952. Accessed February 15, 2014. http://www.nytimes.com/movie/review?res=9501EFDD1E3AE23BBC4E51DFB4678389649EDE.

———. "The Screen; 'Deception,' Warner Film with Bette Davis and Claude Rains, at Hollywood—'Dark Mirror,' New Mystery, at the Criterion." *New York Times*, October 19, 1946. Accessed February 9, 2012. http://www.nytimes.com/movie/review?_r=2&res=9B05E1D61338E53ABC4152DFB667838D659EDE.

"Daphne du Maurier." *My Cousin Rachel*. Fox Searchlight Pictures, 2017. 20th Century Fox Home Entertainment, 2017. DVD.

D'Árc, James V. "'Perfect Manners': An Interview with Olivia de Havilland." In *American Classic Screen Interviews*, edited by John C. Tibbetts and James M. Welsh. 1979. Reprint, Lanham, MD: Scarecrow Press, 2010.

Dargis, Manohla. "Kiss Him Deadly." *New York Times,* June 9, 2017.
The Dark Mirror. Directed by Robert Siodmak. International Pictures, 1946. Olive Films, 2012. DVD.
Davis, Bette. Foreword to *The Films of Olivia de Havilland,* by Tony Thomas. Secaucus, NJ: Citadel Press, 1983.
Deelder, J. A. *Portret van Olivia de Havilland.* Amsterdam: De Bezige Bij, 1985.
de Havilland, Olivia. "Bouboule." *Ladies' Home Journal,* June 1975.
———. "Come out Fighting." *Films and Filming* 12, no. 6 (March 1966): 20–21.
———. "The Dream That Never Died." *Look,* December 12, 1967.
———. *Every Frenchman Has One.* New York: Random House, 1962.
———. Foreword to *Actresses of a Certain Character: Forty Familiar Hollywood Faces from the Thirties to the Fifties,* by Axel Nissen. Jefferson, NC: McFarland, 2007.
———. "I Married a Frenchman." *Los Angeles Times,* May 20, 1956.
———. "Mickey Rooney: The Eternal Boy Wonder." *Time,* April 10, 2014. Accessed December 11, 2017. http://time.com/57843/mickey-rooney-olivia-de-havilland/.
———. "The Role I Liked Best." *Saturday Evening Post,* March 1, 1947.
———. ". . . Where Am I? I'm in France, That's Where!" *McCall's,* August 1961.
de Havilland, Olivia, as told to Alice Craig Greene. "How I Met My Husband." *Motion Picture Magazine,* March 1947.
"De Havilland, Olivia—Actress." Contracts dated March 5, 1941, May 24, 1945, and November 29, 1945. Olivia de Havilland Collection, Margaret Herrick Library, Beverly Hills, CA.
"De Havilland Active for Episcopalians." *Variety,* February 7, 1979.
"De Havilland Film out of London Film Fest." *Los Angeles Times,* November 5, 1965.
Devotion. Directed by Curtis Bernhardt. Warner Brothers, 1946. Warner Home Video, 2011. DVD.
"Dinah! And the Ladies Who Took Home Oscar." *The Dinah Shore Show,* 1977. Accessed June 6, 2015. https://www.youtube.com/watch?v=14Q8tphR2xw.
"Divorce Seen for Olivia de Havilland." *Los Angeles Times,* May 18, 1952.
Dodge City. Directed by Michael Curtiz. Warner Brothers, 1939. Warner Home Video, 2005. DVD.
Dodge City: Go West, Errol Flynn. Taylor Made Entertainment and Warner Home Video, 2005. DVD.
Doyle, Neil. "Olivia de Havilland and Joan Fontaine: Oscar Winning Sisters." *Films of the Golden Age* 22 (Fall 2000): 21.
———. "Olivia de Havilland Was Not Content to Be Merely a Beautiful Costumed Prop." *Films in Review,* February 1962.
"Dragon Ladies." *Time,* March 19, 1965.
"The Duel/Two for Julie/Aunt Hilly." Directed by Ray Austin. Episode of *The Love Boat.* Aaron Spelling Productions, 1981.
Eames, John Douglas. *The Paramount Story.* New York: Random House, 1987.
Edwards, Anne. *Road to Tara: The Life of Margaret Mitchell.* New Haven, CT: Ticknor & Fields, 1983.
Elizabeth and Essex: Battle Royal. Taylor Made Entertainment and Warner Home Video, 2005. DVD.

Eyre, Hermione. "Hollywood's Sweetheart." *ES Magazine,* March 19, 2010.

Fagan, Myron C. *Moscow over Hollywood.* Los Angeles: R. C. Cary, 1948.

Feinberg, Scott. "New Details about the Joan Fontaine–Olivia de Havilland Feud Revealed." *Hollywood Reporter,* December 17, 2013. Accessed December 20, 2013. http://www.hollywoodreporter.com/race/joan-fontaine-olivia-de-havilland-666087.

The Fifth Musketeer. Directed by Ken Annakin. S&T Films Berlin, 1979.

"Films on TV." *Films in Review,* February 1978.

"Fine Costume and Needlework Including the Dior Wardrobe of Miss Olivia de Havilland." *Lodi News-Sentinel,* June 30, 1993.

Finler, Joel W. *The Hollywood Story.* New York: Crown, 1988.

Finn, Natalie. "Joan Fontaine Dies, Olivia de Havilland 'Shocked and Saddened' by Sister's Death after Decades-Long Feud." *Eonline,* December 16, 2013. Accessed December 17, 2013. http://www.eonline.com/news/491543/joan-fontaine-dies-olivia-de-havilland-shocked-and-saddened-by-sister-s-death-after-decades-long-feud.

Flynn, Errol. *My Wicked, Wicked Ways.* New York: G. P. Putnam's Sons, 1959.

Fontaine, Joan. *No Bed of Roses: An Autobiography.* New York: William Morrow, 1978.

"For Olivia, Paris Spells Home." *Variety,* March 16, 1988.

Forster, Margaret. *Daphne du Maurier.* 1993. Reprint, London: Arrow Books, 2007.

Four's a Crowd. Directed by Michael Curtiz. Warner Brothers, 1938. Warner Home Video, 2009. DVD.

French, Philip. "Review: Critics: Philip French's Screen Legends: No. 73 Olivia de Havilland 1916–." *Observer,* November 1, 2009, 12.

"French Fete de Havilland at Her Wedding." *Daily Mirror,* April 2, 1955.

Gabbard, Glen O., and Krin Gabbard. *Psychiatry and the Cinema.* 2nd ed. Washington, DC: American Psychiatric Press, 1999.

Gates, Anita. "The Good Girl Gets the Last Word." *New York Times,* November 7, 2004.

Gaver, Jack. "Along the Great White Way." *Los Angeles Daily News,* August 25, 1951.

Genower, Peter. "Olivia de Havilland . . . Too Busy Living Her Life to Write about It." *Family Scene,* September 10–16, 1977.

Gold Is Where You Find It. Directed by Michael Curtiz. Warner Brothers, 1938. Warner Home Video, 2014. DVD.

Gone with the Wind. Directed by Victor Fleming. Selznick International Pictures, 1939. Warner Home Video, 2004. DVD.

Goodwin, Betty. "Olivia Sets Sail." *Los Angeles Times,* January 18, 1981.

Government Girl. Directed by Dudley Nichols. RKO, 1943. Warner Home Video, 2014. DVD.

Grant, Lee. *I Said Yes to Everything.* New York: Penguin, 2014.

The Great Garrick. Directed by James Whale. Warner Brothers, 1937. Warner Home Video, 2009. DVD.

Grobel, Lawrence. *The Hustons: The Life and Times of a Hollywood Dynasty.* 1989. Reprint, New York: Cooper Square Press, 2000.

Hadleigh, Boze. *Hollywood and Whine.* Secaucus, NJ: Birch Lane Books, 1998.

Hard to Get. Directed by Ray Enright. Warner Brothers, 1938. Warner Home Video, 2014. DVD.

Hark, Ina Rae. "Errol Flynn and Olivia de Havilland: Romancing through History." In *Glamour in a Golden Age: Movie Stars of the 1930s,* edited by Adrienne L. McLean. New Brunswick, NJ: Rutgers University Press, 2011.

Harry Ransom Center. *The Greenwich Village Bookshop Door: Lawrence Langner,* n.d. Accessed June 23, 2015. http://norman.hrc.utexas.edu/bookshopdoor/signature.cfm?item=106#1.

Haskell, Molly. *Frankly, My Dear:* Gone with the Wind *Revisited.* New Haven, CT: Yale University Press, 2009.

———. *From Reverence to Rape.* Harmondsworth, UK: Penguin Books, 1974.

Hawkins, William. "Olivia's 'Juliet' Grows Young Again." *New York World Telegram and Sun,* March 12, 1951.

Head, Edith. "What Are You Going to Wear?" 1945. Edith Head Papers, Margaret Herrick Library, Beverly Hills, CA.

The Heiress. Directed by William Wyler. Paramount, 1949. Universal Cinema Classics, 2008. DVD.

Here's Looking at You, Warner Bros. Directed by Robert Guenette. Robert Guenette Productions, TNT, and Warner Bros. Television, 1991. Warner Home Video, 2003. DVD.

Higham, Charles. *Olivia and Joan.* Sevenoaks, UK: New English Library, 1986.

———. *Sisters: The Story of Olivia de Havilland and Joan Fontaine.* New York: Dell, 1986.

Hillenbrand, Laura. *Unbroken.* New York: Random House, 2010.

Hitchens, Christopher. "O Brother, Why Art Thou?" *Vanity Fair,* May 16, 2005. Accessed July 21, 2017. http://www.vanityfair.com/culture/features/2008/03/proust_fontaine200803.

Hold Back the Dawn. Directed by Mitchell Leisen. Paramount, 1941. Universal, 2010. DVD.

Hold Back the Dawn: Notes Taken at Random while in Mexicali and Calexico. January 7, 1941. Margaret Herrick Library, Beverly Hills, CA.

Holloway, Daniel. "Olivia de Havilland Looks to Revive 'Feud' Defamation Lawsuit." *Page Six,* May 4, 2018. Accessed May 5, 2018. https://pagesix.com/2018/05/04/olivia-de-havilland-looks-to-revive-feud-defamation-lawsuit/?utm_source=email_sitebuttons&utm_medium=site%20buttons&utm_campaign=site%20buttons.

Hollywood Independent Citizens Committee of the Arts, Sciences and Professions. "Statement of Policy," n.d. HICCASP file, Margaret Herrick Library, Beverly Hills, CA.

Hollywood Reporter, December 13, 1985, February 21, 1986, January 8, 1987. Olivia de Havilland Collection, Margaret Herrick Library, Beverly Hills, CA.

Honan, William H. "Marcus Aurelius Goodrich, 93, Writer Known for Naval Stories." *New York Times,* October 22, 1991. Accessed June 23, 2015. https://c01130.mail.live.com/?tid=cmgFENLtoZ5RG9GwAiZMF9dg2&fv=1&fid=flinbx.

Hopper, Hedda. "The Goodriches." N.d. (circa 1950). Olivia de Havilland Collection, Margaret Herrick Library, Beverly Hills, CA.

———. "No Answer—So Olivia and Joan Still Feud." *Chicago Sunday Tribune,* April 10, 1947.

———. "Olivia de Havilland." September 10, 1952. Hedda Hopper Collection, Margaret Herrick Library, Beverly Hills, CA.

———. "Olivia de Havilland." March 17, 1961. Hedda Hopper Collection, Margaret Herrick Library, Beverly Hills, CA.

———. "Olivia de Havilland." 1961. Hedda Hopper Collection, Margaret Herrick Library, Beverly Hills, CA.

———. "Olivia de Havilland Enjoys Bride's Role." *Los Angeles Times,* December 1, 1946.

———. "Olivia de Havilland Here for Film Role." *Los Angeles Times,* January 23, 1963.

———. "Olivia de Havilland Interview." March 1959. Hedda Hopper Collection, Margaret Herrick Library, Beverly Hills, CA.

Hubler, Richard G. "Olivia—The Bellicose Belle." *Coronet,* July 1958.

Hunt, George W. "Gone with the Wind." *America* 178, no. 1 (January 3–10, 1998): 2.

Hush, Hush, Sweet Charlotte. Directed by Robert Aldrich. 20th Century Fox, 1964. 20th Century Fox Home Entertainment, 2005. DVD.

Hush Up Sweet Charlotte. Directed by William Clift. Everything Is Going to Be Just Fine Productions, 2015. Amazon.com, 2018. Streamed.

Huston, John. Autobiographical notes, chap. VI. N.d. John Huston Collection, Margaret Herrick Library, Beverly Hills, CA.

———. *An Open Book.* New York: Alfred A. Knopf, 1980.

Internet Movie Data Base. *The Adventures of Robin Hood* (1938). Accessed March 12, 2015. http://www.imdb.com/title/tt0029843/?ref_=nv_sr_1.

———. *Hold Back the Dawn.* Accessed April 27, 2013. http://www.imdb.com/title/tt0033722/?ref_=nv_sr_1.

———. *My Love Came Back.* Accessed June 20, 2012. http://www.imdb.com/title/tt0032829/?ref_=fn_al_tt_1.

———. *Noon Wine.* Trivia, 2015.

———. *The Snake Pit.* Accessed June 28, 2015. http://www.imdb.com/title/tt0040806/awards?ref_=tt_awd.

In This Our Life. Directed by John Huston. Warner Brothers, 1942. Warner Home Video, 2008. DVD.

The Irish in Us. Directed by Lloyd Bacon. Warner Brothers, 1935. Warner Home Video, 2014. DVD.

"It Isn't Yoga, It's Love." *Sunday Dispatch,* September 21, 1958.

It's Love I'm After. Directed by Archie Mayo. Warner Brothers, 1937. Warner Home Video, 2009. DVD.

James, Henry. *Washington Square.* 1881. Reprint, Harmondsworth, UK: Penguin Books, 1968.

Jancovich, Mark. "'Rebecca's Ghost': Horror, the Gothic and the du Maurier Film Adaptations." In *The Daphne du Maurier Companion,* edited by Helen Taylor. London: Virago Press, 2007.

Johnson, Erskine. "Big Role Lures de Havilland Home." *Los Angeles Daily News*, October 15, 1954.

Jorgensen, Jay. *Edith Head: The Fifty-Year Career of Hollywood's Greatest Costume Designer.* Philadelphia: Running Press, 2010.

Kaplan, E. A. "Classical Hollywood Film and Melodrama." In *American Cinema and Hollywood: Critical Approaches*, edited by John Hill and Pamela Church Gibson. Oxford: Oxford University Press, 2000.

Kass, Judith M. *Olivia de Havilland.* New York: Pyramid Books, 1976.

Kelly-Barton, Casey. "Frankly My Dear . . . The Ransom Center Remembers *Gone with the Wind.*" *Texas Journey*, September–October 2014.

Kenny, Glenn. "Olivia de Havilland Remembers 'The Heiress.'" *Premiere.com*, February 2, 2007.

Kirgo, Julie. "My Cousin Rachel." DVD booklet essay. *My Cousin Rachel*, Twilight Time, 2011. DVD.

Knight, Arthur. "Ghouls Rush In." *Saturday Review*, January 23, 1965.

Kramer, Stanley, and Thomas M. Coffey. *A Mad, Mad, Mad, Mad World: A Life in Hollywood.* New York: Harcourt Brace, 1997.

"Ladd, Olivia de Havilland Suffer Burns." *Los Angeles Times*, September 24, 1957.

Lady in a Cage. Directed by Walter Grauman. Paramount, 1964. Warner Archive Collection, 2013. DVD.

LaGuardia, Robert. *Monty: A Biography of Montgomery Clift.* New York: Arbor House, 1977.

Lane, Lydia. "U.S. Women Aggressive, Says Actress." *Los Angeles Times*, October 13, 1957.

———. "Yoga Helps Olivia Refuel." *Los Angeles Times*, August 27, 1961.

The Last Hunters. Directed by Robert Gist. Episode of *The Danny Thomas Hour.* Thomas-Spelling Productions and NBC-TV, 1968.

"A Law for Olivia." *Variety*, June 4, 1958.

"Leftists' Trickery Told by Olivia de Havilland." *Los Angeles Times*, September 6, 1958.

Leonard, Tom. "Has There Ever Been a Sibling Rivalry More Venomous than This? Now Joan Fontaine Is Dead at 96, Her Sister Olivia de Havilland Will Be Livid She's Stolen the Headlines Again." *Mail Online*, December 17, 2013. Accessed December 22, 2016. http://www.dailymail.co.uk/femail/article-2524952/Joan-Fontaines-d. . . .

"Let Olivia Laugh It Off." *Picturegoer*, June 14, 1941.

Libel. Directed by Anthony Asquith. Metro Goldwyn Mayer, 1959. Warner Home Video, 2011. DVD.

Lichfield, John. "Golden Girl: The Divine Olivia de Havilland." *Independent*, July 14, 2009. Accessed July 15, 2009. http://www.independent.co.uk/arts-entertainment/films/features/golden-girl-the-divine-olivia-de-havilland-1744807.html.

"The Life Story of Olivia de Havilland." *Picture Show*, May 6, 1944.

"The Life Story of Olivia de Havilland." *Picture Show*, March 7, 1953.

Light in the Piazza. Directed by Guy Green. Metro Goldwyn Mayer, 1962. Warner Home Video, 2011. DVD.

Lindsey, Robert. "Olivia's Life Is Buzzing with Change." *New York Times,* November 16, 1977.

———. "Reunion Recalls Those Gone with the Wind." *New York Times,* December 31, 1979. Accessed July 12, 2012. http://query.nytimes.com/gst/abstract.html?res=9405EFDD1538E732A25752C3A9649D946890D6CF.

Lobrano, Alexander. "Catching Up with the Players." *TV Guide,* December 23–29, 2000.

Lumenick, Lou. "De Havilland on Fontaine, 1957: 'She Seems to Need What I Have.'" *New York Post,* August 20, 2012. Accessed December 4, 2015. http://nypost.com/2012/08/20/dehavilland-on-fontaine-1957-she-seems-to-need-what-i-have/.

———. "Sisters in Spite." *New York Post,* August 19, 2012. Accessed July 4, 2014. http://nypost.com/2012/08/19/sisters-in-spite/.

Luther, Claudia. "Joan Fontaine, Star of 'Suspicion' and 'Rebecca,' Dies at 96." *Latimes.com,* December 15, 2013. Accessed December 17, 2013. http://www.latimes.com/obituaries/la-me-joan-fontaine-2013126,0,2145457.story.

Maddaus, Gene. "Olivia de Havilland Says She Never Called Her Sister a 'Bitch,' Despite 'Feud' Scene." *Variety,* September 15, 2017. Accessed September 15, 2017. http://variety.com/2017/tv/news/olivia-de-havilland-bitch-feud-lawsuit-fx-1202560454/.

Madsen, Axel. *John Huston.* Garden City, NY: Doubleday, 1978.

———. *William Wyler.* New York: Thomas Y. Crowell, 1973.

The Male Animal. Directed by Elliott Nugent. Warner Brothers, 1942. Warner Archive Collection, 2012. DVD.

"'The Male Animal,' with Henry Fonda, Olivia de Havilland, at Strand—'Strange Case of Dr. Rx' Arrives at the Rialto." *New York Times,* March 28, 1942. Accessed January 26, 2018. http://www.nytimes.com/movie/review?res=9B04E0DA143CE33BBC4051DFB5668389659EDE.

"Man She Adores Met by Olivia de Havilland." *Los Angeles Times,* November 11, 1952.

Mann, Roderick. "Olivia Keeps Publisher Waiting." *Los Angeles Times,* December 30, 1980.

Manners, Dorothy. "Ups and Downs." *Los Angeles Herald-Examiner,* June 7, 1964.

Matzen, Robert. *Errol & Olivia: Ego & Obsession in Golden Era Hollywood.* Pittsburgh: GoodKnight Books, 2010.

McHenry, Jackson. "Olivia de Havilland Sent a Gorgeous Email about How She Doesn't Watch *Feud.*" *Vulture,* April 18, 2017. Accessed April 19, 2017. http://www.vulture.com/2017/04/olivia-de-havilland-emails-about-how-she-doesnt-watch-feud.html.

McNulty, Thomas. *Errol Flynn: The Life and Career.* Jefferson, NC: McFarland, 2014.

Medved, Harry, and Michael Medved. *The Golden Turkey Awards: The Worst Achievements in Hollywood History.* New York: Perigee Trade, 1980.

Melanie Remembers: Reflections by Olivia de Havilland. Directed by John Rust. Turner Classic Movies, 2004. Warner Home Video, 2004. DVD.

Meroney, John. "The Interview: Olivia de Havilland." *Garden and Gun*, December–January 2015. Accessed March 12, 2015. http://gardenandgun.com/print/article/interview-olivia-de-havilland.

———. "Olivia de Havilland Recalls Her Role—in the Cold War." *Wall Street Journal*, September 7, 2006. Accessed March 25, 2011. http://www.onlinewsj.com/article/SB115757993223555601.html#prin. . . .

Mesinger, Maxine. "De Havilland Sells Collection." *Houston Chronicle*, June 30, 1993.

Meyers, Jeffrey. *John Huston: Courage and Art*. New York: Crown, 2011.

A Midsummer Night's Dream. Directed by Max Reinhardt. Warner Brothers, 1935. Warner Home Video, 2007. DVD.

Mikelbank, Peter. "Olivia de Havilland: A Star Turns 100." *People*, July 18, 2016.

———. "Olivia de Havilland on Becoming the Oldest Person to Be Named a Dame: I'm Extremely Proud." *People*, June 17, 2017. Accessed June 21, 2017. http://people.com/royals/olivia-de-havilland-oldest-to-be-named-a-dame/.

———. "Olivia de Havilland Opens Up about Her Love for Married Errol Flynn—and Her Romance with Jimmy Stewart." *People*, July 7, 2016. Accessed January 20, 2018. http://people.com/movies/olivia-de-havilland-on-romances-with-errol-flynn-and-jimmy-stewart/.

Miller, Julie. "How Jared Leto Charmed Hollywood Legend Olivia de Havilland." *Vanity Fair*, July 1, 2016. Accessed September 6, 2016. https://www.vanityfair.com/hollywood/2016/07/jared-leto-olivia-de-havilland.

Mitchell, Margaret. *Gone with the Wind*. 1936. Reprint, New York: Pocket Books, 1964.

Mooring, W. H. "Hollywood's Normal Girl." *Film Weekly*, August 21, 1937.

———. "Will 'Livvy' Over-Do It?" *Picturegoer*, February 2, 1946.

Morris, Mary. "Lady Olivia." *PM's Sunday Picture News*, March 23, 1947.

Mosby, Aline. "Actress Says She Won't Remarry." *Los Angeles Daily News*, August 1, 1952.

———. "Leading Man Goes to Bat for Olivia." *Los Angeles Daily News*, December 22, 1951.

"Mother of Joan Fontaine, Olivia de Havilland Dies." *Los Angeles Times*, February 22, 1975.

Mrs. Bumpstead-Leigh. Playbill Vault. N.d. Accessed March 25, 2015. http://www.playbillvault.com/Show/Detail/6287/Mrs-Bumpstead-Leigh.

Munn, Michael. *Richard Burton: Prince of Players*. New York: Skyhorse, 2008.

Murder Is Easy. Directed by Claude Whatham. CBS Entertainment Production, 1982. KNM Home Entertainment, 2017. DVD.

Musto, Michael. "Olivia de Havilland and Joan Fontaine Are Still Alive! My Thoughts." *Village Voice*, July 3, 2012. Accessed July 9, 2012. http://blogs.villagevoice.com/dailymusto/2012/07/olivia_dehavil. . . .

My Cousin Rachel. Directed by Henry Koster. 20th Century Fox, 1952. Twilight Time, 2011. DVD.

My Love Came Back. Directed by Curtis Bernhardt. Warner Brothers, 1940. Warner Home Video, 2011. DVD.

Nathan, George Jean. "Theatre Week." *Los Angeles Examiner,* March 26, 1951.
Nemerov, Alexander. *Wartime Kiss: Visions of the Moment in the 1940s.* Princeton, NJ: Princeton University Press, 2013.
Newman, John K. "Straight out of a Story-Book." *Film Weekly,* May 13, 1939.
"The 'New' Olivia de Havilland Says What She Thinks." *Newsweek,* November 4, 1957.
Niven, David. *Bring on the Empty Horses.* New York: G. P. Putnam's Sons, 1975.
———. *The Moon's a Balloon.* New York: Dell, 1972.
Nolan, William F. *John Huston: King Rebel.* Los Angeles: Sherbourne Press, 1965.
Noland, Claire, and *LA Times.* "Mary Anderson Dies: She Played Maybelle Merriwether in 'Gone with the Wind.'" *Washington Post,* April 12, 2014. Accessed August 9, 2015. https://www.washingtonpost.com/entertainment/mary-anderson-dies-she-played-maybelle-merriwether-in-gone-with-the-wind/2014/04/12/d986e3b8-c193-11e3-b574-f8748871856a_story.html?utm_term=.27d645b85328.
North and South, Book II. Directed by Kevin Connor. David L. Wolper Productions and Warner Bros. Television, 1986. Warner Home Video, 2005. DVD.
Not as a Stranger. Directed by Stanley Kramer. Stanley Kramer Productions, 1955. MGM Home Entertainment, 2011. DVD.
Nugent, Frank S. "The Screen; Joe E. Brown Returns in a Merry Film Version of Ring Lardner's 'Alibi Ike,' at the Cameo." *New York Times,* July 17, 1935. Accessed December 18, 2017. http://www.nytimes.com/movie/review?res=9407E2DB1E39E33ABC4F52DFB166838E629EDE.
———. "The Screen; Technicolor Pretties Up a Feud in 'Gold Is Where You Find It,' at the Strand." *New York Times,* February 14, 1938. Accessed March 3, 2015. http://query.nytimes.com/mem/archive/pdf?res=9A05E3D91F39EE3ABC4C52DFB466883629EE.
Nussbaum, Ben, ed. *Gone with the Wind.* Irvine, CA: 1–5 Publishing, 2014.
O'Brien, Kate. *That Lady.* 1946. Reprint, London: Virago Press, 1988.
"Olivia Asks Steepest Terms in History to Play Broadway 'Juliet.'" *Variety,* August 9, 1950.
"Olivia de Havilland." *Candida* program, 1951.
"Olivia de Havilland." *Entertainment Weekly—The 100 Greatest Stars of All Time,* 1997.
"Olivia de Havilland." *Films Illustrated* 1, no. 4 (October 1971): 3.
"Olivia de Havilland Becomes Bride." *Los Angeles Times,* August 27, 1946.
"Olivia de Havilland Contract Ruling Upheld by High Court." *Los Angeles Examiner,* February 3, 1945.
"Olivia de Havilland Free to Wed French Suitor." *Herald Express,* August 28, 1953.
"Olivia de Havilland Heads Cannes Jury." *Hollywood Reporter,* April 20, 1965.
"Olivia de Havilland Honored by Brazil." *Los Angeles Times,* March 13, 1950.
"Olivia de Havilland Kicks Off Omaha Lecture Series." *Box Office,* October 21, 1974.
"Olivia de Havilland: Proust Questionnaire." *Vanity Fair,* March 2005.
"Olivia de Havilland Rises to the Occasion." *Los Angeles Times,* June 17, 2006. Accessed July 12, 2012. http://stylescenes.latimes.com/fashion/2006/06/olivia_de_Havil.html.

"Olivia de Havilland Tells of Breaking L.A. Red Front." *Los Angeles Examiner,* September 6, 1958.

"Olivia de Havilland to Make TV Dramatic Debut." *Hollywood Reporter,* May 25, 1966.

"Olivia de Havilland to Wed Writer Today." *Los Angeles Examiner,* August 26, 1946.

"Olivia de Havilland Wed to French Film Reporter." *Los Angeles Times,* April 3, 1955.

"Olivia de Havilland Will Feature I Am American Fete." *Los Angeles Examiner,* April 20, 1947.

"Olivia Sues for Divorce, Wants Maps." *Mirror,* July 4, 1952.

Osborne, Robert. "De Havilland: Caine Autobiography 'Untrue.'" *Hollywood Reporter,* December 15, 1992.

———. Foreword to *The Making of* Gone with the Wind, by Steve Wilson. Austin: Harry Ransom Center, University of Texas Press, 2014.

———. Introduction to *The Heiress,* directed by William Wyler. Paramount, 1949. Universal Cinema Classics, 2008. DVD.

———. "Rambling Reporter." *Hollywood Reporter,* December 10 and 22, 1987.

"Oscar Win Shocks Olivia; Crawford Says He's Numb." *Los Angeles Times,* March 25, 1950.

Othman, Frederick C. "Olivia Idol of South Pacific Boys." *Citizen News,* March 25, 1944.

"Parental Discretion Revised." *People,* October 19, 1987.

Parish, James Robert, and Don E. Stanke. *The Leading Ladies.* New Rochelle, NY: Arlington House, 1977.

Parsons, Louella O. "Actress Olivia de Havilland Falters in Fight for Health." *Los Angeles Examiner,* April 4, 1949.

———. "Decree Asked by Actress de Havilland." *Los Angeles Examiner,* July 4, 1952.

———. "Louella O. Parsons in Hollywood: Olivia de Havilland." *Los Angeles Examiner,* May 26, 1946.

———. "Olivia de Havilland Dated for August Visit by Stork." *Los Angeles Examiner,* February 18, 1949.

———. "Olivia de Havilland Has Son." *Los Angeles Examiner,* September 28, 1949.

Patten, Dominic. "Ryan Murphy & FX in Legal Feud with Olivia de Havilland, Who Is Suing over 'Feud.'" *Deadline,* June 30, 2017. Accessed July 1, 2017. http://deadline.com/2017/06/ryan-murphy-fx-sued-olivia-de-havilland-feud-catherine-zeta-jones-1202122984/.

Picardie, Justine. *Coco Chanel: The Legend and the Life.* 2010. Reprint, London: Harper, 2013.

"Plan to Marry." *Los Angeles Times,* August 16, 1953.

Poling, James. "Olivia's World Is the Stage." *Collier's Weekly,* January 13, 1951.

Pope Joan. Directed by Michael Anderson. Columbia Pictures, 1972. Hollywood/DVD, 2005. DVD.

Pratley, Gerald. *The Cinema of John Huston.* Cranbury, NJ: A. S. Barnes, 1977.

Pratt, William. *Scarlett Fever.* New York: Collier Books, 1977.

Princess O'Rourke. Directed by Norman Krasna. Warner Brothers, 1943. Warner Home Video, 2011. DVD.

The Private Lives of Elizabeth and Essex. Directed by Michael Curtiz. Warner Brothers, 1939. Warner Home Video, 2005. DVD.

The Proud Rebel. Directed by Michael Curtiz. Buena Vista, 1958. HBO, 1999. DVD.

Rader, Dotson. "Rewards and Regrets." *Parade,* September 7, 1986.

Radosh, Ronald. "How Olivia de Havilland Bucked Dalton Trumbo and Helped Save Hollywood from Itself." *Daily Beast,* July 7, 2017. Accessed July 7, 2017. https://www.thedailybeast.com/how-olivia-de-havilland-bucked-dalton-trumbo-and-helped-save-hollywood-from-itself.

Rafferty, Terrence. "A Heavy Lift onto the Screen." *New York Times,* April 28, 2013.

———. "Let's See What's Inside That Pretty Head." *New York Times,* November 27, 2011.

Raffles. Directed by Sam Wood. Samuel Goldwyn, 1939. Warner Home Video, 2014. DVD.

Raines, Sally Tippett. "*GWTW* Actors Olivia de Havilland, Alicia Rhett Heard from at Cherry Blossom Festival." *Gone with the Wind* booklet, May 4, 2012. Accessed May 6, 2012. http://gwtwbook.wordpress.com/2012/05/04/gwtw-actors-olivia-de-havilland-alicia-rhett-heard-from-at-cherry-blossom-festival/.

Ravitz, Justin. "Joan Fontaine, Oscar Winning Actress, Dies at 96." *Us Magazine* online, December 13, 2013. Accessed December 22, 2016. http://www.usmagazine.com/celebrity-news/news/joan-fontaine-oscar-winning-actress-dies-at-96-20131612.

"Reunion Gladdens Dad, but Joan, Olivia Feud Goes On." *Los Angeles Examiner,* September 2, 1950.

"Review: 'To Each His Own.'" *Variety,* December 31, 1945. Accessed June 25, 2015. http://variety.com/1945/film/reviews/to-each-his-own-1200414634/.

Robinson, Belinda. "Inside the $3 Million Mansion of Hollywood Starlet Joan Fontaine Which Has Been Left to an Animal Charity in Her Will—Along with Her Oscar." *Daily Mail Online,* October 20, 2014. Accessed October 20, 2014. http://www.dailymail.co.uk/news/article-2800256/Sale-Joan-Fontaines-house-aid-animal-group.html#ixzz4qRLN4vvs.

"Romeo and Juliet." *Variety,* January 24, 1951.

Roots: The Next Generations. Directed by John Erman. David L. Wolper Productions and Warner Bros. Television, 1979. Warner Home Video, 2007. DVD.

Rose, Joel. "Tintype of Olivia de Havilland." Paramount Studios, 1964. Olivia de Havilland Collection, Margaret Herrick Library, Beverly Hills, CA.

The Royal Romance of Charles and Diana. Directed by Peter Leven. Chrysalis-Yellen Productions, 1982.

Rubython, Tom. *And God Created Burton.* London: Myrtle Press, 2011.

Santa Fe Trail. Directed by Michael Curtiz. Warner Brothers, 1940. Marengo Films, 2005. DVD.

Scheuer, Philip K. "Olivia Seeks 'Interesting Ambiguity' in Rachel Role." *Los Angeles Times,* August 3, 1952.

Schwartz, Missy. "The Last Star." *Entertainment Weekly: Special Oscars Guide 2015.* January 30–February 6, 2015.

The Screaming Woman. Directed by Jack Smight. Universal Television, 1972. YouTube.

"The Screen; Audiences Learn about 'Wings of the Navy' at Strand—Three Offerings at Foreign Language House." *New York Times,* February 4, 1939. Accessed March 10, 2015. http://www.nytimes.com/movie/review?res=9A02E6D91F3AE433A25757C0A9649C94894D6C.

"A Screen Legend Now Sees Clearly." *Business Wire,* July 28, 2008. Accessed August 9, 2015. https://www.businesswire.com/news/home/20080728005052/en/Screen-Legend-Sees.

"Screen News and in Hollywood; Paramount Lends Sonny Tufts to RKO Studios in Exchange for Maureen O'Hara." *New York Times,* June 9, 1943. Accessed March 23, 2015. http://query.nytimes.com/gst/abstract.html?res=9D03E2D6173DE13BBC4153DFB066888659EDE.

Sennett, Ted. *Warner Brothers Presents.* New Rochelle, NY: Arlington House, 1971.

Server, Lee. *Robert Mitchum: "Baby, I Don't Care."* London: Faber & Faber, 2002.

Sheppard, Dick. "Olivia de Havilland—from Twelve Oaks to Henning, Tenn." *Los Angeles Herald-Examiner,* November 5, 1978.

Shipman, David. *The Great Movie Stars: The Golden Years.* New York: Crown, 1970.

Sikov, Ed. *Dark Victory: The Life of Bette Davis.* New York: Henry Holt, 2007.

"Singular Dilemma of Papa de Havilland and His Japanese Wife." *American Weekly,* May 5, 1942.

Skolsky, Sidney. "A Practical Sentimentalist." *New York Post Week-end Magazine,* November 9, 1946.

———. "Tintypes." *Citizen News,* February 12, 1942.

Smith, Liz, and Denis Ferrara. "Liz Smith: Celebration of Life." *New York Social Diary,* May 6, 2017. Accessed December 9, 2017. http://www.newyorksocialdiary.com/guest-diary/2017/liz-smith-celebration-of-life.

The Snake Pit. Directed by Anatole Litvak. 20th Century Fox, 1948. 20th Century Fox Studio Classics, 2004. DVD.

Spada, James. *More than a Woman.* 1993. Reprint, London: Time Warner, 2005.

Speck, Gregory. "Joan Fontaine." *Interview,* February 1987.

———. "Olivia de Havilland." *Interview,* February 1987.

Spensley, Dorothy. "Victorian . . . with Variations." *Photoplay,* September 1938.

Spoto, Donald. *High Society: Grace Kelly and Hollywood.* London: Hutchinson, 2009.

Stadiem, William. "De Havilland's Bumpy Flight." *Vanity Fair,* May 2016.

Stafford, Muriel. "Olivia de Havilland's Script Reveals Gifted Mind." *New York Daily News,* December 28, 1950.

"Stars' Father to Seek Haven in So. America." *Los Angeles Examiner,* November 16, 1940.

"The Star They Didn't Forget." *Family Weekly,* May 23, 1965.

The Story of Gone with the Wind. New York: National Publishers, 1969.

The Strawberry Blonde. Directed by Raoul Walsh. Warner Brothers, 1941. Warner Home Video, 2012. DVD.

"Strolling with Olivia." *New York Times,* November 8, 1936.

The Swarm. Directed by Irwin Allen. Warner Brothers, 1978. Warner Home Video, 2012. DVD.

Swinton, Dan. "Arrest Confuses Olivia's Admirer." *St. Louis Citizen-News,* May 31, 1947.

Taplinger, Robert S. "Life Story of Olivia de Havilland." N.d. (circa 1935). Margaret Herrick Library, Beverly Hills, CA.

Taubman, Howard. "Theatre: 'A Gift of Time.'" *New York Times,* February 25, 1962.

Tehari, Nidhi. "Cannes Film Festival 2015: Producer Megan Ellison, Actresses Jane Fonda and Olivia de Havilland Honored as 'Women in Motion.'" *International Business Times,* May 18, 2015. Accessed May 21, 2015. http://www.ibtimes.com/cannes-film-festival-2015-producer-megan-ellisonactresses-jane-fonda-olivia-de-1926968.

Thank Your Lucky Stars. Directed by David Butler. Warner Brothers, 1943. Warner Home Video, 2008. DVD.

That Lady. Directed by Terence Young. 20th Century Fox, 1955. YouTube.

They Died with Their Boots On. Directed by Raoul Walsh. Warner Brothers, 1941. Warner Home Video, 2005. DVD.

This Is Your Life. Ralph Edwards Productions, March 1971. Accessed December 28, 2017. https://www.youtube.com/watch?v=jEkmS919cVM.

Thomas, Bob. *Joan Crawford.* New York: Simon & Schuster, 1978.

———. "Olivia Planning to Do Another Stage Vehicle." *Hollywood Citizen News,* June 9, 1952.

———. *Selznick: The Man Who Produced* Gone with the Wind. Los Angeles: New Millennium Entertainment, 2001.

Thomas, Kevin. "Miss de Havilland in Fright Film." *Los Angeles Times,* January 29, 1972.

Thomas, Tony. *The Films of Olivia de Havilland.* Secaucus, NJ: Citadel Press, 1983.

Thompson, Howard. "Testament of a Roving 'Lady.'" *New York Times,* June 7, 1964.

Thomson, David. "Heiress Olivia," *LA Weekly,* June 9–15, 2006.

———. "Olivia de Havilland." In *The New Biographical Dictionary of Film.* New York: Alfred A. Knopf, 2003.

Thornton, Michael. "And the Oscar for Sibling Rivalry Goes to . . . the Nine-Decade Feud between Olivia de Havilland and Joan Fontaine That Is Still Raging." *Mail Online,* September 13, 2010. Accessed March 9, 2015. http://www.dailymail.co.uk/femail/article-1311426/Olivia-Havilland-Joan-Fontaine-their . . .

Thorpe, Vanessa. "Grace Kelly: Screen Goddess, Princess and Enduring Source of Scandal." *Guardian,* May 10, 2014. Accessed May 25, 2014. http://www.theguardian.com/film/2014/may/11/grace-kelly-grace-of-monaco-film-nicole-kidman-controversy.

To Each His Own. Directed by Mitchell Leisen. Paramount, 1946. Universal, 2010. DVD.

Toubiana, Serge, Florence Müller, and Jerome Hanover. *Stars in Dior.* New York: Rizzoli, 2012.

Trétiack, Philippe. "Saint James Paris: A Crazy Chic State of Mind." *Elle Decoration,* n.d.

Vespa, Mary. "Amid Divorce, Disaster Movies and the Feud with Sister Joan, Olivia de Havilland Finds Solace Serving Her Church." *People,* March 5, 1979.

Vieira, Mark A. *Hollywood Horror: From Gothic to Cosmic.* New York: Harry N. Abrams, 2003.

Warner, Jack. *My First Hundred Years in Hollywood: An Autobiography.* New York: Random House, 1965.

Watts, Jill. *Hattie McDaniel: Black Ambition, White Hollywood.* New York: Amistad, 2007.

Welcome to Sherwood! The Story of "The Adventures of Robin Hood." Directed by Jeff Kurtti. Kurtti-Pellerin and Turner Classic Movies, 2003. Warner Home Video, 2003. DVD.

The Well-Groomed Bride. Directed by Sidney Lanfield. Paramount, 1946.

The Well-Groomed Bride (1946). Turner Classic Movies. Accessed June 1, 2014. http://www.tcm.com/tcmdb/title/95302/The-Well-Groomed-Bride/original-print-info.html.

What Ever Happened to Baby Jane? Directed by Robert Aldrich. Warner Brothers, 1962. Amazon Video, 2017. DVD.

White, Armond. "What the Wind Blew In." *New York Times Book Review,* March 1, 2009.

"Why Olivia de Havilland Hates Her Sister Joan." *Inside Story,* November 1954.

Wilson, Earl. "Olivia, Mate Separated, Share Home." *Los Angeles Herald-Examiner,* June 28, 1965.

———. "Separated . . . but Together." *Los Angeles Herald-Examiner,* December 17, 1966.

Wilson, Elizabeth. "Scarlett O'Havilland." *Liberty,* March 15, 1947.

Wilson, Steve. *The Making of* Gone with the Wind. Austin: Harry Ransom Center, University of Texas Press, 2014.

Wings of the Navy. Directed by Lloyd Bacon. Warner Brothers, 1939. Warner Home Video, 2014. DVD.

Withnall, Adam. "*Gone with the Wind* Actress Alicia Rhett Dies Aged 98." *Independent,* January 5, 2014. Accessed September 12, 2017. http://www.independent.co.uk/news/people/news/gone-with-the-wind-actress-alicia-rhett-dies-aged-98-9039751.html.

The Woman He Loved. Directed by Charles Jarrott. Harlech Television (HTV), 1988.

Yeck, Joanne L. "In the State of California: De Havilland, Plaintiff vs. Warner Bros., Defendant." In *American Classic Screen Features,* edited by John C. Tibbets and James M. Welsh. Lanham, MD: Rowman & Littlefield, 2010.

INDEX

SCREEN CLASSICS

Screen Classics is a series of critical biographies, film histories, and analytical studies focusing on neglected filmmakers and important screen artists and subjects, from the era of silent cinema through the golden age of Hollywood to the international generation of today. Books in the Screen Classics series are intended for scholars and general readers alike. The contributing authors are established figures in their respective fields. This series also serves the purpose of advancing scholarship on film personalities and themes with ties to Kentucky.

Series Editor

Patrick McGilligan

Books in the Series

Olivia de Havilland: Lady Triumphant
Victoria Amador

Mae Murray: The Girl with the Bee-Stung Lips
Michael G. Ankerich

Hedy Lamarr: The Most Beautiful Woman in Film
Ruth Barton

Rex Ingram: Visionary Director of the Silent Screen
Ruth Barton

Conversations with Classic Film Stars: Interviews from Hollywood's Golden Era
James Bawden and Ron Miller

You Ain't Heard Nothin' Yet: Interviews with Stars from Hollywood's Golden Era
James Bawden and Ron Miller

Von Sternberg
John Baxter

Hitchcock's Partner in Suspense: The Life of Screenwriter Charles Bennett
Charles Bennett, edited by John Charles Bennett

Hitchcock and the Censors
John Billheimer

My Life in Focus: A Photographer's Journey with Elizabeth Taylor and the Hollywood Jet Set
Gianni Bozzacchi with Joey Tayler

Hollywood Divided: The 1950 Screen Directors Guild Meeting and the Impact of the Blacklist
Kevin Brianton

He's Got Rhythm: The Life and Career of Gene Kelly
Cynthia Brideson and Sara Brideson

Ziegfeld and His Follies: A Biography of Broadway's Greatest Producer
Cynthia Brideson and Sara Brideson

The Marxist and the Movies: A Biography of Paul Jarrico
Larry Ceplair

Dalton Trumbo: Blacklisted Hollywood Radical
Larry Ceplair and Christopher Trumbo

Warren Oates: A Wild Life
Susan Compo

Improvising Out Loud: My Life Teaching Hollywood How to Act
Jeff Corey with Emily Corey

Crane: Sex, Celebrity, and My Father's Unsolved Murder
Robert Crane and Christopher Fryer

Jack Nicholson: The Early Years
Robert Crane and Christopher Fryer

Anne Bancroft: A Life
Douglass K. Daniel

Being Hal Ashby: Life of a Hollywood Rebel
Nick Dawson

Bruce Dern: A Memoir
Bruce Dern with Christopher Fryer and Robert Crane

Intrepid Laughter: Preston Sturges and the Movies
Andrew Dickos

Miriam Hopkins: Life and Films of a Hollywood Rebel
Allan R. Ellenberger

John Gilbert: The Last of the Silent Film Stars
Eve Golden

Stuntwomen: The Untold Hollywood Story
Mollie Gregory

Saul Bass: Anatomy of Film Design
Jan-Christopher Horak

Hitchcock Lost and Found: The Forgotten Films
Alain Kerzoncuf and Charles Barr

Pola Negri: Hollywood's First Femme Fatale
Mariusz Kotowski

Sidney J. Furie: Life and Films
Daniel Kremer

Albert Capellani: Pioneer of the Silent Screen
Christine Leteux

Ridley Scott: A Biography
Vincent LoBrutto

Mamoulian: Life on Stage and Screen
David Luhrssen

Maureen O'Hara: The Biography
Aubrey Malone

My Life as a Mankiewicz: An Insider's Journey through Hollywood
Tom Mankiewicz and Robert Crane

Hawks on Hawks
Joseph McBride

Showman of the Screen: Joseph E. Levine and His Revolutions in Film Promotion
A. T. McKenna

William Wyler: The Life and Films of Hollywood's Most Celebrated Director
Gabriel Miller

Raoul Walsh: The True Adventures of Hollywood's Legendary Director
Marilyn Ann Moss

Veit Harlan: The Life and Work of a Nazi Filmmaker
Frank Noack

Harry Langdon: King of Silent Comedy
Gabriella Oldham and Mabel Langdon

Charles Walters: The Director Who Made Hollywood Dance
Brent Phillips

Some Like It Wilder: The Life and Controversial Films of Billy Wilder
Gene D. Phillips

Ann Dvorak: Hollywood's Forgotten Rebel
Christina Rice

Michael Curtiz: A Life in Film
Alan K. Rode

Arthur Penn: American Director
Nat Segaloff

Claude Rains: An Actor's Voice
David J. Skal with Jessica Rains

Barbara La Marr: The Girl Who Was Too Beautiful for Hollywood
Sherri Snyder

Buzz: The Life and Art of Busby Berkeley
Jeffrey Spivak

Victor Fleming: An American Movie Master
Michael Sragow

Hollywood Presents Jules Verne: The Father of Science Fiction on Screen
Brian Taves

Thomas Ince: Hollywood's Independent Pioneer
Brian Taves

Carl Theodor Dreyer and Ordet: *My Summer with the Danish Filmmaker*
Jan Wahl

Clarence Brown: Hollywood's Forgotten Master
Gwenda Young